GRETA GARBO
A CINEMATIC LEGACY

MARK A. VIEIRA

HARRY N. ABRAMS, INC., PUBLISHERS

To my father and to the memory of my mother.
—Mark A. Vieira

Editors: Elisa Urbanelli, Richard Slovak
Designer: Miko McGinty
Production Manager: Maria Pia Gramaglia

Library of Congress Cataloging-in-Publication Data

Vieira, Mark A., 1950–
Greta Garbo : a cinematic legacy / Mark A. Vieira.
    p. cm.
Includes bibliographical references and index.
ISBN 0-8109-5897-X (hardcover : alk. paper)
1. Garbo, Greta, 1905–
I. Title.

PN2778.G3V54 2005
791.4302'8'092–dc22

2005001051

Printed and bound in Singapore
10 9 8 7 6 5 4 3 2 1

Harry N. Abrams, Inc.
100 Fifth Avenue
New York, N.Y. 10011
www.abramsbooks.com

Abrams is a subsidiary of

LA MARTINIÈRE
G R O U P E

Frontispiece: Greta Garbo poses on the set of the 1929
Metro-Goldwyn-Mayer film *The Single Standard*. Photograph
by James Manatt

Contents

Preface

This is a book about Greta Garbo. You are probably wondering what it can say about her that hasn't been said already. I feel that Karen Swenson's *Greta Garbo: A Life Apart* is the best book ever written about the renowned Hollywood actress. Published in 1997, it is detailed, painstakingly researched, and compassionate. It has competition, too; its bibliography lists twenty Garbo biographies. They span a period from 1932 to 1995. It would appear that the story of the Swedish girl who became a star in her first American film, went on to become an international icon, and then mysteriously gave up her career at the height of her powers has been told often enough.

Yet none of Garbo's biographies appreciate what made her an icon—her films. She did not become an icon by being a debutante, an athlete, or a supermodel. She made Hollywood movies. So did Gloria Swanson and Pola Negri, but it is hard to find their films on DVD. In *Greta Garbo: A Cinematic Legacy*, I write of her movies. I combine a chronicle of their making with a treasury of the images they engendered. Without these images—*without these movies*—there would be no icon.

When Garbo's films were playing first runs, writers were already trying to analyze her. James Agate wrote: "Her beauty is more than beauty. It is strangeness in beauty." Isabel Quigly found Garbo's face "the furthest stage to which the human face could progress, the nth degree of cultured refinement, complexity, mystery, and strength." Bela Balász asked: "Why should this strange sort of beauty affect millions more deeply than some bright and sparkling pin-up girl?" The last word for many years belonged to Kenneth Tynan: "What, when drunk, one sees in other women, one sees in Garbo sober. She is woman apprehended with all the pulsating clarity of one of Aldous Huxley's mescaline jags. Tranced by the ecstasy of existing, she gives to each onlooker what he needs."

After Garbo's death in April 1990, a new generation of authors tried to answer the riddle of the Swedish Sphinx. Sven Broman, Frederick Sands, Hugo Vickers, Diana Souhami, Raymond Daum, and Barry Paris all examined Garbo's life—especially her sexual life—in exhaustive detail. No tale was left untold as they tried to find the secret of Garbo's mystique. Most of these exercises in armchair psychology had the desperation of a child unscrewing the base of a favorite toy in a useless effort to fathom its appeal. All of these authors dismissed Garbo's films, even extravagant, clever, immensely popular vehicles such as *Mata Hari*. Critics had these opinions, too. In 1965 Raymond Durgnat wrote: "To see, in these early films, Garbo breathe life into an impossible part is like watching a swan skim the surface of a pond of schmaltz, and finally with long, slow, persistent strokes, mysteriously as natural as breathing, streak to some unknown horizon."

Granting that Garbo herself had reservations about the films with which Metro-Goldwyn-Mayer capitalized on her sudden popularity, one need only look at Edmund Goulding's 1927 *Women Love Diamonds*. Garbo went on suspension rather than make this film. She felt that the story was stupid and the character unworthy. Seen now, it is not much worse than any number of her silent films, but without her magic at its center this well-mounted movie cannot sustain attention, let alone sympathy. A Garbo biographer may complain about having to sit through the "creaky, banal" *Mata Hari* just to see Garbo, but he or she will invariably sit. This artist does not disappoint. And, yes, some of these are little more than star vehicles, but they boast excellent supporting casts, witty scripts, artful direction, and stylish design, all captured in luminous cinematography.

One of my greatest pleasures—discovered in a 1968 high-school film series—is to project a 16mm print of a Garbo film, especially *Queen Christina*. These days the print is more than thirty years old and the film more than seventy, but, after the audience accepts that, there is a wonderful realization. As illuminated by Garbo, the character is not a glass-encased museum piece but a living being. Because of her artistry, scenes of passion and betrayal in far-off settings assume the currency of online news. Fifty-five years ago, critic Jean George Auriol wrote: "Have you ever thought of the emotions let loose in the cinema's darkness when the countenance of Greta Garbo assumes possession of the screen? What waves of love, jealousy, regret, hatred, pity, renunciation, complaisance immediately reverberate among and cross-infect the spectator?" Worthy of repeated viewings, Garbo's films are worthy of a book.

Another pleasure comes for me after the last image of Garbo, etched in ivory and silver by the gifted cinematographer William Daniels, has faded from the screen. The room lights come up and questions are asked. What was she like? How was the film made? Who was Rouben Mamoulian? Why did she work only at M-G-M? What was the nature of her collaboration with Daniels? With Ruth Harriet Louise? With George Hurrell? How did people react to her at the time? Who were the "Garbomaniacs"?

Garbo made two features in Europe and twenty-four in Hollywood. *Greta Garbo: A Cinematic Legacy* is the first book to study the making of her Hollywood films. No book has ever considered her films as a discrete body of work. Studying them as a unit and giving her credit for that unity is defensible. As Metro-Goldwyn-Mayer's highest-paid star, she had approval of story, costar, director, cinematographer, unit still photographer, and portrait photographer. While she was not an auteur, she certainly knew what she could and could not play. Among her rejected projects were *The Garden of Allah*, *The Paradine Case*, and *I Remember Mama*, all fascinating might-have-beens. Sad as her early retirement is in retrospect, for it deprived us of many more films, it came after she had made twenty-six. Sarah Bernhardt made ten. Katharine Cornell made none.

To comprehend Garbo's artistry, one cannot look at her as an isolated artist. She was part of a film manufacturing company. She had to cooperate in order to sell the product—her image. If *Queen Christina* did not play well in the provinces, Garbo would be shown the door as quickly as if she had been a flash in the pan like Anna Sten, Sari Maritza, or Tala Birell. *Two-Faced Woman*, the first incorrectly manufactured Garbo film, was also the first to fail at the box office. Regardless of her artistic aspirations, she knew that her films, whether well scripted (*Grand Hotel*,

The information on the edge of this negative tells that it was shot on April 23, 1926, for M-G-M production 265, *The Temptress*.

Ninotchka) or slightly silly (*Romance*), were vehicles that conveyed her to her audience by creating not only a world for her but also a universe, one in which her "strange beauty" could bring newness to the boy-meets-girl formula.

What interests me as a student of classic Hollywood filmmaking is the construction of these vehicles, the progression from story conference to premiere. Now, more than ever, it is possible to trace this process, thanks to newly accessible studio files and unique research methods. I wish to mention in particular my method for verifying the production dates that I present in the text. I have been printing original M-G-M studio negatives since the mid-1970s. At that time I observed that each negative had a date and production data photographically imprinted on its edge (see photo above). I asked Clarence Sinclair Bull, the retired head of the M-G-M stills department (and Garbo's favorite portraitist), what this edge code meant. He explained that he had built a small "flash box" so that freshly exposed film could be identified according to date, film, photographer, and exposure before it was processed. Every studio negative was permanently marked in this ingenious fashion on the day it was exposed. (George Hurrell's negatives were never flashed because he preferred to process his own film elsewhere.) I saw that it was possible to trace the making of a film by merely noting the date on the edge of each consecutive still negative. This immutable evidence has made it possible for me to present the most accurate account of Garbo's life at M-G-M yet written. It has untangled the confused production history of Garbo's second American film, *The Temptress*. It has also revealed a mysterious gap in the chronology of Garbo's career, one that has been glossed over by every Garbo biographer, and one that raises previously unasked questions about Garbo's personal life.

In presenting new information about Garbo, I cite only facts than can be verified by this unusual method or by archival documents. I began researching Garbo's films when I was fifteen, when I transcribed sound tracks from television broadcasts to paper with my parents' typewriter. Two years later I persuaded the Catholic boys' high school I was attending to let me program a film series, which was, predictably, dominated by Garbo films. Using film rewinds and a viewer, I was able to study her films, scene by scene, shot by shot—almost frame by frame. Later, when my environment changed to film school and then to a photographic studio, I was still in love with Garbo, using methods both old and new to continue my research. I did not attempt to reach Garbo until I was twenty. I sent her a sixty-fifth-birthday card in 1970. She didn't respond, of course. From that time, though, on I did interview many of her colleagues, including Basil Wrangell, William Daniels, Joseph Ruttenberg, Sydney Guilaroff, Dore Freeman, Clarence Bull, Joseph Newman, Chester Schaeffer, and George Hurrell. I wanted to know how she worked with them and how they worked with her. I wanted to know how movies were made in M-G-M's golden era.

Every book ever written about Garbo has taken a superior, dismissive stance on her films. I beg to differ. From *Grand Hotel* at age seven, I have enjoyed them. I like to think that I am lucky enough to enjoy them as audiences did when they saw them at their initial engagements. I admit that seeing an early talkie on television or a silent film on a 16mm projector in a college classroom cannot approximate the experience of seeing *The Temptress*, for example, in a scented, melody-filled picture palace in 1926.

My viewing of *The Temptress* in 1972 was not like seeing it in 1926, when Gaylord Carter played the organ at the Million-Dollar Theatre in Los Angeles, introduced by a stage prologue that included Paul Whiteman's concert orchestra. I saw it in the concrete-walled screening room at the Pacific Film Archive in Berkeley, California. There were no pots of incense or brocaded velvet curtains, but the print was the original nitrate vault print, and I wanted to believe what I was seeing. The images I saw on that screen were so sharply etched compared to what I had been watching recently in Panavision prints of new Hollywood films that I sat forward in my seat through the entire film. And, of course, the story and its star were quite something for a twenty-two-year-old questioning traditional values. In one scene, Garbo is accused in an intertitle: "Men have died for you—forsaken work and honor—for you!" Many young women in the Berkeley audience clapped when this intertitle flashed her

proud reply: "Not for me—but for my body! Not for my happiness, but for theirs!" Women's lib in 1926? Wow!

That audience found the film as believable as did a 1990 audience at the Director's Guild in Los Angeles. The friend who accompanied me to the 1990 screening was at that time working (somewhat unhappily) on a big-budget Bruce Willis action film. At the conclusion of *The Temptress* she said, "It wasn't great art. But at least it was *about* something. It was about *people*."

So I have no patience with writers who take the attitude that "Garbo should have been doing Ibsen or Shakespeare instead of the rubbishy movies she did for her exploitative Hollywood bosses." As we will read, she acquired a tremendous amount of power over those bosses and made all the films that she wanted to (except for *The Picture of Dorian Gray* and *St. Francis of Assisi*). Furthermore, those bosses could only make films that the public would pay to see. A case in point: three years before M-G-M packaged Garbo, there was a fading Russian star named Alla Nazimova. In one last grasp for success, she produced her own version of Ibsen's *A Doll's House*. It was an awful flop. Sad to say, it is a lost film, so we do not know if it was well made or terrible, but we do know that American moviegoers of 1922 were not ready for Ibsen. Garbo was something else again. As soon as M-G-M saw her, they knew that Garbo had to be presented in a special way. Once M-G-M found her formula, they stuck with it. She did not need Ibsen—or Shakespeare, for that matter. Let Norma Shearer experiment with Shakespeare. Garbo had her formula and used it for sixteen years, generating one hit film after another. Critics and historians write how awful they were, but writers like me find much to admire in them. I wish that she had made more of them. Awful or admirable, this is how they began.

———

"Two Swedish Players Now En Route Here" was the lackluster title of a tiny news item in the *Los Angeles Times* on September 1, 1925. The item, wedged between reviews of vaudeville openings and Charleston contests, stated: "Greta Garbo, 'the Norma Shearer of Sweden,' and Mauritz Stiller, one of the foremost directors of that country . . . have just signed contracts to work in American pictures under the Metro-Goldwyn-Mayer banner and will be met on their arrival by various noted Scandinavians now associated with M-G-M, including [directors] Victor Seastrom, Benjamin Christensen, and [actor] Karl Dane." It did not explain why M-G-M would need a second Norma Shearer. Of course, no one had seen this Greta Garbo—no one, that is, but the thirty-nine-year-old head of the studio, the short, iron-bicepped, bespectacled Louis B. Mayer.

While in Berlin in November 1924, Mayer had made a point of meeting Garbo and Stiller, who were making a splash with their new film, *The Atonement of Gösta Berling*. Accompanying Mayer were his wife, Margaret, and daughters, Edith and Irene. "My father was mad about Seastrom," recalled Irene Mayer Selznick, referring to the director who made M-G-M's first film, *He Who Gets Slapped*, which was then playing to packed houses in the States. (He had been making films in Sweden since 1913 as Victor Sjöström; M-G-M changed his name to Seastrom.) "He had talent and poise, and my father believed every word he said. He was the one that put it in his head to go to Berlin and meet Mauritz Stiller."

A Sunday afternoon screening was arranged at the Universum Film A.-G. (Ufa) Studios in Potsdamer Platz. The petite Irene found the forty-one-year-old Stiller "an awesome physical sight. I likened him to the giant in 'Jack and the Beanstalk'—enormously tall, with a very craggy face; a head, hands, and feet huge by comparison even with his height; his voice had the rumble of something from under a deep mountain." Then she was introduced to the acromegalic figure. "Stiller frightened the life out of me," she said. "When he took my hand, it disappeared. The most striking feature of his face was his eyes—blue they were, and one was disfigured and teared." The lights dimmed and the finely wrought film began to unspool. After the actress portraying the Countess Elizabeth Dohna appeared on the screen for a few minutes, Mayer popped up in his seat: "Who's that girl?"

"Watch the picture! Watch the direction!" Stiller rumbled to Mayer via an interpreter.

"Stiller's fine," Mayer whispered to his family as the film progressed. "But the girl. Look at the *girl*!" After the film ended, he was resolute. "I'll take her without him. I'll take her *with* him. Number one is the girl." After Mayer diplomatically redirected his attention to the continent's most admired new director, Stiller agreed to bring Garbo to the Adlon Hotel to meet Mayer and his family. Mayer and Stiller went ahead, leaving Margaret, Irene, and Edith to run into Garbo. "When we stepped into the elevator," recalled Irene, "a nice-looking but slightly heavy-set woman who looked faintly familiar also entered. She wore a large-brimmed black taffeta hat and a fairly long, dark, full skirt. No one could have possibly guessed that she was between me [eighteen] and Edith [twenty] in age. She got out at our floor, and as we stood together in front of the door to our suite, she smiled shyly at us and we smiled back, but no one introduced anyone." The Mayer women departed, leaving Garbo with Stiller and Mayer.

What took place inside the hotel suite was later described by Garbo: "Louis B. Mayer was in Berlin. He wanted to sign a contract with us for his company. When I met Mr. Mayer, he hardly looked at me. I guess he looked at me out of the corner of his eye, but I did not see him. All of the business was done with Mr. Stiller. Whatever Mr. Stiller said, I knew was always the best thing to do. I would say, 'Is it good?' and

The first photograph made of Greta Garbo in America was taken on the boat deck of the Swedish ship *Drottningholm* by New York photographer James Sileo on July 6, 1925.

if he says, 'It is good,' I would do it." Garbo agreed to a three-year contract at $400 a week, rising at yearly options (to be exercised by M-G-M) to $600, $750, $1,000, and $1,250. As Mayer was known to drive a hard bargain, he must indeed have seen potential in the girl to contract for such generous amounts. His parting advice to Stiller was supposedly that Garbo should diet: "Tell her that in America men don't like fat women."

When Garbo and Stiller arrived in New York on the *Drottningholm* on July 6, 1925, the studio publicity department had budgeted only ten dollars for James Sileo of Apeda Studios to photograph their arrival. This translated into an insulting four plates of film, so Sileo used empty film holders and "pretended" so that his subjects would not feel slighted. His harsh high-noon images of a fuzzy-haired girl in a checked suit standing next to a bug-eyed giant did not say much for Mayer's continental talent hunt. New York was shimmering in a heat wave, and for the next month, tutor

Garbo's first portrait sitting in America took place in a New York hotel room in July 1925. Photograph by Russell Ball

and tyro sweltered in the Commodore Hotel, waiting in vain for "Mister Mayer" to return their calls. Garbo spent much of her time cooling off in a bathtub. "Miss Garbo says she adores America," wrote her first interviewer, "but is it always as hot as this in the summer? She looks forward to her work in Hollywood—if she survives the heat . . . Marvelous skyscrapers here . . . the world's best movies—but heat, *heat*, HEAT!"

Another photo session took place only because a young press agent named Hubert Voight was infatuated with Garbo. He pestered a middle-aged commercial photogra-

pher named Russell Ball to go to Garbo's hotel room. "He was highly skeptical," said Voight, "but when he saw his subject, he changed his mind. He saw greatness in her. He exclaimed later over her wonderful mobility of expression [and how] the little Garbo went through her poses with so much enjoyment." Unfortunately for her, this photographer did not have the skill to compensate for the lack of a hair stylist and makeup artist. Ball's portraits of Garbo were too sharp, harshly lit, and poorly retouched; freckles showed through sloppy squiggles of lead. Her skin looked patchy, her hair matted, and her central incisors crooked. The publicity department in New York was appalled. What on earth had Mayer seen in *this* one?

Voight persevered, however, and a propitious introduction brought Garbo to the studio of one of the great photographic artists of the day, Arnold Genthe. This time her magic was not allowed to escape into the gritty Manhattan air; Genthe caught her evanescent fascination with a new city and a new country. After the prints were retouched and printed, both artist and subject agreed on an important destination. Genthe's status ensured an appointment with Frank Crowninshield, editor of *Vanity Fair*, who questioned paying for a photo of an unknown. Genthe offered the photo for free if "Crownie" would run it as a full page with the caption "A New Star from the North" in the November issue. This was a prestigious placement, but it would not help the actress now, so Genthe offered her a set of prints to send to L. B. Mayer at M-G-M's Culver City studios. Luckily, Mayer did receive them. Once he connected the magnificent creature in the photos with the black-clad girl in Berlin, he put negotiations back on track, and Garbo signed with M-G-M on August 26, 1925.

Garbo and Stiller arrived at the downtown Los Angeles train station on September 10 and were greeted by the "Hollywood Swedes," who included photographer Olof Brinell, actors Anna Q. Nilsson and Warner Oland, writer Harry Behn, and about twenty-five others. The group was snapped by a xenophobic photographer who quickly walked off, waving and saying, "Bye, bye, Swedeys!" A journalist named Dorothy Wooldridge took pains to catalogue Garbo's appearance: "Her shoes were run down at the heels. Her stockings were silk but in one was a well-defined run. As a sartorial masterpiece, she was a total loss."

The funny-looking couple had to check in, not only at the Biltmore Hotel, but also at their employer. As their taxi drove up to the colonnaded M-G-M gate on Washington Boulevard, a group of aggressive young autograph seekers jumped onto the running board.

"Is it anyone?" asked one youth, peering directly into Garbo's frightened face.

"No," answered another one as he scanned her face and body for any resemblance to any contract player at M-G-M. "Nobody," he said disgustedly, as he dropped backward from the running board. Garbo's heart was pounding. She turned to Stiller, lips parted, unable to speak. There had never been incidents like this in Stockholm or Berlin, even though she was appearing in two acclaimed films.

As the taxi dropped them off at the executive offices, people began staring. One of them was future director Joseph Newman. "I remember the day she came into the studio," he recalled sixty years later. "I was in the front office at that time, and in marched this tall, awkward, large-boned young girl. I ushered her and Mr. Stiller into Mr. Mayer's office." With Garbo's twenty-first birthday a year and a week away,

Mayer realized that her mother in Stockholm would have to re-sign the August 26 contract. He assured Garbo and Stiller that all would be well and introduced them to Irving G. Thalberg, his small, dark, and handsome vice-president in charge of production. Thalberg was as reserved as Mayer was extroverted, but even his impassive young face betrayed surprise at the odd-looking man with the big hands and the angular woman with the big feet. Was this supposed to be the "Norma Shearer of Sweden"? Who *was* she?

Greta Garbo was born Greta Lovisa Gustaffson on September 18, 1905, in a cold-water flat in Blekingegaten, the poorest district of Stockholm. Like the proverbial mud-cultivated lotus, she predicted (at the age of five): "I'm going to be a diva, and after that I shall become a princess." When she was fourteen, she had to escort her father to a charity hospital and watch him die of kidney failure. To help support her mother, sister, and brother, she then had to take work in a barbershop, applying lather to stubbly men's faces. She survived her abbreviated youth and grim surroundings in solitude. "As early as I can remember, I have wanted to be alone," she said later. "I detest crowds, don't like many people. I used to crawl into a corner and sit and think, think

Garbo's second American sitting saved her embryonic career. Photograph by Arnold Genthe

Greta Garbo and Mauritz Stiller arrived in Los Angeles on September 10, 1925.

things over. When just a baby, I was always figuring, wondering what it was all about—why we were living. . . . When I wasn't thinking, wasn't wondering what it was all about, I was dreaming. Dreaming how I could become a player."

By the time she was sixteen, she had dreamt her way into the Stockholm theatrical world—by modeling hats in department stores, taking bit parts in advertising films, and entering the Royal Dramatic Theatre Academy. There the inexperienced, morbidly shy girl became a protégée of the worldly, flamboyant, theatrical Mauritz Stiller. He found his polar opposite as he was preparing to film Selma Lagerlöf's epic novel *The Atonement of Gösta Berling.* In Gustaffson he saw the raw material for the great star he had longed to create all his professional life. He renamed her "Garbo," coached her, bullied her, and in the process removed all the gawky, ungainly, unprepossessing attitudes that had caused her teachers and classmates to overlook her. "Stiller's the most generous person I know," Garbo told an interviewer in the midst of her ordeal. "You don't get either angry or upset however how much you get told off. He creates individuals and then shapes them in line with what he wants." In truth, his cruelty drove her more than once to scream at him: "Damn you, Stiller! I hate you!"

Having finally found the ideal subject for his brutal curriculum, he confided to a friend: "You know, she receives instruction excellently, follows orders closely. She is like wax in my hands. Greta will be all right. I believe in her." Applying the same relentless approach to the physical aspects of his film, Stiller paced for days as he waited for icy weather to clear or roared like an animal as flames ate at a full-sized set. He was an eccentric's eccentric. People wondered whether he was in love with Garbo and she with him, but no one dared ask the towering genius. His singular technique made a diffident girl into an actress and contributed to the success of two features: *The Atonement of Gösta Berling* and G. W.

Pabst's German film *The Street of Sorrow.* The unusual Miss Garbo could carry a film, but she was in need of guidance, whether from Stiller or someone else. She was an unsure adolescent, looking to Stiller for every motivation and gesture. He had directed her behind Pabst's back, although Pabst had broadened her horizons, showing her how gentle direction could elicit even more delicate and intuitive playing. But for Garbo, Stiller was God. She called him "Moje."

"Moje did have some simple rules he used to preach," Garbo said fifty years later. "He was concerned that I should grow more self-confident:

Don't take any notice of other people.
Be yourself.
Don't try and be like anyone else.
Every person is unique.
Don't try and be like Norma Shearer."

When Mayer and Thalberg talked with Stiller about projects that would be better for her than for Shearer, Renée Adorée, or Aileen Pringle, they found his English hard to follow and his production methods even harder to comprehend. "Stiller [expected] to work in Hollywood the same way he had worked in Sweden, where the head office didn't know anything more about what he was doing than the title of the picture," recalled Lars Hanson. This did not bode well for a long-term collaboration with Thalberg, who was establishing the story conference as the keystone of the Hollywood studio system.

While Thalberg sought a property for Garbo's debut, Mayer sent her to the studio's beauty experts, who agreed that her right central incisor was too long. The studio dentist went to work on it. Then Thalberg ordered a screen test. Thirty-year-old William Daniels had finished photographing Erich von Stroheim's *The Merry Widow* a few months earlier. "They asked me to come in one Sunday morning," he recalled in 1970, "and make some tests of a Swedish girl. She had just arrived. I didn't like that idea at all. I didn't like working Sunday too well. But I came in, of course. I made a few simple close-ups of her. She couldn't speak one word of English and was terrifically shy. She didn't enjoy it any better than I did. It was an ordeal for both of us." Their mutual discomfort showed in the test; Garbo looked distinctly ill at ease. Looking at footage of the nervous, poorly groomed girl, Thalberg began to question Mayer's judgment in signing her. Stiller was furious. "Fools, all of them!" he fulminated. "Let me make the test. I will show them." Mayer refused. Seeing her mentor rebuffed only made Garbo feel—and look—worse. "You are quite right in thinking that I'm unhappy here," she wrote to her family. "God, how I dislike this shapeless country, and if you knew how ugly their studios are, and everything such a confusion and jumble, just like my poor head at times."

The studio beauticians then tried curling Garbo's hair and giving her a lighter makeup. Howard Strickling, the head of the publicity department, assigned her next portrait sitting to the new head of the portrait department, Ruth Harriet Louise. Her understated skill was an improvement, but there was little rapport between artist and subject. Whatever Mayer had initially seen in Garbo was still hiding from the artists in Culver City. A frustrated Stiller joined a gloomy Garbo at the Miramar Hotel. "They were a melancholy pair," one of the Hollywood Swedes later said. "It was partly because she made no success at all at the start. She was really quite unattractive then. Her hair was kinky and her teeth were not good. Nobody paid any attention to her, and she was very unhappy. So was Stiller. They used to sit on the terrace, staring out at the ocean. I remember we called them 'grandma and grandpa.'" Friends began to echo the studio's attitude. One day she overheard one of the Swedes say: "I don't see why Stiller brought that Garbo girl to Hollywood. It's like bringing a sandwich to a banquet."

Although the studio would not permit Stiller to do anything more than sit in at portrait sessions, they did allow him to supervise a second screen test. The Danish cameraman Henrik Sartov was renowned for the magic he could work with a soft-focus lens he had made himself, and which he had recently been using on Lillian Gish's film *La Bohème*. "I often saw the young Garbo on the lot," recalled Gish. "Stiller often left her on my set. He would take her to lunch and then bring her back, and Garbo would sit there, watching." Gish approached Sartov: "She has such a lovely face," she said to him. "Why don't you make some tests of her?" Perhaps it was because he was European or because Stiller was coaching, but for whatever reason, Garbo responded to Sartov as she had to Genthe. For the first time, a Hollywood camera captured the essence of Greta Garbo.

A few days later, the test reel made its way to a screening room reserved for William Randolph Hearst's Cosmopolitan Productions, the only producing partner Mayer had so far allowed on the M-G-M lot. Monta Bell, who had just directed Hearst's mistress, Marion Davies, in *The Lights of Old Broadway*, was screening newsreels of floods to prepare Cosmopolitan's next project, *The Torrent*. Bell wanted Norma Shearer for the lead role of Leonora, a Spanish peasant who becomes an opera star. He had begun to cultivate Shearer (both on-screen and off) in a series of highly individual films. Having just played a spit-curled moll in *Lady of the Night*, Shearer declined the part. Bell was now faced with the prospect of Aileen Pringle as his leading lady. This was the same tart-tongued Pringle who had said to John Gilbert while the camera filmed him carrying her to a bed on the set of *His Hour*: "If you drop me, you son of a bitch, I'll break your neck." Lip readers all over the country had written angry letters to M-G-M. Yes, it was *that* Aileen Pringle who was up for the part of Leonora in *The Torrent*.

After another reel of storm footage, the projectionist mistakenly threaded the Sartov test of Garbo. Seeing his error flash on the screen, he quickly doused the projector arc. "Go ahead!" Bell shouted into the intercom. "I want to see every bit of that!" When Bell finished watching the test, he went to Thalberg and asked to have Garbo for *The Torrent*. No matter that Mayer had promised Aileen Pringle the part; Bell was confident that the unknown Swedish girl in this test could fill the bill. For Garbo, the news was conflicting. She was happy to hear that she was wanted for a major film. She was unhappy to hear that Mauritz Stiller was not directing the project.

Garbo's first Hollywood sitting captured an unformed persona. Photograph by Ruth Harriet Louise

PART I

THE IMPORT

CHAPTER ONE

Ibáñez's Torrent

Greta Garbo's first American film was not chosen as a vehicle for her or for the rising star Ricardo Cortez. It was meant to capitalize on the name of the Spanish author Vicente Blasco Ibáñez. His marquee value had been established by *The Four Horsemen of the Apocalypse* and *Blood and Sand*, both hit films with Rudolph Valentino. The rights to his novel *Entre Naranjos* (*Among the Orange Trees*) was owned by William Randolph Hearst's Cosmopolitan Productions. Mindful of the current Valentino craze, Cosmopolitan pushed *Entre Naranjos* onto the Metro-Goldwyn-Mayer assembly line in April 1925 and renamed it *The Torrent*. By September, scenarist Dorothy Farnum had completed a first-draft adaptation, which she prefaced with a statement of purpose.

> To dramatize the brief hour of passion, which comes but once in a life. The TORRENT, which rages in youth, and which passes—leaving barrenness behind. To exemplify the eternal conflict of Romance against Respectability.
>
> To argue in favor of Romance—and to call upon people to have the courage to forsake everything else for it.
>
> To tell the story of a Woman of Destiny, a creature born to shine as a Star, to be the light of all Men—but out of the reach of any One.

With a budget of $250,000, *The Torrent* was planned as a medium-sized epic about a small-town politician who misses the big things in life because he cannot say no to his mother. Don Rafael Brull not only lets the lovely, angelic Leonora go off to the big city because Doña Brull tells him to. He also lets her slip through his fingers a second time, when she returns to their town as a famous opera star, "La Brunna," and is still in love with him. The scenario ends years later with a gray, paunchy, unfulfilled man encountering a glamorous, world-weary diva, who barely recognizes him as her childhood sweetheart.

Monta Bell was well suited to this mocking, bittersweet tale. His *Lady of the Night*, with its gentle satire of "good-

Opposite: Greta Garbo, as the Marquesa de la Torre Bianca, descends the stairs of her mansion in a scene from the Mauritz Stiller version of *The Temptress*.

This is the first close-up of Greta Garbo by the cinematographer whose lighting would make her famous. A freak accident promoted William H. Daniels to "first cameraman" on *Ibáñez's Torrent*, and he began working with Garbo on November 27, 1925.

bad" girls, had just positioned Norma Shearer as Metro's most versatile actress. Bell's eye for the subtle gestures that betray desperation came from his tenure as a reporter for the *Washington Herald*. While interviewing a distraught woman whose young son lay dead from a violent accident in the next room, he noticed that she was mindlessly winding and unwinding something around her fingers—a thread from the child's jacket. "These things make movies," said Bell.

Mauritz Stiller had not unreasonably expected to direct Garbo's American film debut. He was her discoverer and her mentor. Only he should direct her portrayal of Leonora. The studio's choice of Bell came as a shock both to him and to Garbo, who at first told him that she would not work without him. Touched by her loyalty, he nonetheless prevailed upon her to accept the part. It was, after all, the lead in a major film, and, in actuality, his fortunes were less tied to hers than hers to his. Furthermore, he promised to coach her privately every night for the next day's scenes. Garbo acquiesced. On November 14, Stiller accompanied her to the studio for costume fittings and makeup tests, and to meet

Sven-Hugo Borg, a young Swedish actor who would be her interpreter. Her earlier visits to M-G-M had been to relatively quiet departments of the vast plant. For the first time now, she entered one of the hangarlike "dark stages," where the sound of construction competed with the chords of a portable pipe organ and gossiping extras. "It was all very strange and terrifying," Garbo later said. "It frightened me— the newness of it, the size, the numbers of people. I could not speak English, nor understand the people around me."

From across the stage where Bell was shooting his first day on *The Torrent*, two young men watched a trembling Garbo clutch Stiller's arm. One was cameraman William Daniels, who had made her first test two months earlier. "There she was," recalled Daniels, "in the midst of a strange people and a strange language, and it must have been a horrifying experience for her." The other was Borg, who heard her say to Stiller: "Oh, Mauritz! It is so terrible and confusing! What am I to do? What do all these people talk about?" Borg approached the isolated couple and introduced himself. Stiller smiled at Garbo. "Here is a man," he said, indicating Borg, "who has nothing to do except to tell you what they talk about." For the next two weeks, Borg worked with Garbo, translating, helping her learn English, and even accompanying her to Louis B. Mayer's office; her improved tests had not escaped his notice. "It was very funny," said Garbo several years later. "Before I started on *The Torrent*, Mr. Mayer called me back into his office and wanted me to sign a new contract with him. But I said, 'Mister Mayer'—I

While working on her first American film, *Ibáñez's Torrent*, Greta Garbo studied English with Sven-Hugo Borg, an interpreter who became a confidant.

could not then talk but a little English and not so good pronunciation—'Mister Mayer, I haf not done yet one picture. Let us wait until I haf been in one pictures.' He wanted me to sign for five years with him. I could not understand it." Nor could she understand why Mayer would not let her work with Stiller. As the day of her first work without him approached, the bewildered girl would implore her newfound friend: "Borg, Borg, do something! Make them let me have Mauritz! Why won't they let me have Mauritz?"

Garbo's first day on the film was scheduled for November 27. "Greta is starting work for a well-known director," Stiller wrote to a friend, "and I think she has got an excellent part. If only she has the energy she will make millions here." At 6 A.M., Garbo had neither energy nor nerve. "For once she wanted me to drive," recalled Borg, "and as she sat beside me in the little car, she would wring her hands and repeat over and over, 'Oh, Borg! Oh, Borg!'" Her first scene took place in a black-and-silver cabaret. She was required to sit at a table, her hair slicked back in a modish Continental cut, and watch a black man sing a song onstage. Her costume was a boldly patterned black-white-and-gold fur coat designed by yet another Scandinavian, Danish Max Rée, as a homage to opera diva Marcella Sembrich. The scene was being photographed by Daniels, who later recalled: "A couple of days before, the first cameraman, Tony Gaudio, fell off a parallel, and cut off his little finger. I was promoted." This time, Daniels and Garbo, with the help of Bell and Borg, did better, although it was still difficult. "She was shy from the very beginning," he said. Yet his first close-ups of her at the table revealed a different person than anyone at M-G-M had seen—a slinky woman of the world. Before the film could be processed and screened, however, Garbo began to sense that she, like other foreigners, was not entirely welcome in post–World War I California.

Walking from the women's dressing room to the stage, Garbo impulsively sampled some fruit from one of the studio's ubiquitous trees. "Don't pull them figs!" a gardener yelled at her. "Whatsa matter? Can'cha read?"

"Beat it!" replied Garbo to the astonished man.

"I didn't learn English quickly," she said later. "The first English I learned was slang. I remember how proud I was when I learned to say 'Applesauce!' with just the right accent." On the set she was treated to more niceties, most of which she overheard and some of which she understood.

"Look at her! Isn't she funny? Imagine that Swede trying to get into pictures!'"

"Hey, Borg! What the hell is wrong? Get that squarehead on the set!"

"Tell that dumb Swede we're ready to start shooting!"

"What makes that big Swede think she can act?"

Garbo's twenty-six-year-old costar was a Viennese Jew (by way of Hester Street) who had changed his name from Jacob Krantz to Ricardo Cortez in order to style himself as a

Garbo's penchant for solitude was evident even on the set of her first American film. Unit still photographer Bert Longworth had to track her down to make on-the-set portraits of her.

Latin lover. His gamble paid off; he had been working non-stop for four years and was considered a threat to Valentino. In his opinion, *The Torrent* was his film, but he at first demonstrated a token courtesy to Garbo. "And what do you think of Hollywood?" he asked her, not knowing the limits of her English vocabulary.

"Ah, he-ll," replied Garbo succinctly.

Cortez was not amused, and from then on did not speak to her. "Cortez resented her from the beginning," said Borg, "[because he] felt himself a great star who had conde-scended to work with this 'dumb' Swede who was nobody. On the set or off, he gave Garbo not the slightest notice." Years later, Cortez recalled his costar: "She was unknown—kind of a gawky individual. Not what we'd consider an attraction." Having decided that Garbo was a nonentity,

Cortez treated her as such. During the shooting of the eponymous rainstorm, both actors were drenched with cold water. Borg was waiting offstage with blankets for Garbo. Cortez came over to him: "Here! Give me those blankets!"

"But they are for Miss Garbo!" Borg protested.

Without another word, Cortez took the blankets from him and walked off. "Let him have them," said Garbo when she saw what had happened. "You mustn't let yourself be bothered about a pumpkin like that." She was not getting much support from Bell either. "In Sweden we are instructed exactly how the scene must be played before the camera is turned," Garbo told an interviewer. "The American director tells his players to act the scene as they feel it—and then he makes suggestions." One of Bell's more pointed suggestions to Garbo was that she stop complaining about shooting

is because of me. . . . The public and the critics have been wonderfully kind, but personally I don't think I was good, so I can't get much pleasure out of that. They don't have a type like me out here, so if I can't learn to act, they'll soon tire of me, I expect." A *Photoplay* magazine interviewer named Myrtle West thought otherwise. "She is a tall girl," wrote West. "Long-limbed like so many Scandinavian women, but with slender grace that is not always seen in that race. Blue eyes, a lengthy blonde bob, a fascinating mouth. A face that you would remember long after the body had crumbled away." This was a curious comment in view of the poignant, powerful last scene of *Ibáñez's Torrent*.

Leonora, the great and ageless opera diva, is leaving another triumph as Carmen while the prematurely aged

Rafael sits by the fire with his careworn wife. As the camera gives us a final caressing close-up of the beauteous Leonora, riding in solitary splendor in her elegant carriage, we are jarred by a cut to a plebeian crone in the street. "She must be very happy," says the old woman. "She has everything she wants." Dorothy Farnum's description—"a Star . . . the light of all Men—but out of the reach of any One"—has been fulfilled, but with the misogynistic fervor of the old grammar-school taunt: "Is that a promise or a threat?" Leonora has harmed no one, and yet the story has punished her with an unrequited longing for an unworthy man. At the fade-out, each character is hopelessly in love with what the other appeared to be in adolescence. Seldom has an actress's debut been so auspicious and so prophetic.

This is "a Woman of Destiny, a creature born to shine as a Star, to be the light of all Men—but out of the reach of any One." So wrote Dorothy Farnum about the character of Leonora, the peasant girl who becomes an opera star. When Farnum wrote these words in September 1925, she was not thinking of the frizzy-haired teenager who had just arrived in Los Angeles—and who at the age of five had declared: "I'm going to be a diva." By the time *Ibáñez's Torrent* was released (in February 1926), Garbo was becoming that woman of destiny.

CHAPTER TWO

The Temptress

A month before the preview of *Ibáñez's Torrent*, two months before its premiere, and long before Metro-Goldwyn-Mayer's accounting department had tallied its $126,000 profit, Irving Thalberg told Louis B. Mayer that he had made a decision. In her second film, Greta Garbo would again essay a character from a Vicente Blasco Ibáñez novel, and William Randolph Hearst's Cosmopolitan Productions would again produce. This time, however, he had been served notice by the ever-obliging Sven-Hugo Borg that Garbo expected Mauritz Stiller to direct her. Thalberg and Mayer put their heads together. They did not say yes; they did not say no. With an adolescent's enthusiasm, never imagining what her next film would really bring, Garbo rushed to finish *Ibáñez's Torrent* (which became known simply as *The Torrent*).

Hearst had serialized a number of Ibáñez stories in *Cosmopolitan* magazine, and owned motion picture rights to several more, so Thalberg checked the M-G-M story department. Since May, the novel *La Tierra de Todos* (*The Earth Belongs to Everyone*) had gone through eight writers, including novelist Alice Duer Miller, playwright Bayard Veiller, and scenarist Dorothy Farnum, who had finally whipped it into a readable story called *The Temptress*. Thalberg studied it with associates Paul Bern and Albert Lewin, and he wondered if *Gösta Berling*'s director could direct this slightly perverse tale without becoming the kind of self-indulgent director that Erich von Stroheim had with *Greed*. This was an experience that Thalberg did not want to repeat: having to rein in a temperamental, extravagant, intractable "genius" while coping with his own health problems. Yet Garbo planned to work with her mentor.

"Then came the happy word," recalled Garbo, "that I was to make *The Temptress* under Stiller. I was overjoyed. We understood each other!" Looking around the set of *The Torrent* in late December, she was unable to contain her happiness and her hope of vindication. She burst out laughing at her translator friend: "With Mauritz I will show them, Borg!" Her usual reserve vanished, and she almost spat out her words: "*The Torrent*? Bah! You wait!" Later that day, when Stiller received the news of his assignment, he, too, was overcome. "At last they'll see what Greta can do!" he

In January 1926, Greta Garbo posed reluctantly with Jackie the Lion, who was known to moviegoers as Leo the Lion, M-G-M's mascot. Garbo was terrified of the regal creature—and of his bosses. In a year, their positions would be reversed. The beastly corporation would be fearful of this strange Swedish girl.

shouted at Lars Hanson. "We'll show them a thing or two!" Garbo's only reservation was about the story. Leonora in *The Torrent* had not really been unsympathetic, but Elena in *The Temptress* was a vamp in the tradition of Theda Bara, an inscrutable siren who leaves a trail of desiccated victims from Paris to Argentina. Ibáñez wrote: "Like another Helen of Troy, she laid the world to waste and set men at war in a far country." Garbo had already told Mayer and Thalberg that she did not want to play what she called "bad womens." She even told an interviewer: "Some time I would like to play good girl." To put her mind at ease and to prepare the public for her imminent debut in *The Torrent*, the studio devised a wholesome publicity campaign: no mantillas, black satin, or eye shadow.

Photographer Don Gillum brought Garbo to the University of Southern California, where he posed her in a skimpy track suit with the track-and-field team. Then he took her to Olympic Stadium and posed her with prizefighters. The ultimate indignity involved a cold January drive to Gay's Lion

Farm in El Monte, where Gillum introduced Garbo to Jackie the Lion, the mild-mannered animal who appeared at the beginning of each M-G-M film as Leo the Lion. She could not bear to enter his enclosure. "That poor girl was almost paralyzed with fear," said Gillum. "Suddenly she made a bee-line for the restroom and I had to drag her out. She had to be thrust into the cage!" Locked inside, Garbo shrank from the pointedly indifferent king of the beasts. "I have never been so afraid in my life," she wrote to a friend. "If I ever become as great as Lillian Gish, I shall have it in my contract that I am to be spared such idiocies." It wasn't long before the word traveled up the steep wooden steps of the M-G-M publicity department. "No more pictures of this Swedish dame," said head publicist Pete Smith to Larry Barbier, head of the publicity art department. "She's been complaining to Stiller and Stiller's been complaining to Mayer. Talk to me before you do anything more with her." The lion photos and the USC photos were added to the key set photos from *The Torrent* and were, of course, printed by the thousands, but Garbo's attitude left a distinctly bad taste with the corps of hardworking studio publicists; unknown foreigners did not refuse publicity.

Stiller, meanwhile, was rewriting Dorothy Farnum's script of *The Temptress* with what he felt were better intertitles. His poor command of English was not demonstrably aided by a translator. A typical title read: "You must go out there as you would go to war. A spoiled luxury doll like your wife could not stand it there—those men out there, rugged and untamed as the elements in nature they are fighting." To save Ibáñez's writing, Thalberg put Farnum back on the script, which she finished by February 18, 1926. However, Stiller had a new vision. He wanted to open the film with a visually impressive scene, a private circus party set in Paris, which would introduce both the hero and the audience to Elena, the Marquesa de la Torre Bianca. On March 24, the first day of shooting, the script was still unfinished but Stiller was at last ready to direct his discovery in Hollywood. This was, after all, the whole point of their trip and their M-G-M contract.

The first scene to be filmed would show the Argentine engineer Manuel Robledo (Antonio Moreno) visiting the mansion of his old friend, the Marquis de la Torre Bianca (Armand Kaliz). This is the morning after a wild party at which Robledo has been entranced and seduced by a mysterious young woman who refuses to tell him her name. Now, the morning after, *she*, of all people, descends the grand staircase, and the Marquis introduces her to Robledo—as his wife, the Marquesa.

The mood on a movie set on the first day of shooting can traditionally make the barometer needle nervous, but when the director brings as many problems with him as Stiller did, the needle can spin. Even before he arrived, he started an argument with the male star of the film, thirty-eight-year-

old Antonio Moreno, who (unlike Ricardo Cortez) was an authentic Spaniard, born in Madrid, a veteran of more than ninety films. As soon as Stiller looked at him, he insisted that Moreno shave off his mustache. Moreno said that his fans expected him to wear it. Stiller demanded that it come off. Moreno, in deference to this important new director, submitted. Then Stiller strode onto the set.

"I saw fifty people standing around. 'Who are all these people? What are they doing here?' I was told that one was an assistant director, another was an assistant producer, one was somebody called a script girl, and so on. 'Take them away. I don't need them. All I need is a camera and actors.'" Observing this unorthodox behavior was Garbo's translator, Borg, who later said, "When Stiller refused to have a supervisor, an assistant director, etc., Mr. Mayer became afraid that he had made a mistake." The scene to be shot was a fairly simple one, since it only involved the three principals, a butler, and a maid. Even so, Stiller had problems with Moreno. Rilla Page Palmborg, a visiting journalist, wrote that when Stiller grew agitated, he mixed languages and transposed words. "When he wanted action before the camera, he would shout 'Stop!' [instead of 'Action!'] Then he would wave his hands and pace back and forth, shouting in Swedish." Moreno complained to Thalberg. Fortunately, the actor was not involved in the filming of the "Paris Cirque" sequence in the first two weeks of April.

As visualized by Stiller and designed by art director James Basevi, the circus party set was undeniably a marvel, with its bold black-and-white tones, contrasting shapes, and suggestive symbols. It is the setting for the extravagant party thrown by the disgustingly rich banker Fontenoy (H. B.

Garbo was also afraid of the horse she rode in her second American film, *The Temptress.* When asked if she was comfortable, she provoked frantic laughter by replying: "I am so unhappy on the top of this horse."

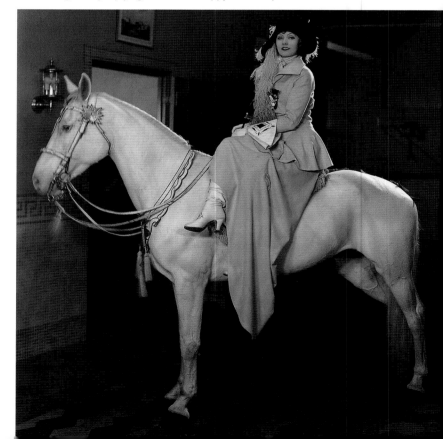

Director Mauritz Stiller had his camera operator film Greta Garbo and Antonio Moreno with a hand-held camera on April 17, 1926, for the nightclub tango in *The Temptress*. The filming of this scene was interrupted five days later by a disturbing telegram.

Warner), who is revealed to be keeping Elena, the Marquesa, as his mistress. The center of the event is a sawdust ring surrounded by trapeze artists performing on flaming hoops. There is a fanfare, a drum roll, and a huge white horse enters the ring, bearing Elena. She is dressed in a tailored white riding outfit, complete with stenciled boots and a kinky riding crop. Perhaps Stiller thought that this would compensate for Monta Bell's lackluster introduction of Garbo in *The Torrent*.

If so, he was right. This was Hollywood showmanship at its most profligate. Borg, still working as Garbo's translator, said, "Metro intended to spare no expense in its setting for the new jewel. Hundreds of extras, colorful costumes, magnificent settings, and around the ring, mounted on a huge white horse, rode Garbo." All the settings were sparkling, but Stiller was having trouble getting them onto film; he just could not communicate. He was mumbling, fumbling, and gesticulating. He was still saying "Stop" instead of "Action!" When Garbo rode in, he wanted the extras to applaud. He roared through his megaphone: "Now: all explode!" With a pained expression, Garbo quietly said, "I am so unhappy on the top of this horse." The cast, crew, and extras exploded, all right—in hysterical laughter.

In spite of the Tower of Babel atmosphere, Garbo was happy to be working with Stiller; it showed in her characterization of the languid, seductive Elena. As photographed by cameraman Tony Gaudio and unit still photographer Bert Longworth, she looked as lovely as she had in *The Tor-*

rent. She had a screen presence without precedent. There was only one problem. When looking at the rushes, Mayer and Thalberg could not tell what scenes went where. Thalberg asked Hanson, who was working on *The Scarlet Letter*, to look at the footage with him. "Is the man mad?" Thalberg asked. "Has he ever been behind a camera before?" Hanson hesitantly tried to explain Stiller's working methods as he had experienced them in Sweden. "He had his own particular way of making a picture," said Hanson. "He shot scenes as he wished, not necessarily in sequence and not necessarily the ones he intended to use. He liked to shoot everything, and then make the film what he wanted it to be by cutting." This was why Mayer and Thalberg found the unedited footage indecipherable. "Why should things always be so difficult for Mauritz?" Garbo wrote to a friend. "He is one of the best directors there is. You know, I could have cried when I saw the opposition growing up around him and how it became more and more difficult for him to concentrate." Irene Mayer later said, "My father was tortured by the Stiller situation. It was heartbreaking." She recalled her father pleading with Thalberg: "Give him another chance."

Thalberg called Stiller to his office, and, according to Hanson, "Thalberg talked to Stiller and tried to get him to work in a more orderly way. [But] Stiller, because he could speak hardly any English, wasn't able to explain what he was doing and satisfy them." When Hanson next saw Stiller, the sad-eyed director told him: "They brought me here to direct because they liked my methods. They say they are something special. Then they won't let me use my methods. Instead they try to teach me how to direct."

Stiller had already incurred the displeasure of his leading man, which was not a wise move, considering that Moreno was liked by Hearst, Mayer, and audiences everywhere. Having deprived Moreno of his prized mustache, Stiller had taken to blaming him when scenes did not play correctly, waving his huge hands at him, and saying in one of the few English phrases he had mastered, "Ah, that is bad, very bad. I think I go now." Moreno could tolerate the babbling of a foreign director witnessed only by coworkers; every night he went home to a mansion called Crestmount in the Silver Lake district and laughed about it with his millionaire wife, the former Daisy Canfield Danziger. What he could not abide was the affront to his screen image that Stiller now proposed.

In the nightclub scene where Fontenoy declares to a large party that Elena has ruined him and then drinks poison, Stiller wanted to show the decadent Parisians caressing one another's feet under the table. The juxtaposition of Moreno's and Garbo's feet made his look smaller than hers; Stiller's solution would be to put oversized shoes on Moreno's feet, which, according to Moreno, all his fans knew were exquisitely shaped and sized. On Thursday, April 22, Stiller and Moreno reached an impasse. Moreno stormed off the set.

Garbo could see trouble as the assistants whom Stiller had earlier scorned stood around talking in hushed tones, eyes averted. Before long, a calmed Moreno returned to the set and resumed work on the nightclub scene. He and Garbo were executing the tango, which she had been taught a few weeks earlier, when a messenger boy appeared at the edge of the set, spotted Stiller's head over the top of the crowd, pushed his way through the extras, and handed him an envelope. Borg later wrote:

I saw Stiller raise his arm brusquely, as with a gesture he stopped the action. Garbo, at his motion, came up. Silently he handed her the envelope. She opened it and read it. Then, with a little cry she sank into a chair. His arm supported her. The message told her that her sister, her beloved Alva, was dead in Sweden. . . . The set was hushed in sympathy as the word spread. For a few moments, Garbo sat silent, holding her head in her hands. Then she rose to her feet. "Come, Mauritz. Let us go on."

After Stiller was replaced as director of *The Temptress,* a disconsolate Garbo managed to finish the film with the help of two kind men. Sven-Hugo Borg (left) was her interpreter and friend. Fred Niblo (right) was her considerate director.

Garbo managed to act a few more takes, but she finally had to be assisted from the set and driven to her apartment at the Miramar Hotel. She could not come to work the following two days, but the studio wanted her back on Monday. She was torn. She obviously could not travel to Sweden, but the notion of "The show must go on" was unknown to her. Out of loyalty to Stiller, she returned to work. "I was in agony," she said later. "I was tired, sick, broken. But there was nothing [to do] for it but to go on." What she did not know until many years later was that Stiller had received the

This absinthe-slurping slut is none other than Elena, the temptress who has come to a bad end on the sidewalks of Paris. When Elena's greatest love asks her if she recognizes him, she replies, "I meet so many men." The disillusioned man foolishly gives her money for a drink. Absinthe causes hallucinations. After her fifth, Elena sees an unlikely patron in the sidewalk café . . .

. . . Jesus Christ listens as Elena asks to be forgiven for her sins and . . .

. . . Jesus accepts her guilty gift of a very valuable gem . . .

. . . but the "blind drunk" Elena does not see that she has bestowed her worldly wealth on an unscrupulous denizen of the underworld.

telegram informing him of Alva's death twenty-four hours earlier. For reasons known only to him, Stiller chose to have the messenger deliver it to the set at precisely that moment. This manipulator of destinies was about to feel a tap on his own shoulder.

On Thursday, April 29, after one more scene, and two months of shooting, Stiller was summoned to Thalberg's office, which overlooked an alley. Thalberg's assistant Al Lewin happened to be walking down the alley that night and caught sight of Thalberg and Stiller in the lit-up window. Lewin recalled:

> I couldn't hear what was being said, of course, but it was plain that a very lively discussion was in progress. It was a curious sight, a kind of dumb show. As I stood there, I saw Garbo walking up and down the asphalt street alongside the old wardrobe building. She would look up into the office where Irving and Stiller were talking, watch the characters inside for a moment, and then walk away again. I watched her for quite a time as she continued that pacing up and down, up and down. She was obviously very agitated. . . . She was still pacing when I finally walked away.

There is no record of how long Garbo waited in that dark alley, but eventually Stiller did leave Thalberg's office and did give Garbo the news: Thalberg had fired him from *The Temptress*. "I was heartbroken—and so was Stiller," said Garbo. "I didn't think I could go on."

On Monday, May 3, Fred Niblo, the director who had pulled *Ben-Hur* from the mess of its Italian production, took charge of *The Temptress*. The first scene he filmed was a fresh one, showing Robledo arriving in the Argentine camp. After a series of meetings with Mayer, Thalberg, and Farnum, it was decided that he would continue to film the script as it stood. Thalberg then decided to scrap and rewrite *all* of Stiller's scenes. He also decided to replace cameraman Tony Gaudio with William Daniels, to replace H. B. Warner with Marc MacDermott (as Fontenoy), and to restore Moreno's mustache. It looked as if everyone would be happy—except the lead actress and the deposed director.

Stiller, the maker of stars, the dynamo, the giant genius, had sunk into a deep depression. He now sat alone in Santa Monica, listless, deflated, seeing no one. For the first time since 1923, Garbo was left to fend for herself. On Tuesday, having lost first her sister and then her mentor, Garbo returned to M-G-M and reported to the wardrobe department, bereaved, hurt, and alone. If watching her father die and then being forced to lather men's faces at fourteen was not the most traumatic experience of her life, this certainly was. Quotes from subsequent interviews only hint at her abject misery:

"I was frantic when Mr. Stiller was taken from the picture."

"How I was broken to pieces, nobody knows. I was so unhappy I did not think I could go on."

"[But] I never missed a day. I was never late to work. Week in, week out, from seven until six."

Back at the Miramar Hotel, Garbo's Swedish friends tried to comfort her. She closed her door to them. Without Stiller to guide her, she was beside herself. Years later, an anonymous neighbor recounted her distraught behavior. "She walked the floor until daybreak and sometimes in desperation she would knock her head against the wall."

Bruises on her scalp would not show under *Temptress* hats and hairstyles, so Garbo went on like this for a month, acting like an impassive flame by day and a dying moth at night. In truth, she *was* dying. The Gustaffson child of the cold-water slum was dying, as she had to, if the adult Garbo was to survive in what she saw as a cold, hostile environment. "You know these Americans haven't the faintest idea what to do with Europeans," Garbo wrote to her friend Lars Saxon on June 7. "You know how they are. So both the film and I got a new director. He spent all day asking if I was happy. After everything that's happened lately, this was a little nerve-wracking, to say the least." Niblo's attempts to cheer Garbo were not to be discounted. He was, after all, showing her far more consideration than Monta Bell ever had. And the task he had to accomplish, while not as daunting as the completion of the mammoth *Ben-Hur*, was formidable. Three months of shooting and reshooting lay ahead of him. If *The Temptress* was to make a profit—or just break even—he needed to be inventive, work quickly, and put some life into the dispirited young woman Stiller had left behind.

"For six months, from morning 'til night," Garbo later exaggerated to a reporter, "over twenty gowns to try on, over and over again. I care nothing about clothes, and there were numberless dresses for each part." To listen to her, Garbo suffered through endless costume fittings, and had no sympathy for the people who were poking and prodding her, but when costumer Max Rée quit during the production, Garbo told Borg that she would not continue without him. Rée wanted more money than Mayer would pay. "Niblo at last agreed to get Rée," said Borg, "if he had to pay him out of his own pocket, which I know he did."

Part of Garbo's difficulty with Niblo (and everyone else on the set) was the language barrier. "I could not understand the English directions," she admitted two years later, although she did manage to communicate with her cameraman, albeit haltingly. "I did not teach Garbo to speak English," recalled Daniels, "but we used to talk a lot, and I would correct her on certain things. We understood each other. We talked about things we both knew—movie talk." It is doubtful that Garbo told the moody technician, who sometimes had alcohol on his breath in the mornings, how she really felt as she spent day after day in front of glaring blue-white arc lights portraying the heartless Elena. "It has made me so very unhappy being so far from my own people," she wrote to Saxon in the same letter of June 7.

> Having to be here without being able to do anything for one's nearest and dearest has been very difficult. I won't tell you what I have been going through, but it would have been a relief to me if I had been able to be with the other people affected by the same thing. I have become afraid of life. I have been given what millions envy me for but the shocks that life holds in store for you can make you frightened. I don't understand and cannot learn to understand why God suddenly meant me such harm. It's as though a part of me has been cut away.

In the same letter, Garbo mentioned that she would have a break of a few days from shooting. She spent most of it with her constant companion, Borg, who was now regarded on the set as a Mayer operative. Still Garbo confided in him.

On Tuesday, June 8, they decided to go to lunch and then to the beach. Garbo said to him, "I am so homesick and lonely, Borg. I wish I was home with my poor mother. I wonder if this is all worth it." The couple entered what he later described as an Italian restaurant and ordered their "first tamales." Other patrons looked at them, not because she was Garbo, but because they were a striking pair of Swedish beauties, golden-limbed, tawny-haired, with perfectly sculpted features and clear blue eyes. The film had not yet been invented that could do justice to their almost illusory good looks. Was there a sexual chemistry between them? In a later interview Borg did admit to pinching Garbo's naked leg once when she was late for work, but that was the extent of their intimacy. Now she fixed her gaze on him. "Borg, people say that I am in love with Mauritz, don't they? That is not true, like they think. Borg, I have never been anything to any man, not even Mauritz. I do not love him that way, nor he me. . . . You have seen me, Borg, sit on his lap like a child and smoke with him the same cigarette. You have seen him hold me like a child. It is so good when his arms are around me, for sometimes I am afraid. But it is not love, Borg." Now Borg had another tidbit for Mayer.

At the beach, Borg watched Garbo frolic and gambol, sing and dance like a carefree child—in fact, like the fourteen-year-old that she had never been. "On those long, lazy afternoons at the beach that was the only time that I have ever seen Garbo truly relax and be herself." As soon as she noticed the tenants of one of the beach houses watching her, she froze up. Borg suggested that she make her need for privacy a requirement at the studio. "I know you are not acting, Greta, but just the same, it is something that fits your personality, to be mysterious and secretive. By playing it up you will kill two birds with one stone. You will get your privacy and you will get people talking about you."

Lying next to him on the warm Santa Monica sand, Garbo pondered it for a moment. "You think so, Borg?" Then she was quiet. "Yes. Maybe it is a good idea."

When Garbo returned to the film, Niblo had finished all the scenes of Robledo and his men trying to keep a mighty dam from breaking after the villain Manos Duras (Roy D'Arcy) has blown a hole in it, with a sneering intertitle: "Beautiful lady . . . My songs could not touch your heart—perhaps a symphony in dynamite will be more to your taste." Now Garbo had to endure the reshooting of all the scenes that she had already made with Stiller. Only now they were being made according to a template established by Thalberg, Farnum, Niblo, and Daniels. In this version Elena is introduced not on a white horse but in a darkened opera box at a masked ball. She is shot in silhouette against the kaleidoscopic patterns of the ballroom, as the imposing figure of Fontenoy enters the shot and raises a long, threatening arm to intimidate her. After a terse confrontation, she escapes

This costume was designed by Max Rée for Stiller's production of *The Temptress*. After Stiller was fired, both the scene and the costume were discarded.

A portrait of Garbo made by Ruth Harriet Louise on July 14, 1926, to publicize *The Temptress.*

him, running through the crowd of revelers. She is followed by a moving camera that is not on a standard camera dolly; the cameraman is copying Stiller's innovation and shooting the scene with a hand-held Bell and Howell Eyemo camera while being pushed on a wheeled platform. Drunken revelers try to ravish her in a moonlit garden, but she is rescued by an imposing man in a cape and a domino mask (Moreno). The sequence of shots in which she and Moreno remove their masks was wonderfully directed by Niblo to express the awe of looking for the first time at a future love's face.

This entire opening sequence was reshot by Niblo and Daniels in the second week of July. Was it inferior to Stiller's? Could a heartsick, traumatized, twenty-year-old tell? The answer to both questions, even from an eighty-year remove, is a resounding no. The assuredness and elegance of this sequence and of the banquet sequence, with its over-the-table tracking shot and under-the-table foot-fondling,

give the lie to the legend that Niblo was a hack, tacking on inferior material to some great artistic invention. But Garbo had decided that Hollywood was a cold place. Now that she was an adult, she was going to fight ice with ice. In actuality, where *was* this ice? Garbo's coworkers appeared more cheerful than cold, but even this irritated her. "In America you are all so happy," she asked. "Why are you all so happy all the time? I am not always happy. Sometimes yes, sometimes no. When I am angry, I am very bad. I shut my door and do not speak." Stuck on a busy movie set when she wanted to be alone, she wrote to her friend Vera Schmitterlöw: "I never see anybody look unhappy here [at M-G-M]. They smile and smile all day and sometimes I get angry. I would like to say: 'Shut up.'"

Mayer had tried to save Stiller. Now Paramount wanted Stiller to direct a Pola Negri film, *Hotel Imperial.* M-G-M needed to apply for an extension to Stiller's work permit if the studio wanted to profit by a loan-out. In mid-July, an ominous memo arrived from William A. Orr of M-G-M's New York office saying that "the Department of Labor had heard something antagonistic to Stiller. I was not able to find out what it was, and I can only assume that it was possibly an anonymous letter sent to the Department by someone who wanted to see him out of the country." Mayer lost no time in calling Borg, who could only speculate, although there had been gossip, as there is about anyone involved in theatrical circles. Borg did admit that in his opinion Stiller was "a strange man, of strange passions," but he tried to soften the news by saying that "his gratifications came as a theoretical, not a practical sensualist. His fine, artistic soul, loved the finer, more subtle forms of passion, and it is doubtful if he ever loved a woman, any woman." Mayer inferred that someone was trying to shake down Stiller as an "invert," or homosexual. If this reached the press, it would cause problems for the studio with the Hays Office and could even affect Garbo's career. Ultimately, the work extension, the loan-out, and possibly even a blackmail payment took place. The blood of creativity began to course through Stiller's veins anew, and he threw himself into *Hotel Imperial* with a fervor that the Hollywood Swedes had not seen since *Gösta Berling*.

Perhaps a little envious, Garbo finished *The Temptress* on July 26, a full four months after she had started it. She was numb with exhaustion, drained of emotion, and as cold and hard as the character she had been playing. And as Borg noticed, she was beginning to act as an entity independent of Mauritz Stiller. She paid a visit to Thalberg, who confirmed the April 19 news item that she would be costarred with matinee idol John Gilbert, the studio's most popular star, in something called *The Undying Past*. Instead of thanking him, she berated him for assigning her another temptress role and for making her go to work on another film so soon. She left his office with her complaints unresolved. She did not care much for Mayer, but if she needed to see him, he was the court of last appeal. "I've worked five—six months [*sic*] on my second film until a week ago and am now going to be thrown straight into another," she wrote to Lars Saxon. "I'm so sick and tired of everything, all I want is to run away. I've had trouble with Metro-Goldwyn, been forced to turn to the manager and tried to talk to him although I don't know anything about how to run his business. I've become so nervous that one day I will make a scandal and leave everything. If you knew how hard you have to work here. . . . But no increase in salary yet. Those greedy people!"

In late August, Garbo, Stiller, and the other Hollywood Swedes attended a preview of *The Temptress*. Stiller was riding high at Paramount and consequently not happy to see his scenes reshot with bold American flair by Niblo and Daniels. After the screening, the irate giant confronted the much shorter Thalberg in the lobby of the theater, ranting in angry German, "Es ist ein Skandal!"

"Ja . . . ja . . . ja," answered Thalberg, who was for once not behind his elevated desk, and now looking up a full foot and a half at Stiller's distorted face.

Stiller stalked off and said to Hanson, "When I was at Metro, that fellow pretended not to know any German. Now I find he speaks it fluently." Fortunately he did not look back to see the knowing smile Thalberg was bestowing on his date, Norma Shearer.

Garbo was of the same opinion as Stiller. She described *The Temptress* to Saxon: "Dreadful! The story, Garbo, just absolutely frightful. This is not an exaggeration—I was beneath contempt. And I've only got myself to blame. I was feeling low, tired, I couldn't sleep, everything was crazy, but the basic problem is that I'm not really an actress." Thalberg agreed to a certain extent because he did make retakes, one of which was an alternate ending.

Not completed until a week before its premiere, *The Temptress* ended up costing $669,211, far too much for its earning potential. The editing and publicity departments worked around the clock, and the film premiered at the Capitol Theatre in New York on October 10, 1926. It immediately broke box-office records, and why not, with Robert Sherwood writing in *Life* magazine:

> I want to go on record as saying that Greta Garbo in *The Temptress* knocked me for a loop. I had seen Miss Garbo once before, in *The Torrent*, and had been mildly impressed by her visual effectiveness. In *The Temptress*, however, this effectiveness proves positively devastating. She may not be the best actress on the screen—I am powerless to formulate an opinion on her dramatic technique—but there can be no argument as to the efficacy of her allure. . . . *The Temptress* is a lavish, luxurious picture with all known forms of audience appeal. It would, however, be pretty dreadful were it not for the individual and unassisted efforts of Greta Garbo, who qualifies herewith as the official Dream Princess of the Silent Drama Department of *Life*.

In the fall of 1926, Garbo was the Dream Princess of many a young man and woman. *The Temptress*, for all its tortured progress, was a stirring spectacle and genuine entertainment, and, as any Hollywood film should be, a tight vessel for its star. For a second film, it was quite a vessel. In spite of lost months, discarded scenes of white horses and stenciled boots, replaced actors, and a fired director, *The Temptress* eventually grossed an amazing $965,000. Garbo had no way of knowing what M-G-M was getting, but she did know what *she* was not getting. More importantly, she knew how she could get it.

PART II

THE LOVE MATCH

CHAPTER THREE
Flesh and the Devil

As Greta Garbo approached her third American film, it became obvious to her friends and coworkers that she was deeply conflicted. She wanted to excel in the performing arts, to be an actress, even a star. This, of course, required her to be around people and in front of people. Whether in motion pictures, in radio, or in a puppet show, one could not work alone; one had to work with people. And yet this young woman—who turned twenty-one on September 18, 1926—had an aversion to people. It was not merely shyness or stage fright, and it was not a ploy. The perspiration on her forehead, the rigidity of her body, and the manic blinking of her eyes were not produced at will. Her fear was real. Whether of one person or a crowd, she was terrified of people she did not know. How could an actor with such gifts be afraid of the very people she wanted to reach?

She did lose her inhibitions if she allowed herself to know someone, but even then she was formal and wary. She would not trust anyone beyond a certain point. She required every new friend to abide by a set of rules that she had formulated years before. "If you and I are to remain friends," she wrote to one when she was fifteen, "you must keep away from my girlfriends as I did from yours. I'm sure you wouldn't like it if you met me with your most intimate friends and I completely ignored you. . . . I am arrogant and impatient by nature, and I don't like girls doing what you have done. If you hadn't written, I should never have made the first move toward reconciliation."

Five years later, Garbo was even more secretive, more proprietary, and, if she thought a confidence had been betrayed, more vindictive. As a result, her circle of friends had not expanded beyond the Swedes who had welcomed her to Hollywood. "I do not care much for many people," she told a journalist. "Never do I go out in evening. I do not like to go. I would rather stay at home." In an industry that depended on constantly increasing contacts, this was unhealthy. Garbo did not care. "I cannot go to work after I party and all that. I have not energy enough. People take energy from me, and I need it for pictures." A watchful Mauritz Stiller tried to help by taking her to subdued social functions. One was a dinner given by German producer Erich Pommer. Garbo was seated next to director Rowland V. Lee, who recalled:

> She spoke very little English. Sometimes she pretended to know even less. But when Jack Gilbert's name came up—he was the hottest thing in pictures then—her eyes lit up. Then when I told her I knew Jack Gilbert, that I had practically brought him up, she roused herself to a pitch of excitement. Her English became better, but it was still a struggle. She asked me question after question about him. Jack Gilbert was all she wanted to talk about, how marvelous, how wonderful, how charming he was.

It was odd, then, that when Garbo encountered the rambunctious and likable John Gilbert between dark stages on the M-G-M lot, she acted as if he were a masher. Gilbert told his coworkers at lunch, "The Swede isn't a bad looker. Bones are too large but she has amazing eyes. I ran into her the other day and said, 'Hello, Greta,' and I'll be damned if she didn't freeze. 'It is *Miss Garbo*,' she said, then turned on her big flat feet and walked off. Imagine—upstaging *me*."

The actor's egotism was not entirely pretense; the show-business veterans who sat in the commissary with him—screenwriters Frances Marion and Bess Meredyth, directors King Vidor and Monta Bell—welcomed the millions of dollars his films were bringing M-G-M. In 1924, Vidor had established Gilbert as a star in *The Wife of the Centaur*. *The New York Review* wrote of it: "Gilbert adds to his growing laurels . . . not because he is probably the handsomest man on the screen today, but because of his undeniably genuine and versatile ability." The 1925 film in which Garbo (and nearly everyone else in America) had seen Gilbert was *The Big Parade*. Also directed by Vidor, it was the first to look at the Great War through the eyes of the average enlisted man. Its novel approach and Gilbert's sincerity made it a $5 million hit. Playwright Donald Ogden Stewart marveled at Gilbert's newfound celebrity: "I never went with him to a public restaurant that some man didn't leave the woman he

Opposite: While making *Flesh and the Devil*, Greta Garbo and John Gilbert showed Hollywood what a love affair could really be. "Those two were alone in a world of their own," said director Clarence Brown. Photograph by Bert Longworth

In 1970 cinematographer William Daniels recalled: "In *Flesh and the Devil*, for the arbor love scene I just wanted a faint glow to illuminate Greta Garbo and Jack Gilbert's faces." His ingenious device can be seen in Gilbert's hand, and while the glow was simulated, the actors' excitement was not.

was with and come to our table and try to pick a fight with him. Jack was a flaming, radiant person in those days, a bright and shining star. *The Big Parade* had just shot him into the sky."

Gilbert followed this blockbuster with another hit, Erich von Stroheim's *The Merry Widow*. "Not since Rudolph Valentino," wrote a *Photoplay* magazine reviewer, "has there been such a performance of a glowingly romantic role as Gilbert's." The *New York Times* review of his next, *La Bohème*, conveyed the thrill of a Gilbert film: "Mr. Gilbert's acting aroused applause last night." His leading ladies had included the volatile Mae Murray, the stately Eleanor Boardman, and the beloved Lillian Gish. Now Irving Thalberg, who had been his friend since the days when Gilbert was a writer, was teaming him with Garbo.

A new Gilbert script had been in the works since November 1925, when staff writers Frederica Sagor and Max Marcin took on a Hermann Sudermann novel called *The Undying Past*. "Keeping in mind," Sagor wrote in a memo to Marcin, "that it was to be a vehicle for Jack Gilbert and had to be laid in Prussia, I tried to give the role of Leo as much of a romantic flair as possible. . . . I do feel that Sudermann's heavy mood should be thrown aside for a lighter, more entertaining story." In April 1926, Thalberg turned it over to the accomplished freelance writer Benjamin ("Barney") Glazer. Glazer turned in a "continuity," or readable script, on July 27, only a day after Garbo had finished *The Temptress*. "I did not like the story," Garbo said. "I did not want to be a silly temptress. I cannot see any sense in getting dressed up

and doing nothing but tempting men in pictures." She had gotten nowhere in her last meeting with Thalberg, so this time she met with Louis B. Mayer. She felt that she had valid reasons for requesting sick leave. "My sister had died while I was making *The Temptress*," she later said. "My poor body wasn't able to carry on any longer. I was so tired, so sick, so heartbroken."

Garbo had not taken into account Mayer's own expectations. In his mind, M-G-M was a family business and he was the benevolent father. She had been part of the family for a year—a year in which he had spent a great deal of money to make her a star. Not once in all that time had she come to his office to thank him, to ask advice, or to tell him about her bereavement. She was a stranger in her own home, and now it was a little rude to ask for favors.

"Mister Mayer, I am dead tired. I am sick. I cannot do another picture right away. And I am unhappy about this picture—"

"That's just too bad," replied Mayer. "Go on and try on your clothes and get ready."

"I am sick," Garbo said quietly. She saw that Mayer was ignoring her, and then, without another word, she left his office. She next turned to Stiller for guidance. This time the embattled artist could not help her; he was fighting for his American career with *Hotel Imperial* at Paramount. According to Hanson: "She had developed no thoughts or opinions of her own at that time. Whatever thoughts she had were thoughts she borrowed from Stiller. She was still just a little girl from the South Side of Stockholm. For her, life was like walking on a marsh." When Stiller was finally able to break free and meet with her, he told her to be strong. "You are now a great star, Greta, and in America, great stars do not work for $400 a week. Tell them that until they give you more money, you will not return to work."

"But Mauritz, they will send me back to Sweden."

"Not they. They will not dare."

The production, tentatively retitled *Flesh and the Devil*, was scheduled to start shooting in less than two weeks, so Garbo was due for costume fittings. She showed up but quarreled with costumer Clément André-ani, who reported: "She has many dislikes. She will wear nothing with fur on it. She wants neither lace nor velvet garments. She goes in for flaunting bizarre collars and cuffs." Garbo stopped going to fittings. She also missed rehearsals with director Clarence Brown. She did not answer her telephone, and on August 4, a messenger delivered an M-G-M memo to the Miramar Hotel.

You are hereby notified and instructed to report at 4:30 pm today at the office of Mr. Irving G. Thalberg, for the purpose of receiving instructions with reference to the part to be portrayed by you in "Flesh and the Devil," about to be produced by us. If for any reason this notice is not delivered to you on time to permit you to report to Mr. Thalberg this afternoon as instructed, then you are notified and instructed to be in his office at 10 o'clock AM tomorrow. Failure by you to comply with this demand, particularly in view of the attitude heretofore displayed by you, and your general insubordination, will be treated by us as a breach of your contract of employment with us dated August 26th, 1925, and we shall take such action in the premises as may be necessary to protect our interests.

Garbo did not appear at M-G-M on the afternoon of August 4. Five days later principal photography commenced on *Flesh and the Devil*, but it was at Lake Arrowhead and on scenes that did not involve her. Mayer sent Sven-Hugo Borg to visit Garbo. Borg had to use a code to be admitted: one long and two short knocks. He soon sensed a change in her. She was not leaning on Stiller for a solution, and she appeared not to care what happened. When Borg asked her what she planned to do, she answered calmly, "I think I will go home." Borg relayed her message to Mayer and Thalberg. Mayer was incredulous. Actresses did not behave this way. Was it really possible that this willful child might break her contract and leave? He turned to Thalberg. "She could hop a boat to Sweden!"

"In that case, I intend to let her," replied the imperturbable Thalberg.

On August 13, Mayer dismissed Garbo from *Flesh and the Devil*. Garbo did not reply; she hired a lawyer. When the company returned from the lake, Gilbert heard about the dispute and asked: "Who the hell *is* this dame?" With only a few days left until Garbo's scenes were to be shot, Mayer called his special agent in again. "Borg," said Mayer, "that girl thinks that I am a hard, unreasonable man and that I am paying her a salary far below what she is worth. She forgets that it is I who took all the risk. . . . Tell her that to me she has acted as a simple and ordinary dishwasher. Tell her that she can go back where she came from. I'm through!"

When Borg arrived at Garbo's apartment the same day, she was in pajamas. "Hello, Borg! Come in! Hurry!" she exclaimed as she ran back to the bed after admitting him. "Now tell me the bad news!" After Borg relayed Mayer's ultimatum, Garbo called her lawyer. "Maybe I better go back to the studio," she said. "I have rested two days. It does not make any difference here whether I am tired and sick and have lost my sister. I do not understand [but] I will go back." On August 17, Garbo gave in. "I went back and I said nothing," she recalled. "And there I met for the first time (except to nod to him) John Gilbert."

The railroad siding on the back lot was dressed as a German railway station. When Garbo arrived, director Brown diplomatically suggested to Gilbert that he walk over to her and introduce himself. "To hell with her," snapped the actor, who was making $10,000 a week. "Let her come meet *me*."

After a brief rehearsal, Brown began directing the scene, which called for Leo (Gilbert) to arrive from military school with his friend Ulrich (Hanson) and meet Felicitas (Garbo) as she enters the carriage of her rich husband (Marc McDermott). Filming proceeded without incident, although Gilbert began to stare at Garbo. On the following Sunday, Garbo was visiting Stiller's Santa Monica home with their Swedish friends Erik and Irma Stocklassa. "While we were making lunch," their daughter Ingrid recalled, "Garbo whispered to me in confidence that she had met Gilbert. . . . 'Well, what did you think of him,' I asked.

"'Ah!' was her only reply. But there was so much feeling in that one little word that I realized that it was love at first sight." Borg saw it, too. "Some instant spark, some flash seemed to pass between them the instant they looked into each other's eyes. If there was ever a case of love at first sight, that was it." Gilbert's star behavior began to evaporate, and, with it, Garbo's air of grim resignation. Gilbert became as courtly and thoughtful as the character he was portraying, which, according to Vidor, was to be expected. "John Gilbert was an impressionable fellow," wrote Vidor. "He had submerged his own individuality and personality in his career. Whatever role he was playing, he literally continued to live it offscreen. If his new assignment were a dashing Cossack officer, Jack would hire Russian servants in his household, and guests would be entertained with a balalaika orchestra while they were served vodka and caviar."

Gilbert was brash, extravagant, and mercurial. Ten years of writing, directing, and acting in more than eighty films had refined his skills; his concentration on a role bordered on possession. Garbo, too, submerged herself in a character during production. "I know the person I am in the picture," she explained, "and I feel that I am that person for the time being. How I get what you call effects, I do not know. I do not know how I do it." In this film she was playing a character more sensual than Leonora, more predatory than Elena, and more erotic than any yet depicted in a Hollywood film. After seeing the electricity between Garbo and Gilbert in the first few days' rushes, Thalberg assigned Frances Marion to rewrite scenes with an eye for passion. "He was so terribly good to work with!" Garbo said of Gilbert. "Every morning at nine o'clock he would slip to work opposite me. He was so nice that I felt better. I felt a little closer to this strange America." Marion had not finished her rewrites when Brown directed the first love scene, and, as he later put it, "the buttons began to pop."

At thirty-six, the prematurely graying Brown had two engineering degrees and twelve popular films to his credit; the most recent were *The Eagle* with Valentino and *Kiki* with Norma Talmadge. He had learned filmmaking from the great French director Maurice Tourneur, who introduced chiaroscuro to the silent screen. From him, Brown had learned to create depth in the frame by putting a totally dark

In August 1927, Florence Nicholai of San Francisco wrote to *Motion Picture* magazine: "*Flesh and the Devil* was advertised oh, so well—little clever touches anent the Garbo-Gilbert romance—frequent use of the adjective 'subtle' in describing the love scenes. Subtle? Oh, ye gods. Poor Greta Garbo. As Felicitas, she was chiefly occupied in being the 'other half' of kisses *and* kisses *and* kisses. Now, I have no objection to these osculatory salutations. No, indeed. This is no plea for 'nice' pictures, with Miss Garbo as a sort of sublimated Salvation Nell. Life is what we want, and, since wickedness, sinfulness, and what have you are still rampant down here, we'll have them, too. Just a little more finesse, please, and a little less of the flapper's delight."

object in the foreground, how to create suspense by diminishing the number of frames in consecutive shots, and how to coax performances from frightened actors such as the aging Pauline Frederick in his own *Smouldering Fires*. Brown was ideally suited to direct Garbo. He was the first director since Stiller to see the distinctly cinematic possibilities in her technique, the first who was sensitive enough to elicit a subtle performance from her, and the first who was capable of creating something more than a diverting melodrama. As Garbo worked with him, she began to see that he respected her and would give her the time and latitude she needed. "Mr. Brown had a style that allowed us to . . . find our own characters," recalled Barbara Kent, who played a young girl infatuated with Leo. "He was a very quiet man, and would talk to us in the softest voice. He was especially careful with Garbo and would almost whisper his instructions to her." This was Brown's first film with William Daniels, who believed that the cinematographer should be "an inventor of detail, adding to the imagination of a director with his own scientific skills."

The story they had to tell was a torrid fable. Leo and Ulrich's morbidly intense friendship is ripped apart by Felic-itas, who seduces Leo, lets him kill her husband in a duel, and then marries Ulrich so she can ensnare Leo again. Garbo and Gilbert would have to work together in more than fifteen of the script's thirty-odd scenes. In their second scene together, they are dancing, the cynosure of all eyes in a crowded ballroom. In their third scene together, they seek the seclusion of a moonlit garden. Felicitas asks for a cigarette. Leo lights it for her, the match in his hand revealing the desire in her eyes. She blows out the match. Leo says, "You know . . . when you blow out the match . . . that's an invitation to kiss you . . . ?"

The impact of the scene depended on the contrast of inviting shadows and flickering light. It was impossible to capture the subtle light of a match on the slow orthochromatic film in use at that time. Daniels had to find a way to approximate it. "For the arbor love scene," he said, "I just wanted a faint glow [of the match] to illuminate Greta Garbo and Jack Gilbert's faces. So I gave Gilbert two tiny little pencil carbon [arc bulbs] to hold. His hand shielded the mechanism from the lens." The scene, of course, ended with a series of kisses. After filming the first take, Garbo and Gilbert both burst out laughing, something that still

photographer Bert Longworth made them pose again for the slow-shuttered 8x10 camera. Then they grew passionate. "It was the damnedest thing you ever saw," said Brown. "It was the sort of thing [Jazz Age novelist] Elinor Glyn used to write about. When they got into that first love scene, well, nobody else was even there. Those two were alone in a world of their own."

Garbo and Gilbert next had to play the scene in which Leo visits Felicitas for an afternoon of lovemaking. According to Brown: *Flesh and the Devil* had a horizontal love scene—one of the first. Toward the end of the scene, Gilbert, playing Garbo's lover, throws a cigarette out the window. Marc McDermott, playing Garbo's husband, is getting out of a cab when the cigarette falls at his feet. He looks up at the window, so the audience knows that he's prepared for something. When he bursts in on them and finds them in this compromising position on the couch, I put the camera down by McDermott's hand. I shot through his fingers at Garbo and Gilbert as he clenches his fist." This time Garbo and Gilbert performed even more convincingly. "Their lovemaking was so intense," recalled Brown, "that it surpassed anything anyone had seen, and made the technical staff feel their mere presence an indiscretion. Sometimes they did not even hear my 'Cut!' but went on, to the cameraman's amusement." After another week and a few more scenes (the duel, a clandestine meeting in the park, Leo's first visit to Ulrich and Felicitas), "I had a romance going," as Brown recalled, "that you couldn't beat, any way you tried." Gossip sped through the studio. Why was this shy girl making a show of herself? What did Gilbert, the "Great Lover," see in her? They were, at first glance, mismatched—a gloomy, friendless introvert and a reckless, romantic extrovert. On closer inspection, they had much in common.

Both Garbo and Gilbert had been forced to find work at fourteen. Gilbert had been born to traveling actors in Utah, deserted by his father, and resentfully dragged from town to town by his mother, after she had unsuccessfully tried to give him away—the day after he was born. While the teenage Garbo was lathering men's faces, the teenage Gilbert was trying to sleep in a filthy hotel room while the prostitutes who fed and housed him plied their raucous trade. Both Garbo and Gilbert had pushed their way into show business and held on with a fierce grip. Both felt lonely in the midst of Hollywood's manufactured hysteria. Garbo was grieving her sister and working without Stiller, who was a surrogate father as much as a mentor. Gilbert had an infant daughter, but he was unable to be a father to her since his marriage to actress Leatrice Joy had been dissolved a year earlier. And both Garbo and Gilbert were at odds with Mayer.

Beyond these similarities, there was the overwhelming attraction of two healthy young adults, their constant propinquity, and the love scenes that Thalberg urged Brown to create for them. According to *Motion Picture* magazine's

Doris Markham, "Clarence Brown says that he has been getting the greatest love scenes that have ever been screened. He is working with the raw material. They are in that blissful halcyon stage of love that is so like a rosy cloud that they imagine themselves hidden behind it, as well as lost in it. They are not even self-conscious—yet."

On September 9, Brown was directing Garbo, Gilbert, Hanson, and Barbara Kent in a scene that would occasion much comment. In it, the four are kneeling at an altar rail to receive communion. Leo drinks from the communion chalice, and, as is customary, the minister rotates it before the next parishioner drinks from it. In a bold, scandalous gesture, Felicitas turns the chalice backward so that her lips can touch it where Leo's lips touched it. Visiting the set that day, Markham recorded: "[Garbo] was kneeling at a communion rail, John Gilbert beside her. Again they were caught up in the magic cloud of their own making. They played a love scene that tightened your throat with its intense beauty, even there in that most prosaic and disillusioning of all places, a motion picture set. 'They have done that in every love scene they have played,' said Clarence Brown. 'It's marvelous.' The scene was over and Greta slipped down from her knees into a pathetic little heap on the altar steps. Her face was dead white. Her eyes, big and solemn and tragic."

Markham took advantage of Garbo's momentary availability to ask her some questions. "I can only talk to you in little words," said Garbo as they walked to the edge of the set. "I can say yes or no, but I cannot explain much in your English." Borg was, of course, nearby to clarify if needed. Gilbert overheard and joined them.

"Don't let them Americanize you," Markham cautioned Garbo.

"And why not?" Gilbert asked. "Why shouldn't she learn our ways? The world doesn't go to see her because she is Swedish, because she has a fascinating accent. They can't hear her talk. They want to see her because she is an actress. Nationality has nothing to do with it."

Garbo was slumped in a canvas-backed chair. "I don't see how you can work so much and play so much, too," she said to Gilbert, yawning. "Me, I am so sleepy I cannot go to parties. I must go to bed. I get so tired I cannot do it. To be on the set at eight o'clock in the morning—that is terrible. I just brush my hair back. I haven't time to think what I shall wear." She turned to the smartly dressed Markham. "Clothes! Oh, I wish they were bags, all alike, just to jump into, quick! On the screen, oh, yes, I would wear beautiful things—but for myself, just simple. I do not think about them much. I haven't time!"

Before Markham could formulate another question, Garbo was going on: "And, oh, I do not want to be bad woman—on the screen, you know. That is my only trouble in America. People say I am what you call—'vamp type.' I know what they mean but I do not think I am. I do not like to play

By September 16, 1926, when this scene was filmed, Gilbert was in love with Garbo. "There is something eternal about her," said Gilbert. "And dangerous, too. When she comes into a room, every man stops to look at her. And every woman, which is more remarkable." Garbo was no less enthralled with Gilbert. "He is a great artist," she said. "He lifts me up and carries me along with him. It is not scenes I am doing. I am living."

'bad woman!' Oh, much rather I played good women—good but interesting—you know?"

"That can't be," Gilbert laughed at her.

"Yes, it can be true!" she insisted. "You are all mistaken and I do not think the people like the bad women—and I—I know I do not like to play them. I do not *want* to play them. When people see me on the screen, they will think I am like that." Gilbert laughed again and Garbo leaned toward him. "Oh, yes, they will!" she said. "They will write me letters about it. That is why some days I am sad. But most days I am very, very happy." Markham caught the look that passed between Garbo and Gilbert. "I am very happy," Garbo smiled at him.

"Garbo!" called the assistant director from the new camera setup at the altar. "Garbo!"

"Coming," Garbo answered dutifully.

As the entire studio watched and whispered, filming continued, giving Garbo and Gilbert further occasion to enact what everyone suspected was taking place nightly. The September 16 love scene set in a lodge was the most torrid thus far, with Garbo lying on top of Gilbert and practically devouring him. This was considered scandalous, even by the standards of an era that was challenging Victorian strictures. A woman was making love to a man—to the Great Lover. And, more shocking than that, she was enjoying it as much as he. This had never before been shown in a Holly-

wood film. What would the censor boards say? How would audiences react? Marion was pleased, as were Brown and Thalberg. Here was the essence of cinema, what film conveyed better than anything: sex. And it was real.

Gilbert felt more than mere lust for Garbo. The care that Gilbert could not show his infant daughter, Leatrice Jr., he was bestowing on Garbo. "Jack helped her enormously," said Brown. "He watched everything she did and corrected it. Garbo was so grateful. She recognized his long experience in the movies and hung on his every word." Surprisingly, Garbo acknowledged his help. "If John Gilbert had not come into my life at this time," she later told a Swedish journalist, "I should probably have come home to Sweden at once, my American career over." Journalist Adela Rogers St. Johns wrote: "There was a very real side to Jack under a kind of schoolboy wildness." When Gilbert was asked about his new friend, he enthused that she was as "capricious as the devil, whimsical, temperamental, and fascinating. Some days she refuses to come to the studio. When she doesn't feel like working she will not work. Garbo never acts unless she feels she can do herself justice. But what magnetism when she gets in front of the camera! What appeal! What a woman!"

Opposite: A critic named "Fred" wrote in *Variety*: "If they don't star this girl after this picture, Metro-Goldwyn doesn't know what it is missing. Miss Garbo, handled properly, should be as great a money asset as Theda Bara was to Fox in years past. This girl has everything."

Gilbert was not quite so enthusiastic when Garbo refused to come to his Spanish-style home at the summit of Tower Grove Road in Beverly Hills or to social functions such as the September 8 wedding of King Vidor and Eleanor Boardman. When he began to propose to her—in public—she went to her hotel and would not answer calls, which caused Gilbert to drink and drive to friends' homes seeking consolation. Then he would tell the press: "She is a wonderful girl. We are merely good pals."

On September 18, Garbo turned twenty-one and her contract raised her salary to $600 a week. There was no time for a party. Stiller was rushing to complete *Hotel Imperial* by September 25, and Garbo was still walking on air—except in her last scene in *Flesh and the Devil*, which would finish September 28. In that scene she walks on the icy surface of a frozen lake, trying to stop Leo and Ulrich from shooting each other. "In the end I fall through the ice so the play can go on," she told a British interviewer. "They want me out of the way. That is the kind of part I have. It seems too bad when I love nothing more than for everyone to like me— much!"

Flesh and the Devil premiered at New York's Capitol Theatre on January 9, 1927, heralded by an ad campaign that titillated Americans with creamy soft-focus photographs of ardent lovemaking. For months fan magazines, gossip columnists, and radio broadcasts had been talking about the big love affair. Now the 5,000-seat flagship of the Loew's theater chain had to turn away customers from every show. Americans wanted to see two people who were really in love make love on a thirty-foot-high screen. A *Variety* reviewer was the first to break the news: "Here is a picture that is the pay-off when it comes to filming love scenes. There are three in this picture that will make anyone fidget

in their seat and their hair rise on end—and that ain't all. It's a picture with a great kick, a great cast, and great direction." The *New York Herald Tribune* was full of praise: "Never before has John Gilbert been so intense in his portrayal of a man in love. Never before has a woman so alluring, with a seductive grace that is far more potent than mere beauty, appeared on the screen. Greta Garbo is the epitome of pulchritude, the personification of passion." *Photoplay* made no secret of the film's appeal: "Here is the picture filmed when the romance of Jack Gilbert and Greta Garbo was at its height. Naturally, the love scenes (and there are several thousand feet of them) are smoulderingly fervent."

In two weeks, *Variety* reported that, in spite of winter weather, the sensational film had set a house record for attendance, bringing in $132,505. Not every audience in America was ready for such undiluted passion. A letter to *Picture Play* said: "I am disgusted at Metro-Goldwyn's officials for putting before the public a film such as *Flesh and the Devil*." *Picture Play* also reported that some moviegoers were laughing at Gilbert, and *Picturegoer* magazine cited "titters and disrespectful comments." *Motion Picture Classic* said that "the audience roars with laughter in the wrong places." This kind of reaction was more typical of midwestern audiences, for whom M-G-M shot an alternate ending for the film: after Garbo dies, Gilbert marries Kent, the ingenue. In spite of giggles, blushes, and occasional censorship, *Flesh and the Devil* would eventually turn a profit of $466,000. It also contributed to the institution of a censorship code known as the "Don'ts and Be Carefuls," made an international star of Greta Garbo, and created a romantic team, Hollywood's first in the Golden Twenties. All told, the combined talents of Thalberg, Marion, Brown, and Daniels had taken what could have been a conventional matinee feature and transformed it into a fable of desire and destruction, a landmark in cinema sexuality.

A critic in Stockholm paid Garbo a rare compliment: "It is a pity that [Swedish playwright August] Strindberg is no longer alive, for he would have applauded her satanic Felicitas who throws over and betrays her lover just to live a life of luxury and ease. The film could just as well have been called 'The Dance of Death.'" There was another Swedish review that may have caused her to smile. It came from Anna Gustaffson, her mother. An interviewer asked her what she thought of her daughter's performance in *Flesh and the Devil*. "Oh, I thought her good, of course," answered Mrs. Gustaffson. "But they didn't need to kiss so much."

By the time Garbo read this (which she surely did, since she was already collecting every article written about her), she had plenty of time to read reviews. She was not working. Neither was she returning to Sweden. She was on suspension. *The Temptress* had ended her childhood. *Flesh and the Devil* had ended her innocent youth. Her next assignment nearly ended her career.

Garbo had no double to take her place for her last scene in *Flesh and the Devil*, and the water was not heated. "Miss Garbo may be a torrid siren through most of the scenes," wrote critic Edwin Schallert, "but her death will elicit a fervid sympathy."

CHAPTER FOUR

The Scrapped *Anna Karenina*

Even before its release, *Flesh and the Devil* brought many things to many people. To Clarence Brown it brought a friendship with Louis B. Mayer, one that would endure for thirty years. To Irving G. Thalberg it brought a "Garbo formula." In every film henceforth, Garbo would be an ageless, mysterious beauty encountered in a picturesque setting by an idealistic young man who soon discovers that she is married to (or being kept by) an older man. Now Mayer was eager for Garbo to sign a five-year contract so that he could cash in on the formula and the new romantic team. Last but not least, to those team members, Greta Garbo and John Gilbert, the enchanted weeks of make-believe on the dark stages of *Flesh and the Devil* brought a real-life romance.

In September 1926, the members of Gilbert's cultured social circle saw a dashing twenty-seven-year-old in love. His close friends included screenwriters Barney Glazer, Carey Wilson, and John Colton; directors Jack Conway and King Vidor; producers Thalberg and Paul Bern; and stars Colleen Moore, Edmund Lowe, and Norma Shearer. As they gathered at 1400 Tower Grove Road for tennis and lunch, they observed that Garbo was spending more time there than at her hotel. Gilbert proudly showed them how decorator Harold Grieve had converted the guest room from a replica of a monk's cell to a blue-and-gold setting fit for a Louis XVI princess. Garbo, however, had not liked her reflection on the bathroom's black marble walls; workers put fluting in the marble, bringing the room's cost to $15,000. This satisfied her and amused Gilbert's friends, who were in no position to criticize his extravagance. These children of lower-class immigrants and middle-class midwesterners were also earning thousands of dollars weekly, and spending it without the hindrance of income tax.

If this was the "Era of Wonderful Nonsense," no place in America was more nonsensical than Hollywood, where stars worked six days a week and danced on the seventh. Even

On September 30, 1926, Greta Garbo attended the premiere of the King Vidor film *Bardelys the Magnificent* with (from left) Howard Strickling, Norma Shearer, Irving Thalberg, and John Gilbert.

October 13, 1926, was the last time Greta Garbo was photographed by M-G-M—or anyone—for six months, due to a mysterious disappearance. On this day, Garbo and Antonio Moreno acted in a new scene for *The Temptress*, which had finished shooting on July 26. The scene showed Elena happily reunited with Robledo at the dedication of his dam. This alternate ending was shipped as a separate reel to exhibitors who did not want the film to end with Elena staggering down the streets of Paris.

Garbo admitted: "Perhaps it is your America. But I cannot go to sleep at nine. So I dance. God! By myself in my room I dance your Charleston." At one of Mae Murray's Sunday tea dances, Garbo and Gilbert saw directors Dudley Murphy and William K. Howard abscond with Murray's cream Rolls-Royce. It had a black patent leather collapsible top, sable lap rug, and a yellow tonneau fitted with solid gold and cloisonné. When they returned, the car was filled with flowers. Inside the house, operetta composer Rudolph Friml filled the music room with lilting melodies and more flowers. Murray noticed that Garbo looked ill at ease as the "celebrated of two continents danced, chatted, and flirted in the light from giant candles." Garbo answered that she did not like the films M-G-M was giving her. Half-listening, Murray misunderstood. "You should have a dressing room right on the set, as I do, darling," said Murray. "A chaise longue, flowers, a burning candle."

The air of unreality that hung over Hollywood like the scent of orange blossoms did everything for Gilbert and nothing for Garbo. It intoxicated him and urged him to greater excess; it made her want to escape to the ocean. "I do not like parties," she said pointedly. "I never know what I am going to do next when I am not working. I walk on the beach for many miles. But I never know what time I will do it. I stand on the beach and watch the sea for an hour, perhaps two." Her sudden disappearances vexed the insecure Gilbert. "I went to see her. Her maid told me she had gone to the beach. I jumped in my car and motored for miles, way out beyond Santa Monica. I found her at last. She was all alone

and just coming out of the surf. She didn't see me, so I just watched her to see what she would do. She stood on the beach, all by herself, and just looked out at the ocean. And she remained so, without moving, for fifteen minutes." When she returned to Hollywood, Garbo had to think about her next film and about Stiller, who completed *Hotel Imperial* on September 25. Stiller had read about her romance; it was hard not to, since Gilbert's wooing was as often as not conducted in public.

"Gilbert pleaded and begged that they should marry," recalled Brown, "but Garbo just did not want to. I heard her say, while she looked at him and shook her head, 'John, you're such a child.'" Gilbert lamented to writer Adela Rogers St. Johns: "She keeps saying, 'You're in love with Garbo the actress.' And you know what I say? 'You're damned right.'" Sven-Hugo Borg spoke with Stiller about Gilbert, and in his opinion, "Stiller's attitude toward other men was not that of a jealous man, but of a father who would shield his daughter from hurt." Garbo sensed Stiller's concern and spent more time with him, causing the insecure Gilbert to fuss and fume. She placated him by making the great concession of going with him, Norma Shearer, and Thalberg to the September 30 premiere of his and Vidor's new film, *Bardelys the Magnificent*. On such evenings, these exultant Metro stars, resplendent in tuxedos, minks, and orchids, personified glamour for a worshipful public. Garbo had begun to know Thalberg socially because of his close friendship with Gilbert, yet her innate reserve kept her from relaxing with him or with Shearer, his occasional date.

On October 13, 1926, Garbo was once more costumed and made up as the temptress Elena, only this time with a saving grace. She was being filmed in an alternate ending for *The Temptress*, one in which she, instead of ending up a pathetic wreck, turns away from wickedness and helps Robledo complete the great dam. The reel containing this scene would be sent with the rest of the film, giving Midwest exhibitors a choice of resolution. "I hope they leave the happy ending on *The Temptress*," said Garbo. "It isn't right for so young a girl to go down so far. It is better they give her a chance—a hint of something better, maybe, later on." A still photographer made the necessary photographs of her and Antonio Moreno after they had finished the scene, and Garbo went home, not knowing that this was the last camera shutter she would hear for half a year.

The trouble began two weeks later, when the studio sent Garbo the script for her next film, *Women Love Diamonds*. The scenario by Lorna Moon and Waldemar Young told the story of Mavis Ray, a girl of uncertain character and profession whose uncle keeps her in a penthouse, furs, and finery. When an earnest young man wants to marry her, the uncle takes him aside and tells him Mavis's Unholy Secrets—her parents were not married and he is not her uncle. Mavis lives down her disgrace by raising the children of a chauffeur of whom she is enamored. He later finds her working in a hospital and offers to marry her. Although the story followed Thalberg's new Garbo formula, Mavis Ray was conceived of cardboard and the plot was preposterous.

On November 2, Garbo made up her mind. "I could not do that story," she said. "Four or five bad pictures and there would be no more of me for the American people." Stiller was in New York and Gilbert was working on a Tod Browning film called *The Show*. Gilbert suspected that Mayer, who had always disliked him, had assigned it to him as punishment for his latest drunken escapade. Garbo was unsympathetic, so a petulant Gilbert renewed an affair with his *Big Parade* costar, Renée Adorée. Garbo suddenly found herself alone. "I did not know what to do," she said. "No one would tell me." Stiller's New York attorney, Joseph S. Buhler, advised Garbo to ignore any threats that the studio might make. Garbo was afraid, but she complied. "I went to the hotel and I sat down and waited. I did not know what else I could do. I wanted to be home in Sweden."

On the morning of November 3, Garbo received a telephone call from the wardrobe department, asking her to come and look at some costume sketches and to meet the director, Dmitri Buchowetski. She had heard from Murray, Stiller, and others that he was untalented and prickly. Garbo informed the startled wardrobe assistant that she would not be coming in, that day or otherwise. "It was the first time I had not done what they wanted," she said, somewhat inaccurately. On November 4, Mayer sent two messages to her hotel. Garbo did not respond. On November 5, a messenger delivered a registered ultimatum.

> Yesterday you were notified by telegram as well as by letter to report at our studio this morning at the hour of ten o'clock AM. You have disobeyed this instruction and we have not heard from you either directly or indirectly. In view of this situation and considering particularly the shortness of time left to us before commencing the photographing of the photoplay *Women Love Diamonds*, which was to be your next vehicle, it will be impossible for us to cast you in this picture. We desire you to know at this time that it is our intention to engage another artist to play the part assigned to you.
>
> Until further notice you are instructed to report daily at our studio at the hour of nine o'clock AM. Failure on your part to comply with the provisions of this notice will be deemed to constitute a willful disregard of your obligations under your contract of employment with us and during the period of any insubordination on your part your compensation under said contract will be discontinued.

When Garbo did not answer Mayer's letter or report to work, Mayer ordered her salary suspended, effective November 5. Then Thalberg sent Buchowetski to the Miramar.

"Greta met him in the lobby of her hotel, quite casually," said Gilbert. "But he immediately cornered her and argued interminably, like a self-winding phonograph, as to just why it was to her advantage to work under his direction. After all his talk, she turned to him coldly and said, 'But I do not wish to work for you.' Naturally, he was horribly insulted." Buchowetski returned to the studio empty-handed. He was replaced by Edmund Goulding, who rewrote *Women Love Diamonds* and cast the contract player Pauline Starke as Mavis Ray; it would not be a success.

Paramount thought that *Hotel Imperial* would be a hit and invited Stiller to make another film. On November 17, M-G-M paid Stiller $2,166.66 to end his contract so that he could accept one at the rival studio. He now spent what time he could with Garbo, and he did not like what he heard. She and Gilbert were not getting along. Something was wrong.

More than one of the Hollywood Swedes had seen evidence of Garbo's maternal instinct. At a restaurant in June, a baby crawled across the floor toward her. "With arms outstretched, she talked baby talk to him," recounted her companion Borg. After the baby's mother retrieved it, Garbo told him: "Borg, someday I want a little one like that—all my own." She spoke to a journalist about her voyage from Sweden. "I did not talk to anyone but a tiny boy," she said. "Little Tommy. I wanted so madly to give him cakes. But he had never eaten cakes. His mother and father were very careful." She also spent a great deal of time playing with the children of her artist friends the Stocklassas. "She was devoted to children," recalled their daughter Ingrid. "You can say intelligent things to children," Garbo once said. "When you talk silly things, they just look at you, and you feel they are thinking, 'Why are you saying such silly things?' Children are very sensible persons." Garbo had broached the subject of children to Gilbert. He did not take it well. "She hates Hollywood and everything that is in it," he told writer Adela Rogers St. Johns. "She wants to buy half of Montana or whatever state it is that has no people in it and turn it into a wheat farm and raise wheat and children. Frankly, I don't want to marry some dumb Swede and raise wheat and kids miles from civilization." When quotes like this reached Garbo's friends in Stockholm, they asked her for reassurance. "I suppose you have read in the papers about me and a certain actor," she wrote to Lars Saxon, "but I am not, as they say here, 'going to get married.' But they are crazy for news. That is why they have picked on me."

Since the premiere of *The Torrent*, Garbo had been increasingly aware of her value to the press, and in particular to the gangs of freelance photographers who waited outside expensive restaurants, train stations, courthouses, and movie stars' homes with pockets full of film holders and flash powder. Garbo's peers regarded photographers as an annoying but necessary part of celebrity. She looked on them as a gazelle looks on a gang of hyenas. She could not, *would* not cooperate with these relentless, intrusive picture snatchers who would just as happily shoot a man being executed. And if they could capture a forbidden image like that, they could surely catch Garbo coming out of Gilbert's house in the morning. They could alert the public if she was driving to the beach, Palm Springs, or Mexico, catching a train, or boarding an ocean liner. If she left her hotel or John Gilbert's house, 5x7 Graflex cameras could freeze her action and isolate any aspect of her appearance. They could catch her looking not so much like a movie star. If she was hung over, beat up, drug-addicted, pregnant, recovering from an abortion or a nervous breakdown, they could capture it—and the tabloids would run it. Garbo's war of nerves with M-G-M was the biggest story in Hollywood in the fall of 1926. The newspapers were not about to lose it.

As a nervous and wary Garbo dug in her heels, her relations with Gilbert did not improve. Angry with her because she would not marry him, he took a train to New York to accept a *Photoplay* magazine award and stayed much longer than he said he would. She could have gone with him. She did not. As the frustrated photographers could attest, she did not go anywhere. She stayed hidden, and if she traveled from his house to her hotel after he left, she most likely did so under a rug in the back of a domestic's car. Writing to Saxon in late November, she hinted that the studio was threatening to use her immigrant status against her.

> You cannot imagine how many things have happened since you heard from me last. Twice I have turned my back on the studio and gone home. Threats! Nothing has helped. I will not return until I calm down. I was given a part right after finishing my second film. I was tired and nervous. Besides, it was a "vamp" part. I asked to be spared it but they said no. I stayed home for more than a week but then I went back and played it. Believe me, that was a big scandal. They think I am mad. Then there was still another ugly part with one of the worst directors there is. And Garbo went home the second time. This is something nobody does here. But I get so nervous over these idiotic things that I lose my head. People say that they are going to send me back home. I don't know what will happen. Haven't shown up at Metro for over a month. Uh oh.

In early December, Garbo met Harry Edington, the M-G-M account executive who was also Gilbert's personal manager. Edington was recommended to both actors by scenarist Carey Wilson, who had known him since working in Italy on *Ben-Hur*. "All I wanted was no trouble and just a chance to make good stories," said Garbo. "So I went to see Mr. Harry Edington, and, after talking to me almost every day, almost, for over a week, and coming to believe that I was not all the papers had said about me, he said he would handle . . . my contracts, my money, my work—everything."

Only Edington's status at the studio prevented him from being thrown out when he informed Mayer and Thalberg of the terms on which Garbo would return.

"GRETA GARBO SAYS $5,000 OR NO WORK" was *Variety*'s headline on December 15. The studio immediately assumed the role of an aggrieved parent, an attitude happily espoused by the *Los Angeles Examiner* columnist Louella Parsons, who portrayed Garbo as peevish, stubborn, and avaricious, and by *Photoplay* editor James Quirk, who called her everything but an ungrateful immigrant and suggested that she learn English. "They had a cartoon of me in my country holding out my hand for many American dollars," recalled Garbo. Mayer assumed that Gilbert was behind Garbo's strike but controlled his temper when speaking to Victor Seastrom, whom he respected perhaps more than any other director working for him. Seastrom agreed to take Mayer's case, not to Garbo but to Stiller, whose response was succinct: "These fools at Metro will ruin her." Nonetheless, he promised Seastrom he would talk with Garbo. The result was a December 18 letter to Mayer on her behalf. In it Stiller said that he had been able to persuade her to sign a five-year contract in which she would ask less than Edington had: $500 less per week for the first two years, and $1,000 less per week for the remaining three years.

> The reason that Miss Garbo has been so unhappy here, notwithstanding her success, is the number of vamp roles that she has been forced to play and which she keenly feels are outside her sphere. You saw her in *Gösta Berling* and you know it was because of her great success in this production that you gave her a contract. In this picture she was an entirely different type—an innocent girl—not a vamp. Believe me or not, Mr. Mayer, I have been the only one who consoled her and I explained to her that the roles she portrayed for your company, whether they were vamp roles or others more suited to her, made absolutely no difference whatsoever. I also told her that I had expressed my opinion to Mr. Thalberg and he personally assured me there would be a change and Miss Garbo need have no fear that she had to play vamp roles in the future.

Mayer's comment was terse: "If I had granted her wishes in that direction, I can tell you that her career would have ended then and there." He made sure the following quote showed up in *Photoplay*: "Miss Garbo is a type. She cannot play guileless, sweet heroines any more than Gloria Swanson can play them. If we let her have her way, she would be ruined quickly." Oddly, on December 18, M-G-M put Garbo back on salary, releasing a statement to the effect that Garbo would soon return, and under the terms of her original contract. Why? Had Edington been able to talk studio sense to Garbo? Or was there some other process at work? Garbo was, as the saying goes, unavailable for comment. When she wrote home, the upcoming premiere of Stiller's *Hotel Imperial* was on her mind. "I hope that Stiller, who did not get much kindness at home, will become one of the best, if not the best here. He is now with Paramount. I have to stay at Metro, where no one cares about me, sad to say." On December 30, M-G-M took Garbo off salary again.

Stiller agonized over his premiere, according to Lars Hanson, and was "so worn out and wrought up when we talked with him in the lobby before the picture started that he began to cry and ran into the lounge to compose himself." Garbo was supposed to attend the premiere; however, as there were a dozen hungry photographers waiting for her, and as no photographs were published showing her there, she most likely did not appear. The same thing happened on January 9 when *Flesh and the Devil* premiered in New York. Then she had a visitor from Sweden, the journalist Lars Saxon. "My first impression," Saxon later wrote, "was that she looked as though her eyes were sore from crying. She looked careworn." Mayer invited him to the studio and told him about the wonderful production of Count Leo Tolstoy's *Anna Karenina* that was being prepared for Garbo. Mayer was complimentary and diplomatic, almost going as far as to offer Saxon a job if he could effect a reconciliation, but the bewildered visitor was of little help. Saxon later wrote that Garbo treated him to dinner at the Ambassador Hotel. Did she?

Once again, waiting photographers never saw her. No photos were published.

Nor can any press photographs of Greta Garbo from this period be found in archives or private collections as proof that she indeed went to Edington's office, Stiller's premiere, the Ambassador Hotel, or anywhere else she was reported to have gone after October 13.

This lengthening seclusion was indeed peculiar. She was not a fugitive from justice; she was conducting a legitimate strike for better wages. Why the protracted disappearance?

One thing was certain. On January 24, 1927, when Garbo was required to report for work on *Anna Karenina*, she did not. Edington, Stiller, and Gilbert (who was now on better terms with her) all advised her to hold out. "I did not say anything or do anything," she said. "And the papers always said I want money. I was terribly restless. I figured out that maybe the next moment I would be packing my trunks. I was so low, as you say, that I thought I would break. But it's like when you are in love. Suppose the man you love does something to hurt you. You think you will break it off; but you don't do it." Louella Parsons reported that Garbo and Gilbert appeared together at the Hollywood premiere of *Flesh and the Devil* on February 3. Once again, in spite of Parsons's breathless description of flashbulbs and newsreel cameras, no photos appeared in the press.

On April 21, 1927, Garbo was photographed for the first time in six months. She had just returned to M-G-M to star in *Anna Karenina*, and was visiting Lillian Gish on the set of Victor Seastrom's *The Wind*. "I heard one day that she had lost her only sister," wrote Gish, "and I sent her flowers and a note. Garbo [later] came to thank me, but she could not speak English. Tears came to her eyes, but I could not speak Swedish so I put my arms around her and we both cried. I knew how I would feel if I had lost my darling sister and could not get to her from a strange, far land."

Two days later, Universal News Service correspondent Dorothy Herzog released an item that appeared from coast to coast: "GRETA GARBO ALMOST WEDS." Herzog reported that Garbo and Gilbert "eloped to Santa Ana to be married a short time ago, only to be halted at the altar by the chill, though beautiful actress's exercise of woman's prerogative—she changed her mind at the last minute—it became known last night." If Garbo had married Gilbert, she would, of course, have instantly deprived M-G-M of the threat of deportation. The source for this story was not revealed; there were no eyewitness interviews or photographs. The same dubious journalism qualified Louella Parsons's February 14 story, "GILBERT WEDS GARBO, SAY FRIENDS." Gilbert made an official denial of this story nine days later, after returning to the studio from a Glendale hospital, where he had been admitted "for observation."

As strange as this sequence of events was in the face of Garbo's calculated withdrawal, M-G-M's laxity was more so. The strike had been going on for almost four months. This intransigent young woman was costing the corporation thousands of dollars in wasted preproduction, lost revenues, and good will. M-G-M's lawyers could have filed a restraining order, an injunction, or a lawsuit. Garbo could, after all, still hop that boat to Sweden. The usually purposeful Mayer chose not to act. And on February 15, he ordered Garbo's salary reinstated. To the public, Garbo was on strike. But these inconsistencies in policy continued to occur—in private.

On February 21, Thalberg ordered an accounting of the strike. (That he had to investigate this on his own suggests that he was uninformed of certain aspects of the strike.) To his surprise, the accountant's report revealed that since Garbo had walked out, she had been suspended for only $6\,1/6$ weeks, and on "Lay-Off" for 7 weeks. She had in fact been paid $1,400 (roughly $28,000 in today's dollars) for $8\,1/3$ weeks of "Idle Time." This made no sense; Garbo had *refused* to work.

Thalberg immediately sent word to Garbo: she was to report for work in a week. She did not. On February 26, her salary was again suspended. For reasons that were equally vague, the studio was now pretending that the last four months had not happened and that Garbo simply could not begin to act in this manner. After all, not even Mae Murray could defy the studio and get away with it. After filming most of *Valencia* a few months earlier, the giddy star had suddenly decided that she could not live without Prince David Mdivani and had sailed to Europe with him, leaving Thalberg and director Buchowetski to finish the film with a double. Her contract canceled by a vengeful M-G-M, Miss Murray could find work at no other studio. Her stardom was ended.

On March 2, Garbo sent a note to Mayer claiming that she had not been told to report for work. A day later, Mayer replied that such an excuse was "not in good faith" because she had been aware of the *Anna Karenina* start date, yet had waited four days to contact them. Edington was well acquainted with the power elite of M-G-M's parent company in New York, Loew's Inc. At this point, he decided to go over Mayer's head and have Garbo appeal directly to the studio's "secretary," New York boss J. Robert Rubin. Her March 6 cable read in part:

> A five-year contract was ready several months ago, the terms of which were impossible, and I immediately told them I could not sign it. The result was that every newspaper published long articles about my temperament and my refusal to play any roles. They also said that I refused to take the part of Anna Karenina, which is indeed a false assertion as I asked them to let me take that part. But I leave it to you if you have ever seen a star contract like that. When the new contract was drawn up, I was fighting not to play three roles a year because my constitution is not strong, and, if I were to play as many roles as they see fit, I know I would break down under the strain and fail to do my work as it should be done. . . . To my deep regret, I see that Metro-Goldwyn has no understanding nor consideration for my situation though I have always tried to do my best in my pictures.

Garbo's salary was reinstated in a week and a press release prepared. *Variety* was foolish enough to believe it, reporting on March 18: "Greta Garbo will play the part of a chorus girl in *His Brother from Brazil*, the first costarring vehicle of Lew Cody and Aileen Pringle." Even more incredibly, Garbo later told an interviewer that she had gone to the studio. "I did not say a word," she recounted, "but tried on the dresses and was all ready to play the little part in the picture when Miss Pringle said she would not do it. Then they called me and said I was impossible and could not be handled. For the first time I answered Mr. Mayer back. I said I had all my clothes fitted and was ready to play the little part. What more did they want?" The fans who were watching this bizarre charade wanted to know what it meant. Garbo supporting Pringle as a *chorus girl*? It made no sense. No one would be watching Pringle!

Most of M-G-M's costume test photographs survive in archives. None has ever been found to substantiate the chorus girl story.

Further complicating matters was Garbo's inconstant relationship with Gilbert. On the same day as the *Variety* item, Louella Parsons claimed that Garbo had been caught leaving her hotel by reporters, and had said: "I think a lot of Mr. Gilbert. I admire him very much indeed—as a friend. Not as a possible lover or husband."

Lionel Barrymore cut a striking figure as Karenin in the early scenes of *Anna Karenina*, but Garbo was more subdued than the role required.

No new press photos of Garbo had appeared in print since early October. Contrary to what was being written for publication, Garbo was still not going out in public.

Whatever was going on where Garbo was hiding out, it suddenly changed. On March 30, Edington and M-G-M, through Rubin's mediation, reached an agreement. Garbo's new twelve-page contract, retroactive to January 1, gave her $2,000 a week the first year; $4,000 a week the second year; $5,000 a week the third year; and $6,000 a week the fourth year. In addition, she was freed of the necessity of endorsing commercial products. The contract did not free her from interviews or posing for poster art in the portrait gallery. Nor did it give her a choice of director, cameraman, or script.

Now, for the third time, the studio put *Anna Karenina* into production, with Buchowetski still in place as director and Merritt Gerstad on camera (instead of William Daniels, who was shooting *On Ze Boulevard*). Ricardo Cortez was cast as Count Vronsky and Lionel Barrymore as Karenin. Garbo had reason to be happy, even to gloat. By holding out as she had, and waiting for the box-office returns of *Flesh and the Devil* to affirm her value, she had forced Mayer to capitulate. His need to impose order on a corporation had been bested by a lone immigrant. Friends said that Garbo had survived her siege by simply not caring, that she would have been equally happy returning to Sweden. If so, why did she stay in Los Angeles? Would not caring make a human being isolate herself for six months?

On April 11, in the wee hours of the morning, Gilbert roared into the Beverly Hills police station, claiming that Stiller had tried to kill him. When he would not be quieted and began to wave a pistol around, he was arrested. In actuality, Gilbert had been pestering Garbo the previous night and the much taller Stiller had pushed him away, first from his car and then from a low balcony. Gilbert served a day in jail for disturbing the peace. The most disturbed party was Garbo. Gilbert's drunken episodes were increasing in inverse proportion to her tolerance for them. "Garbo said he drank too much—for her," related his daughter, Leatrice Gilbert Fountain. But she stayed. "She was in love with him," wrote Adela Rogers St. Johns, to whom Gilbert confided too much one night over a glass of Scotch whisky. "When in sheer desperation he threw her off the balcony and she rolled down the Beverly hillside, she climbed back up over rocks and through burrs and tumbleweed." Worse than this, according to Sven-Hugo Borg, M-G-M story editor Samuel Marx, and actors Colleen Moore and John Barrymore, firearms were also an element of these passionate quarrels. Gilbert, perhaps unable to differentiate between the melodrama on an M-G-M stage and the cool drama of Garbo's withdrawal, on several occasions threatened her with a gun.

Garbo and Gilbert both reported to the studio on April 18, she to begin *Karenina*, and he to begin a rum-running

In this scene with Dorothy Sebastian, Garbo's posture betrays her growing fatigue. When Sebastian introduced herself before the scene, Garbo asked her how she felt. "Tired," said Sebastian. "I'm glad that you are tired," Garbo smiled wanly. "I like tired people."

drama called *Twelve Miles Out*. "When I was starting work on *Anna Karenina*," said Garbo, "the wardrobe department sent me flowers. I was so pleased. I know in a big factory-studio they cannot send you flowers and do things for others. But it made me feel a little closer." Garbo felt so confident about her homecoming that she consented to pose with Lillian Gish and Seastrom on April 21 on the set of their film, *The Wind*. She was wearing a dark, shapeless, all-concealing coat. This was the first time Garbo had been photographed at M-G-M since posing with Moreno after retakes on *The Temptress*.

It was also the first time she had been photographed by anyone—since October 13.

Gilbert was not as happy to be back, as his leading lady, Joan Crawford, soon found out. "John Gilbert wasn't interested in this film," she wrote. "He was madly in love with Garbo, the love affair wasn't going well, and he was obsessed—a caged lion. . . . The moment he finished a scene, he'd rush to her set, to her dressing room, or he'd attempt to call her. Thwarted, he was fury incarnate. He resented every minute on the set away from her."

Buchowetski began *Anna Karenina* with a banquet scene. Visiting the set, journalist Dorothy Calhoun transcribed the conversations of dress extras in Czarist uniforms and 1870s gowns. An elegant older woman playing a dinner guest at the Karenin banquet fumed as two o'clock rolled around and Garbo had not yet arrived. "She is getting away with murder, that girl! But *they* won't stand for it."

"Her success in holding up the company is going to her head," said another extra. "But if anyone can get away with anything around a studio, then more power to her!"

"They're all afraid of her," said a third. "They don't dare find fault with her for fear she'll turn around and go home."

"A foreigner!" sniffed the grand older woman, who was making a few dollars a day parading herself in borrowed finery. "To get high-hat! What people see in her! When she lies back on pillows in a picture with her mouth half open and her eyes half shut, is that acting, I ask you? Or is it simply sex?"

"What's the difference as long as people pay to see it?" yawned a wise young man.

The word had spread that *Flesh and the Devil* was a runaway hit, so Garbo could be forgiven her peremptory new manner. She now had no patience for the long hours she was spending in costume fittings with costumer Gilbert Clark. A dressmaker's dummy was out of the question, but a stand-in was not. A dress extra who bore an uncanny likeness to Garbo soon took her place in fittings. When Garbo first saw Geraldine Dvorak, she exclaimed: "Gott! She looks like me!" The inevitable rumors surfaced; perhaps Dvorak had doubled for Garbo in public during her six-month hideout. Her absence was still being discussed at the studio, especially when it became obvious that Garbo's physical dimensions had changed since her fittings for *Flesh and the Devil*. Anyone watching the rushes of *Ann Karenina* would surely have observed that Garbo's hips were slightly wider and that her breasts were noticeably fuller, particularly in the form-fitting ball gown. The womanly contours diminished slightly in the coming months, but her figure never again looked as it had in her first three films.

Being studied so intently by everyone with whom she worked, Garbo began to exhibit her usual nervous symptoms. Now she had the power to remedy them. "Garbo insisted that she could not act if anyone watched her," recounted a witness. "She even asked if the set could be fenced in so the electricians would have to stay outside. This was tried, but it proved impractical." She also tried to have visitors prevented from entering the stage. In spite of Garbo's temperament, tardiness, and absences, Buchowetski managed within ten days to film more than five long sequences with her. "I like her," said Cortez, who was more polite to her than he had been on *The Torrent*. "She never talks scandal. She never talks personalities. She never talks at *all* to speak of." The journalist who interviewed him commented on Garbo's "lack of vitality." After less than two weeks of shooting, Garbo fell ill. An April 30 item reported that a Dr. Gustav Bjorkman had diagnosed her illness "as an intestinal affliction, probably ptomaine poisoning. Dr.

Bjorkman stated last night that X-ray pictures were taken yesterday to determine the exact cause."

An internist consulted by the author offers the opinion that X-rays would be useless in diagnosing ptomaine poisoning.

On May 7, Louella Parsons reported that Garbo was still quite sick and not expected to return to work for three weeks. Buchowetski filmed a few more scenes, shooting around Garbo, and then Thalberg shut down the production.

Years later, Cortez gave this account of the filming: "We were on it for six weeks [*sic*] and she became ill, and Mr. Thalberg asked me to wait around. [Finally] he called me in and said, 'I don't know how long this girl's going to be out, and I'd like to put you in a film with Lon Chaney. It's a good part, entirely up to you.' She was down with anemia of sorts. So I went into [Benjamin Christensen's *Mockery*]." Garbo's intuition about Buchowetski had been right; Thalberg did not like his *Anna Karenina* footage. On May 18, *Variety* announced that *Anna Karenina* was being scrapped. The project would be restarted with the new title of *Love*; a new director, Edmund Goulding; a new cameraman, William Daniels—and John Gilbert as Vronsky. Garbo's mysterious and as yet undisclosed illness was not mentioned as a primary cause of this turn of events—which cost M-G-M in excess of $100,000 (more than $2 million in today's money). On May 21, Garbo returned to the studio, apparently recovered. On June 1, she officially (and at last) signed her new contract. When she reported to the set of *Love* on June 22, the saga of her strike and the scrapped *Anna Karenina* finally came to a close—well, not quite.

Garbo quietly informed her new director and returning cameraman that she would no longer shoot close-ups during her "time of the month." She believed that her face would not match the previous week's film; she was right. As the years progressed, this became a challenge for both camera crew and production manager. "She might look like hell for a week at a time," wrote producer David Lewis in 1977. "You'd have to shoot around her or not do close-ups. She would get very thin-faced and gaunt." However, when the company tried to schedule shooting around her menstrual cycles, she was forced to admit that they were now irregular. They had also become painful and debilitating. With extreme reluctance, she finally confided the cause: a recurring ovarian infection. No one dared ask her what had initially caused it, but M-G-M gossip blamed an abortion performed by a studio doctor.

Opposite: Garbo sat for a close-up in a dinner party scene in *Anna Karenina*. "The heavy-lidded droop of her eyes seems not provocative, as the critics say, but weary," wrote journalist Dorothy Calhoun. "The languid grace they call seductiveness is merely low vitality." Within two weeks, Garbo was seriously ill.

This production still shows cameraman Merritt Gerstad and director Dmitri Buchowetski with Garbo and Ricardo Cortez during the first days of work on *Anna Karenina*. She should have been happy to be working on her own terms, but she looked unwell.

abuse her, causing a miscarriage and complications? Did he shoot her? Did she shoot him, causing him to be hospitalized "for observation"? Was her April illness (and her subsequent female trouble) a result of this stress? Was her fear of strangers indicative of a more serious psychological disorder? Did she have a nervous breakdown as a result of the combined trauma of her sister's death, her separation from Stiller, her too-sudden romance with Gilbert, a possible pregnancy, a possible abortion, and the strike?

There have been numerous stories of the studio's collusion with the Culver City Police Department, Los Angeles district attorney Buron Fitts, and various corruptible physicians to cover up studio employees' misbehavior. Any of the possibilities mentioned above are both plausible and possible, since they did occur in other M-G-M stars' careers and were indeed covered up. The question here is which of these events (or what combination of them) caused Garbo's eight-month eclipse.

Garbo may have confided something at a later time to screenwriter S. N. Behrman, who knew her intimately for more than forty years. In an unpublished 1962 interview with a television producer, Behrman supplied the only clue to this mystery ever to be put on paper. A stenographer's notes read: "Mr. Behrman said he thought she might have had a couple of abortions and that this had given her a terror of sex."

The whole story, of course, could only have come from Garbo, Gilbert, or Mayer. It is conceivable that no one else— not even Thalberg or executives such as Pete Smith, Eddie Mannix, or Howard Strickling—knew it. There is also a question about Harry Edington's role. Every Garbo biography states that Edington did not collect an agent's fee for representing Garbo, only a bonus after the completion of each of her films. Yet Behrman said unequivocally: "He was her manager. He even got Metro to pay his agent's fee when she once went on a seven-month strike." In May 2004, the author sent the manuscript of this chapter to Edington's widow, Barbara Kent, who may be the last person living who has an insider's perspective on Garbo's private life in the 1920s. Although Miss Kent had granted interviews in recent years to three other writers, she responded to this author with the following: "I did not know Greta Garbo very well, and do not feel that I would be much help in providing you with information for the book that you are writing about her films."

Unless there is someone else who was privy to these events or who heard them recounted by someone who was, we shall never know what really happened to Greta Garbo seventy-nine years ago.

As incredible as it sounds, the photographic and archival evidence cited here suggests that an easily recognizable motion-picture star completely and totally disappeared from sight from October 13, 1926, to April 18, 1927, was then gravely ill after only ten days of work, and was again unseen from April 28 to June 22. That new absence brought her total time away from the studio to eight months. Contrary to what has been written elsewhere, no single event or combination of events related to a salary strike would be sufficient to cause this extraordinary disruption of lives.

Almost eighty years later, there are too many unanswered questions. Was the salary strike a smoke screen for some potential scandal? If not, why was Garbo not seen in public for six months? Did Mayer use publicity to aid the smoke screen? Was Thalberg kept ignorant of this entire process? Did he grow suspicious in mid-February? Did he accidentally discover the anomaly in the accounting records? Did he then demand that Mayer and Garbo end the pretense? What was really behind it?

Did Gilbert get Garbo pregnant in August 1926? Did she have a child prematurely and give it up to be raised by Swedish friends? Did she have an abortion? Did Gilbert

CHAPTER FIVE
Love

After the tumult of the past eighteen months, the production of *Love* was the well-ordered effort that Greta Garbo had come to expect of Louis B. Mayer and Irving Thalberg. They could not have done better for her than to hire Frances Marion as the first writer of her new formula. At thirty-nine, Marion was the most prolific, respected, and highly paid scenarist in the industry, having apprenticed with director Lois Weber in 1912 and written for the powerful Mary Pickford since 1917. In the 1920s she crafted star vehicles for Marion Davies, Rudolph Valentino, and Lillian Gish; the successful and much-praised *Scarlet Letter* was made from her script. Marion knew that there was no way to condense Count Leo Tolstoy's 1877 novel *Anna Karenina* into a formula film without reducing it to its love story. Worse, the supervisor (unnamed in her memoirs) who was originally assigned to the project emphatically disliked the story. "It stinks," said the supervisor after Marion told him of the aristocrat who ruins Anna's life and the lives of everyone around her in order to experience passionate love. "Who's going to care about stuff like that?"

"It's a classic," Marion answered.

"Classic, my foot! I tell you it stinks. Hope we didn't pay a lot of dough for it. The whole damn thing will have to be rewritten."

As soon as Marion could escape from this boor's office, she went to Thalberg and asked him to personally supervise the film. He was unable to drop his other obligations, but he did take the film away from the boor and give it to a supervisor who could also direct. "When [Thalberg] told me that Edmund Goulding was going to direct the picture," wrote Marion, "it was welcome news, as I had known this clever and amusing Englishman since the end of the World War, when [writer] Anita Loos (to whom laughter was manna) introduced him to our circle. Goulding's spontaneous wit, Chesterfieldian manners, slightly manic behavior at times, and supreme self-confidence gave him an air of insouciant romanticism." Garbo took to the former actor immediately. He was sensitive to her need for privacy, her preference for as few rehearsals as possible, and to the instability of her relations with John Gilbert. Hoping that the romance would last as long as the filming, the studio changed the film's title

so that theater marquees would read: "Greta Garbo and John Gilbert in *Love*."

Filming commenced on June 22, 1927, with a scene at a roadside inn where Garbo and Gilbert seek refuge from a snowstorm. She removes a veil and a hat, stunning Gilbert with her beauty. When she removed the hat, her hair was not photographing as well as William Daniels liked, so Goulding stepped in with a comb and a few hairpins and made it right. Within a week, Garbo and Goulding were getting along famously. "Every day at lunch and every evening at dinner while *Love* was being filmed," said Goulding. "she, Jack Gilbert, and myself were together. We talked of nothing but the picture. I knew how I wanted it done, but I didn't give Garbo orders. She was given to understand that it was a mutual responsibility, this thing of directing. She rose to the suggestion like the great woman that she is. The actual directing was done over the dinner table, not on the sets.

Director Edmund Goulding, shown here with Greta Garbo and John Gilbert, waxed enthusiastic about Garbo's work in the 1927 film *Love*. "She is superbly simple," he said. "Shrewd, yet quite untouched by pettiness, jealousy, or unimportant concerns. Her vocabulary is chiefly 'Yes,' 'No,' 'I like,' 'No, I not like.' She looks at you in questioning silence and expects you to know what she means."

"Garbo and Gilbert in *Love*," was the catchphrase that would sell this film. It was up to still photographer William Grimes to capture images that would affirm the celebrated romance, but . . .

When we assembled for work in the morning, it was all settled what we were going to do."

The first few scenes—the inn, an Easter service in a Russian Orthodox cathedral, and a ball—were all staged on large sets with many people present. Garbo could no longer abide the curious looks that came from extras and workers on the periphery of the dark stage. Daniels suggested that the tall black flats used to block lens flare could serve as screens to isolate her work area. He tried them and Garbo approved them. "I was the one who insisted on closed sets for her," said Daniels. "No visitors, and so on; no one present except the director and the crew, and no executives. I was trying to help her, especially because it took her a time to speak English, and she was shy, *so shy*. I did it to *protect her*. And then, she had never been on stage, so she wasn't accustomed to acting in front of an audience, and she was, quite simply, suffering constantly from stage fright."

In addition, Garbo tried to have journalists barred from her sets. "Interviews! How I hate them! When I get to be a big star, I will never give another." This was where Pete Smith put his foot down. He could not sell a film without publicity, and poor English or not, people wanted to know what Garbo thought. She disagreed. "Oh, please, let's not talk of me," she told an interviewer. "I was born. I grew up. I have lived like every other person. Why must people talk about me?" There was a good reason to talk about her, according to journalist Malcolm H. Oettinger.

She was in the arms of John Gilbert when I first saw her. The air was surcharged. As they embraced, unaware of my presence, the heat curled the walls, blistered the chairs, all but stifled in its intensity. Slowly Greta's arms encircled his

shoulder, gradually she lifted her chin, suddenly their lips met. It looked for all the world like a close-up. In fairness to the interlocked pair let it be said at once that it *was* a close-up. But it was not received with the ordinary calm attending such routine affairs. Scene shifters edged nearer during the amorous passage. Calloused prop men paused to watch the tableau, script clerks blushed enthusiastically, and even extras awakened from their lethargy long enough to study the action.

The stills released from these first weeks of shooting showed that Gilbert was still in love with Garbo, passionately and possessively. Like the character of Vronsky, he did not want to share her with anyone—even with their director. "Gilbert was feeling his oats," said an onlooker. "He wanted to show Garbo how clever he was. Every scene meant his interfering with Goulding. He insisted on trying to direct the picture." Goulding, mindful of what had happened to Stroheim, Stiller, and Buchowetski, graciously let Gilbert have his way. Even when *Photoplay* printed an item that Gilbert had directed all of the love scenes, Goulding kept his mouth shut and cashed his sizable paycheck. Gilbert, on the other hand, could not keep his criticism to himself. "We are making a Russian picture now built around the lavishness and splendor of the days of the Czar," he said. "The appropriation for the picture is $125,000. It can't be done on this sum. That's all there is to it." His remarks were not only rude but also inaccurate. The film's budget was $488,000, and while its scope did not equal that of 1927 epics such as *Sunrise, In Old San Francisco,* or *The King of Kings,* it had its share of

. . . the romance was not always going well.

spectacular scenes. Did Gilbert really think that audiences would come to this film just to see a violent horse race? When they did come, in December 1927, they came to see Garbo and Gilbert in love, giving the handsome film an equally handsome profit of $571,000. After *Ben-Hur*, *The Big Parade*, and *The Merry Widow*, *Love* would be M-G-M's most profitable silent film.

Love was everything that the studio and Garbo had hoped for. The team made a huge hit and she got to leave the vamp roles behind, a victory lauded by the Swedish film critic Dr. Bengt Idestat-Almquist, who, under the name of "Robin Hood," wrote: "In her first American pictures she was something different from this: a sensual body, thin and wriggling like an exotic liana, plus a couple of heavy eyelids that hinted at all kinds of picturesque lusts. But gradually Miss Garbo has worked her way toward becoming a real artist, an actress of depth and sincerity." *Variety* looked at the team: "Peculiar combination this Gilbert-Garbo hook-up. Both sprang up suddenly and fast, Miss Garbo from nowhere. The latter isn't now as big as she should be or will be, always remembering it's the stories that count. . . . Miss Garbo and Mr. Gilbert are in a fair way to become the biggest box office mixed team this country has yet known. Both are strong away from each other and have proved it. But combine that double strength with a reasonable story and who or what can stop it?"

And what was this team doing at Tower Grove Road? The same thing that was on the screen? Garbo laughed when asked about Gilbert by an interviewer. "Love? Of course I have been in love. Love is the last and first of a woman's education. How could you express love if you have never felt it?" When the interviewer pressed too hard, Garbo drew the line. "Marriage? I have told many times: I *do not know*. I like to be alone, not always with some other person. There are many things in your heart that you can never tell another person. They are you. Your joys and your sorrows. And you can never, never tell them. It is not right that you should tell them. You cheapen yourself, the inside of yourself, when you tell them." A less tactful interviewer asked about Gilbert and got a sharp retort.

"Is it that Americans have no love affairs themselves," asked Garbo, "that they always want to hear about other people's? God! If one looks at romance, it is bruised. If one touches it, it is broken. You think if I have a romance I tell everybody? No! I hide it!" As Thalberg sought a suitable story for the next Garbo-Gilbert movie, his reticent new star was perhaps saying too much. The romance was indeed bruised—and breaking.

Garbo and Gilbert waltzed to their own music on the set of *Love*.

THE SMOLDERING SILENCE

The Divine Woman

Producing Greta Garbo's films had become a many-layered challenge for Irving Thalberg. He needed a director who could work around her increasingly anomalous work habits. He needed a charismatic leading man, but not necessarily John Gilbert. He needed to honor his newfound Garbo formula, even though he had promised not to cast her as a vamp. He certainly did not want to cast her as an ingenue; her fans wanted to see her in sensational roles. Perhaps she could do all of these in one film. Why not have her play a naive girl who becomes a glamorous actress? In this way, he could honor both the formula and his promise. Garbo could play Sarah Bernhardt, the most famous actress of the nineteenth century. The studio owned a 1925 play called *Starlight*, a romanticized version of Bernhardt's life. Thalberg hired its author, screenwriter Gladys Unger, to adapt it. "The Divine Sarah" had died four years earlier, at the age of seventy-eight, after sixty years of stardom. Known for her "golden voice," Bernhardt was in her late fifties when she began to see films as a way to preserve her celebrated performances in *Camille* and *Queen Elizabeth*. When she saw herself on the screen, she cried out: "I am immortal! I am a film!"

Bernhardt was born the illegitimate daughter of a Dutch Jewish courtesan, was educated in a convent, and then entered the Conservatoire de Musique et Déclamation. Her dedication to her craft would suit Garbo's requirements for a new type of character, but her slow, steady ascent to stardom would make a dull film, so her life was gradually rewritten to suit the formula. Thalberg rejected Unger's first draft and turned the project over to the reliable Dorothy Farnum. Garbo's countryman Victor Seastrom then began to rework the script, first with Paramount producer Erich Pommer and then with Farnum and scenarist Frances Marion. After five drafts, Thalberg approved the script, but then he decided it still was not ready for the cameras.

There was also the question of a leading man. It now appeared that the Garbo-Gilbert team might not be available for this project. No one knew, of course, that *Love* would

be the most profitable Garbo film of the 1920s. They did know how eagerly anticipated the next Garbo film was (thanks to the pair's offscreen romance), and there was no underestimating Gilbert's box-office draw. Douglas Fairbanks, Charlie Chaplin, and Ramon Novarro had huge followings, but none of them had Gilbert's direct, electric appeal. Since Rudolph Valentino's death in August 1926, Gilbert was the screen's unchallenged Great Lover. "In the time of Hollywood's most glittering days, he glittered the most," wrote his friend, screenwriter Ben Hecht. "He was as unsnobbish as a happy child. He went wherever he was invited. He needed no greatness around him to make him feel distinguished. He drank with carpenters, danced with

With her 1928 film *The Divine Woman*, Greta Garbo began a new phase of her career. She was no longer a vamp. A few fans expressed dismay at seeing her as an illegitimate country girl, but most enjoyed the sweetness of her early scenes. *The Divine Woman* is considered a lost film. When MGM embarked on a preservation program in the 1960s, both the negative and the vault print of the film were found to have suffered total nitrate decay. One reel was found in Russia in the 1990s, but there is little hope of ever seeing this film as it was originally presented.

Opposite: Russell Ball used a vignetter to make Garbo dissolve into a white background in this 1927 portrait. For the next two years it was the most widely reproduced image of Garbo.

waitresses, and made love to whores and movie queens alike. He swaggered and posed but it was never to impress anyone. He was being Jack Gilbert, prince, butterfly, Japanese lantern, and the spirit of romance."

After finishing *Love* in July 1927, Garbo and Gilbert went from working and living together to just living together, and, although their schedule was less intense, their relationship was not. Gilbert was vocally frustrated at Garbo's unwillingness to commit herself, often lamenting to writer Adela Rogers St. Johns the pain of being in love with an illusion. "You are in love with *Garbo*," Garbo would correct him, referring to the persona she had created with Stiller and M-G-M.

"I told her yes," said Gilbert. "I am in love with *Garbo*. I want to marry *Garbo*. She wants to leave the screen and buy a wheat ranch and have seventeen children—and don't think she can't. I love people and cities and conversation—so I say that I will not marry her unless she goes on being Garbo. She says she will not marry me unless she can leave the screen forever. So there we are." When their arguments went nowhere, Garbo drove off. "I do not like the loud talk, the shout," she said. "And when I hear it, I go away." At this point, even M-G-M's East Coast publicity boss could hear it. "I was one in whom Gilbert confided," wrote Howard Dietz. "He told me that Garbo was too much for one man and often left his side on evenings when lovers should be together." Gilbert, who had no inkling of Stiller's private life, assumed the worst. "[Stiller] was her first friend and her first god," Gilbert reasoned. "Stiller discovered her. He taught her to act. And he understands her, knows what she is up against.

She can be happy with Stiller. I don't think I was ever Stiller's real rival with Greta." Left alone, Gilbert began to drink, and then continued drinking in public. One night Dietz encountered him looking glum in Luigi's Saloon in Hollywood, and asked him what was wrong. Gilbert said that he had tried to make Garbo jealous by saying, "I'm going out to sleep with Anna May Wong!" Garbo did not react as he had hoped.

"I'll leave the door open, Jack," was her sole reply. This indifference was taking its toll. "During the past year," said Gilbert, "I have been miserably unhappy in both mind and body." When Garbo sent Sven-Hugo Borg to speak with Gilbert, the actor cursed and wept. "She doesn't love me," he said desperately. "It's Stiller." Then Gilbert buried his face. "Oh, Borg. I'm awfully sorry, really I am. I do love her." Following their one-year anniversary in August, Gilbert went to Washington, D.C., to costar with the already-legendary Jeanne Eagels in a Monta Bell film called *Man, Woman, and Sin*. Garbo's new film would have to do without him, as would she, since he was reportedly having an affair with Eagels.

After seven drafts, *Starlight* became *The Divine Woman*, the first Garbo film to be written as a solo starring vehicle. Farnum's continuity still bore a slight resemblance to Bernhardt's life. Marah, the heroine, comes to visit her mother, Rosine, a kept woman. For the first time since *The Torrent*, Garbo would have an on-screen mother, although this one was quite different from the little old lady in that film. Rosine's sophistication would contrast with the vulnerable young Marah. To introduce this new Garbo, Farnum and Seastrom planned a scene that would play without intertitles.

A strange creature has invaded Rosine's drawing room—a young girl in the quaint but clumsy costume of the province of Auvergne. She is moving like a hummingbird from one lovely thing to another. She smooths a silken curtain. She reaches on tiptoes to touch the glittering crystals of the chandelier. THE CAMERA MOVES UP CLOSER. She walks to a magnificent mirror. THE CAMERA KEEPS MOVING UP until it holds her in CLOSE-UP just as she looks at herself in the mirror. For the first time we have seen her face. She is Marah, and her eyes are full of wonder.

"Hog woman!" says Marianne (Garbo) to Zizi (Dorothy Cumming), the mother who abandoned her. "In Brittany that's what they call those women who leave babies in the fields for hogs to find!" Zizi's "friend" Legrande (Lowell Sherman) looks on in amusement.

By the time this scene was filmed, Garbo's graceful entrance had been rewritten into a conventional medium shot made through a doorway, Marah had become Marianne, her mother had become Zizi, and the script had become a fabrication. "It is no lie," Seastrom said later, "that I and Metro's own script writer, Frances Marion, wrote the story eight times before it was accepted. By that time nothing remained of the original material, and every trace of the Divine Sarah had been obliterated. Instead she had been debased to a pretty ordinary shopgirl who falls in love with a soldier. We made him that because uniforms suit Lars

Hanson." Garbo now had a Swedish director, Seastrom, and a Swedish leading man, Hanson, who was her costar in *The Atonement of Gösta Berling*. Conspicuous by his absence was her Swedish mentor, Mauritz Stiller.

Although his *Hotel Imperial* was doing well, two years of anxiety and disappointment had affected Stiller's health. He was suffering from respiratory ailments and found himself unable to surmount the technical and political problems of his latest Paramount film, *The Street of Sin*. A few days into it, the hapless artist suffered a physical breakdown. Paramount dumped him; Pommer, his producer, could not restore him. Stiller hoped that there was a chance he could direct Garbo, if she was powerful enough to ask for him. She may not have been, or she may have seen that he was too ill. Her letters to friends in Sweden gave no indication. When Thalberg finally approved Seastrom's *Divine Woman* script and assigned him to direct it, Stiller gave up and announced that he was going back to Sweden. Garbo was about to lose the strongest, the most intelligent, and the most benevolent influence she had ever known. With the M-G-M factory humming loudly in her ears, though, she had little time to think about it.

The Divine Woman began filming on September 28, 1927, with Garbo playing Marianne in a peasant blouse, skirt, and velvet cape. Portraying her mother was Dorothy Cumming, who had just played Mary in Cecil B. DeMille's *The King of Kings*. She was only six years older than Garbo. Playing the theatrical producer who elevates Marianne to stardom (for a price) was the thirty-nine-year-old Lowell Sherman, a master at suggesting lechery. William Daniels was not available to photograph Garbo this time due to studio politics. (Norma Shearer was marrying her boss, Irving Thalberg, on September 29. Her first film after their one-week honeymoon would be a comedy, *The Latest from Paris*, and she wanted Daniels to light it.) Garbo got Oliver Marsh, who had worked with Daniels on *The Merry Widow* and was known for his ability to create luminous close-ups by placing silk diffusers on fill lights below the camera lens as well as on either side of it.

Seastrom hoped that he and Marsh could rework Garbo's image, transforming her from a hard-edged vamp into "a softer, more easy-going woman." Recent advances in photographic technology helped them do this. The orthochromatic film used to photograph Garbo's first four films had made her blue eyes look very light and her red lips very dark. "Ortho" was overly sensitive to blue and could not "see" red. Heavy makeup was supposed to compensate for this, but it sometimes gave Garbo a contrasty, vampiric look. Panchromatic film, which could reproduce the entire color spectrum in black-and-white, had been invented at the turn of the century but was not manufactured for use in motion-picture cameras until much later. By this time Eastman Kodak was making it available to studio cameramen on a limited basis.

"Life is short—so short," says Marianne to Lucien (Lars Hanson) as his departure for Algeria draws near.

Shortly before the "All-Talking, All-Singing, All-Dancing" pictures, there was an all-Swedish picture, *The Divine Woman*, which had Lars Hanson, Greta Garbo, and Victor Seastrom (actually Sjöström) working together in Hollywood.

In mid-1925, Lillian Gish had prevailed upon Thalberg to use it in *La Bohème*, and it had occasioned much comment. It eliminated the "dead-white" skin associated with silent films; in its place was a balanced, natural skin tone.

The most dramatic example of this transition could be seen in *Love*, which had two different endings. "When the picture got into the small towns," Thalberg explained, "they didn't understand the unhappy ending. It was unbelievable to them. There was such a demand for a happy ending and there was a great deal invested in the picture, and, as it seems pointless to argue with the public, we acceded to the

This photograph was made in August 1927, between *Love* and *The Divine Woman*, by Russell Ball, who had done Garbo's first American portraits two years earlier. Because she was making films back-to-back, her portrait sessions were often scheduled without regard for costumes from respective productions. This session's wardrobe comprised a gold lamé cape, a pair of white pajamas, and a black bathrobe.

demand." The big cities saw Garbo commit suicide on ortho, the same stock used for the rest of the film. Smaller cities saw a different last reel. This ending was shot with pan film; Garbo suddenly looked soft, creamy, *real*. The remarkable new film would be used to shoot *The Divine Woman*. Sure enough, Marsh's first shots of Garbo, in which she was leaning out a window, made her look as if she were glowing from within.

Most of the first week's filming, which Seastrom accomplished quickly, were scenes of Marianne bidding a poignant farewell to her sweetheart, Lucien (Hanson). The young lovers pass their time in her little apartment with a sense of dread, since Lucien must return to his regiment at nine o'clock that night and leave for Algeria the next day. Trying to ignore the clock on the mantel, they play, sing, and run

around the room. Lucien starts to go, but Marianne stops him in the doorway and pulls him back to her. Their embrace ends on the floor. Marianne bends over Lucien, kisses him, and says, "For you I would toss the whole world into the—soup pot!" Then, repeating what he has written to her in a love note, she says, "Life is short—so short." A lap dissolve to a clock on the mantel suggests that they are making love—and that Lucien has missed his deadline. He is now a deserter. Marianne and Lucien sit in the window seat, she illuminated by streetlamps, he with his face in shadow so that he cannot be detected by the soldiers marching below. "Sing to me, Lucien," she says. "The funny little soldier song!" Lucien begins, his eyes filled with tears. "How brave a lad was I," he sings, "when the drums went by!"

Garbo was working on an exterior set when the American journalist Rilla Page Palmborg, whose husband was Swedish, awaited a privileged interview.

> She and Lars Hanson were enacting a scene on a street in Paris. It was a street paved with cobblestones and lined with quaint shops. Gendarmes sauntered up and down the narrow pavement. There came a shy little girl and a young officer walking slowly down the street. They paused in a doorway. The officer asked a frowsy innkeeper for lodgings. The girl looked up shyly at the officer. She hesitated a moment, raised up on her toes, and kissed him on the cheek. Then she hurried past him, up the stairs. "Cut!" shouted the director. Garbo, wrapped in the long, high-collared cape she wore in the picture, picked her way across the rough cobblestones to join me. Extras, electricians, and carpenters followed her with their eyes.

Having watched Garbo emote with a new leading man, Palmborg, true to her profession, wasted no time in asking her if she missed Gilbert. "I will be very frank with you," Garbo answered. "The only American I have gone out with at all is Mr. Gilbert. But it is only a friendship. I will never marry. My work absorbs me. I have time for nothing else. But I think Jack Gilbert is one of the finest men I have ever known. He is a real gentleman. He has temperament. He gets excited. Sometimes he has much to say. But that is good. I am very happy when I am told I am to do a picture with Mr. Gilbert. He is a great artist. He lifts me up and carries me along with him. It is not scenes I am doing. I am living." Then, as if regretting that she had said even this much, she concluded the interview and went back to her make-believe Paris.

In a sly reference to her recent fight with M-G-M, the script of *The Divine Woman* had Marianne become a temperamental star whose love life compromises her art. The impresario Legrande snarls at her: "The world has tossed you up but one little push from me and back you go into nothing!"

Lucien sits in shadow so that his regiment, marching below, will not see that he has deserted in order to make love with Marianne.

"Push then," Marianne dares him, and, with an indifference that echoes Garbo's, says, "I don't care!"

"I'm willing to end everything if you are," threatens Legrande. "Including our contract!"

Marianne storms out of Legrande's theater, and the spurned lover makes good his threat. Marianne is reduced to poverty, ignominy, and, finally, the worst fate that can befall a star. "Fame is a witch with two heads," says John Colton's intertitle. "For a short time, people wondered where the great Marianne had vanished to. Soon nobody cared!" The devastated has-been turns on the gas in her wretched hotel room. She is lying in a hospital when Lucien finds her. "You're going to live, Marianne!" he tells the inert woman. "You must live—live for me!" She does, and so *The Divine Woman* has a happy ending.

Filming ended on November 7, and Seastrom had nothing but praise for Garbo. "She never once came to the set without having prepared herself down to the last detail," he said, "and if one gave her directions, she accepted them quite gladly, even though she was a big star even then." There occurred at least one incident in which he had to acknowl-

edge Garbo's idiosyncrasies. The scene called for her to stand on the stage of a large theater, surrounded by floral tributes, and make a thank-you speech. She did not want to film it with extraneous personnel watching her. Seastrom reassured her in Swedish, the language in which they conversed and in which she would deliver the speech. Then he had the crew hang up a bedsheet. "On the other side of the sheet," related Seastrom, "Lowell Sherman stood with the rest, listening intently. After the first take, he came up to me and said, 'I don't understand a word of your language, but I can tell that that girl is uncannily gifted.'" The Swedish director agreed with the stage veteran. "She thinks above her eyes," Seastrom later said. "Certain great actors possess what seems to be an uncanny ability to register thought. Lon Chaney was one. Garbo is another. They seem literally to absorb impressions. Garbo is more sensitive to emotion than film is to light."

In keeping with the studio's practice, Seastrom and his wife, Edith, attended a preview of *The Divine Woman* in an outlying area of Los Angeles County. "At the preview," recalled Seastrom, "the management came up and paid me

General Alexandroff, played by Gustav von Seyffertitz, toasts Tania (Garbo). During the anti-German frenzy of World War I, the Austrian Seyffertitz had found it necessary to change his name to G. Butler Clonebaugh.

Garbo was indifferent to this news, preoccupied as she was with Mauritz Stiller's recent departure. In particular, she was brooding over a letter he had given her at the train station. "I am now leaving Hollywood," he wrote. "And the worst of it is I am leaving you here. Leaving you your freedom. Perhaps you—when I am gone—will blossom anew. Perhaps your face will get its peace back; your mouth, your lips will get their strength again. Perhaps your eyes won't tear as often. I am gone, obliterated from your life. . . . And you shall not think about me. You don't even have to repeat 'Poor Moje' every time we meet. You are free!"

If freedom, privacy, and solitude were Garbo's obsessions, she found little comfort in them after reading Stiller's letter. According to Karen Swenson, Garbo expressed profound guilt in a subsequent letter to Mimi Pollak, her friend in Stockholm. "No woman could possibly feel as sad and inferior as she now felt," writes Swenson. "[Greta] castigated

herself for being bitter, mean, and mad, but she appeared resigned to what fate had decided for her. Seemingly devoid of emotion, she dramatically declared that something had died within her, and she faulted herself for selling out to Hollywood. Last of all, Greta admitted to feeling nothing like a movie star." Once again, Garbo went into eclipse. *War in the Dark* was not ready for her, so she stayed away from the studio, which was surprisingly unconcerned. At that moment, the possibility of having to train all its stars for talking pictures was more important to M-G-M than Garbo's time off. She was kept on salary and left to her own devices, which meant occasional (and witnessed) excursions with Gilbert but mostly solitary walks in the Hollywood hills. "Whether I'm filming or not," she wrote, "I'm tired and slightly unhappy and don't want anything. I'll soon be a little old woman. I live like I was seventy years old. The others here are a bit piqued because I never go out and won't take part in their so-called social life. Perhaps I'll end up living all by myself on a desert island."

After six months, Garbo joined William Daniels and Fred Niblo, who had directed *The Temptress*, on the set of *War in the Dark*. They began shooting on May 8 with a slightly less outré version of the scene in Christensen's treatment: the opium cigarette had been deleted, but candlelight, a grand piano, and rain-swept windows were much in evidence on M-G-M's Stage 6. The assistant director's production report for the day read: "WAR IN THE DARK—May 8, 1928. Called 9-30. Started 10-15. Waiting for Miss Garbo. Had to have her hair fixed up on account of rain. Rehearsing 10-15. Int. Tania's Apt." The next day she was late again. "Miss Garbo 30 min. late on set. From 9-30 to 9-45 Mr. Niblo talking over story with actors. Rehearsing 9-45. Script scenes [shot]: 7. Added scenes: 4." The next day she was forty minutes late but managed to be on time for a week after that. Niblo was often fifteen minutes late but made up for it with a healthy number of camera setups each day. Once working in a regular rhythm, Garbo did not like to be interrupted or distracted.

The transition from ortho film to panchromatic film had increased the number of incandescent lights on the set. This technological jump resulted in the founding of a Hollywood lighting company called Mole-Richardson. Mole lights, whether the "double broads" used to throw soft light or the spotlights used to throw hard light and sharp shadows, made it easier for Garbo to see the perimeters of the shooting area. The gaze of starstruck extras bothered her more than ever, and she could immediately detect the arrival of an unauthorized visitor. Louella Parsons, a columnist syndicated in William Randolph Hearst's newspapers, could hardly be described as an intruder but, on the second day of shooting, Garbo treated her as such. "Greta was in a temperamental mood," wrote Parsons. "She ordered a screen placed in front of the script girl where I was standing. I stepped to one side. Then she ordered the screen placed in front of the musicians. Again I walked to the other side of the room. Finally, the property boy placed the screen directly in front of me." Parsons took the hint and left.

On another day, a board member of Loew's Inc. asked L. B. Mayer to escort him to Garbo's set so he could see her work. At the first sight of Mayer, Garbo walked to her dressing room and closed the door. Niblo sent his script clerk, Virginia Kellogg, to plead with Garbo. "No!" Garbo said through the door. "They posed me in a track suit. Now let them bend their rusty knees." Mayer apologized to the New York executive and left.

Marion Davies, one of his biggest stars, was not quite so acquiescent. Davies was working with director Robert Z. Leonard and Dutch actress Jetta Goudal on the set of *The Cardboard Lover* at the other end of the same stage as Garbo. The amiable, much-liked Davies had noticed Garbo

observing them. Before she could welcome Garbo to her set, the shy visitor had vanished. Davies got the notion to visit Garbo's set. As soon as she set foot on it, Garbo glared at her and stopped working. Davies followed her to her dressing room, where Garbo proceeded to busy herself with her hairdresser, pointedly ignoring Davies, who was the lady love of America's most powerful publisher and as big an M-G-M star as Garbo. Furthermore, Garbo had already been a guest at La Cuesta Encantada, the mansion at San Simeon where Hearst and Davies held court on weekends. Davies was too good-natured to bring this up. Her attempts at conversation were cut short.

"Why don't you go back to your set?" asked Garbo.

"I understand you're a wonderful actress," stammered Davies. "You were nice enough to come to my set. I thought I'd repay the courtesy."

"You're very funny," said an unsmiling Garbo. "You make me laugh, but I didn't come over to see you. I came over to see a great actress, Miss Goudal."

"She's a very good actress," agreed Davies, "but she's stealing my stuff. I don't like it."

"They're calling you on your set," said Garbo coldly.

"I don't hear any call," said Davies, ignoring her cue.

"You're wasting my time," said Garbo, impatiently. "Get off my set before I have to kick you off. Go back to your set. I won't act. I don't like anybody watching me."

"Well, that goes both ways," said Davies. "Don't you come to my set either."

"You're very funny. But it's very peculiar. To me you are null and void. Is that the word?"

"The melancholia which seems to rest upon her," wrote Danish director Benjamin Christensen in a treatment for this film, "only seems to enhance this woman's strange charm."

The camera crane had not yet been invented, so William Daniels used a forklift to have his camera descend the stairs with the actors in *The Mysterious Lady*. Director Fred Niblo is at his right.

"Uh huh," nodded Davies.

"I don't care about your acting. I just like to visit."

"Well, so do I. And I'm going to stay here."

"Oh, no you don't," said Garbo. "It's going to cost the company money. And you're going to be blamed for it. They'll put it on your production."

"Then I'll leave," said Davies, who scarcely needed to worry over a few idle minutes when Hearst's millions were underwriting her films. That Garbo would act in this manner in quick succession to the two most powerful people on the lot was deplorable, but, as always, the company tolerated her, as it tolerated her latest demands. She refused to wear a gown designed by Gilbert Clark because she thought it too revealing. An argument ensued. Garbo locked herself in her dressing room until notified that she need not wear the offending garment. Clark walked out of the fitting room and

off the lot; a designer named Gilbert Adrian would soon replace him. Garbo was no longer working past 5:30 P.M., and though she was still contractually required to grant interviews, she was no longer giving autographs—to anyone, anywhere, under any circumstance. And if anyone with whom she worked asked for one, she refused.

"I had a big part in the film," said actor Gustav von Seyffertitz, "yet very seldom did I get the opportunity of meeting and getting to know her. She was very shy and always sat by herself, somewhat disconcerted by her surroundings, or so it seemed to me." Conrad Nagel, who after more than twenty films for M-G-M was popular enough to take Gilbert's place as Garbo's leading man, gave her the benefit of the doubt. "She concentrated more strongly on her acting than almost anyone I ever worked with," recalled Nagel, "and so naturally at the end of the day she was tired and said, 'I tank I go home.' She wasn't the only one. We all wanted to go home at the end of the day." What he failed to mention was that even when Garbo was more than half an hour late, she still could leave by 5:30; everyone else had to work until evening.

War in the Dark was deemed an uncommercial title. After toying with titles such as *Love in the Dark*, *The Devil's Bargain*, and *The Glorious Sinner*, an unnamed studio writer won a $50 bonus for *The Mysterious Lady*. Its thirty-one days of shooting ended on June 15, with only two days of minor retakes and a final tab of $336,973. The film

This sylvan setting was filmed on June 13, 1928, on M-G-M Stage 15, one of the glass stages inherited from Thomas Ince's Triangle Company. That day's production report read: "Discovered this A.M. that top of set had to be diffused [on] account [of] sunlight and cameraman wanted trees sprayed as they blended into the background." Wider angles of the loving couple's day in the woods were filmed in Griffith Park and in the area known then as the Verdugo Woodlands and now as Eagle Rock.

premiered on August 4. The story of a languorous and ambivalent spy was obviously an excuse for scene after scene in which William Daniels used pan film and Mole lights to paint glowing images of a performer whose presence was so unusual that reviewers and coworkers alike had difficulty describing it. "She was unassuming," said von Seyffertitz, "yet possessed a mysterious power of attraction." Betty Colfax of the *New York Evening Graphic* wrote: "Miss Garbo takes to a close-up like no other star in Hollywood. She overcomes the handicap of an atrocious wardrobe, big feet, and widening hips with a facility of expression and a charm which still keep her in a class by herself." A review in the *New*

York Morning Telegraph said: "This Garbo girl seems to develop just a little more of that intangible 'it' with each picture, and the love scenes between her and Nagel are what might be termed burning. There are love scenes by the score, many of which are in close-up, with the famous La Garbo kiss given full sway as well as full camera focus." Confirming his earlier appraisal, Robert Sherwood wrote in *Life*: "She is the dream princess of eternity, the knockout of the ages." With reviews like these, where was there left for Garbo to go? Her fans wanted her to go back to John Gilbert. The Great Lover was only too happy to oblige them.

CHAPTER EIGHT
A Woman of Affairs

or her seventh film in America, Garbo wanted something different. Her previous films had presented her as an exotic personality, usually from an earlier era, and always from another country, whether Spain, Russia, or France. True, she did not look like the home-grown "flappers" or "baby vamps" populating the screen in the Golden Twenties—Colleen Moore, Gloria Swanson, and Norma Talmadge among them—but there was no reason why she could not portray an English-speaking modern woman, especially as talking pictures might soon have her speaking in fact. By the time of *The Mysterious Lady*'s August 1928 premiere, M-G-M had released a film with synchronized music and sound effects, *White Shadows in the South Seas*; and Warner Bros. had released an "All-Talking Vitaphone Picture," *The Lights of New York*. Irving Thalberg believed that sound films could coexist with silent films, but no one believed that sound films would go away—not until eager audiences had heard every silent star's voice. Garbo made certain that Harry Edington conveyed two messages to Louis B. Mayer: (1) she would not make a sound film without a rider to her contract; and (2) in her next film she wanted to play the lead character in the best-selling novel *The Green Hat*. The contract proved the easier hurdle.

Published in mid-1924, Michael Arlen's *The Green Hat: A Romance for a Few People* was an international cause célèbre. The glittering, world-weary novel was set on the Continent and spanned a period from 1910 to 1923, but it soon became emblematic of the social changes taking place in 1920s America, where women were now able to vote and hold jobs. Its heroine, Iris March, is an independent, self-possessed young woman whose greatest problem is that the men who swarm to her are not her equals. One by one they disappoint her. Her sweetheart Napier breaks off their engagement to placate his conservative father. The clean-cut Boy Fenwick jumps from a hotel window on their wedding night after telling her an awful secret. Her devoted brother Jeffry disowns her when she will not reveal the secret; she will only say that Boy died "for decency."

An unnamed male narrator tries to reason with Iris when he hears that she has been trawling the Riviera trying to forget her failed affairs. Iris answers him: "I am not the proud adventuress who touches men for pleasure, the silly lady

who misbehaves for fun. . . . It is not good to have a pagan body and a Chislehurst mind, as I have. It is hell for the body and terror for the mind. There are dreams, and there are beasts. The dreams walk glittering up and down the soiled loneliness of desire, the beasts prowl about the soiled loneliness of regret."

The Green Hat was published simultaneously in London and New York, and the M-G-M story department immediately reviewed it. "It is sordid and filthy and entirely impossible for screen consideration," wrote a reader named Nina Lewton (the sister of Alla Nazimova and mother of writer Val Lewton). Another reader wrote Thalberg: "This is a

A Woman of Affairs was adapted from the Michael Arlen novel *The Green Hat*, a story of a freethinking British woman who runs afoul of her conservative upper-class peers. In the film, former producer Hobart Bosworth played Morton Holderness, implacable nemesis of defiant Diana Merrick (Garbo). *Photoplay*'s Leonard Hall wrote a year later: "In the greatest scene Garbo ever played—the renunciation scene in *A Woman of Affairs*—she wore a slouchy old tweed suit and a squashy felt hat. She never looked more mysterious, more alluring, and she never acted with greater authority or arrogant power."

naughty one—ooh la la!" Readers found the novel's topicality hard to resist. "Your generation is a mess," says a stuffy upper-class character to a member of the so-called Lost Generation, then offhandedly asks: "Have some brandy?"

"It's absurd to talk 'generations,'" replies the younger man. "Slack novelists do it to get easy effects. All generations are a mess. Thank you."

What really made *The Green Hat* a best seller was Iris March's head-held-high approach to situations that would have caused Victorian heroines to faint dead away. Even in daring 1924, the revelation that came at the end of Arlen's novel could not be spoken in mixed company, or even aloud. Boy Fenwick's secret was shocking, and the entire plot turned on it, but because of new censorship policies, it could not be filmed. Undeterred, Thalberg consulted with Will H. Hays, the Protestant bureaucrat known as the "Czar of Movie Morality." As Thalberg knew, Hays's two-year-old Motion Picture Producers and Distributors Association (MPPDA) used what it called the Formula, which judged the novel unfit for the screen. On November 8, Thalberg sent a cable to J. Robert Rubin: "Agree with Hays [about his stand on] *Green Hat* but [he is] not consistent. Paramount doing *Little French Girl* which he likewise prohibited and which [is] just as censorable as *Green Hat*; Paramount always able to do wrong and [later] apologize." By December 1, *The Green Hat* was headed for Broadway, but the Hays Office still would not allow Thalberg to option it. "This looks to me like another *Flaming Youth* from comment I am hearing from entire reading public," he cabled Rubin, alluding to a scandalous best seller that Hays had let First National buy.

In less than a year, Katharine Cornell was starring on Broadway in *The Green Hat*. The A. H. Woods production ran for 231 performances and was just as notorious as the book. One of the many New Yorkers affected by the glamorous, fatalistic Iris March was the society gadfly Mercedes de Acosta. "This period seemed to produce people with an inner violence and an overcharged excess of emotion that marked them for a tragic end," she later wrote. "[*The Green Hat*] completely symbolized the spirit of this time. A spirit that went overboard in bravado, sentimentality, and taste. It was a play in which the heroine was utterly reckless but always gallant. *Gallant* and *dangerous* were in a sense the passwords of the twenties. One could do anything then, as long as one lived gallantly and dangerously."

Although the story was set in London, the jaded attitude of the novel was international, a lingering effect of the Great War. "Practically everyone of my generation was influenced by this story," Acosta recalled. According to her friend F. Scott Fitzgerald, hers was a generation bereft of Victorian bulwarks, one that had "grown up to find all gods dead, all wars fought, all faiths in man shaken." Replacing tradition was an atavistic pleasure-seeking, an elegant rebellion set to the new music being played in Harlem speakeasies and Montmartre cabarets. "There was a rhythm," wrote Arlen. "There was syncopation. It had a beat like the throbbing of an agonized heart lost in an artery of the Underground. Dolorous it was, yet the phantasm of gaiety lay twined in it." It may have been W. C. Handy's "St. Louis Blues," James P. Johnson's "Charleston," or George Gershwin's "Fascinatin' Rhythm." The world was buying stock to it, dancing to it, and making love to it, led by a brash United States, where an unprecedented prosperity promised to put two chickens in every pot, two cars in every garage—and one hip flask in every pocket. Prohibition had made drinking illegal, but bootleggers made liquor ubiquitous. Hollywood was making equally intoxicating products, films with labels like *Dance Madness*, *Our Dancing Daughters*, and *Dancing Mothers*. Moviegoers wanted to live what they saw on the screen: "Brilliant men, beautiful jazz babies, champagne baths, midnight revels, [and] petting parties in the purple dawn." Fitzgerald summed it all up: "America was going on the greatest, gaudiest spree in history."

It was high time, then, that Garbo bade farewell to vamp roles and played a "modern." She was all for it, as early as December 1927. "Will you immediately make every effort [to] secure for us *Green Hat* for Garbo," Metro executive L. A. Shaw cabled Rubin. "We are absolutely stuck at this moment and this would be a marvelous solution." *The Green Hat* proved slippery. The Fox Film Corporation, hoping Hays would clear the title, optioned the play from Woods, who now held rights to the novel. Hays would not clear it, perhaps fearful of public opinion. He was receiving letters about Fox from exhibitors and censor boards. "Is it possible for you to request that *The Green Hat* be eliminated from motion pictures?" wrote the amusement inspector in San

In this scene, Neville Holderness (John Gilbert), his wife, Constance (Dorothy Sebastian), and their friend Hugh (Lewis Stone) visit Diana in the sanitarium where she is recovering from a breakdown.

A behind-the-scenes photograph by James Manatt shows William Daniels (at camera) and director Clarence Brown (in foreground) as they film a close-up of Garbo over Gilbert's shoulder on August 24, 1928.

Antonio, Texas. "I saw somewhere it was to be filmed. The drama was here recently and I deplored greatly that talent should be wasted on such poor, disgusting material."

What some found disgusting and others found titillating could not be filmed, according to the Formula. It was the revelation at the end of the story, the reason Boy Fenwick jumps not into bed but to his death. It is disclosed by Napier, who has loved Iris since childhood. "She wanted people to think as well of Boy as people can of a suicide," he tells his father. "She just didn't care what people thought of her and so she said that Boy had died 'for purity.' That might mean anything, and so of course we all took it to mean the worst thing as regards Iris. Oh, she knew we would. Well, Boy did die 'for purity.' . . . He—he had syphilis when he married her, and went mad when he realized what he had done. That's all. There's your Boy Fenwick. There's Iris. That's Iris!"

As everyone knew, there was no way that the word *syphilis* could be projected onto a movie screen, even in the Roaring Twenties. If M-G-M was going to snatch the property from Fox and make it a Garbo vehicle, it would have to appease—or circumvent—the Formula. Thalberg assigned Bess Meredyth to the scenario. Then Hays (perhaps pressured by Mayer) suddenly decided that M-G-M could film *The Green Hat*, but only if: (1) the plot point of syphilis was eliminated; (2) the title and character names were changed; and (3) neither the source novel nor the play was mentioned

in credits or advertising. Thalberg sent an interoffice cable: "Confident can make picture within Formula. Of course don't look for Sunday school proposition."

On June 11, as Garbo went into her last week of work on *The Mysterious Lady*, Fox Film, still under the impression that *The Green Hat* would have to be changed beyond recognition, let its option lapse. On June 15, M-G-M took a month's option on *The Green Hat* while Meredyth tried various approaches to it. The next day, Garbo went on an expensive layoff; time was a-wasting. On June 25, Thalberg sent Hays a story outline in which Iris's sacrifice covers up not venereal disease but financial misdeeds. "I am confident," he wrote, "that you will find that we have treated the matter in a way that will avoid any censor [*sic*] on anyone's part. It is practically a new story, taking all that is fine and worthwhile in the book, but building it on a new, clean foundation."

On July 11, after reading a more detailed treatment, Hays gave M-G-M permission to proceed. Within a few hours, M-G-M bought all rights to *The Green Hat* for $50,000. Thalberg fully expected the property to make a million for the studio, especially since Meredyth's smooth, speedy adaptation cost only $10,000. Rubin sent a memo to Mayer with this assurance: "We have instructed the publicity department not to use the title *The Green Hat* in their publicity." Mayer's secretary forwarded it to Pete Smith of the publicity department with a caveat written in grease pencil: "Mr.

scene filmed on August 21, where constant camera movement around the stark white set made it easier to use a soft, flat light on Garbo caressing a bouquet of roses. Instead of shooting the close-up with the usual 75mm lens and using a conventional key-and-fill-light scheme, Daniels shot with a much shorter lens, which almost (but not quite) distorted Garbo's face as she drew close to it, a startlingly effective way to convey the character's disorientation.

That Garbo was supremely photogenic was also confirmed by Edward Steichen. The esteemed *Vanity Fair* photographer was working in Los Angeles on an advertising assignment during the first week of August, so his editor booked a sitting with Garbo and Gilbert at M-G-M. Steichen set up a shooting area on Stage 2, outside the Deauville hotel room set. Garbo was dressed in widow's weeds, and her hair was combed flat on top, parted, and fluffed on the side. She straddled a chair that Steichen had covered with his black focusing cloth and, still wound up from a dramatic scene, went into poses. "And then I started to photograph," said Steichen later. "She would turn her head this way and shake

Diana visits Neville a few days before he is to be married to Constance. *A Woman of Affairs* was the third pairing of Garbo and Gilbert, but not everyone was looking forward to their love scenes. After seeing the film's trailer, a young woman wrote to *Film Weekly* magazine: "It is evident that this picture will be full of the rather nasty exhibitions of osculation which are present in most films featuring this pair, and, for which, apparently, they are famous. Even modern girls have shreds of modesty left and when seeing films like this accompanied by a man friend, well . . . I simply squirm in my seat."

her head in this way. And this wasn't the Garbo I was interested in. This was the regular Hollywood Garbo. So I said, 'It's too bad we have to photograph all these things with the hairdo you're wearing, this Hollywood hairdo.' She said, 'Oh, this *hair*.' She put her hands up to her head and brushed [it] back. 'Now let's make a photograph of *that*,' she said." The resulting image, in which two floodlights cross Garbo's face in potentially unflattering competition, caused much comment when it was published. It was not a glamour photo. It was a character study of a strange young woman whose hands were flattening her hair and guarding her head.

After Steichen had finished his session (which included a couple portrait with Gilbert), Garbo hugged the photographer and exclaimed: "Oh, you should be a motion picture director. You understand." This was taking nothing away from Brown. With his understated manner and carefully designed sequences, he was fast becoming her favorite. "He directed by the subtlest of suggestions," Fairbanks told Karen Swenson in 1992. "He never demanded. He just kept going until we got it right." Steichen witnessed this, too, as the methodical Brown "continually tried to explain" to Garbo how to walk to her husband's suicide window as the camera pulled back to the edge of the set. "For me, Garbo starts where they all leave off," said Brown in 1967. "She was a shy person; her lack of English gave her a slight inferiority complex. I used to direct her very quietly. I never gave her a direction above a whisper. Nobody on the set ever knew what I said to her. She liked that."

A Woman of Affairs brought another artist to Garbo. She had not gotten along with costume designers Clément André-ani or Gilbert Clark. André-ani had run afoul of studio protocol when he made unflattering remarks about Garbo in a widely published interview. "She has foreign ideas about clothes that do not go well in American pictures," he said. "She wants short skirts when she should have long ones . . . And her figure—it is difficult to dress." After André-ani and Clark had been shown the door, M-G-M hired a designer who would not need to assert his ego. Fortunately for the studio and for Garbo, this designer would prove to be the most talented and influential in the entire industry.

Gilbert Adrian was scheduled to come to M-G-M with Cecil B. DeMille in August 1928, when the producer would move onto the lot in an arrangement like that of William Randolph Hearst's Cosmopolitan, but Adrian was so badly needed that M-G-M could not wait; he was inducted in June. By the time Garbo was ready for her green hat, Adrian was ready to take her out of Clark's droopy medieval designs and into lively, jazzy outfits. Adrian believed that costumes should not merely reflect trends but anticipate them. Given the interval between a film's design and its release, this was a vital aspect of his work. Before long he would be setting his own trends, but at this point the studio was loath to tamper

In this posed publicity still, Clarence Brown indicates to Garbo the efficiency of bringing a Victrola to Busch Gardens to play mood music. M-G-M customarily provided a string trio and organist on its sets to inspire emoting stars, but it appeared more economical to bring this console to Pasadena. There was already a generator there, since the Mitchell camera used by William Daniels (at right) was now motorized.

with Garbo's image. "They feared she would lose all her allure if she came down to earth," he said. "Her natural aloofness and the manner of her bearing make it possible for her to put meaning into simple clothes. . . . In *A Woman of Affairs* I put her in sport clothes, and so amazingly beautiful is her face, she is just as intriguing in a sweater." Production of the "new Garbo" film ended on September 11 without incident or undue expense. The final tally for *A Woman of Affairs* was $328,687.77, and it premiered in New York on January 19, 1929, while Mayer and Thalberg waited to see how the public would respond.

"A sensational array of screen names," wrote *Variety*'s reviewer, "and the intriguing nature of the story from which it was made, together with some magnificence in the acting of Greta Garbo—by long odds the best work she has ever done—will carry through this vague and sterilized version of Michael Arlen's exotic play. Superb technical production and admirable photography count in its favor. But the kick is out of the material." Critic Pare Lorentz argued in *Judge* magazine that morality was not a matter of semantics.

> The heroine's white feather was borne for the proud fact that her suicide husband suffered from the same ailment enjoyed by our most popular kings, prelates, and prize-

fighters. Well, sir, Bishop Hays changes that to "embezzlement." And for some strange reason, instead of using the word "purity" (the boy died for purity, according to Iris March) they substituted the oft-repeated word "decency." To anyone who can show me why "purity" is a more immoral word than "decency," I'll gladly send an eighty-five cent Paramount ticket, to be used at your own risk.

The *New York Times* was unconcerned with the Hays compromise. "Not only is the narrative [well] translated with changes where it was necessary to circumvent censorial frowns, but Miss Garbo gives a most intelligent and fascinating impersonation of that 'sad lady.'" *Photoplay* magazine went further: "Despite the change of title, despite the Hays ban, despite new names for old characters, it is still Michael Arlen's *The Green Hat*. And it is corking!"

The magazine's constituents agreed, according to exhibitors. "Comments from the patrons were that it was a good picture," said the manager of the H & S Theatre in Chandler, Oklahoma. "Some were slightly disappointed in the ending. However, from a moral standpoint it could not end otherwise." The manager of the Dayton Theatre in Dayton, Ohio, called *A Woman of Affairs* "the finest picture I have had the pleasure of playing." Others felt that the story shortchanged

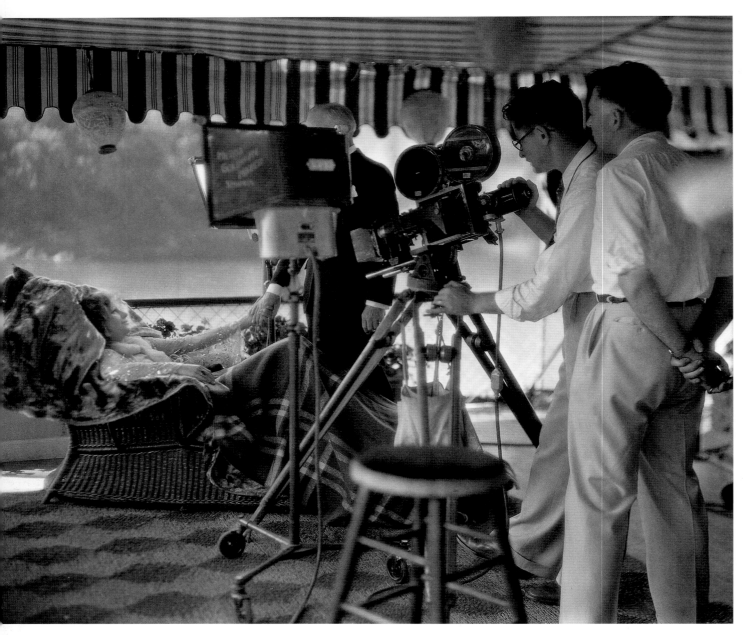

M-G-M built and launched a houseboat on the shores of the Franklin Canyon reservoir for *A Woman of Affairs*. In this photo, Brown and Daniels are filming a scene on the upper deck with Garbo and Lewis Stone on August 7. When asked by a Swedish reporter who was her favorite director, Garbo said, "After Stiller, I suppose Clarence Brown. He isn't such a strong personality, but he usually gets a good result." This was faint praise for a craftsman who went out of his way to accommodate her obsession with privacy.

their favorite team member. "John Gilbert, idol of the flappers, has an utterly blah role," wrote *Variety*. "Most of the footage he just stands around, rather sheepishly in fact, while others shape the events. At this performance, whole groups of women customers audibly expressed their discontent with the proceedings." Naysayers notwithstanding, both the new Garbo film and the new Garbo were an unqualified success. *A Woman of Affairs* was on its way to earning a profit of $417,000. Better yet, Garbo was willing to make a third film in 1928 if M-G-M would let her go to Sweden for Christmas to visit her mother and see her beloved Mauritz Stiller. In September 1928, as Garbo prepared for her next film, three months did not look like a long time to wait.

Opposite: Garbo was convincing as a fabulous invalid in *A Woman of Affairs*. Critic Pare Lorentz wrote in *Judge* magazine: "The movie is a good dramatization of the novel and for the first time I respected the performance of Greta Garbo. She shuffled through the long, melancholy, and sometimes beautiful scenes with more grace and sincerity than I have ever before observed."

PART IV

THE SWEDISH SPHINX

CHAPTER NINE

Wild Orchids

I rving Thalberg's formula for Greta Garbo's scenarios required her to be a woman of mystery, tied to an older man but desired by a younger man. Deciding that in Garbo's eighth film the formula would best be served by an original story, he turned to a treatment that had just been turned down by Lillian Gish. It was by M-G-M contract writer John Colton and was titled *Heat*. In 1928, Colton had also written intertitles for Gish's film *The Enemy*, as well as for Garbo's *The Divine Woman*, John Gilbert's *The Cossacks*, and the much-talked-about part-talkie *White Shadows in the South Seas*. Colton was a natural for the latter, since he specialized in stories about exotic places.

The forty-two-year-old playwright had been born in Minnesota but raised in Japan; his father was an art importer. One of his earliest memories was of being left asleep in a Yokohama teahouse. "Nobody in that region had ever seen a white child," wrote a *New York Times* interviewer, "and the unfortunately impervious Mr. Colton woke up to find himself surrounded by a garden of pervidly admiring geisha girls. Mr. Colton screamed in terror." The collision of occidental and oriental sensibilities was the dominant theme of Colton's writing, expressed in controversial plays that were also star vehicles. His 1922 play *Drifting* had matinee idol Alice Brady smuggling opium. In the same year he adapted a W. Somerset Maugham short story about a San Francisco prostitute stranded in the South Seas. "Miss Thompson" became *Rain*, which made a star of Jeanne Eagels. His latest Broadway hit was *The Shanghai Gesture*, which starred Florence Reed as a Chinese madam called Mother Goddam. Now Colton sat in a small office in the wooden M-G-M writers' building, burning the midnight oil to create a vehicle for Garbo. Story editor Samuel Marx recalled in 1989 that one of Colton's eccentricities was his preference for writing late at night.

Three years had passed since Garbo's arrival in the United States. In her seven films there, she had portrayed only women of foreign extraction. Colton's story made her an American, a San Francisco resident named Lillie Sterling. *Heat* was the story of a devoted young wife who travels with

Opposite: As 1929 drew to a close, Greta Garbo was one of the last stars who was still making silent films.

In October 1928, Greta Garbo and John Gilbert made cameo appearances in the M-G-M comedy *A Man's Man*. Their scene, arriving together at a movie premiere, was a studio in-joke.

her sedate older husband on a business trip to Java. There she finds her mettle tested by the sultry climate—and her fidelity, by a Javanese prince. Instead of developing this triangle into a scenario, Colton turned the story over to Thalberg and went back to writing titles. *Heat* was then adapted by Willis Goldbeck, a former journalist who had written *Mare Nostrum* for Rex Ingram, and rewritten by contract scenarist Josephine Lovett, who suggested an opulent houseboat as a setting. "We wish to add allure to the scene: music, dancing, dripping tropical trees at landings, moonlight, etc. The secluded part of the raft where Ferdinand [the prince] enshrines Lily could be gorgeously seductive—incense that intoxicates burning constantly, dim light, etc." The final script had the seductions begin on an ocean liner, continue in the palace, and end in the jungle.

Garbo was no doubt acquainted with John Colton through John Gilbert. In the early twenties, Colton, Gilbert,

am really going home, I can hardly wait to get there. I will be home for Christmas. Christmas in Sweden is wonderful. I adore the great piles of snow. Everyone says I will freeze after living so long in California. But I will love it."

Palmborg hesitantly broached the subject of Garbo's late sister.

"It has been hard to believe that she is really gone," said Garbo. "When I get home I will find that it is true."

As if with foreboding, Palmborg asked about Stiller. Of course, Garbo planned to spend time with him.

"I owe all of my success to Mr. Stiller," Garbo said. "If it were not for him, I would not be here now." There was a call from the set: no longer an assistant director's rude yell, but a respectful request to return. "I expect that we are wasting a lot of money," Garbo said to Palmborg with mock concern, and then excused herself.

Two days later, Garbo received a wire from Sjöström. "Your message made Moje happy," he wrote. "He sends his love. His condition, however, [is] absolutely hopeless, dear Greta. Seemingly only [a] question of a few days." She put the unbelievable message out of her mind and reported to

This scene was shot early in the morning of November 9. Garbo had spent a sleepless night crying, as evidenced by her eyes.

M-G-M, thirty minutes late as usual, to film a scene in which the prince's servants outfit her in a gaudy native costume.

In the early afternoon of Thursday, November 8, the company was filming a scene in which Lillie is trying to adjust herself to the lavish suite in the prince's palace. She is taking off her coat when the prince enters and resumes his blandishments. During a break in the filming, an office boy named Max Sarnoff walked up to Garbo and handed her a telegram. Something about the unexpected delivery caused everyone to watch. As Asther recalled, "Greta turned deathly white after reading the wire, and for a moment I thought she was going to faint." An unnamed crew member later told Palmborg: "Slowly she walked over to the other side of the building, as though she did not know what she was doing. She stood there with her hands pressed against her eyes." Historian Raymond Daum later wrote: "A string trio that had been playing background music was suddenly silent. Wanting to linger, Sarnoff wandered over to a partition, tried nonchalantly to lean on it—and fell through, collapsing a wall of South Seas scenery. It was real-life comic relief, as everyone, including Garbo, with tears in her eyes, roared with laughter."

Garbo tried to continue with the scene, but Franklin sensed that something was very wrong. Once she told him the contents of the telegram, he dismissed the company for the day. It was 2:50 P.M. Word began to filter through the company. The telegram was from Sjöström. Mauritz Stiller was dead.

After some conversation with Franklin, Asther began to walk outside. Something stopped him. "As I passed Greta's dressing room, I heard the sound of laughter. Just then the door flew open and she asked me to come in. 'I have something to show you, Nils,' she said. She was still trembling, but suddenly she laughed, holding a small perfume bottle in one hand. The tiny bottle was half filled with brandy. Attached to it was a note from Louis B. Mayer, saying, 'Dear Greta, My sympathy in your sorrow. But the show must go on!'"

Garbo reported for work the next day, and the next, walking through her scenes. She was still in shock. "After Moje died," she confided to a friend years later, "I could not eat or sleep or work. For me it was a time that was very black. I wanted to drop everything and go back to Sweden but the studio said no. They shook their heads and said, 'You must be faithful to us and to your work.' I said to them, 'You will have something dead on the screen. It will have no life.' But they wouldn't let me go."

During the week of November 12, Garbo began arriving later than usual. Asther also became tardy, sometimes as much as an hour. Franklin, who was polite and professional, found Garbo uncommunicative. "Our relationship, which wasn't too good to begin with, deteriorated. The deterioration also involved the other actors, Lewis Stone and Nils Asther, and soon I was working with an apparently hostile cast." As Asther recalled: "Sidney Franklin came over to us—a nice guy, but not a great director—and said, 'Oh, Miss Garbo, do you think you can manage it? Do you feel inspired?'"

"Yes," she answered. "If you'd only leave the studio."

After working with Shearer and Davies, Franklin was unprepared for this type of treatment. "It became so difficult," he wrote, "that I went to Irving and asked him to take me off the picture. The result, I explained, could never be good if we continued under these circumstances. He refused to relieve me, and I struggled on as best I could to the end." The scenes that remained to be shot consisted mostly of Garbo being oppressed by heat and by Asther's violent advances. Her depressed state, instead of taking away from her performance, made it more convincing.

Garbo finished her work on *Heat* at 7:50 P.M. on November 23. For the next five days, Franklin used Dvorak, Stone, Asther, and a tiger to film the climax. "It was not a happy picture," he recalled in 1970. "The result showed it." Thalberg agreed and scheduled retakes for December 3. Garbo did not show up. Assistants found out that she had left for New York. On December 4, M-G-M sent a cable to the Santa Fe Chief, Train 20, Car 206. "There is still time for you to return to Culver City," it read, "and make Sweden in time for Christmas. Return or great loss will be caused us. Louis B. Mayer." Garbo did not respond. On December 5, Mayer put her on suspension. Three days later, Garbo sailed for Sweden on the SS *Kungsholm*. Thalberg could not improve *Heat* with retakes, so he turned it over to the publicity department, from which hysterical laughter soon emanated. How could M-G-M sell this film with a straight face? The ads would read: "Greta Garbo in *Heat*." A new title was hastily affixed: *Wild Orchids*.

News reports soon detailed Garbo's shipboard friendship with Prince Sivgard of Sweden, her triumphant return to Stockholm, her tearful reunion with her mother, and the hysterical adulation of her countrymen. There were also reports of a solitary visit to Mauritz Stiller's grave and to his home. Mostly, though, there was the endless replaying of the thing that bedeviled her in California—attention from staring strangers. She had been sadly mistaken to think that Sweden would be any different. Still, being away from the Hollywood "factory" lifted her spirits and momentarily helped her grief.

Years later, Garbo would tell publicist Howard Dietz that she hated Louis B. Mayer, not for anything he had done to her, but for what he had done to Stiller. Why hate Mayer and not Thalberg? Mayer had, after all, tried to retain Stiller. It was Thalberg who had dismissed him. Was this perhaps transference of the blame she assigned herself for remaining at M-G-M while Stiller returned to Sweden a failure? Did she feel guilty for not using her considerable clout to reinstate him? Had there indeed been some kind of love affair?

Nils Asther, who played the prince in *Wild Orchids,* had known Garbo in Sweden. He later told historian Kevin Brownlow: "Garbo was a nice girl, but she didn't give, you know? I have worked with much more interesting actresses. She could have developed into a very good actress, I'm sure, if Stiller had remained and directed her."

Had Stiller died of a broken heart? For whatever reason, Garbo never truly recovered from the shock of Stiller's sudden, premature death. As if in defense, she returned to America with a cold resolve. She would continue to make films for Mr. Mayer, but she would make him and his studio do things her way and her way alone.

Hubert Voight, the studio's New York publicist, was still infatuated with the memory of the shy, sweet young girl he had welcomed in July 1925. When she arrived in New York on the *Drottningholm* on March 19, 1929, he found Garbo had become a self-contained young woman. "She was sort of a recluse," said Voight. "She was sort of strange about people. They had been cruel to her." Four years earlier, Voight had begged people to pay attention to Garbo. Now he had to keep them away from her. Even Nicholas Schenck, president of Loew's, who in 1925 had shown no interest in her, presented her with flowers. One reason for the frenzy was that *Wild Orchids* was in release—playing concurrently with *A Woman of Affairs*; in some districts, *The Mysterious Lady*,

Rilla Page Palmborg watched Sidney Franklin and William Daniels film this scene on November 5, 1928. "The set was a stateroom on an ocean liner," wrote Palmborg. "It was night, and the husband was sleeping peacefully. Garbo, the wife, was tossing restlessly on her bed. She was gorgeously dressed in orchid satin pajamas. Stealthily she slipped out of the bed, wrapped a silken robe about her body, and stole from the room. The scene was taken over and over." The main reason for the many takes was that Garbo's mind was elsewhere.

Left: Lillie awakes from a dream in which the prince is whipping her. "Sex is the meat and marrow of its drama, the protagonist of its characters," *Variety* wrote of *Wild Orchids*. "The dames will probably feel that having their marital fidelity tested and tempted by so natty a sheik as Asther is a possible source of pleasurable tremors."

The Divine Woman, and even earlier Garbo films were being trotted out by exhibitors on odd nights. The public could not get enough of Greta Garbo, even if reviewers had a difficult time making *Wild Orchids* sound exciting. The best that Mordaunt Hall of the *New York Times* could say was that the film was "pleasingly imaginative" and that Garbo's acting was "well-timed and, as usual, effective." If the film had not followed a series of scintillating films with Gilbert, it would have been judged more fairly. Franklin's direction made the most of the story's inherent suspense, aided considerably by Lewis Stone's authoritative performance. And William Daniels found still new ways to put Garbo's beauty on the screen.

While in New York, Garbo went to a few gatherings with Voight. One was a party for Metropolitan Opera baritone Lawrence Tibbett. Recalled Voight:

> Garbo threw off her reserve in the center of all these charming people and laughed with more gaiety than the rest. This is sort of cute—she got a wee bit tipsy on champagne and she was singing in Swedish so adorably that everyone was excruciated. I sat there watching her. I saw a new sophistication—a polishing off of the rough corners, but there, underneath—not bothering to remain hidden, was the real Garbo, a marvelous friend, and a child of the sun and of joy. She was the most beautiful creature I have ever seen that night, simply shining with life.

On March 26, Garbo arrived at the train station in Glendale, where she was met by a beaming John Gilbert. It was not long before he resumed his proposals of marriage, and less time before Garbo rebuffed them. Gilbert, seeing a new intransigence, grew angry.

"You are a very foolish boy, Yacky," Garbo said. "You quarrel with me for nothing. I must do my way, but we need not part."

"Not this time," said Gilbert ominously. "This time it's going to be all or nothing." On April 10, a prominently placed article in *Variety* announced that M-G-M would not be co-starring Garbo and Gilbert again. A spurned lover had dissolved the most popular romantic team in cinematic history.

CHAPTER TEN
The Single Standard

Greta Garbo's first film after her Swedish vacation was her ninth American feature. In the "part-talking" spring of 1929, *The Single Standard* was silent; but then, so was Garbo. She had lost patience with fan-magazine interviewers who made her feel self-conscious. "I don't like to talk to people because I can't express myself satisfactorily," said Garbo. "I don't say the things I mean." When she did say the things she meant, some writers quoted her phonetically with phrases like "Ay t'ank ay go home."

In that home was a pink enamel breakfast tray. "On the tray," an employee named Gustaf Norin later disclosed, "were always the two morning papers, the *Los Angeles Times* and the *Los Angeles Examiner*. She would turn to the theatrical section of each of the papers to see if there were any items about her. If she found any, she would cut or tear them out and put them away in the drawer of one of the little tables at the head of her bed." Later she would send them to Harry Edington for inclusion in a comprehensive scrapbook. She did not stop at newspapers.

"She was always anxious to get all the American motion-picture magazines," recalled Norin. "Often she would send me down to the drug store for them days before they were due. Sometimes she would walk down to inquire for them herself at a Beverly Hills drug store. With her hat pulled way down on her face and dark glasses hiding her eyes, she didn't think that the druggist knew who she was. But he knew her, all right." When Garbo read the interviews and began to comprehend their snide, cartoonish impressions of her, she said to John Gilbert: "People look at me like I am some *animal*. 'Exotic? Weird?' If I am that way, then I wish I should shoot myself. They make damn fool out of me!"

Now that interviewers were banned, reporters tried to take up the slack. A friend asked Garbo how she dealt with them. "Run like hell," she replied. Some reporters got the bright idea of ambushing her at the Beverly Hills Hotel. She eluded them by sending scouts to make sure that the coast was clear. One day, she heard that a well-dressed girl had been pestering the hotel clerks and was lying in wait in the lobby. After scanning the lobby, Garbo strode through it, got into her chauffeur-driven Lincoln, and rode quietly down the driveway to Sunset Boulevard. Suddenly a girl jumped out of a hedge and threw herself onto the pink gravel in front of the car. The driver braked—just short of her. The girl scrambled to her feet and jumped onto the running board.

"*Gott*! Are you all right?" Garbo asked, then saw an autograph book. The driver pulled the determined girl away from the car, demanding to know why she had endangered all three of them.

"I love her," cried the girl, who was found to be the daughter of a Milwaukee dentist. She was not the only one who tried this tactic. According to M-G-M publicist Ralph Wheelwright, "A reporter kept jumping out at [Garbo] from behind doors and bushes. When he finally accosted her, all she said was 'Damn!' It became famous as the 'one-word interview.'"

One interview Garbo could not duck in 1929 was the *New York Times*. Film critic Mordaunt Hall wanted to know what role she would most like to play. "Joan of Arc," she answered. "But it probably wouldn't go so well. I would like to do something unusual, something that has not been done. I would like to get away from the usual. I don't see anything in silly

In John S. Robertson's 1929 film *The Single Standard*, the free spirit Arden Stuart (Greta Garbo) takes her chauffeur (Robert Castle) for a ride, much to the dismay of her admirer (John Mack Brown).

In spite of the turmoil in her personal life, Garbo enjoyed working with Nils Asther and the crew of *The Single Standard* on a lumber boat off the coast of Catalina Island.

lovemaking." Hall brought up sound films. *The Trial of Mary Dugan*, which was Norma Shearer's first all-talking film and M-G-M's second, was about to open. The studio had six more in the works, one of which was *The Hollywood Revue of 1929*. Garbo had been approached for this all-star variety show, which would be the vocal debut of John Gilbert, Joan Crawford, and almost every M-G-M star but Lon Chaney, who was ostensibly holding out for a solo sound debut. Garbo used her contract to avoid doing a skit in the film. The contract specified that she must be costarred only with a male and that she did not have to speak. She was in no hurry to do so. "If they want me to talk, I'll talk," she said. "I'd love to act in a talking picture when they are better, but the ones I have seen are awful. It's no fun to look at a shadow, and somewhere out of the theater a voice is coming."

Even so, Garbo prepared herself for the inevitable. On her arrival in New York in March, she had asked publicist Hubert Voight about a Eugene O'Neill play. "She begged me to get her a Swedish version of *Anna Christie*," recalled Voight. "I could buy only an English version, so I had the little interpreter who had gone to the boat that day translate it into Swedish for her." In the meantime, Garbo had at least one more silent film to make. Its source was *The Single Standard*, a *Cosmopolitan* magazine serial by Gilbert's friend Adela Rogers St. Johns. The Hearst journalist was the daughter of San Francisco criminal lawyer Earl Rogers and had learned about life, as she later wrote, from "pimps, professional prostitutes, gamblers, bank robbers, poets, newspapermen, jury bribers, millionaire dipsomaniacs, and murderers." Her story looked at society through the eyes of Arden Stuart, a San Francisco girl "as much of our day as

radios and bobbed hair." Arden wants to bury the double standard and enjoy the same freedom that men have. She begins an affair with her chauffeur, who kills himself when Arden's family objects. She then takes up with a good-looking rogue named Packy Cannon, a champion prize-fighter who is also an award-winning painter and a skilled seaman. Should Arden sail to the South Seas with him on his yacht—without marrying him?

> Arden Stuart stood where few women have ever stood, face to face with the wholly abstract question of virtue, of righteousness for the sake of principle, of sheer moral integrity unforced by any consequences, of whether women are, after all, any different from men. Many women, from now on, will face that question—as to whether women were ever actually purer, better, than men, or whether they were simply held by fear and custom and convenience.

Arden sails with Packy and falls in love with him, but he sees the idyllic affair only as an image to be preserved, not unlike one of his paintings. Arden goes home and tries to live down her adventure, but only one friend, a young society man named Tommy, stands by her. She marries him, has a child, and then Packy returns. Still true to her standard, she wants to leave with Packy again. Will she desert her husband and child for the single standard?

M-G-M had bought St. Johns's novel in 1927. After Joan Crawford's newfound stardom in the fall of 1928 (in *Our Dancing Daughters*), it was considered for her. But its protagonist was a woman even more daring than *The Green Hat*'s Iris March. In 1929, the "modern woman" had a right to such behavior, wrote Mildred Adams in a *New York Times* article, "Now the Siren Eclipses the Flapper."

This simple scene was the result of all the hubbub in the photograph above.

[The modern American woman] no longer has to bother about smashing tradition or demonstrating her superiority to convention. In this she is the flapper's debtor, for that young person . . . established the feminine right to equal representation in such hitherto masculine fields of endeavor as smoking and drinking, petting, swearing, and upsetting the community peace. They need no longer be the subject of crusades. Indeed, the incurable flappers who go on fighting for them are as absurd as the good ladies who carry the hysteric air of martyrs in the cause of women's rights.

In this tolerant environment, anything was possible, or so M-G-M set out to prove, with Garbo as the avatar of freedom. "Miss Garbo has [until now] mostly portrayed princesses of small, nebulous countries," wrote an uncredited (and inaccurate) *New York Times* staffer. "In the greater number of her pictures she has gone her own way—or the way of the part—and has bothered not for tradition." This was not entirely true. Although she was a foreign enchantress in most of her eight American films, five ended with her in a traditional marriage. How would she handle a "100 percent American" role? And when the final fade-out came, would she choose her own way or tradition?

The scenario of *The Single Standard* was begun by Josephine Lovett and finished by Alice D. G. Miller, the daughter of *The White Cliffs of Dover* author Alice Duer Miller. Supervisor Hunt Stromberg dictated notes to Miller as specific as if he were writing the story himself. In one scene, Arden has been living with Packy for two years, far from her husband and child. "We open up," wrote Stromberg, "on a rendezvous in Italy's Bohemia. Artists! Colonists! Dreamers! Adventurers! Life in the raw—just such a life as this Packy Cannon, this rover and philosopher, would pursue. We pack this sequence full of attraction and color . . . the songs of Old Italia . . . the music of Venetian nights . . . revelry . . . glorious abandon! It is in this place and in this mood that we dramatize Arden's lifeless spirit, something of the disintegration that was inevitable." Arden is disillusioned with her rootless existence not because she is guilty or homesick but because Packy reserves the benefits of their lifestyle for himself. At a café society soiree, he humiliates Arden by flirting with a girl in front of the entire party.

Intercutting with this would be flashes of groups commenting on Packy's amours . . . his utter disregard . . . dramatizing in Arden's reactions the realization that she is nothing more than a mistress, possessing the duties of a wife, but certainly not the privileges, nor the common respect. This scene [is] intended as a striking example to Arden of the differentiation between men and women.

By the Single Standard, the man can go on . . . drawing friends . . . admiration.

"What some girls do and a lot more would like to, Greta Garbo does in *The Single Standard*," wrote a reviewer about Garbo's South Seas idyll with Nils Asther.

By the Single Standard, a woman must stop . . . drawing judgment . . . condemnation.

The sophisticated, college-educated Stromberg was well suited to this project, respecting Garbo's uniqueness by not making the story too sentimental or too sensational. He allowed the actress who preferred solitude to play a character who escapes society on a yacht called the *All Alone*. There was also an effective scene of Arden strolling in the rain. A pushy middle-aged man intrudes on Arden's privacy, and she tells him: "I am walking alone because I *want* to walk alone." A few years earlier Garbo had told a journalist: "I like it when it rains. Because when I walk in the rain I am separated from the world."

The Single Standard went into production on April 15, 1929, directed by John S. Robertson, who was best known for a series of Richard Barthelmess vehicles at that star's own Inspiration Pictures. Robertson had also worked with Lars Hanson and William Daniels on the 1927 M-G-M film *Captain Salvation*; Garbo's two friends may have recommended him. Daniels was busy lighting Norma Shearer's sound films, so Oliver Marsh photographed *The Single Standard*. Cedric Gibbons designed the film's imposing sets, which, like those in *Our Dancing Daughters*, were inspired by the 1925 Exposition Internationale des Arts Décoratifs et

Industriels Modernes in Paris. Arden's mansion was not the gingerbread edifice that a San Francisco setting would imply, but a "Moderne" marvel of soaring sandstone setbacks and geometric black-and-gold interiors. Gilbert Adrian made Garbo's athletic angularity stand out in bold relief from this contrasty backdrop with ensembles that had geometric patterns and prints in softer shades of gray. All these elements helped Garbo portray a girl who was as individual as she was, if not as solitary.

Filming went smoothly for the first three weeks, even with Garbo's habitual tardiness. She was more at ease on the set, perhaps because she already knew Dorothy Sebastian, John Mack Brown, and Nils Asther. She was even spending time with Asther after work. He was one of the first to see her new home at 1027 Chevy Chase Drive in Beverly Hills, and to meet her domestic help, a pleasant young Swedish couple named Gustaf and Sigrid Norin. He even got to see her chow dog, Fimsy; her parrot, Polly; and her naughty black kittens, Half Pint and Large Pint, who nestled together in an expensive bed—the silken folds of a Chinese ceremonial robe that hung to the floor from an otherwise bare wall of Garbo's bedroom. Adrian was also invited to Garbo's

In *The Single Standard,* Arden Stuart visits an art gallery. Unit still photographer James Manatt made this portrait of Garbo on the set between scenes.

home. He soon realized that he had been invited there to rearrange the bland furniture that came with the house.

Garbo had moved little more with her than a trunk, a few boxes of books (still unpacked since her 1925 arrival), and the simple, almost mannish clothes she favored. The gowns that Lilyan Tashman had helped her choose for her vacation hung unworn in her closet. "She was sorry she had bought them," said Sigrid Norin. "In her closet Garbo kept the old checked suit she wore when she went on location in Turkey with Mauritz Stiller [in November 1924, after meeting Louis B. Mayer in Berlin]. She cautioned me to see that it was kept free from moths. When Mrs. Victor Seastrom called on her, Garbo brought it out, explaining how proudly she wore her new suit on her first location trip."

There was one piece of furniture that Garbo prized. It was a chest of drawers that she had bought at an auction of Stiller's belongings. As she showed it to Asther, to Adrian, or to Harry Edington, she would lapse into an emotionless, almost singsong recitation of her mentor's demise. "He was only forty-five," she said quietly. "He died at one o'clock in the morning. Only a nurse was with him. If he had recovered, he would have started filming in Paris. He had pus in his lung. The doctors wanted him to go to Switzerland to rest." She spoke these facts as if still trying to comprehend them. On the set, she would occasionally say to herself, "He says I must do this," or "He doesn't want me to do that." Some bystanders wondered if she was referring to John Gilbert.

Garbo's only mention of her ex-lover came when he passed her in his car one day. "*Gott,* I wonder what I ever saw in him," Garbo said to a companion. "Oh, well. I guess he *was* pretty." Those who had witnessed the romance felt that there was unfinished business. "She'd had enough of his craziness and she was glad to be through with him," an unidentified actress said, "but Gilbert was still in love with her."

In late April, while Garbo worked on the silent *Single Standard* to the sound of a whirring camera and mood music, Gilbert was working on Fred Niblo's *Redemption* in the unnatural quiet of a new soundstage, playing his first sound role. It was not going well. For some reason, the playbacks did not sound like him. The new M-G-M sound engineers made take after take, but his timbre did not materially improve. The technology was too new and Gilbert was too nervous. Lionel Barrymore was brought in to retake some particularly poor sequences. After work Gilbert distracted himself by fanning the flames of a new romance.

Ina Claire was informally engaged to screenwriter Gene Markey, but something had happened when she first saw Gilbert. It was at a Hollywood party in early March. "He was playing craps on the floor with some people," she recalled. "And he said something derogatory about himself. Not exactly derogatory, but [as if he saw] himself as a kind of joke, as a sex symbol. . . . It made me laugh, and I thought, I wouldn't have expected that from him." Claire was

Arden Stuart's San Francisco mansion was designed by Cedric Gibbons to underscore her modernity.

thirty-seven, the star of a string of Broadway hits, and famous since 1913 for being the first actor to forsake traditional stentorian delivery for naturalistic line readings. She was a real stage star—elegant, witty, and ready to conquer the talkies. By late April, Claire was filming *The Awful Truth* at the Pathé studio in Culver City and seeing a lot of Gilbert at nearby Metro. As a stage actor, she had definite opinions of Hollywood histrionics, Gilbert's included. "I'd thought he was kind of a ham, and I wouldn't be falling for a ham!" Still, there was talk of marriage. "I'd only known him six weeks!" Claire recalled. "But it was because he was so nice."

Not everyone thought Gilbert was nice. Some friends thought he was using Claire to get at Garbo, most noticeably at a party thrown by Basil Rathbone and his wife, Ouida Bergere, on April 27 at the Beverly Hills Hotel. As described by Laurence Olivier, who was not there, but who knew many who had been, it was "an unkind, empty gesture on his part, taking advantage of a young female's flattered fascination simply in order to snap his fingers at her as he paraded her in front of Garbo. Garbo, of course, wore a more mocking expression than ever, doing the slow nod and keeping it up pretty steadily, for all the world like an automatic model in a shop window, while poor Gilbert went ma-a-a-d."

On May 8, the *All Alone* set sail from San Pedro, bound for Catalina Island to film Arden and Packy in the South Seas. The next morning Garbo was chatting with coworkers on the former lumber boat when someone came aboard from the island and directed her attention to a news item in the *New York Times*. It read: "John Gilbert, star screen actor, and Ina Claire, noted chiefly as an actress of the legitimate stage, surprised their friends who have been expecting Gilbert to marry Greta Garbo when they took a train tonight for Las Vegas, Nev., with the announcement that they would be married there tomorrow." According to an onlooker, "She turned white as she glanced at it, then read with interest. Finally she smiled, handed back the paper, and thanked the lender. Then she resumed her gaiety and was literally the life of the party."

Later that day, screenwriter Lenore Coffee was arriving early for an appointment with Garbo's manager, Harry Edington, when a dramatic scene unfolded before her. The door to Edington's inner office was ajar, and he was engaged in such an intense conversation that he did not notice Coffee coming in. The writer felt awkward about eavesdropping, but she did not want to interrupt him. "Some of the M-G-M telephones were very sensitive and I could tell it was

The past returns to haunt Arden Stuart during a party at a yacht club. *The Single Standard* was photographed by Oliver Marsh, whose lighting was slightly softer and flatter than that of William Daniels. Marsh fell ill during filming and was temporarily replaced by Peverell Marley, who lit this shot.

a woman's voice on the other end. I could almost tell which woman. . . . This is what I pieced together: A woman, in a state of great emotion, was telling him that this marriage of Jack Gilbert to Ina Claire could not take place." Edington was trying to talk, but the woman wasn't listening. Coffee could see drops of perspiration on her manager's forehead as the crying grew louder. "The voice on the other end [of the line] was unmistakably Garbo's," recalled Coffee. "And she was sobbing. Edington asked Garbo why on earth she'd waited until the last minute when everyone had known about it for days. She said she'd been on a yacht making a movie and hadn't heard until now." Edington was wiping his face with his handkerchief, trying to reason with her, but Garbo was not listening. "[She was saying that] Jack belonged to her—they never should have separated—what had been between them was too real, too deep," recounted Coffee years later. "If I hadn't heard it myself, I wouldn't have believed it."

"You know I'd do anything for you," Edington pleaded, "but how can I stop a wedding which is to take place in a matter of hours? What excuse or reason can Jack give?

Please, you know how devoted I am to you, but you must be reasonable. You must not ask for the impossible. I'm Jack's manager, not his guardian. There is only one person who can stop this wedding and that is yourself." Edington was shaking as he hung up the phone. Then he realized that Coffee had been there all the time, just outside the open door. "My God! Did you hear all that? Do you think she'd do anything? Can you imagine what the papers would do with it?"

Coffee tried to calm Edington and promised not to tell anyone.

"Jack would kill me if he knew this," he said. "What a scandal! His career is in enough trouble as it is. Yet I feel guilty as hell. But what could I do?" As accustomed as he was to Garbo's increasing sense of entitlement, Edington spent an anxious night. The wedding took place without incident. To stop it, Garbo would have had to confront her own fear of strangers and public scenes. She would have had to admit that something was more important than her privacy.

On Catalina Island the next day, a persistent reporter buttonholed her and informed her of Gilbert's marriage. "Thank you," she replied in her most offhanded Iris March–

Arden Stuart manner. "I hope Mr. Gilbert will be very happy." A reporter who approached Ina Claire, now the second Mrs. John Gilbert, got a more pointed response. "How does it feel to be married to a great star?" asked the reporter.

"I don't know," smiled the glamorous blonde. "Why don't you ask Mr. Gilbert?"

All of Garbo's scenes at Catalina took place on the yacht, so she was temporarily removed from studio gossip. In keeping with the name of the craft, she spent her time off "all alone." She would swim, row, or zoom about Avalon Bay in a speedboat, inviting no one to accompany her. Her ease in this lovely setting was well translated to film by Robertson and Marsh, whose scenes of her lounging on the deck of the *All Alone* made stunning tableaux. She worked well with Asther, too. What time she did not spend alone, she spent with him, speaking in Swedish. She never mentioned Gilbert to him, but she did warn him when she was in one of her moods. "I had an awful row with God this morning," she said to him one gloomy day after they had returned to Los Angeles.

"Arden Stuart was altogether a woman of her times. Upon her slim, tanned young shoulders could be placed the great question as to whether, after all, women are so different from men." So wrote Adela Rogers St. Johns in her serialized novel *The Single Standard.* The other great question was how different Greta Garbo was from Arden Stuart.

"I used to stand behind the camera and watch her act," said Asther. "Her motions and gestures seemed ungainly and crude, but when seen on film they were marvelous." One scene they were shooting involved the strikingly handsome seaman's attempts to convince Arden to run away with him. Asther was wearing a great deal of makeup for the role and looked epicene in the extreme. He was already subject to the backstage gossip that afflicts unmarried young actors who are too handsome. One day, when he wrestled Garbo into a clinch during rehearsal, she pulled loose and snapped at him: "Stop that! It's not a sailor you've got in your arms." The remark made the rounds of the studio, causing Asther some embarrassment. In defense, he attempted to give the impression of an offscreen romance with Garbo. He even offered her marriage at one point, but she would not take him seriously, aware as she was of his homosexual tendencies.

The Single Standard finished production on June 4, but Stromberg was not satisfied with the scene in which Arden returns from the South Seas to find a chilly reception in a San Francisco ballroom. "The Stafford-Hanley party must be played in an entirely different key than the one shot," wrote Stromberg. "The sequence in the picture now is dull, awkward, and stupid. The tango is a joke. Arden's appearance

Garbo liked this outfit so well that she took to wearing it around M-G-M. Women did not wear pants in 1929, but no studio employee would criticize someone bringing the company more than a million dollars a year (when a million bought twenty times what it does now).

This scene was visualized by supervisor Hunt Stromberg as a punctuation mark to a stuffy party. Garbo, shunned by hypocritical socialites, leaves the ballroom in search of only she knows what.

[is] insignificant, and Tommy's acting [is] like a dose of salts."

Stromberg visualized retakes that could be shot on standing sets. "I see Arden," he wrote, "leaving the room following the conflict with her brother. Possibly she marches straight through the crowded ballroom, and in this way, gets over something of her contempt for the hypocritical sophisticates. I see her going out into the garden and the moonlight—to be alone—forever alone—free from the nasty little tricks of this nasty little set." The scene was shot to better effect on June 10 and 11, and the new footage was rushed into the around-the-clock editing sessions that M-G-M used to honor exhibition contracts. With amazing alacrity, *The Single Standard* opened on July 27.

"What some girls do and a lot more would like to, Greta Garbo does in *The Single Standard*," wrote a reviewer in *Variety*, who predicted that "thousands of typing girlies and purple-suited office boys will find this made to their order." The review also mentioned the way Garbo slipped in and out of both romantic entanglements and Adrian's costumes. "Throwing off the cloak of conventionalism for free plunges claimed so common in spots here and on the Continent, the

actress is almost unfeline in her brazen directness. While censors probably expected to leap on this point, when the picture gets to them, they will find no show except a veiled peep at Arden's garters." As most critics noted, all of Arden's iconoclasm was redeemed at the final fade-out. M-G-M, knowing that the public would not condone a Garbo heroine deserting a toddler, ended the film with Arden and Tommy reunited and the double standard firmly in place. *The Single Standard* made $81,600 in its first week at the Capitol Theatre, which was excellent for a silent film. Its eventual profit, though, was $330,000, not as good as Garbo's pairings with Gilbert, and not nearly as good as every M-G-M talking picture so far. Garbo still had not committed to a contract amendment, so one more silent film was readied for her. If she continued to delay her sound debut much longer, her film career would be in jeopardy.

Opposite: This June 1929 portrait of Garbo marked the end of her work with Ruth Harriet Louise, who would soon leave M-G-M to marry director Leigh Jason and start a family. By this time, Garbo finally had a home, too.

"And I am indifferent to public opinion," says Garbo in the courtroom scene.

versions of films such as Norma Shearer's *The Trial of Mary Dugan*. A French (or German or Spanish) cast and crew would utilize the same sets and shoot the same scenes, but in their native language. The parallel version, titled *Le Procès de Mary Dugan*, and directed by Feyder, would then bring revenue from France and French-speaking territories.

So far, only Rosay had gotten work in Hollywood, and that was in the Fox Film Corporation's last silent film, *The One-Woman Idea*. Feyder had his own idea for a woman, a treatment called "The Kiss." Emil Jannings read it and saw a Garbo film in it. "We knew that she had a great deal to say about the pictures she made," said Loder. If she liked the story, she could suggest Feyder to M-G-M. So Jannings contrived to have the Feyders and the Loders camped in his living room when Garbo made an informal but not unexpected appearance. She came to play tennis, and, in spite of the strangers present, she did. Perhaps because she trusted Jannings or because of Rosay's lofty manner, Garbo began to relax. Loder recalled: "After a delicious dinner of German dishes, [Jannings] came over to me rubbing his hands together and smiling. 'Everything is going fine,' he said. 'Garbo is listening to Jacques's story. She likes it. I think she

will make it and that Jacques will be the director.'" Feyder's story was a clever one. Instead of being torn between an older man and a younger man as she was in her M-G-M formula, Garbo would have three men vying for her: an older husband, a lover her own age, and a male ingenue. While Feyder worked with M-G-M to adapt his story, he helped Garbo make another friend.

At a black-tie party at Lubitsch's home, Garbo was the only woman not wearing an evening gown. Sitting next to Feyder in her slightly wrinkled suit, she caught the attention of German actress Salka Steuermann. Feyder introduced Salka as the wife of Berthold Viertel, who had directed Feyder's wife in *The One-Woman Idea*. Garbo dropped her bored reserve and warmed to Salka Viertel. Soon she was a frequent visitor to the Viertels' home at 165 Mabery Road in Santa Monica. This half-timbered retreat would one day be known as Hollywood's premier literary salon, but at this time, Salka Viertel was still adjusting herself and her young sons to California. When Garbo showed up at her kitchen window—always without warning—Viertel would put her chores aside and take a long walk on the beach with her new friend. "She told me," wrote Viertel, "that she was pleased that I had only seen her in *The Atonement of Gösta Berling*, as she did not care much for her other films. She was very funny, caricaturing the repetitiousness of their seduction techniques." The two women discussed films in depth. Sixteen years Garbo's senior, Viertel was astute and opinionated. She was surprised to find out that Garbo was a frequent moviegoer.

"She often went to motion-picture theaters all by herself," confirmed Gustaf Norin. "She never allowed me to drive the car up to the entrance of the theater. She would get out a block or two away. Then, with her hat pulled down over her eyes, the collar of her heavy tweed coat turned up around her neck, and her hands thrust into her pockets, she would hurry inside. In two and a half hours, I would be waiting to pick her up." No doubt Garbo heard an exchange like this as she waited in line at the box office:

"Is this a talking movie?"

"No. It's with music."

"Thank you. We'll go somewhere that's showing a talking movie."

Americans wanted all-talking films, and they wanted their favorites in them; some stars were holding out. "I am not sympathetic to this 'sound business,'" Ronald Colman wrote to Samuel Goldwyn. "I feel, as many do, that this is a mechanical resource, that it is a retrogressive and temporary digression insofar as it affects the art of motion picture acting." The reception accorded Colman's velvety voice in his first talkie, *Bulldog Drummond*, proved him wrong. Charlie Chaplin, perhaps the most popular movie star in the world, was making a silent film called *City Lights*. When asked what he thought of talkies, he replied: "I loathe them. They

This scene was eliminated from the final cut of *The Kiss* because it slowed the film's pace. Cedric Gibbons's art direction and William Daniels's lighting were both saved for posterity by James Manatt. Garbo knew which of her scenes were missing from the finished film. Her employee Gustaf Norin drove her to see it. "I remember that she saw *The Kiss* three different times," said Norin. "Once in Los Angeles, again in Pasadena, and a third time in Long Beach."

are spoiling the oldest art in the world—the art of pantomime. They are ruining the great beauty of silence." On March 25, 1929, William Fox announced that Fox Film would make no more silents. Chaplin owned his own studio and could take three years to make a silent movie if it pleased him. Garbo, on the other hand, had to be aware of M-G-M's release pattern.

In March, three M-G-M silents and two part-talkies were released; in April, three silents and two all-talkers; in May, four silents and no talkies. In June there were suddenly no silent films—just one all-talkie. By mid-July it was obvious that the only silents being released were those of holdouts such as Lon Chaney and Garbo. The talkies were coming out at a rate of one a week, and if silent stars were not willing to do them, stage actors were. Ruth Chatterton (or Ina Claire) might soon eclipse Garbo if she did not commit to talking pictures. Waiving negotiations for a contract amendment, Garbo agreed to take the plunge. Her current project, tentatively titled *The Woman Accused*, would be her last silent film. Her talking debut would be in Eugene

O'Neill's play *Anna Christie*, the story of a Swedish-American girl—who speaks with an accent. "It's a gorgeous story," Garbo told an interviewer. "And we'll see to the accent." What she did not say was that her first impression of *Anna Christie* had been a negative one; she had sent Harry Edington to see Thalberg. "She says it portrays Swedes as low characters," said Edington.

"If she turns down this role," said Thalberg, "I will stop her paycheck." Low or not, Garbo agreed to play Anna.

In *The Woman Accused* she played a wealthy young woman named Irene who is unhappily married to Guarry, a dyspeptic older man. She is in love with André, a lawyer, but cannot leave her husband. Enter a coltish young man named Pierre, a friend of the family whose infatuation with Irene leads to a compromising scene. The kiss of Feyder's title is a platonic favor granted by Irene to Pierre on the eve of his departure for college. Pierre is overcome by passion and wants more, just as Guarry comes home. Guarry attacks him. Irene tries to stop Guarry from killing Pierre. At this moment, the camera pulls back from the struggle, and the

Clarence Bull conducted his first portrait session with Greta Garbo on August 27, 1929. He did not know what to expect, and, as it turned out, neither did she.

door closes in front of it, a device that scenarist Hans Kräly no doubt learned from his frequent collaborator, Lubitsch. The next scene reveals that Guarry is dead, but the audience must wait until Irene is tried for murder and then acquitted to learn what really happened behind that black Art Deco door.

While Kräly and Feyder were crafting this polished piece of cinema, John Gilbert was looking at *Redemption*, his first talking film, which was neither polished nor cinematic.

After seeing the first cut, he asked Irving Thalberg to shelve it. It was hard to believe, but his voice did not sound like him. "He was a fine actor," recalled Conrad Nagel, who was also in *Redemption*. "He had a distinct and forceful way of talking. Whenever he spoke to you, he was extremely powerful about it, but unfortunately, with that microphone, his voice came out funny." The film was based on Leo Tolstoy's *The Living Corpse*, and its scenes of drinking, depression, and suicide were unflattering reflections of Gilbert's moody excesses.

Even with Lionel Barrymore's retakes, *Redemption* was a dubious choice for a sound debut. Exhibitors all over the country were expecting a Gilbert feature in September. Something had to be done.

On June 11, Gilbert rejoined Lionel Barrymore on a soundstage, hoping that they could do better than *Redemption*. Instead of giving Gilbert a modern American piece, Thalberg assigned him a Ruritanian romance called *Olympia*. The most popular talkies were urban dramas that crackled with vernacular jabbering, not mythical-kingdom romances laden with flowery orations. Hungarian playwright Ferenc Molnár had written *Olympia* as a light comedy; the script read like a novel by Elinor Glyn. But this was what M-G-M's "Great Lover" was getting for his sound debut. Predictably, his voice problem was not helped by the stilted dialogue he had to recite, or by the limited equalization of the still-primitive recording equipment. "Now if they had just been wise to this," said Nagel, "they would have slowed him down a little bit and had him talk lower." Barrymore, a veteran of both stage and screen, should have been able to help Gilbert, but day after day the playbacks sounded thin and flat.

Ina Claire was also a master of elocution, but Gilbert resisted her attempts to coach him. "Ina wanted so badly to help him," recalled Eleanor Boardman, who was in *Redemption*, "but she seemed to go about it in the wrong way, correcting his pronunciation, giving him little hints about 'pear-shaped tones' and telling him he had a 'white voice.'" This harsh expression was theatrical terminology for the type of voice that emanates from the throat instead of from the diaphragm. "I tried once to explain to him," Claire recalled. "You see, I was being reasonable and this was something new to him. But his masculine pride . . . his *professional* pride . . . I was the *last* person he wanted to tell him about acting."

Olympia lurched on, inexplicably renamed *His Glorious Night*. Hedda Hopper played a supporting role in it. "I watched Jack Gilbert being destroyed on the soundstage by one man, Lionel Barrymore," wrote Hopper. "Talking pictures had to be approached cautiously. Lionel had plenty of experience on the stage. Gilbert had none. By the time sound came in, 'love' was a comedy word. Use it too freely and you got a belly laugh. Whether by diabolical intent or careless accident, I'll never know, but Jack's very first [*sic*] speech in *His Glorious Night* was 'I love you, I love you, I love you.'" In fairness to Barrymore, he had not written the script or chosen the property. Furthermore, the fifty-one-year-old actor was trying to launch a career as a director because of increasing pain from an undisclosed leg ailment—and he was taking morphine.

His Glorious Night finished filming on July 11, just as *The Woman Accused*—which was first retitled *Jealousy* and later *The Kiss*—was about to commence. Albert Lewin had written new scenes for Garbo, deciding that Irene should not kill herself over the triangular mess she has caused. Conrad Nagel was cast as André. "What do you mean, 'Woman of Mystery'?" he asked an interviewer, referring to *The Mysterious Lady*. "The only mystery about Greta was in the title. I found her to be a thoroughly enjoyable person." Nagel cited an ongoing game in which he and Garbo would bring a new joke to the set each day.

Jealousy went into production on July 16. Nagel was not needed for its first few scenes. In these, Feyder gave William Daniels new opportunities to capture Garbo's beauty. One scene began with a very close close-up of Garbo looking directly into the lens and applying lipstick. The camera pulled back slowly, revealing that she was sitting at her dressing table. It was a spectacular and expertly executed shot, one that could only have worked with the combined talents of Garbo and Daniels. Feyder was showing himself to be an artist of equal stature.

Lewin was producing with the assistance of his trusted adviser, Paul Bern, who suggested an untried actor for the pivotal role of Pierre. Lew Ayres was barely twenty, a recent alumnus of the Henry Halstead Orchestra, which had opened the Beverly Wilshire Hotel. "The great stellar personalities I admired in my youth were Valentino and John Gilbert," said Ayres. "It was—it truly was—my secret ambition to be a part of their world. I tried to find a way into it, and one of the things I did was to become a musician. I learned to play the guitar, the banjo, and several string instruments." While visiting musician friends at the Hollywood Roosevelt tea dance one day, he asked actress Lili Damita for a dance. A burly man suddenly came up to them, and, instead of threatening Ayres, asked him: "Are you an actor?"

"No, but I'd like to be," replied Ayres. "I'd like very much to be an actor."

The man was Ivan Kahn, who was forming a talent agency. He secured Ayres a stint at Pathé, where the teenage musician met Bern, who was temporarily producing there. Now Bern tapped Ayres for a role at M-G-M. In it, Ayres, who idolized Gilbert, was to play a love scene with Gilbert's inamorata, Greta Garbo. It was a bit much for Ayres. "I was flabbergasted to find myself working with Garbo," he said. "She was the most glamorous woman."

On July 20, the day of their first scene together, Feyder began by showing Ayres how to hold and kiss Garbo. Half a day passed before anyone thought to introduce him to her. Apparently she sensed his awe, because she turned to Feyder and asked him, "Can't Mr. Ayres and I have a cigarette and a chat first? How can we play such a scene when we have never seen each other before?" The conversation was formal but slightly self-mocking, according to Ayres: "I remember her saying, 'I'm the woman who's unfaithful to a million men.'" In this scene, Pierre asks Irene for a photo to take to college as a keepsake. Then he asks her for a good-bye kiss. It so excites him that he loses control. Guarry (Anders Randolph) bursts in on them and, without asking for an explanation, tries to kill Pierre, repeatedly knocking Irene to the floor in the process. This was the most physically violent scene Garbo had yet played.

Not surprisingly, holding an 11x14 print of Garbo by Ruth Harriet Louise gave Ayres ideas. He asked Garbo for an autographed photo, perhaps unaware of her stricture against such conduct. "Some day you will get one," she answered noncommittally. About the same time, she noticed the finely made shirt Ayres was wearing. "I like that," she said. "I wish I had one like it." In short order, Ayres came to the set with several shirts just like it and presented them to Garbo. She was pleased—until he again asked for an autographed photo. "I gave you my shirts," he reasoned. "You should give me your picture." Garbo walked away from him, and from then on, "Garbo had very little to say," said Ayres. "She seemed quite meditative."

A few days later, Mordaunt Hall of the *New York Times* visited Garbo for an interview. "I play the wife of a rich silk manufacturer," Garbo explained. "And, I am sorry to tell you, I kill my husband. As everything has to be paid for, I have to pay in the end for that deed." This revelation was not very sporting of her, since the film does not tell who killed Guarry until the last few minutes of its last reel. In it, Garbo again goes her own way—this time scot-free. (Evidently no one feared that giving away the ending of a murder mystery would spoil its box office; both Hall's and *Variety*'s respective reviews revealed that Irene did it.)

The atmosphere on the set of M-G-M's last silent movie was wistful. "There was a mood orchestra on the set during all scenes," recalled Ayres. "Five pieces, including a violinist and a man who played a small organ." These musicians were about to lose their jobs. The studio, which was paying them ninety dollars a day, would no longer need them, now that sound films mandated totally silent sets. But Garbo's sets were different from any other, given her need for total concentration and absolute privacy. Ayres thought her "far more shy than I'd ever been. In the love scenes, which were considered quite intimate at that time, no one was permitted to watch her except the director. That was Garbo's demand, not a request. She insisted on a screen that would hide her from the crew. She did that, not because she was temperamental. She was just embarrassed. She said she felt more relaxed doing her love scenes as privately as possible." Nagel also observed Garbo's ground rules. "She always quits promptly at five-thirty," he said, "while many of us lesser souls sometimes have to work all night. Greta won't work one minute overtime. I admire her for it—and I'd do the same thing if I were important enough to get away with it."

Filming of *Jealousy* ended on August 25. More than ten scenes never made it into the film's final cut. These included scenes that more fully established Pierre's infatuation with Irene, her husband's affection for her, and the protectiveness of Pierre's father; a long sequence between Pierre, Irene, and André in a hotel room; and several dramatic scenes of Irene facing a magistrate and languishing in jail. The advantage of a sixty-four-minute film was that exhibitors could squeeze more showings out of it per day.

Happily, Garbo completed the film without having to endure any offscreen drama. It was enough, perhaps, that she was saying good-bye to the sound of live music on the set, and to the gentle chattering of sprockets and film inside the movie camera. When she had first arrived, Daniels had been hand-cranking it. Now the Mitchell camera was motorized. Soon there would be a silver cover to keep it from competing with the voices of M-G-M actors. A way of life was ending.

Two days later, Garbo made the short trip that took place at the completion of each film. She walked to the editing building with her maid Alma and her hairdresser Billy following in her Lincoln, climbed the outside staircase, and, carrying her costumes, entered the portrait gallery. This was her first sitting with Clarence Sinclair Bull, who was the head of the stills department. Bull was thirty-four, short, soft-spoken, and afflicted with a pronounced limp, the result of a childhood illness. He had been after Pete Smith for some time, asking to do a session with Garbo. Bull had shot an occasional scene still on Garbo's sets since the days of *The Temptress*, but he wanted to get her into the portrait gallery, where he could create something special.

The problem, of course, was that Garbo was used to Ruth Harriet Louise. Furthermore, Garbo no longer wanted to shoot more than one still photo session per film. It was bad enough that she still had to shoot "poster art" in front of a blank background with her leading man, assuming stylized and often silly positions from which artists could paint advertising art. Instead, she required that all portraits made of her be in character. She did not want M-G-M to take photos of her as herself. "If they want to send out pictures of me dressed in the costumes I wear in my pictures, I can't stop that," she told Gustaf Norin. "But none of my personal photographs will be distributed all over the world. Those are for my friends alone." These "personal" photos included the snapshots she took with a Kodak Brownie she carried to work. When she was in the mood, she handed the camera to whoever was standing nearby and instructed this person to snap a picture of her and a coworker in the open shade between stages. Sometimes she would snap a picture of something she thought interesting. One day it was a turkey that was being used in a scene on a neighboring stage. "I want to send the picture home to my mother in Sweden," she explained to an onlooker. These pictures were mailed to Stockholm in her weekly package, along with magazines, a letter, and numerous photographs from her current film.

"The day Garbo walked into my portrait gallery she looked like a frightened schoolgirl," wrote Bull.

What she didn't know was that I was just as scared as she. For over three hours I shot her in every pose and emotion that beautiful face could mirror. Actually, I had no control over myself and I wondered when she might say she'd had too much. She said nothing, so I went on shooting. Finally I ran out of film. There had been no break. She hadn't asked for even a glass of water. As she rose and moved to the door, obviously tired yet somehow showing she had enjoyed our efforts, she said, "I was quite nervous, Mr. Bull. I'll do better next time." At the door, I reached for her hand. It was as moist as mine. "So will I, Miss Garbo."

Bull had exposed more than two hundred sheets of 8x10 sheet film in their session. These were processed that night and proofed the next day. Bull then met with Garbo to show

Bull did not know if he would have a second chance to photograph Garbo, so he used every effect he knew.

her the unretouched proofs. It was customary for M-G-M actors to tear the upper right-hand corners of poses that they did not want released. The remaining proofs would then be sent with the corresponding negatives to the retouching room, where each image would, depending on the size of the face on the negative and the sharpness of the lens used, undergo from two to eight hours of lead retouching. For Garbo's sitting, Bull had mostly used a soft-focus lens, so that except for some contours under her eyes, not much retouching would be necessary; the proofs looked soft and creamy. Neither Bull nor Garbo recorded impressions of this first "proof pass," but it is likely that she was surprised at the difference between his work and that of the head portrait photographer. It is unlikely that she tore the corners off any proof.

Ruth Harriet Louise tended to flatten subjects against a wall with uncomfortable poses and harsh lighting. She routinely cropped her images by shooting copy negatives, thus making the final prints look even flatter. Clarence Bull created depth, roundness, and warmth, first by posing his subject against an out-of-focus neutral background, and then by using a double-broad covered with framed silk screens as his key light. He balanced its milky highlights with a smaller softlight placed below the camera, imbuing its shadows with a subtle glow. When he used a spotlight, he put a conelike "snoot" on it so that the sharp-edged circle of light did not stray from Garbo's face.

William Daniels used a cloth filter or glass diffusion disk on the movie camera's lens to create small soft-focus halos in Garbo's close-ups. Bull used a soft-focus lens on the still camera to put large, liquid-looking halos around the highlights in her hair. The overall effect was painterly, dreamy, and—more than any previous portrait work—expressive of Garbo's enigmatic presence. The artist had a presence, too, a quiet dignity. Garbo would not have worked with him for three hours had he been abrasive, loud, or just forceful. She liked him because, like Clarence Brown, he spoke softly—if at all. Most of the session was conducted in silence, except for the Victrola that his assistant, Virgil Apger, constantly fed new records. Bull was the ideal collaborator for this sensitive soul. Their first set of proofs showed it, a portfolio of accomplished images that would be printed, published, reprinted, and seen all over the world.

Garbo's last silent film was also M-G-M's last silent release. By the time of its November 16 premiere, its title had become *The Kiss*. In the country's most prestigious review, the *New York Times*'s Mordaunt Hall wrote more about Garbo's appearance than her performance. His usual review was unimaginative, consisting of a bland rehash of the plot and a few innocuous comments on the performances. For him to go on about a performer's looks was a departure. "She first appears in a modish hat," he wrote, "one of those creations that seems to have been inspired by fliers' headgears.

Not a curl or even a strand of hair protrudes under the hard line around her face. She may not look pretty, but she is fascinating, and as the scenes pass along, Miss Garbo becomes increasingly attractive, especially in the closing glimpses, where she is arrayed in black." *Variety* allowed that *The Kiss* was "one of Miss Garbo's best, without stretching the elastic of kindness. Though this is silent it may be stronger that way than with dialog. Few actresses could weather the series of close-ups required of Miss Garbo in this one. In each she registers an individual perfection."

A reviewer in *Motion Picture* magazine addressed the issue on everyone's mind. "The last stand of the silent pictures, the last hope of those who like 'em quiet, is Greta Garbo. . . . The question of Miss Garbo's appeal is still unsolved by this picture. In spite of unworthy stories, in spite of her stubborn silence in this talkie day, I would gladly pay for my own ticket to see a Garbo picture—which is the greatest compliment a reviewer can pay!" Whether he paid or not, *The Kiss* did surprisingly well for a silent, grossing $448,000. This must have cheered Chaplin, who did not finish the silent *City Lights* for another year. And if Garbo's farewell to silents could make that much money, what would her first sound film make? That would depend, of course, on how she sounded.

The Hollywood Revue of 1929 had opened in late August. Audiences listened closely as John Gilbert and Norma Shearer essayed an excerpt from the balcony scene of *Romeo and Juliet* and then stepped out of character to chat with director Lionel Barrymore, who had them reprise the scene in Jazz Age lingo. All three sounded natural and relaxed, their voices registering nicely for the microphone. But how would Garbo sound? The only hint came from Hall's July interview. "If any voice suits a personality," he wrote, "it is that of Miss Garbo. It is deep in tone and her utterances are always distinct." *Anna Christie* was scheduled to start shooting in October. Garbo studied her script, rehearsed, and prepared herself for the microphone. If she was not nervous already, something happened in late September that would have paralyzed the most seasoned performer.

Opposite: Garbo liked what she saw in Bull's two hundred proofs. So did the M-G-M publicity department, which put this pose on the poster for *The Kiss*.

PART V

THE VOICE

CHAPTER TWELVE

Anna Christie

Wilhelm Sörenson was young, good-looking, and rich, the son of a Swedish lumber millionaire. In December 1928 his friend Prince Sivgard introduced him to Greta Garbo, who was visiting Stockholm. She sized up the baby-faced twenty-three-year-old and then asked him: "What kind of a sailor are you?" When his hesitant reply assured her that he was not an aggressive ladies' man, she allowed him to become her friend. They began to correspond after her return to America. Eventually, Sörenson grew eager to see if everything he heard about America was true—the grandeur, the freedom, the ubiquitous opportunity. He had a secret ambition to get into movies, so why not travel to Hollywood?

The summer of 1929 was the most propitious time that Sörenson could have chosen to see the United States. The "great god business" was smiling on every industry in sight, and it looked as if the pursuit of happiness need go no farther than the local stockbroker's office. Everyone was investing in the stock market—captains of industry and their factory workers—buying shares on margin by putting 10 percent down and paying off the rest in installments. Fueled by reckless speculation, the boom began in March 1928, survived a few setbacks, and in the spring of 1929 saw the number of shares traded in a day surpass the unthinkable five million.

"Be a bull on America!" came the exhortation if anyone asked how long this unreal prosperity would last. Hollywood was not deaf to the promise of quick millions. After all, a great many stars earning thousands a week had been waiters and chorus girls only a few years earlier; they knew that

Opposite: A microphone hangs like the Sword of Damocles over Greta Garbo and Clarence Brown on the set of her first talkie.

October 14, 1929, was Greta Garbo's first day on a talking picture. The silhouette in the foreground belongs to Clarence Brown, who was directing this version of Eugene O'Neill's *Anna Christie*.

anything was possible, so they (and their chauffeurs and butlers) also bought stocks. "The prosperity band wagon rolled along with the throttle wide open and the siren blaring," wrote historian Frederick Lewis Allen. Drawn by this siren, Sörenson wrote Garbo, asking if he could visit in the late summer of 1929.

"If you really wish to come," Garbo wrote in reply, "you are heartily welcome, but I must warn you that you may never understand me completely—how I really am and what makes me so. If I am working on a movie when you are here, we would not see much of each other because then I must be alone." Sörenson was planning to arrive in late August, when Garbo would be finishing *The Kiss* and preparing for *Anna Christie*. Having visited the new soundstages, she knew that making a sound film was a very different process, but she downplayed her anxiety to Mordaunt Hall of the *New York Times*. "She said she had no qualms about the recording of her voice, neither was she in the least intimidated at the idea of speaking lines before the microphone." Garbo was more candid with Sörenson. "They are making sound movies here now," she wrote, "and nobody knows what is to happen to me. Perhaps I will not stay here much longer. Already some of the top stars intend leaving Hollywood, and it is questionable for how long I can remain a film tramp." The stars to whom Garbo referred were Conrad Veidt and Emil Jannings; both spoke English with a heavy German accent.

Garbo did not tell Sörenson not to come. In fact, she surprised him by boarding his ship to welcome him and by showing him around town. She took him to lunch at the Ambassador Hotel on September 18, her twenty-fourth birthday, and to her birthday dinner at the home of the Paramount director Ludwig Berger. To prepare herself for the party, she went to the hotel's hair salon and came out looking like a half-opened parasol. "She looked like Clara Bow," said Sörenson. When Garbo arrived at the party, she was roundly complimented on her hair. "You know," she

When the Maharajah of Kapurthala visited the set of *Anna Christie*, he could not have known that he was the last visitor to M-G-M with whom Garbo would stand for a photograph. After this film, she no longer posed for publicity photos or poster art.

responded, "one often makes mistakes in life." Sörenson was seated next to the mannered star Pola Negri at dinner. When he tried to make conversation by asking her about her well-publicized romance with the Georgian Prince Serge Mdivani, she snapped at him: "That's all over now. You must remember one thing, young man. One always makes mistakes in life."

"What nonsense are you two talking about?" Garbo asked, then said to Sörenson: "Now, Sören, that's no concern of yours."

Anna Christie was a crucial project for M-G-M, so Irving Thalberg supervised it himself. It was not his first choice for Garbo's sound debut. Knowing that she had seen and liked the 1927 French film *La Passion de Jeanne d'Arc*, he toyed with the idea of engaging Danish director Carl Dreyer to remake it as a sound film for her. Thalberg also considered George Bernard Shaw's play *Saint Joan*, but the renowned Irish playwright was unwilling to sell the rights. *Anna Christie* had won a Pulitzer Prize for Eugene O'Neill in 1922 and had been filmed by Thomas Ince's company in 1923 with Blanche Sweet as Anna. The film was still well regarded, and O'Neill's heroine was, if superficially, a character Garbo resembled.

O'Neill's playscript read: "ANNA CHRISTOPHERSON enters. She is a tall, blond, fully-developed girl of twenty, handsome after a large Viking-daughter fashion but now run down in health and plainly showing all the outward evidences of belonging to the world's oldest profession. Her youthful face is already hard and cynical beneath its layer of makeup. Her clothes are the tawdry finery of peasant stock turned prostitute." Garbo had played vamps, temptresses, and naive girls gone wrong. She had never played a prostitute, and, aside from short speeches and scenes at the Academy in Stockholm, she had never essayed a theatrical role. Norbert Lusk of *Picture Play* magazine wrote: "In choosing *Anna Christie* for her audible debut, the Swedish star attempts one of the most difficult roles in contemporary theater. The part is almost a monologue, a test for an actress experienced in speech, a brave feat for one who is not."

Beyond the demands of the role, there were marketing considerations. If M-G-M wanted Garbo's film to reach the widest possible audience, it was choosing an odd vehicle. Its adult situations and rough language might offend some moviegoers, not to mention the local censor boards, who could cut and splice it at will. At one time, Will Hays's Formula might have forbidden filming it altogether. As it was, a Production Code was in the works. This improvement on the Don'ts and Be Carefuls was being drafted by a committee that included Catholic priests and publishers, Jason Joy of the Studio Relations Committee, and Thalberg himself. Until the document was ratified by the MPPDA, however, Thalberg was free to film *Anna Christie*. The trick was to make it acceptable for a family audience without compromising its

In Garbo's first talking-picture scene, Larry the bartender (Lee Phelps) admits her to the back room of a waterfront bar. She filmed the scene on October 14, wearing a rakish beret and a sluttish attitude.

dramatic integrity. Thalberg assigned the adaptation to the accomplished Frances Marion. She knew that Garbo still felt that the play characterized Swedish-Americans as stupid and vulgar. "You don't suppose we'll end up having to make them Americans," Marion asked Thalberg.

"They're American citizens," he smiled. "That might soften the blow."

Marion finished her *Anna Christie* script in mid-September. As Garbo read it, she wondered about Anna's accent. Her own was nothing compared to the thick Swedish accent indicated in the dialogue. Would people think that was how she really talked? Harry Edington told her that she if she was worried, she could take elocution lessons at the studio.

"What do I need lessons for?" Garbo asked indignantly. "They know how my voice sounds, and I intend to talk English the way I do now." Garbo's confidence made sense, given the vocal debuts of most silent film stars thus far. Norma Talmadge, Marion Davies, and Colleen Moore had all made successful transitions, if one well-received film was any indication. At M-G-M, Joan Crawford, John Gilbert, and Ramon Novarro would soon have their talking-feature premieres. Every talking picture so far had been hugely profitable. There was no reason to think that these would be any different. The future looked as rosy for M-G-M as it did for

the stock market, which hit a new high in the last week of August. The *Wall Street Journal* cited "bullish enthusiasm" as both a cause and an effect, proclaiming that "the outlook for the fall months seems brighter than at any time in recent years." In the midst of this brazen, unchallenged optimism, M-G-M released *His Glorious Night*. Advertised as John Gilbert's first talking film, it was, in truth, his second; *Redemption* was waiting in the wings.

A strange thing happened at the September 28 opening of *His Glorious Night*. An audience full of Gilbert fans started whispering, talking, and finally laughing out loud. The first scene to get this reaction was played by Gilbert and a stage actress named Catherine Dale Owen. In it, Gilbert had to speak lines to her that would have tested John Barrymore: "Oh, darling! Oh, darling, dearest one, what have I done but wait, wait, wait ever since I've known you. . . . I love you. I've told you that a hundred times a week. I love you." This unbelievable dialogue made *His Glorious Night* look and sound like a parody of *His Hour*, the Elinor Glyn story that had made Gilbert a star. The film was supposed to be a sophisticated romantic comedy, but it was nothing but a succession of silly tableaux. Any lightness it might have had was lost to Lionel Barrymore's flat direction. Playing *Romeo and Juliet* for laughs a month earlier had not hurt Gilbert; audiences had laughed with him, not at him. This was awful. The bad reports coming from movie patrons did not blame the script or the direction. They blamed Gilbert's voice.

On October 21, Garbo reshot this scene because she was not happy with her costume or performance in the first week's footage.

A Milton Brown portrait of Garbo as Anna, the "Viking daughter" gone wrong.

Critics were careful not to confuse issues, so every review took pains to describe the voice in question. "His voice is pleasant but not one which is rich in nuance," wrote Mordaunt Hall. "Gilbert has not yet hit quite the perfect note of intonation for the microphone but, barring a certain over-resonant delivery of lines, his enunciation is crisp and fine," wrote Edwin Schallert of the *Los Angeles Times*. "Obviously John has been spending some time with voice teachers," wrote a reviewer in *Motion Picture Classic*. "His accents are a trifle affected and self-conscious. But his voice is pleasing to hear, and is not lacking in a certain warmth which may well be considered essential."

As the news spread, more fans went to see *His Glorious Night*, which was fast becoming the most ironic title of the year. "White-hot love speeches brought only snickers from the first-run audience at Loew's here," reported *Film Spectator* magazine. "Snickers, too, which threatened more than once to become a gale of laughter." The *New York Post* wrote: "Mr. Gilbert repeatedly says, 'I love you, I love you, I love you.' It's all a lot of play acting and I don't believe a word of it. The audience did not always find it possible to take seriously the laughably stilted and affected dialogue." Hedda Hopper, who also acted in the film, said: "Jack was young and virile . . . [and] handsome but his face just didn't fit

those words. When sound came on the screen from his lips, a strange meeting took place between his nose and his mouth which made him look more like a parrot than a lover. In silent pictures you never noticed." One Hollywood correspondent tried to explain what had changed since the silents: "Studios have found that the hooey [that was] going over in titles won't go in talkers. Someone in the audience titters and it's all off."

The news continued to spread—not that the film was laughably bad, but that Gilbert's voice was high pitched. Director William C. de Mille, who was also at M-G-M, said: "It was not Jack's voice that was bad; it was not. It was just not the voice his audiences had heard in their mind in *The Big Parade*, or the voice that made love to Garbo in *Flesh and the Devil*." This voice was difficult to describe. In some scenes it sounded flat; in others, thin and reedy. It never sounded *exactly* high pitched. It sounded more as if it were being played through wet cardboard or at the wrong speed. No one thought to compare its quality to that of a newsreel, where the sound could not be equalized, and every voice had a flat, metallic timbre. Surely M-G-M's sound engineers, headed by Douglas Shearer, could have improved Gilbert's voice through equalization. Whatever the cause, his voice was entirely wrong for this foolish movie. Every scene became a temptation to laugh. Gilbert's fans struggled to contain themselves as they watched and listened in disbelief. "Quite obviously they were at a loss to know what had happened to their idol," wrote *Film Spectator*. "Most of them seemed a little ashamed of themselves for laughing. But they laughed, and all the talking pictures in the world, all the fine salary, all the publicity puffs, all the paid reviews, can never undo that laugh."

With her first day before the microphones only a week away, Garbo could not have been encouraged by news of Gilbert's debut, but she still refused a voice coach, preferring to run lines with her Swedish visitor. "I was amazed at how easily she learned and at her good memory," said Sörenson. "If I ventured once in a while to add some dramatic touch to my part in reading, she would quickly pull me down to earth, saying 'Don't fiddle-faddle! Just read it straight!'" Garbo had approved Clarence Brown as director of *Anna Christie*. She also had a say in casting, and she had heard of a Broadway actor named Charles Bickford who might be effective as the sailor Matt Burke. The rough-hewn Bickford, a new type for M-G-M, was currently working in Cecil B. DeMille's *Dynamite*. At a lunch with Mayer and Thalberg, *Anna Christie* was proposed to the actor. "I was bothered about the vehicle," wrote Bickford. "I knew the play. The role of Matt was about as thankless as a leading part could be." Bickford managed to overcome his reluctance, possibly because Garbo had made an overture, albeit in her own quirky way. Bickford was aware that she had been observing him from the shadows of the *Dynamite* set. When he saw her slip out one day, he followed her. She broke into a run, and he gave chase, finally catching up with her at her dressing room. "I'm sorry for chasing you like that," he said, panting. "My mistake. I thought you were a rabbit." Garbo laughed at this. "What were you doing on my set, Miss Garbo?"

"I wanted to see you act."

"That's very flattering. Did you like what you saw?"

"Very much."

"Thank you. Why did you run away?"

"I was embarrassed to have you see me there."

The ice was broken, and the two became acquainted. The other roles to be cast in *Anna Christie* were Anna's neglectful father, Chris, and Marthy Owen, the aged wharf rat who is his erstwhile girlfriend. George F. Marion, who had played Chris on the stage and in the silent version, was invited to reprise the role for the talkies. For Marthy, Frances Marion suggested Marie Dressler to Brown. "He brushed the idea

Anna's reunion with her father (George F. Marion) is a tentative process.

aside," recalled Marion, because Dressler was known as a roughhouse comedienne. No one believed her capable of pathos. So Marion, who had Thalberg's ear, got him to authorize a screen test of Dressler. The sixty-year-old comedienne later gloated: "To everybody's surprise—except Frances Marion's—my test came out favorably!"

Dressler, George F. Marion, Frances Marion, and Charles Bickford all reported to Stage 1 at 9:00 A.M. on Monday, October 7, 1929, to begin a week of rehearsals, which was an unheard-of practice for M-G-M, or for any studio at the time. When Garbo arrived, she said to Clarence Brown, "I have learned my lines, Mr. Brown. I am ready to rehearse." Brown later recalled: "She hated to rehearse. She would have preferred to stay away until everyone else had rehearsed, then come in and do the scene. But you can't do that—particularly in talking pictures." Rehearsals and camera tests took the full week. On Monday, October 14, Brown directed George F. Marion and Marie Dressler in the film's first scene, which took place in the cabin of Chris's coal barge. On Tuesday they moved to Stage 7 for scenes in the waterfront saloon set. Garbo's first day before the microphone was scheduled for Wednesday.

On the evening before, she telephoned Sörenson, who had not seen her in a while. "This is it, Sören!" she said. "Tomorrow's the day when silent Greta gets a voice!"

Sörenson thought he had heard the last of her after he hung up. To his surprise, she called him at 2:30 A.M. and said: "Come over here immediately and drink coffee with me. Step on it!" No one refused Garbo, even at that hour, so he joined her.

We sat in the living room and talked about trivial matters. Then, before either of us had realized it, the clock had struck six, and a few minutes later the two of us were on our way to the studio. Suddenly it occurred to me that she must have stage fright, though she didn't betray herself with a word. I did not say anything either, but just stared straight ahead. Then I heard a voice from underneath the rug beside me in the car. Instead of a deep, rich timbre, I heard the moving plaint of a little girl. "Oh, Sören, I feel like an unborn child just now."

Young as I was, I could feel sympathy for someone whom fate had made a world figure—someone who at heart was just a charming and very nervous young girl.

Awaiting Garbo in her dressing room were Alma, her colored maid, and Billy, her beauty expert. Both of them adored Garbo and on that morning their faces showed acute apprehension. I almost expected Alma to break into a wailing Negro spiritual, but Garbo would have none of this Doomsday atmosphere. Her manner had again changed and now she was gay and light-hearted about the whole thing. "You must go now, Sören," she told me. "But please stay in the studio so we can have lunch together later on."

In his second portrait sitting with Garbo, Clarence Bull used props from the set of *Anna Christie*.

Just before noon, Sörenson was summoned to Garbo's dressing room. He found her in good shape. "Well, it wasn't really so bad," Garbo said, "though I became a little scared when I heard my own voice." It was customary to check the disc after each take to make sure there was no distortion. The playback came through large speakers in the sound booth. Brown invited Garbo to listen. "I almost jumped out of my chair when I heard those lines played back to me," Garbo laughed.

"My God! Is that my voice?" she had asked Gavin Burns, the sound engineer. "Does that sound like me—honestly?"

Garbo was obviously pleased with herself as she described the scene to Sörenson. "But you should have seen how the others reacted," she said. "Alma makes a dramatic gesture towards her forehead and starts appealing to the Lord. Billy gets hysterics and runs out. Some of those tough boys on the set start clearing their throats. Brown comes up, gives me a big kiss, and says, 'Wonderful, Greta!' After that, the sound engineer signals to the mixing room 'Okay for sound.'"

The scene they were shooting was Anna's entrance, both to the saloon and to the film. In it, the exhausted girl hesi-

tantly comes through the back door, walks cheerlessly across the room, sinks into a chair, and hails the bartender. Marion's script did not deviate one word from O'Neill's text.

ANNA
Gimme a whisky—ginger ale on the side.
(*then as Larry turns to go, forcing a winning smile at him*)
And don't be stingy, baby.

LARRY
(*sarcastically*)
Shall I serve it in a pail?

ANNA
(*with a hard laugh*)
That suits me down to the ground.

Adrian costumed Garbo in a cheap outfit he had found at a store in downtown Los Angeles. The beret she was wearing was somewhat similar to the one she had worn in the tennis scenes in *The Kiss*, but the ensemble was shoddy. Surprisingly, she felt secure enough in this outfit to allow a visitor to the set, the Maharajah of Kapurthala. She even allowed herself to be photographed with him. "One of the most interesting things about *Anna Christie* was the chance it gave me to observe Garbo at close range," wrote Marie Dressler, who worked alone with Garbo for the rest of the week. "I have never seen her display any great interest in anything, except once, when I suggested making a film about Queen Christina of Sweden. About that she became almost enthusiastic; but otherwise she appeared totally indifferent to her surroundings—simply bored to death."

There may have been a reason for Garbo's aloofness; she was unhappy with both her appearance and Brown's interpretation of the Swedish-American character. On Saturday she arrived with Harry Edington in tow and had a lengthy discussion with him and Brown about "characterization." As a result, shooting was postponed until Monday, October 21, and Garbo went back into rehearsals. When she returned on Monday, she was wearing a cloche hat instead of a beret. All the footage she had shot from October 16 through 18 was reshot. "No one else in pictures has made me work so hard," said Dressler. "Greta works almost to the point of exhaustion, and her capacity for work is contagious. The fact is, an actor must put forth every last ounce of effort every minute of his working time, or his role will fall short miserably in comparison to Greta's uniformly splendid work." On October 22, Garbo came to the set with a head cold and was promptly sent home. The new medium was apparently a little more stressful than she admitted to her friends; as before, she responded to stress with psychogenic illness. She returned the next day to play the poignant scene where she meets her father after a fifteen-year separation.

"Garbo was so inspiring that she brought out the best in those acting with her," George F. Marion later said. "She has genius where characterization is concerned. She falls in love with the intellectual aspect of the part and by reason of this sympathy literally slips into her characters." Frances Marion was also on the set, ready to rewrite lines of dialogue if needed. "It was always fascinating to watch Garbo," she wrote. "Her economy of gesture, the constant changing of moods revealed by luminous eyes that never played the little physical tricks used by so many actresses—flashing sidelong glances or opening wide to show the entire iris. Her lashes were so long and thick they veiled her eyes, giving them an expression of 'smoldering passion,' according to the fan magazines. But when she was bored by anyone they burned dully, like candles in daylight."

The production was going well enough for M-G-M executives to study her contract. "Garbo's present contract is still a 'silent' one," said an October 24 memo, "as she has never signed an agreement to talk. In this respect, she is the one exception in our stock company. The question of her signing was discussed with the advent of sound pictures, but she declined to sign, giving as her reason, as I recall, lack of confidence in the English tongue."

October 24 was Garbo's last day of work with Dressler, a scene set in a Coney Island café. Dressler's portrayal of Marthy was embellished with all sorts of vaudevillian scene-stealing, but Garbo held her own. Between scenes, Dressler said to Frances Marion: "She has the basis for comedy: perfect timing and dramatic ability." Dressler said good-bye to Garbo at 5:30 P.M. and finished her own shots just before 6:00. She later said of Garbo:

> I made up my mind about her long before we finished the picture and I have had no occasion since to revise my opinion. Garbo is lonely. She always has been and she always will be. She lives in the core of a vast, aching loneliness. She is a great artist, but it is both her supreme glory and her supreme tragedy that art is to her the only reality. The figures of living men and women, the events of everyday existence move about her, shadowy, insubstantial. It is only when she breathes the breath of life into a part, clothes with her own flesh and blood the concept of the playwright that she herself is fully awake, fully alive.

Garbo was sent home again the next day. Filming resumed on October 28 with a rhythm to which none of these actors was accustomed: two days shooting, three days rehearsing, five days shooting, two days rehearsing, and so on. While they were rehearsing on the 29th, news came from New York that an event even more cataclysmic than the talkie revolution was taking place.

On this day, soon to be known as "Black Tuesday," 16,410,030 shares of stock were dumped in a mindless panic. As Frederick Lewis Allen later explained, "The gigantic edifice . . . honeycombed with speculative credit, was breaking under its own weight." The stock market crashed. Many an M-G-M employee had to dash to the telephone that day. If he managed to reach a stockbroker's office, a stomach-turning scene awaited him. In one day, billions of dollars of both paper wealth and real wealth, the accumulated profits of years of speculation, turned to nothing; within a few months, this disaster was to affect everyone in America, even movie stars who were earning $5,000 a week.

Production on *Anna Christie* finished on November 18, and, as editor Hugh Wynn assembled a rough cut, Frank Whitbeck of the Fox West Coast Theater chain came to Thalberg's office with a large portfolio. In it was a set of paintings representing the film's advertising campaign. Its luscious posters and billboards were based on Clarence Bull's portrait sitting for *The Kiss*, since portraits shot at the completion of *Anna Christie* had not yet been retouched or printed. Whitbeck set the poster boards on chairs that stood along the walls of the office, and Thalberg walked back and forth along the row of chairs, his sloping shoulders squared, his hands behind his back, inspecting the artwork. Usually he would shoot Whitbeck a quick appraisal. This time he kept walking and contemplating. "It's a good campaign, Frank," he finally said, "but it's just not what I want." He stopped walking. "And I can't even tell you what it is I *do* want!"

Whitbeck and Thalberg tried to find out what it was. After two hours of back and forth, they still did not know. All they did know was that Garbo's beauty was not going to sell a talking film about a prostitute. Then Whitbeck spied a used manila envelope on Thalberg's desk. He picked it up, grabbed a pencil, and drew a picture on it. The picture showed a mammoth billboard, large enough to hold a 24-sheet. On the billboard were emblazoned just two words: GARBO TALKS.

"That's it!" exclaimed Thalberg. He whacked Whitbeck on his back, then remembered the benches full of people outside his office—writers, directors, and stars, all waiting to see him. "Now get the hell out of here."

The subject of this campaign was back in her self-contenting routine, visiting friends, secluding herself, and spending so much time with Sörenson that journalists mistakenly assumed a romance. She went to a Beverly Hills theater with him on a Sunday afternoon to see *The Love Parade*, Ernst Lubitsch's first talkie, which introduced the team of Jeanette MacDonald and Maurice Chevalier. After the film, Garbo came out of the theater, sat down on the curb, rested her chin between her hands, and stared ahead for a few minutes. Sörenson asked her if she was all right. "I must sit and think," she answered. "I am so happy to know that pictures like that can be made." She jumped up and had Sörenson look for a florist.

An hour later, when Lubitsch opened his front door, he was startled to have five red roses thrown at him by an ebullient Greta Garbo. "Ernst, I love you!" she said, wrapping her arms around his neck. "I love you for this picture!" It was not long before Garbo found out how her own talking debut had turned out. "She usually went to the previews of her pictures alone," recalled Gustaf Norin. In this case, she turned down the invitation to attend the preview with Thalberg, Brown, Mayer, Dressler, William Daniels, and Frances Marion. The theater Thalberg had chosen was in San Bernardino, and its patrons expected to see *The Kiss*. They knew something was up when Leo the Lion roared audibly and the opening titles of *Anna Christie* flashed on the screen. Taking advantage of the momentary confusion, someone in the working-class audience hollered: "I tank I go home." The nervous audience laughed until an M-G-M employee yelled at them: "Shut up!"

The theater calmed down and the film got under way. Garbo did not appear on the screen until fifteen minutes into the film. When she walked into the saloon, the entire audience held its breath. Two reels later, Thalberg whispered to his row of compatriots: "Garbo is holding them in

the palm of her hand." At the conclusion of the ninety-minute film, San Bernardino wholeheartedly applauded Garbo. "It's in the bag!" Mayer exclaimed. "Garbo's a winner!" On the way back to Culver City, Thalberg declared his intention to release the film without retakes or cuts, a highly unusual and complimentary reaction to a preview.

The premiere of *Anna Christie* took place at the Fox Criterion Theatre in Los Angeles on January 22, 1930. "I went to the opening of *Anna Christie* with Marie," said Dressler's friend Claire Dubrey. "We held hands in our nervousness and her ring was imprinted on my finger for days. But we need not have worried." The first volley of praise came from Hearst columnist Louella Parsons. "Eugene O'Neill might have written *Anna Christie* with Greta Garbo in mind," she wrote, "so superbly does the role fit M-G-M's heretofore silent Swedish star." Parsons described the opening-night audience as a "young army that descended upon the theater to hear with their own ears whether or not Garbo could talk."

Garbo did not see *Anna Christie* until the next day. Although she appeared to be pleased with the film as it unreeled, she said to Sörenson outside the theater: "Isn't it terrible?! Who ever saw Swedes act like that?" She was far more impressed with Dressler's performance and drove to her house at 718 Milner Road in Whitley Heights to present her with a bouquet of chrysanthemums. Had she wrapped them in newspaper, she would no doubt have seen her name. "Garbo Talks" was in print for months to come, since the film did not open in New York until March 14.

"Great artistically and tremendous commercially," wrote *Variety*. "In all departments a wow picture. Its box office strength has already been tested to smash trade in various cities. Opened Friday in New York to a tidal wave of standees at the Capitol." And what did they hear as they stood expectantly in the huge theater's aisles? "La Garbo's accent is nicely edged with a Norse 'yah,' but once the ear gets the pitch it's okay and the spectator is under the spell of her performance. She can read lines. It alters her personality oddly but she is not less glamorous thereby." The *New York Times* reviewer was surprisingly descriptive. "Miss Garbo's voice from the screen is deep toned," wrote Hall, "somewhat deeper than when one hears her in real life. The low enunciation of her initial lines, with a packed theater waiting expectantly to hear her first utterance, came somewhat as a surprise yesterday at the Capitol, for her delivery is almost masculine." The *New York Herald Tribune*'s Richard Watts Jr. wrote: "Her voice is revealed as a deep, husky, throaty contralto that possesses every bit of that fabulous, poetic glamour that has made this distant Swedish lady the outstanding actress of the motion picture world." Norbert Lusk in *Picture Play* was more affected. "The voice that shook the world!" he wrote. "It's Greta Garbo's, of course, and for the life of me I can't decide if it's baritone or bass. She makes it

In this scene from *Anna Christie*, cinematographer William Daniels used cross-lighting and diffusion to transform a Coney Island café into a pearly setting for the drama being enacted by Garbo, Marie Dressler, and Charles Bickford.

heard on the screen for the first time in *Anna Christie*, and there isn't another like it. Disturbing, incongruous, its individuality is so pronounced that it would belong to no one less strongly individual than Garbo herself."

Frances Marion was one of the few to remain objective. "No pyrotechnical display ever drew more oh's and ah's than when Garbo talked. After so much publicity, heaven only knows what the public expected to come out of her mouth, whether bird twitter or trumpets blaring, but people kept saying, 'Isn't it unbelievable? Garbo talks like any other actress, only with a Swedish accent.'" No one at M-G-M was complaining about the hubbub. In its first week at the Capitol Theatre, *Anna Christie* broke the house record, earning $109,286. In its second week, it earned $92,100; in its third, $76,727. "'Garbo Talks' is, beyond quarrel, an event of major box-office significance," reported *Variety*. Spurred by a clever campaign and sustained by word of mouth, *Anna*

Christie went on to become the highest-grossing film of 1930, bringing the studio more than $1 million. The most pointed comment on Whitbeck's campaign came when he walked unannounced into Metro executive Benny Thau's office one afternoon and found Garbo sitting in conference. "Miss Garbo," said Thau, "I think it is high time you met the man who first said: 'Garbo Talks!'"

Garbo looked up at the startled publicist. "Aren't you ashamed?" she asked him.

Thanks to Whitbeck's two words, she was now the pre-eminent Hollywood star, at least according to the magazines she continued to peruse. Riding one day in Sörenson's secondhand Buick convertible, Garbo saw Joan Crawford drive by in her chauffeur-driven limousine. Garbo turned to Sörenson and laughed: "I read last night that I was queen of the movies, and look at me now, riding around in this old car. *Gott*! What a funny joke!"

CHAPTER THIRTEEN

Romance

After Greta Garbo's brilliant transition to talking pictures, Irving Thalberg looked for vehicles with which to sustain her lucrative momentum. *Anna Christie* had, in a curious way, honored the Garbo formula. As usual, her ardent young suitor had to contend with an older man. This time it was not a wealthy protector but her father. Of course, there were also the specters of the men she had known in the house of prostitution. Garbo's dream of playing Joan of Arc—or anything besides a tarnished woman—melted into ether as the M-G-M story department searched for glamorous characters with foreign accents.

A 1926 report by Franclien MacConnell synopsized a play by Edward Sheldon called *Romance* that was then being revived on Broadway with its original star, Doris Keane. "Ned" Sheldon had written it for Keane in 1913 when they were engaged. The wedding was called off after Keane dated one of the play's backers, claiming that Sheldon had told her, "I would make a very poor sort of husband for you." While *Romance* shot Keane to international stardom, the thirty-year-old Sheldon came down with a form of arthritis that rendered him bedridden and blind. Instead of letting this disability conquer him, Sheldon continued to write plays and became an inspiring father figure to numerous theatrical talents, among them Helen Hayes, Ruth Gordon, and Katharine Cornell.

Romance told the story of Tom Armstrong, an upright young cleric who falls in love with Margherita Cavallini, an Italian prima donna. Sheldon describes her as a "bewitching, brilliant little foreign creature—beautiful in a dark, Italian way. . . . She speaks in a soft Italian voice, with quick, bird-like gestures. She seems herself a good deal like an exquisite, gleaming little hummingbird." Cavallini was based on the real-life opera star Lina Cavalieri, who collected starring roles and jewels with equal ease. In contrast to this glittering figure was the young rector of St. Giles Cathedral. "He is about twenty-eight," says the text, "healthy, positive, and determined. He is dressed very simply and a little shabbily. He has a very hearty, genial quality, but no humor." Cavallini will not marry Armstrong because of the open secret that he alone fails to acknowledge: she is the mistress of one of his church's benefactors, Cornelius Van Tuyl.

In her second talking film, *Romance*, Greta Garbo played an Italian prima donna. The film was so well publicized and so widely seen that the Empress Eugenie hat she wore in it started a fashion craze.

MacConnell's report (coincidentally written when Garbo was portraying a Spanish opera diva in *The Torrent*) cited the 1920 United Artists version of *Romance*, which starred Keane: "This has already been done in pictures but could be done much better." M-G-M purchased the play and assigned it to contract scenarist F. Hugh Herbert, who wrote a silent scenario from it in early 1928. One scene read: "She shakes her head, warning him that he ought not to make love to her, but nothing can stop him. He says very earnestly: TITLE: 'I want to know you right down to the very bottom of your soul.'" By the time Bess Meredyth finished her continuity, it was for a talking picture. One of the speeches that she adapted told of Cavallini's loss of innocence. "Love," the prima donna sighed. "It is made of keeses in the dark, of 'ot breat' on de face an' 'eart beats jus' like terrible strong blows! It is a struggle—ver' cruel an' sweet—all full of madness an' of vhispered vords an' leetle laughs dat turn into a sigh! Love is de 'unger for anoder's flesh—a deep down t'irst to dreenk anoder's blood—Love is a beast dat feed all t'rough de night—an' vhen de morning come—*Love dies!*"

Broadway had already seen Bela Lugosi in *Dracula*, so Meredyth and her collaborator, Edwin Justus Mayer, softened the speech. Cavallini, now renamed Rita, says: "I wish I'd died before I ever heard those words 'I love you.' What is love? It's made of kisses in the dark and hot breath on the face and a heart that beats with terrible strong blows. Love is just a beast that you feed all through the night. And when the morning comes, love dies." When the screenplay was ready to show Garbo, she had decided opinions.

"Garbo is keenly interested in the talkies," said her friend John Loder. "Before they came she used to say that most of her pictures were silly. She was in them for the money. Now she thinks there are wonderful possibilities for great dramas enacted upon the screen." Garbo was seeing many films in January 1930. "She never likes to miss a picture Gary Cooper is in," said Wilhelm Sörenson. "She enjoys the so-called he-man type he always plays." Garbo also liked the lounge-lizard looks of Rod LaRocque. She was so impressed with the performance of the young comedienne Fifi D'Orsay in the Fox Film comedy *Hot for Paris* that she had Jacques Feyder arrange a dinner for them at the Russian Eagle restaurant. Within weeks a Los Angeles columnist wrote: "Greta Garbo and Fifi D'Orsay have become inseparable friends. Everywhere that Greta goes Fifi is sure to tag along and vice versa. Greta stays in her shell and is so reserved that Hollywood has been greatly amused and interested in this dalliance. Fifi is Greta's first pal since Lilyan Tashman and Greta parted company." Since Tashman was eliminated from Garbo's circle for giving one interview about her, it was inevitable that the loquacious D'Orsay would eventually be frozen out. Garbo's friendship with the older, more discreet Salka Viertel continued. "Why don't you write?" Garbo asked Viertel one day. Viertel soon became Garbo's colleague, but as an actress; the writing would come later.

Garbo knew that *Anna Christie*'s success was limited to English-speaking countries unless it could be filmed in another language. Because of her social circle, she was increasingly fluent in German. Arthur Loew, vice-president of Loew's Inc., had recently announced that M-G-M was budgeting $2 million for foreign-language versions. "Jacques Feyder will direct two pictures of Greta Garbo in German," said Loew. "Miss Garbo being a Swede, and not speaking a perfect German, will be given a part as a foreigner in Germany to account for her imperfect knowledge of the language." Garbo's following in Europe mandated a foreign-language version. A script of *Anna Christie* in German was sent to Garbo, along with a script of *Romance*. She

Garbo and Gavin Gordon play a scene for director Clarence Brown, cameraman William Daniels, and assistant director Charles Dorian on the set of *Romance*, Garbo's twelfth Hollywood film. Photograph by Milton Brown

was more interested in the German project, in spite of negative fan mail. "Right now," said Loder, "she is getting letters from all over the world, criticizing her for playing the part of a 'bad woman' in *Anna Christie*. 'You will make the whole world think that all Swedish girls are bad,' is the gist of these complaints. . . . Greta laughs at that sort of letter." She agreed to do a German-language *Anna Christie*. She would not, however, commit to *Romance*. "Garbo didn't want to make it," recalled Gustaf Norin.

> Her business manager [Harry Edington] used to come over to the house and argue with her over it. For some reason or other the studio was not ready to start work on the German version of *Anna Christie*. One day her manager brought Bess Meredyth, who wrote the scenario for *Romance*, over to the house to talk with Garbo. They had a long conference. When it was ended, Garbo had agreed to make the picture. The next day she regretted that she had let them persuade her to do it. She called her manager on the telephone, and there was another argument. She finally banged down the receiver, saying: "All right! I will do as I agreed."

Garbo's emotional seesaw was increasingly discernible to her servants and to her friends, especially Sörenson, who was somewhat dependent upon her for social activity; his parents had cut off his allowance shortly after his arrival in Hollywood. After four months he had come to realize that Garbo had few friends—and she was unwilling to share even those. She grew proprietary about time he spent with Norin, who was doing his best to work around her moods. "After a gay time," Norin said, "Garbo often lapsed into a moody spell. Then she would stay in her bedroom for days, coming

George Hurrell photographed Garbo on the set of *Romance* as well as in the portrait gallery.

out only to swim or take walks at night . . . Garbo didn't want to talk to anyone when she was in one of her moods." She did brighten at the prospect of *Anna Christie* and insisted on rewriting the script with John Loder's wife at their Malibu beach house. "Nearly every afternoon her car would drive up to our door," said Loder. "After the girls had worked two or three hours, Garbo would get into her bathing suit and take a brisk hike along the beach. Then she would go in for a swim. I never saw anybody enjoy the sea as much as she does."

Feyder would not be available to direct the German-language film until July, and M-G-M needed to sate a Garbo-hungry public. Producer Paul Bern (the term "producer" had recently been substituted for "supervisor") approved the final script of *Romance* on February 20, 1930, and Garbo got the project rolling. First she approved Clarence Brown as director. Then she had to approve a leading man. Gary Cooper could not be borrowed from Paramount, so Garbo settled on an unknown twenty-nine-year-old named Gavin Gordon.

Gordon's first scene with her was scheduled for March 17. The understandably nervous actor was driving to the studio on Washington Boulevard when a car pulled out of a side street and hit him. The impact threw him onto the road, where he landed on his shoulder. A doctor was called to the scene and tried to convince Gordon not to go to work. "If they know I'm hurt, they'll never let me start," Gordon groaned. He managed to get to M-G-M, where he put on his costume and makeup and reported to the set. By the end of his first scene with Garbo, the pain of a broken collarbone was too much. Gordon collapsed in a dead faint. When he awoke, he was in a hospital. Garbo was standing at his bedside. He told her that he wanted to come back immediately; he did not want to lose the role. Garbo assured him that he would not. "If you are good and take care of yourself," she smiled, "we will wait for you."

There were a lot of raw nerves in Hollywood that month. John Gilbert was fending off bad publicity from all sides. On February 10, he had been involved in a nightclub brawl with

Hurrell deviated from his dramatic lighting schemes to make Garbo's portraits for *Romance* look as if they had been taken in 1867.

Vanity Fair writer Jim Tully. Ina Claire, whose film career was not doing as well as she had hoped, was trying to pretend that all was well at Tower Grove Road, but there were numerous blind items about her fights with Gilbert, who, along with a lot of other stars, had lost money in the stock-market crash. The market had appeared to rally in late 1929, but in the first quarter of 1930, it started to slide again. The first effects of the crash could be seen in diminishing productivity all over the country and in a corresponding loss of jobs. Garbo's home saw another kind of employment crisis. In early March, Gustaf and Sigrid Norin gave her their two weeks' notice.

"But you can't leave me like this," said a disbelieving Garbo. "There will be no one to look after the house." She promptly called Harry Edington, who attempted to dissuade the Norins by offering them a higher salary. Money was not the issue. "We were tired of working as servants," said Gustaf. Edington then tried to convince Gustaf to stay on as chauffeur, but he would have none of it. As Gustaf recalled: "I felt like telling him I was very tired of having him call me a liar, as he often did when I insisted that Miss Garbo was not at home, and he knew that she was and knew that I knew that he knew." The Norins quit on schedule; Garbo's studio maid Alma agreed to look after her until new servants could be found. Gustaf's last recorded comment on Garbo was not complimentary. "Neither of us will ever forget the months

we lived in the same house with this strange girl," he said in 1931. "Day after day we saw the real Garbo without pose or pretense. Yet we never felt that we actually knew her. There was something distant and aloof about Garbo that neither of us could penetrate. She is different from anyone we have ever known."

Garbo was equally inscrutable on the set of *Romance*. Clarence Brown's manager Fritz Tidden and the *Los Angeles Times* film critic Phil Scheuer were visiting Brown as he directed an 1867 ballroom scene. Garbo was scheduled to appear at the end of the scene. "You'll have to leave now," said Brown, growing tense. "She's coming." Instead of leaving the soundstage, Scheuer and Tidden walked quickly to the far end of the ballroom set and positioned themselves behind extras. Sure enough, Garbo saw them and refused to continue until they had left.

Romance finished filming on April 25, and then it was time for portraits. Garbo had complained about having to assume statuesque poses with Charles Bickford and George F. Marion in a poster-art session for *Anna Christie*. Edington struck a deal with Howard Strickling, the new head of M-G-M publicity: Garbo would work an entire day shooting portraits if she had to do it only one time per film. There would be no more posing for poster art with costars. The

Garbo ignored Hurrell's loud music and fantastic carryings-on in the gallery, and gave him studied, almost prosaic poses.

artists would have to design posters from scene stills or just from her face. As Garbo nailed down one aspect of her publicity, another came loose. Her portrait session for *Romance* would not be photographed by Clarence Bull or by Ruth Harriet Louise, who had left the company on January 1. The new head portrait photographer was a twenty-six-year-old firebrand named George Hurrell, who had been hired at the behest of Norma Shearer. Bull was the head of the stills department, but Hurrell could go over his head and snatch a sitting with Garbo from him. He did, giving Bull one more reason to dislike him. Early on April 27, Garbo dutifully walked ahead of her chauffeur-driven Lincoln, carrying one of her flowing velvet costumes because it would not fit in the car with the rest of them. "I took a look at those costumes," recalled Hurrell, "and thought I'd try something like one of those old daguerrotypes. There was a skylight there, so I first tried putting natural light on her, to get that feeling of an old portrait."

The feeling that Hurrell got was as distant and unapproachable as an old portrait. His trademark ebullience was rubbing Garbo the wrong way. In the four months since he had replaced Louise, he had done well with his loud, unpre-

In the German-language version of *Anna Christie*, Garbo was allowed to look like a run-down streetwalker.

dictable, theatrical routine. It relaxed his subjects. When he jumped up in the air, said silly things, and capered like a monkey, he made actors forget that they were in front of a camera without a character to play—the thing that most of them dreaded. Garbo liked to play records by Sophie Tucker, "The Last of the Red-Hot Mamas," to cheer herself, but she did not like Hurrell's repertoire of dance music or, for that matter, his dancing. "She just sat there like a stone statue," said Hurrell. "You couldn't get her to do anything but lean." Hurrell raised the tempo of the music and amplified his performance, but Garbo continued to move to her own rhythm. ""She was pensive," he recalled. "She did not respond very much to my popular recordings. . . . I was getting very little reaction."

Hurrell continued to shoot dozens of plates, but he could not break through Garbo's reserve. "It may have been because we didn't meet on common ground in some way; because I was wild and yelling, hollering, and she wasn't particularly amused by it; it didn't do anything to her." Hurrell finally got her to smile, but only by performing an artful pratfall. When the floodlights went out, Garbo scooped up her costumes and headed for the door. On her way down the outside stairs, she ran into Bull's assistant, Virgil Apger. "There's a crazy man in there!" she huffed. Hurrell was no more pleased with the experience than she was. "I didn't do too well with Garbo," he later said. "I always liked to work with people who would put themselves in my hands—somewhat. She was pretty much self-styled. . . . She was going to do what she was going to do, and that was that. There was never any give and take." The resulting photographs should have been poor; they were anything but. Hurrell's portraits of Garbo created a stir, and one of the hats she wore, an Empress Eugenie, started a fashion trend.

"After the picture was finished," said Sörenson, "Garbo knew she didn't like *Romance*. She had made it against her own judgment. She felt that it was not the play for her." Nor was Thalberg satisfied with it; he ordered more scenes. Furthermore, there were censorship issues to consider. Jason Joy headed the Studio Relations Committee (SRC), which was the local branch of the Hays Office, the regulatory body of the film industry. Joy asked that one scene be rewritten and reshot to conform to the newly instituted Production Code, a set of rules designed to keep films safe from butchering by state censor boards. The scene in question was the revelation of Cavallini's involvement with Van Tuyl. She blurts out to Armstrong: "Until de night I meet you—I vas 'is mistress!" Joy told Thalberg that the word "mistress" had to go, at least as spoken by Garbo. (In an earlier scene, another character refers to her as Van Tuyl's "mistress . . . She's lived with him for years!")

Retakes commenced on May 8, with a young actor named Eddie Woods being replaced by Elliott Nugent in the film's prologue, where Armstrong is seventy-five and reminiscing with his grandson. On May 22, Bern approved the changed revelation scene; two days later, Garbo was filmed saying: "Until de night I meet you—I vas his—" Stone cut her off with "Rita!" before she could mouth the offensive word. Filming was finally completed on May 26 with a tobogganing scene staged in front of a Dunning screen; the snowy background would be added later by the optical printer.

The first preview of *Romance* took place in San Bernardino. "The audience cheered and stamped their feet with delight," said Sörenson, who accompanied Garbo to the Fox Belmont Theatre in Los Angeles for a second preview. "Garbo could have wept when she heard her supposed Italian accent," reported Sörenson. "Trying to speak with an Italian accent, she lapsed into a Swedish accent. She thought it was terrible. At times she couldn't understand her own words. She knew she had made a mistake."

Production of the German *Anna Christie* commenced on July 9, with Jacques Feyder directing Salka Viertel, who recalled: "I was cast as Marty [*sic*], a waterfront whore, admirably played by Marie Dressler in the [English-language] film. Being twenty-five years younger, I was not too eager for the part, but Feyder persuaded me that Marty could be of any age. Also he wanted me to help him with the German dialogue." Garbo's influence got Viertel into the studio, but Garbo was nowhere around when Viertel had to face the cameras. "I was frightened when my first scene had to be shot," she wrote. "I hated my costumes, my makeup seemed all wrong, and there was no time to change it. But Feyder made everything easy. He made me play a long scene just as I would have done it in the theater, without interruption; blinded by lights, I forgot that three cameras were shooting it from different angles. The stagehands applauded after he said 'Cut.'"

Feyder was a considerate director who usually signaled the end of a take by waving a white handkerchief. Garbo liked him and spoke German with him on the set. William Daniels had to resort to a German-English dictionary at times, but so did Garbo. "Playing *Anna Christie* for the second time," wrote Viertel, "Garbo had to conquer the difficulty of still another language. She worked hard, with precision, and her German was almost without accent. She was a most patient, appreciative, and considerate colleague." She did, however, have one unnerving habit: she would mutter to herself. "He says this," Feyder heard her whisper. "He does so and so." Feyder learned that "he" was the late Mauritz Stiller, from whom Garbo was still taking direction. Feyder worked around his unseen codirector, referring to him as "the green shadow."

Shooting ended on August 16. Since Garbo's costumes in this version of *Anna Christie* were almost the same as in the other, there was no point in making portraits of her in them, but Strickling needed new portraits for American fan magazines. Garbo tried to get out of her obligation, but Strick-

In this production still from the German-language version of *Anna Christie*, Jacques Feyder, Garbo, and William Daniels show the confusion of a Belgian director, a Swedish star, and a cameraman from Cleveland all trying to work in German. According to assistant film editor Chester W. Schaeffer, when Garbo watched the rushes and heard her pronunciation, "She laughed out loud at herself—very deep. A guffaw, almost."

ling prevailed. On August 18, Garbo had her third portrait session with Clarence Bull, the only one in which she wore clothing that did not come from a film; Adrian and the wardrobe department augmented Garbo's own clothes with a sporty ensemble for the sitting, but she was so unwilling to be photographed out of character that she almost had to be dragged to the gallery. Once there, of course, she and Bull worked in exquisite harmony. Four days later, *Romance* was released. Garbo braced herself for critical rejection.

The *New York Times* was the first to comment on her accent. "Greta Garbo's peculiarly deep-toned voice and her broken English are better suited to the part of a Swedish contralto rather than that of Rita Cavallini, the 'Golden Nightingale,'" wrote Mordaunt Hall. "While one may find Miss Garbo's intonations not a little disappointing, her appearance and grace are bound to elicit admiration." *Variety* wrote: "When Garbo gargles on the low ones, it's hard to accept her as the operatic high-soprano." This reviewer was willing to suspend disbelief. "Greta Garbo is a trickster deluxe at emoting. She does it double or triple. In *Romance* she often repeats a mood but never the expression. Once she'll look sad with her eyebrows and again with her chin. In [an Earl] Carroll musical, heaven only knows what she could do." Writing in *Picture Play* magazine, Norbert Lusk expressed the feeling of most when he said that the film was "slow, draggy, and lack[ing] climaxes."

Now that he was directing talkies, Clarence Brown (who had been a silent-film innovator) appeared to be overawed

On August 18, 1930, Garbo and Clarence Bull collaborated on a portrait sitting that was not thematically connected to her latest film. M-G-M needed to meet increased demands from photo editors all over the world. The studio needed more Garbo films too. Even Louella Parsons craved more. "I hate to admit being a Garbo fan," Parsons wrote. "A reviewer shouldn't be carried away by even so fascinating a person as the gorgeous Greta. But after an hour and a half at Loew's State Theatre watching Miss Garbo as Rita Cavallini in *Romance*, I came away wondering when her next picture was due to be shown. It's one comfort to know I wasn't alone in that unethical mood. [Movie star] Bebe Daniels accompanied me to the theater, and she was just as entranced as I was."

by the written word. In scene after scene, he let the camera shoot one indifferent angle as Garbo, Stone, and Gordon slogged through endless speeches. Gordon was a problem, too; his portrayal lacked both humor and intelligence. The combination of a dull leading man and a suddenly ineffectual director made *Romance* an unworthy vehicle for Garbo. Her fans did not mind; seeing her shake her curls and smile as she delivered quaint speeches was enough for them. "Hollywood's favorite adjective 'marvelous' is the word that first comes to mind on viewing Greta Garbo," wrote Lusk. "Her performance is a thing of pure beauty, an inspiring blend of intellect and emotion, a tender, poignant, poetic portrait of a woman who thrusts love from her because she considers herself unworthy of the man who offers it."

The German-language *Anna Christie* opened in Cologne on December 22, 1930. According to everyone who knew her, Garbo was happier with it than with any film she had made in recent memory. Its success, and that of *Romance*, made M-G-M consider a Swedish-language version, but that might have slowed the output of Garbo's English-language films. That was something to be avoided—like exhausting the goose that laid the golden egg. M-G-M had enough star problems in 1930.

In April, John Gilbert's second talking release, *Redemption*, was treated more cruelly by critics and columnists than

his first. Unlike *His Glorious Night*, it flopped. Articles questioning his future in films began appearing regularly. On August 26, Lon Chaney, the studio's highest-grossing star, died of cancer. On August 31, newspapers carried the sad but none too surprising announcement that Ina Claire and John Gilbert were separating. At about the same time, Garbo decided that she, too, needed more privacy and told Wilhelm Sörenson to go back to Stockholm; her sensitive young friend hid his hurt feelings and departed. The local papers, meanwhile, were full of Garbo's triumphs, noting that M-G-M had not one but three projects lined up for her: *Red Dust*, *Inspiration*, and *Mata Hari*. There was no comment from Garbo, especially as she had fewer friends to leak stories to the press. She kept her own counsel and kept to herself, declining invitations as usual. There was one she should have accepted.

It took place at the Beverly Wilshire Hotel. B. P. Schulberg, head of Paramount production, was giving an engagement party for Irene Mayer and producer David O. Selznick. The elite of Hollywood's two greatest studios were enjoying fine food, wine, and dance music when there came an interruption. "There was suddenly a silence," remembered Irene Mayer Selznick, "a suspended silence, not the clarion call of bugles, but its equivalence in soundlessness. Then these high double doors at the end of the ballroom opened and in walked Marlene. No one had ever laid eyes on her before. She entered several hundred feet into the room in this slow, riveting walk and took possession of the dance floor like it was a stage." Marlene yes, but Marlene *who*? Schulberg spoke from the dais, acting as if the engagement party had become an exhibitors' convention: "Ladies and gentlemen, Paramount's new star, Marlene Dietrich." Years later, Selznick said: "I can't think of any greater impact she ever made. It was like something out of a dream, and she looked absolutely sensational." Dietrich had recently been signed to a Paramount contract for $1,750 a week. Although unknown in America, she was enjoying a huge European success in Josef von Sternberg's Ufa film, *The Blue Angel*. The stated purpose of bringing her from Berlin was to make her "Paramount's answer to Greta Garbo." As Garbo began work on *Inspiration* with Clarence Brown, Dietrich worked with Sternberg (and Gary Cooper) on her American debut, *Morocco*. The Queen of Hollywood would soon have competition.

Opposite: Bull's third session with Garbo etched images as magical as her on-screen close-ups.

Bull was still using a soft-focus lens to make portraits in late 1930, but he shot this pose with a standard "commercial" lens.

Garbo had approved Robert Montgomery as her leading man after seeing him in Norma Shearer and Joan Crawford films. At twenty-six, the tall, athletic, and intelligent Montgomery was a far more promising presence than Garbo's last leading man, but he was soon constrained by the part of André. There was no way he could bring complexity to a spineless, self-contradictory cipher. Garbo insisted on keeping her distance from him, and whatever chemistry might have existed between them was diluted in a series of foolish dialogue.

"I can't decide whether to sit here, where I can see you, or there, where I can hold your hand," says André to Yvonne.

Brown did not attack the script with a blue pencil, as some directors would have. What Brown did was coach Garbo and Montgomery through the silly scenes as respectfully as if they had come from the pen of Eugene O'Neill. Not even the clever passages got special interpretation. His background was in engineering, not in theater; this accounted for his innovative approach to camera movement in films like *The Eagle*, with its celebrated over-the-table tracking shot. On *Inspiration*, he was less interested in dialogue than in an elevator that would lift him and the camera crew up the center of a stairwell as Garbo and Montgomery played two scenes there; the newly invented "camera crane" had not yet come to M-G-M. This staging of this scene was novel, but

the dialogue spoken in it was not. Fortunately, most of his cast members were seasoned stage performers who knew how to brighten a line. "Half the men in Paris are crazy about her—and the other half are trying to forget her," says the aging cocotte Lulu (Marjorie Rambeau) to the naive Liane (Karen Morley).

"There are tricks in every trade," snarls the jealous model Odette (Judith Vosselli).

"You ought to know, dearie," replies Lulu. "Your trade is the oldest."

Garbo glides through the decadent Parisian art world with her trademark world-weariness, wearing a black velvet Adrian gown, its train trailing inches in front of her admirers, all of whom live only to light her cigarette, pour her champagne, and enshrine her in their art. "Look at her!" says Odette. "The queen of the studios!"

"Listen, dearie," says Lulu. "She makes the rest of you trollops look like scrubwomen."

Garbo may have seen that Marjorie Rambeau was getting all the clever lines, but she worked at her usual pace for the first two weeks. The script was unfinished, but at least the daily pages were complete. She came to the set with her lines letter-perfect, expecting to film every scene in one take. When Brown decided that the script needed to be revised on the set, Garbo tolerantly rehearsed and shot each scene as

Bull used the soft-focus lens for this shot; a few months later, he abandoned it.

This scene of Garbo and Robert Montgomery was shot at Busch Gardens on November 12, 1930. The much-used movie location was created in 1905 as one of the many estates owned by Adolphus Busch, cofounder of the Anheuser-Busch beer empire.

many times as it took. "Garbo is often called a 'pallid anemic' type," said Daniels at the time, "which is more than amusing to those of us who watch her work constantly. She uses up tremendous energy before the camera. I think the stage crew would collapse from exhaustion long before she would tire herself out, once she gets going in a dramatic sequence."

After four films with Brown, Garbo worked well with him. She should have; he and Daniels were in many ways responsible for her stardom. Outside the studio she had no contact with them, unless at a preview or an emergency script conference. "Socially, I don't see her at all," said Brown to *Screenland* magazine. "Only when she invited me to work on a script did I learn that I had been living directly across the street from her for almost a year!" Even on the set, where she was literally "queen of the studios," she could not relax.

Brown was convinced that the change from ortho film and klieg lights to pan film and "inkies" that coincided with (but was not related to) sound films had aggravated her paranoia. "In silent pictures, we used so much light that the rest of the set was a void of blackness," said Brown. "When talkies came and the lights weren't so strong, you could see past the scene. Garbo's eyes would peer around the set, and there would be a pair of eyes staring at her and a person

thinking, 'So this is the great Garbo.' She'd stop acting and start looking at the eyes. When she finished the scene, she would look at me and say, 'Oh, those people.'"

No one had visited a Garbo set in a year, not even a maharajah, but Garbo was taking no chances. "We put up screens around the set," said Brown. "I finally found myself behind a flat, looking through a crack in the screen and directing her scenes." Not even actors were spared Garbo's strictures. "Don't *look* at me," she instructed newcomer Karen Morley, who was supposed to look at Garbo in the scene they were playing. This was not surprising. Garbo did not want to look at herself. "We could never get her to look at the rushes," said Brown. "When sound arrived, we had a projector on the set. This projector ran backward and forward so that we could match scenes and check continuity. When you run a talking picture in reverse, the sound is like nothing on earth. That's what Garbo enjoyed. She would sit there shaking with laughter, watching the film running with laughter and the sound going *yakablom-yakablom*. But as soon as we ran it forward, she wouldn't watch it."

One Saturday morning, Garbo was not the only person wearing a grim expression. Brown looked glum. "What is the matter, Clarence?" Garbo asked him.

"I want to go to the game," he said, referring to a University of Southern California football game being played that afternoon; Brown was scheduled to work until 5:00 P.M.

"You have the tickets?"

"Yes," he answered with an air of resignation.

"Okay," said Garbo, rising from her canvas-back chair. "You go. Now Garbo is sick. She cannot work any more today." Brown and the rest of the cast stared incredulously as Garbo bent over, put her hand to her forehead, and did a melodramatic impression of illness. "Garbo is sick! Garbo is sick! No more work!" Filming was shut down for the day, and although Mayer knew the reason there was nothing he could do about it. As Hall wrote in *Photoplay*, "Greta gets away with personal idiosyncrasies that would send other stars' fans shrieking away in droves. But everything's all right. It's Garbo. And Garbo can do no wrong."

Daniels was protective of his prized subject. "Temperamentally Garbo is no different today than when she first walked in front of my camera," he said a few months later.

"She is shy and timid, and evidently devoid of false illusions. She is warm and sincere, an actress who believes in her work and strives her utmost to portray a role successfully. She does not merely come on the set to do a day's work. She is a creative personality." About three weeks into the filming of *Inspiration*, Garbo felt her creativity being stymied. The last of Markey's rewrites had arrived. She found them unspeakably bad—and unspeakable.

"That's silly," she said after trying to say a particularly awkward sentence. "I never heard people talk like that."

Brown was not about to tamper with the line, and Markey, unlike Frances Marion, was not on the set to help. Brown asked Garbo to say the line as written. Garbo was not happy about it. She walked over to Marjorie Rambeau, who was holding the Pekingese dog who portrayed Boo Boo in the film. "Excuse me, Miss Rambeau," said Garbo, "but your dog must have some fresh air." Garbo took the dog from the startled actress and walked off the set. A few minutes passed. Brown sent Charles Dorian to fetch Garbo. "Not yet," said

This production still shows how the camera setup in the preceding photograph was accomplished. William Daniels and Clarence Brown are on the camera platform at left. Karen Morley, Arthur Hoyt, and Lewis Stone are at the balcony above them. Marjorie Rambeau is with Garbo and Montgomery below.

Garbo, avoiding the stares of various passersby who saw her standing in an evening gown outside a soundstage holding a perplexed Pekingese. "Not until the dog is all right." A few more minutes passed. Clarence Brown emerged into the Culver City sunlight.

"Greta, the script will be just as you want it," he said softly.

"The little doggie is okay now," said Garbo, tucking the creature under her arm and following Brown inside.

The next time Garbo hit a snag in the script, the dog was not present. Brown offered a compromise. "Well," he said to Garbo, "we'll shoot the scene two ways—yours and mine—and we'll see which is better." Garbo usually cooperated, but not always. When she would not, Brown would walk to the farthest black flat—there were many on the stage—and stand behind it for a few minutes, alone. Garbo's fellow actors would then attempt to engage her in conversation, asking about Sweden and the Academy. To their surprise, she admitted an ambition: "I should like to go on the stage."

"But what would you do about rehearsals? You don't like them."

"I wouldn't do them," said Garbo. "You see, I'd have the whole cast rehearse and have another woman do my part. Then, when it was ready I'd come in and play the role."

When Brown returned to the set, he and the ensemble tried to make awkward scenes play by rehearsing them and improvising new lines. Garbo did not like this. "When does the next boat leave for Sweden?" she growled.

An unnamed crew member later said: "Garbo did not like her role in *Inspiration*. She did not like her lines. She did not like the conception of the woman she played. She did not like working in the picture." Garbo could not be blamed. Yvonne's love for the priggish André was totally unbelievable. Montgomery, who was on his way to being M-G-M's best actor, was struggling with lines that would disgrace a high-school play. Was this the best that the studio could do for its queen?

What M-G-M could do better than any movie studio on earth was to make Garbo look radiant and to give her settings of surpassing opulence. In addition to Cedric Gibbons's breathtaking sets, the natural splendor of Busch Gardens, and Adrian's gowns, there was William Daniels's lighting. As always, he was modest, giving credit to Garbo.

> Photographically she is perfection itself. Her coloring and finely chiseled features lend themselves to all manner of lighting effects. There is nothing to be overcome with reduced or increased lighting. She is patient and sympathetic beyond all measure, and is willing and anxious at all times to stand in for camera or lighting adjustments. One of the few things Garbo demands of the camera is golden blonde hair. Most actresses blondine their hair if it seems "muddy," but Garbo is reluctant to take any liberties with nature's coloring. As a matter of fact, her hair is typically Swedish blonde, but on film [it appears] darker unless properly lighted.

To hear him describe it, Daniels had the most enviable job in Hollywood. Garbo had no equal. Or did she? On November 9, while he and the company were working in Pasadena, this item appeared in the *New York Times*: "Marlene Dietrich, German star who is now in Hollywood, will be given an early opportunity to show whether she is the long-sought rival for Greta Garbo. According to present plans, Miss Dietrich is to be starred in a film based on the life of Mata Hari, which is also the subject of Garbo's next." It was common knowledge that Paramount had completed *Morocco*, Dietrich's American debut. However, the mention of M-G-M's Mata Hari project, which had been in script development since May, was a surprise. So was the proliferation of posters heralding Dietrich as Paramount's Great New Star. "Marlene Dietrich Expected to Become Screen Star Overnight" was the headline seen in numerous New York newspapers. Paramount, guided and goaded by Dietrich's autocratic director, Josef von Sternberg, was spending a great deal of money to acquaint America with Dietrich. The question, both spoken and unspoken, since no one had yet seen her in *The Blue Angel*, was if she could really pose a threat to Garbo. On November 14, 1930, *Morocco* premiered at the Rivoli Theatre in New York. Within a week, it was breaking house box-office records, Dietrich was getting raves, and Sid Grauman's Chinese Theatre was planning to pay *Morocco* the unprecedented compliment of a second American premiere.

On November 18, on the set of *Inspiration*, Garbo and Montgomery sat in front of a false fireplace and waited for artificial snow to start falling outside the windows of the set. A makeup artist touched up Montgomery's face. "Don't you think, Miss Garbo, that this is a silly occupation for a man?" he asked.

"Yes, I do," she replied. The snow finally began to fall, and she contemplated having to speak more ridiculous dialogue. "I am very tired," she said to no one in particular. "Very, very tired." Six days later, the production was shut down. Ted Le Berthon in the *Los Angeles Record* reported that "banal claptrap [was responsible for ending the] production rather suddenly and mysteriously. Brown is through as Greta Garbo's director, and King Vidor will direct her next pictures, starting with *Susan Lenox*." On the same day, L. B. Mayer called an emergency meeting of all M-G-M employees in the studio's largest soundstage. Outside the self-contained world of his company, alarming things were happening. The stock-market crash had left more rubble and instability than anyone dreamed possible. Business was down by 28 percent, and more than 6 million Americans were unemployed. America was sinking into a depression.

This portrait of Marlene Dietrich was the first made of her when she came to Paramount Pictures in the spring of 1930. Could this woman—lit exactly like Garbo—pose a threat to her? Photograph by Eugene Robert Richee

This portrait of Dietrich was made by E. O. Hoppé in late 1930, by which time Lee Garmes and Josef von Sternberg had discovered the lighting scheme that made her look like no one else. Before long, even Garbo was asking: "Who is Marlene Dietrich?"

Mayer bade his employees to continue their work without fear of layoffs. That night Paramount premiered *Morocco* on Hollywood Boulevard.

"Famous Actress Wins Acclaim at Chinese Opening" was the title of Louella Parsons's much-read review, which referred to Dietrich as famous because of *The Blue Angel*'s success in Europe. When that film opened in Hollywood two weeks later, Dietrich had the limelight. The invidious comparisons began. "There is a definite likeness to Greta Garbo," wrote Parsons, "although Miss Dietrich is prettier." Wilton Barrett in *National Board of Review Magazine* described Dietrich as a "symbol of glamour like whom there is but one other in motion pictures, and when you see *Morocco*, you will be reminded who that is."

This was not something that Paramount wanted to hear after a campaign that stressed Dietrich's uniqueness. According to her cameraman, Lee Garmes, that uniqueness was not innate.

> I didn't have sufficient time to make tests of Marlene Dietrich [before starting *Morocco*]. I had seen *The Blue Angel*, and, based on that, I lit her with a sidelight, a half-tone, so that one side of her face was bright and the other half was in shadow. I looked at the first few days' work and I thought, "My God, I can't do this. It's exactly what Bill Daniels is doing with Garbo." We couldn't, of course, have two Garbos. So, without saying anything to Jo Sternberg, I changed to the north-light effect. He had no suggestions for more changes. He went ahead and let me do what I wanted.

Watching *Morocco*, it was possible to spot the scenes where close-ups shot with the new lighting scheme had been added later; in them, Marlene had the look of an icon. "The Dietrich face was my creation," said Garmes in 1970.

"I didn't create a 'Garbo face.'" Daniels said about his lighting schemes. "I just did portraits of her I would have done for any star. My lighting of her was determined by the requirements of a scene. I didn't, as some say I did, keep one side of the face light and the other dark. But I always did try to make the camera peer into her eyes, to see what was there."

Not surprisingly, Dietrich was distressed by the constant mention of Garbo in her reviews. "If they had only shown *The Blue Angel* first," said Dietrich in a *Los Angeles Times* interview, "then people would not say these things. There I was not a very nice girl, a little tough. I was not like Garbo. I

Opposite: Elizabeth Yeaman of the *Hollywood Citizen-News* penned a curious review of *Inspiration*. "She is a rather gaunt Garbo in this latest effort," wrote Yeaman. "Her new frizzy hairdress rather accentuates the hollowness of her cheeks, and her extreme and clinging attire gives her a wraith-like appearance. . . . There is something about the appearance of Garbo which suggests a vitriolic past and an empty future. As Walter Pater so aptly said of da Vinci's painting for the *Mona Lisa*, 'She has been a fisher in deep seas and the eyelids are a little weary.'"

was myself. In *Morocco* it is different. Maybe I do look a little like her, but I don't try to. If I do, I can't help it, and I think that it is cruel of people to say such things." The alleged resemblance went back as far as Dietrich's 1929 German film *Ich Küsse Ihre Hand (I Kiss Your Hand, Madame).* "Why has she been given the coiffure of the Swedish star?" asked Hanns G. Lustig in *Tempo* magazine. "Why has she been put into Garbo's clothes? True enough, this German girl (who has really not all that many German characteristics) has a similar and curiously alluring expression of immobility and indolence." Though Garbo most likely read all this, her only comment on her would-be rival was a disingenuous "Who is Marlene Dietrich?"

A week later, *Inspiration* began retakes; it finally finished on December 10. "I would not direct Miss Garbo again under the same conditions that prevailed during the last picture," said Clarence Brown. "We would begin by having a completed script before we started. But for Miss Garbo, personally and as an artist, I have the greatest respect and admiration." On December 12, Garbo went to see the other Clarence (Bull). She worked all day with him in her puffed-out hairdo and slinky *Inspiration* gowns. At the conclusion of the session, she took him aside and told him that she had not liked Hurrell. "The afternoon Garbo told me I was to be the only lensman to take her portraits," wrote Bull, "even I began to think I was a fair photographer." Why wouldn't Garbo work again with Hurrell? Why only with Bull? "Well," Howard Strickling told a reporter, "because she's used to him. She works best with people she's used to. If she went in for a sitting with some other photographer—no matter how good—she'd probably 'freeze up.' She'd lose all the naturalness, all the ease, all the glamour which is Garbo, and become merely another camera-conscious person."

Inspiration premiered on February 6, 1931. Its disappointed reviewers included "W. B." in the *New York Telegram,* who reported a "mediocre and tiresome narrative," and the *Times*'s Mordaunt Hall, who felt that the "chief failing in this film, aside from the fact that its Parisian atmosphere never seems far removed from the Pacific Coast, is that of having Robert Montgomery cast as the young French consular service student. . . . This young lover needed to be played by an actor of more experience to lend credulity to the romance. Virtually all Mr. Montgomery succeeds in impressing upon the audience is his embarrassment." Norbert Lusk of *Picture Play* faulted the writing. "Handicapped by the material provided for her," he wrote, "Greta Garbo still shines with such brightness that it is only when the picture is well under way that one realizes the weight and dreariness of her burden. For not even the greatest artist maintains effulgence in the murk of a poor picture."

"The theater yesterday was crowded to the doors with Garbo devotees," wrote Louella Parsons. "How her admirers adore her!" They must have; the film grossed $1 million,

Clarence Bull may have already seen *Morocco* when he used Dietrich's lighting scheme for this unusual portrait of Garbo. In late 1930, Dietrich was Paramount's answer to Garbo; Dietrich's talent would be the answer to Garbo's question.

bringing M-G-M a reported profit of $286,000, even in 1931's grim new economy. Garbo spent the winter alone, waiting for her next script. She had time for as much socializing as she cared to allow. It is likely that a message came to her from her friend Emil Jannings in Berlin; he was riding high on the success of *The Blue Angel,* even though Dietrich had supposedly stolen it from him. He wanted Garbo to meet Dietrich. Perhaps he thought that Garbo might bring Dietrich down a couple of notches. If he indeed suggested that they meet, the introduction most likely took place at the home of Ernst Lubitsch, who also lived in Santa Monica.

There is no record of their meeting, but two months later, Dietrich asked an interviewer: "Why do people call me a Greta Garbo? Why do they associate my name eternally with lovemaking? I have met Greta Garbo. I have seen her films. We are not the slightest bit alike. I do not concentrate on lovemaking on the screen. I am as happy to play the part of a charwoman." Granted that Garbo was not likely to portray a charwoman, Dietrich was secure in her newfound stardom, especially after the April 4 release of her second American film, *Dishonored,* which reviewers praised for both her acting and her allure. It looked as if Garbo at last had a real rival for the public's affection. *Susan Lenox* was scheduled to go before the cameras in May. For the sake of the "queen," it would have to be better than *Romance* and *Inspiration.*

CHAPTER FIFTEEN
Susan Lenox: Her Fall and Rise

A s Greta Garbo read the reviews of *Inspiration* and waited for the script of her next film, she might have recalled her oft-stated resolve not to play vamps or "bad women." She had just played a prostitute in *Anna Christie*, a rich man's mistress in *Romance*, and a courtesan in *Inspiration*. What had happened to Joan of Arc and the other "different" roles to which she aspired?

In spring 1931, British society photographer Cecil Beaton was in Hollywood making portraits of stars such as Dolores Del Rio and Tallulah Bankhead. Beaton desperately wanted a sitting with Garbo, but she had been saying no for more than a year. The best that Beaton could do was to chart her progress through well-connected acquaintances such as M-G-M writer Anita Loos. "In many ways," he wrote in his diary, "Garbo is in a position to, and does, dictate to the directors of her films, but in regard to the plots she plays, they are adamant. They know the financial success of Garbo as a vamp." Two years earlier, the studio could have taken a chance on a new kind of role for Garbo, but not now.

The film industry, at first untouched by the depression, was finally feeling shock waves. In the year since the stock-market crash, weekly movie attendance had dropped from 90 million to 60 million. This falloff, coupled with the expensive transition to sound, had pulled M-G-M's profits from a yearly $10 million to just $5 million by the end of 1930. In early 1931, studios with smaller profit margins (RKO-Radio, Warner Bros., and Universal) began laying off employees. Paramount began selling its theaters—those that had not already closed. Every studio looked for some magic formula to restore the lost audience. They had only to look to M-G-M, where the highest-grossing films of 1930 were two sex dramas, *Anna Christie* and *The Divorcee*. *Variety* was philosophical about the resulting trend: "As figures at the box office dwindle, the boys underline the sex angle the more. And who's to blame them?"

There were women's clubs, churches, and reformers to blame them, not to mention the studios that had abided by the Production Code. "Why should some studios," asked the *Hollywood Reporter*, "follow its dictates and find themselves with a lot of sweet pictures that will not draw flies at any box office while others, disregarding the Code, cash in on box-office smashes?" After *Little Caesar* and *Public Enemy*

launched the "gangster cycle," a wave of films dealing with fallen women and kept women introduced the so-called bad-girl cycle. Among them were Fox Film's *Bought*, M-G-M's *The Easiest Way*, and Paramount's *Tarnished Lady*. Jason Joy of the SRC tried to forestall this cycle, but having just quashed the gangster cycle, and faced with a horror cycle, he was failing, as he admitted to colleague Joseph I. Breen. "With crime practically denied them," wrote Joy, "with box-office figures down, with high pressure being employed back home to spur the studios on to get a little more cash, it was almost inevitable that sex, the nearest thing at hand and pretty generally sure fire, should be seized on. It was."

The audience for this sinful cycle was not men who suddenly found themselves unemployed and able to attend matinees. According to the trade journal *Exhibitors Herald-World*, the audience was 75 percent women. "Female

Marlene Dietrich's *Dishonored* dropped a bomb on Garbo's kingdom in the spring of 1931.

Susan Lenox: Her Fall and Rise was M-G-M's attempt to show that Garbo could display more facets of womanhood in one film than Dietrich. In this scene, sparkling with raindrops, Garbo catches the beam of a flashlight (in actuality a small spotlight held by electrician Floyd Porter).

picturegoers decide the fate of motion pictures," declared a reporter. "There can be no argument with the accepted fact that women patrons make or break a picture, because women make up a majority of the vast motion picture public, particularly at the matinee performances." Apparently, the angry letters from women's clubs did not indicate the true disposition of female cinema patrons. In an article entitled "Sinful Girls Lead in 1931," *Variety* reporter Ruth Morris wrote: "The smug and contented housewife subconsciously envies the glamour that surrounds cinema mistresses. Luxury, excitement, dangerously stolen romance are an alluring opposition to her own conventional life. She experiences them vicariously in the film she patronizes." Another *Variety* article, "Dirt Craze Due to Women," theorized that far from being dragged to sexy movies by low-minded men, women were going on their own. "Women love dirt. Nothing shocks 'em," said the article. "Women are responsible for the ever-increasing public taste in sensationalism and sexy stuff. Women who make up the bulk of the picture audiences are also the majority readers of the tabloids, scandal sheets, flashy magazines, and erotic books."

Joy had required seven changes in the script of *Dishonored*, Marlene Dietrich's second American film, before he would approve it, but her character was still a leggy prostitute. And the film was a success, making Dietrich a household word. Not surprisingly, rumors began to spread that Garbo was considering retirement. "It has been said that she is always threatening to go home," said director Clarence Brown. "All I can say is that she has never threatened me. If, after working on a picture from nine in the morning until late in the afternoon she does announce that she's going home, it is only because of real fatigue. She is not a very strong person." Not satisfied with this, reporters tracked down Harry Edington. "The rumors of her retirement originated with Garbo herself," Edington admitted. "She has frequently referred to her plan of going home. And she can quit whenever she wants to. She has saved enough to be financially independent for life. Her money is all invested in substantial American securities. If Garbo retires, it will not be because of a loss of popularity. She may be restless." The most persistent reporters worked for the *New York Times*; they managed to corner Garbo and ask her directly. "Greta Garbo broke her customary silence long enough the other day to declare, in response to questions, that she never has considered retiring from the screen or taking up a stage career," reported the *Times*.

"But when my contract arrangements permit," Garbo added, "I may return to Europe and make a few pictures there." Garbo's contract had less than a year to run, which made Louis B. Mayer nervous and Paramount pleased. The official M-G-M attitude was to avoid mentioning Dietrich, but reporters pressed Clarence Brown: "They do say, Mr. Brown, that Marlene Dietrich is going to be a dangerous rival."

"Anyone who knows them both," answered Brown, "would not mention Marlene Dietrich in the same breath with Greta Garbo, who gets her effects from her own mind. All the director must do is indicate the way and she follows it unerringly. Dietrich is all director. Her work gives the impression that a man is standing over her with a gun, forcing her through every action, all the time." Brown was alluding to the much-discussed relationship between Dietrich and Josef von Sternberg, the director of her last three films.

Maria Magdalene Dietrich was born in 1901 on the outskirts of Berlin to a Prussian police officer and the daughter of well-to-do jewelers. Like Garbo, she lost her father at an early age; she was six when he died of injuries sustained in an equestrian accident. Unlike Garbo, she gained a stepfather whom she learned to love. More important to her upbringing than affection, though, was obedience. This virtue, so different from Garbo's stubborn resistance, would lead Dietrich to fame.

Stardom was slow in coming. Four years older than Garbo, Dietrich spent the 1920s bouncing between musical

A few weeks before her real-life vacation on a lake in the Sierra Nevadas, Garbo filmed this scene on the Franklin Canyon reservoir.

theater and silent films, just another hardworking actress with a husband and child until a Hollywood director was lucky enough to see her on the stage of the Berliner Theater in the musical comedy *Zwei Krawatten* (*Two Bow Ties*). The director, von Sternberg, became Dietrich's mentor. He was domineering, exacting, and cruel, making Mauritz Stiller look polite by comparison. "Look at that light stand," Sternberg would say to Dietrich, directing a close-up in which she was supposed to be looking at her leading man. "Look at it and count backwards from twenty-five. I told you to look at the light stand! Look at it as if you couldn't live without it! Can't you count? *Dummkopf*! Do it again!"

The reward for this regimen was "overnight" international stardom for the twenty-nine-year-old Dietrich. She got even better reviews for *Dishonored* than for *Morocco*. "How much of her defiance as a streetwalker," wrote a critic in *Picture Play*, "her terrible charm as the secret service decoy, her gaiety and abandon in the peasant disguise is due to brilliant direction and how much to Dietrich's personality is unimportant. She is unique." A fan letter said: "Marlene Dietrich has everything that Garbo has and something else besides—humor!" Richard Watts Jr. in the *New York Herald Tribune* wrote: "Her hasty rise to film celebrity was the result of neither luck, accident, nor publicity. Her almost lyrically ironic air of detachment and, to be as frank about it as possible, her physical appeal, make her one of the great personages of the local drama." In addition to this physical appeal, there was Dietrich's ability to put over a song. If she

meant to eclipse Garbo, she was qualified to do so. Thus, it was not enough that Garbo's next film flout the depression. It also had to put Dietrich in her place—second place. To accomplish this, Garbo would once again have to portray a "bad woman," even if it meant a slight variation on her formula.

The most likely property for her fourteenth film was *Susan Lenox: Her Rise and Fall*, a 1917 novel by David Graham Phillips. Known as a muckraking social realist, Phillips had been gunned down in New York in 1911 after finishing *Susan Lenox*. (The assassin claimed that his sister had been libeled by Phillips's last novel, *The Fashionable Adventures of Joshua Craig*.) A 1925 M-G-M reader's report described the posthumously published *Susan Lenox* as an "intimate story of a prostitute; how, being illegitimate, she is hounded into prostitution by society's wolves, how she shrinks, how she struggles to rise above her environment, and how, at last, she conquers." Script reader Ross Wills wrote: "If this touching and magnificent story could only reach the screen, maybe people would understand better such tragic characters; it's the truth!" Two years later, the Phillips estate lawyer wrote Irving Thalberg, asking if he was still interested in *Susan Lenox*. Thalberg took an informal poll of the secretaries outside his office: "Who is Susan Lenox?"

"Wasn't there a book about her?" asked his secretary, Vivian Newcom. Mildred Kelly, secretary to Harry Rapf, thought so.

"It was something about her rise and fall, or maybe the other way around," said Stanley Partridge, Eddie Mannix's assistant.

Garbo wore a huge hat and black velvet tights for a montage in which she makes the transition from fugitive farm girl to carnival showgirl.

Garbo spent a great deal of time in June 1931 filming scenes that were not included in the final cut of *Susan Lenox*. This scene with an unidentified actor was part of a sequence in which she hides out from Clark Gable.

"We'll buy it," said Thalberg to his secretary. In 1930, he assigned several writers to work on it simultaneously and told John Gilbert that he could have the lead. Gilbert's sad outing in *Redemption* had been followed by the hopelessly bad *Way for a Sailor*. Each of these films cost the studio $250,000 in salary to Gilbert, yet no one seemed able to secure a decent vehicle for the star. Perhaps being teamed with Garbo again would break the chain of failures. Gilbert tried to be sanguine as he waited at Tower Grove Road. "Jack would put a glass of Scotch and soda on the mantelpiece of his long living room," recalled his friend Gene Markey. "His manservant would put another glass at the far end of the room, and Jack would stride between them, talking, warming up to his themes, sipping the liquor he liked best, on into the night. . . . I had a feeling that Jack would have preferred to be a writer. He held no high opinion of acting, and his imagination offered a world of books, plays, and essays to be written."

Perhaps Thalberg should have let Gilbert take a crack at the script of *Susan Lenox*. It was not doing well. In early 1931, after Garbo had expressed her displeasure with Brown, Thalberg had put director King Vidor on the project and changed the subtitle to *Her Fall and Rise*. After weeks of

long story sessions with writer Mildred Cram and producer Paul Bern, Vidor brought the material to Thalberg, who shuffled through papers on his desk while Cram read him their material. "No, you've missed it," said Thalberg suddenly. "Entirely. The formula we're after is this: love conquers in the end! We're not interested in defeat. No one is! You've got this girl down, but there's no 'rise.' Try again."

The script was also being worked on by contract writers Wanda Tuchock, Wells Root, Zelda Sears (a sometime actress who had played Robert Montgomery's aunt in *Inspiration*), and Martin Flavin, whose play *The Criminal Code* would soon boost Boris Karloff's career. All these adaptations of the book had language and situations that the Production Code would never allow. One of Root's scenes had the hapless Susan Lenox forced into a relationship by a sleazy carnival owner who tells her to get ready for bed. "There's a pint of gin with your name on it under your pillow," he says. "Snap into it, baby." Joy's colleagues at the SRC returned this material as unacceptable. By the time *Susan Lenox* was scheduled for shooting, more than twenty writers had worked on it, and it still was not finished.

The incomplete script did not prevent Bern from preparing the production. The most important consideration was a leading man. Breaking his promise to Gilbert, Thalberg offered Garbo half a dozen possibilities. She chose Clark Gable, who had been at M-G-M only six months but whose appearances with Joan Crawford in *Dance, Fools, Dance* and *Laughing Sinners* created a stir. "A star is in the making," wrote W. R. Wilkerson, publisher of the *Hollywood Reporter*. "A star, that to our reckoning, will outdraw every other star pictures have ever developed. Never have we seen audiences work themselves into such enthusiasm as when Gable walks on the screen." Gable was shocked when he got the news of the casting. "The big thrill came up at Monterey," he told a reporter. "I had been out swimming. When I came into the hotel, I picked up a paper and saw the headline: 'Clark Gable to play opposite Greta Garbo.' That was one of the thrills of my life." After he recovered from it, he complained to his agent; he knew how Garbo's leading men usually fared.

Filming commenced on May 25, 1931, with Robert Z. Leonard directing. King Vidor had withdrawn from *Susan Lenox* when he saw himself outnumbered by writers and outvoted by producers; he was happier working for Samuel Goldwyn, where he had some hope of autonomy. At forty-two, Leonard was one of M-G-M's most dependable directors, storyboarding each shot in the script before he filmed it. The first scenes to be shot took place in the dreary farmhouse where Susan's cruel uncle (Jean Hersholt) tells her she must marry bestial Jeb Mondstrum (Alan Hale). As soon as the uncle is out of sight, Jeb steals his jug of whisky, gets drunk, breaks into Susan's room, and tries to rape her. Leonard shot these scenes with a cinematic flair

This cut scene had Garbo saying good-bye to Clark Gable at the lodge before vanishing into the night.

In this cut scene, Garbo welcomes her long-lost love to a dinner party in her penthouse. Eddie Kane and Hale Hamilton watch from the right. The dinner scene, in which Gable realizes that Garbo is a kept woman, was shot twice.

that surpassed the best of his work on the twenty-four silent films he had made for his ex-wife, Mae Murray. Every shot was beautifully composed and lit by William Daniels, and every shot provided just enough information before relinquishing its place to the next shot. Leonard and Daniels took special delight in using the new camera crane that M-G-M had bought; its giddy flight through crowded soundstages gave scenes a new depth. For texture, atmosphere, and power, these were the best sequences in a Garbo film since Jacques Feyder and *The Kiss*.

The sets were also outstanding, the work of a Russian art director named Alexander Toluboff. "Our aim," he said, "was to reflect as closely as possible the varying moods of the girl in constructing these sets—to set off by the atmosphere of the film the different emotional reactions experienced. In the Minnesota farmhouse, for example, there was not a single piece of lumber not off plumb. The object was to make the set as grim as possible, without resorting to exaggeration. We tried to create a mood of jarring angularity and we used grim color tones to strengthen the mood."

Working with Garbo for a week, actor Jean Hersholt (possibly because he was Danish) broke through her reserve. "Some persons have the mistaken idea that because she does not like publicity she is conceited and undemocratic," said Hersholt. "That is not true at all. She has moods when she talks very little—most Scandinavian people are like that—but then again she will sit down and talk two or three hours at a time. She is a very delightful person and I think one of the few real artists of the screen."

Edington brought records to the set for Garbo to listen to between takes. There was much comment when the singer was identified as Marlene Dietrich, warbling her songs from *The Blue Angel*. Garbo was already in a bad mood. Having gotten past the stark, wordless scenes of the first sequences, she once again found herself trying to speak dialogue that sounded as if it had been written by amateurs. In some scenes she was a monosyllabic farm girl; in others, she was witty and biting. Nothing was consistent because the character of Susan Lenox was obviously a mystery to every writer who had labored on the script. In addition, Garbo had to cope with the constant arrival of new scenes that Bern was dictating and then having a writer translate into dialogue. "Plenty of turmoil at Metro during the production of *Susan Lenox*," reported *Variety* in early July. "Twenty-two writers worked at different times on the story before it went in, with some still working while production was on. Greta Garbo, topping, has done six walks off the set, at different times finding fault with the story. Several halts were made as a result to revamp, with the ending also changed several times."

On Friday, July 3, one of the days when she was playing hooky, Garbo went to visit her friend Salka Viertel. There she encountered a society woman from New York who was working as a screenwriter at RKO. The woman's name was Mercedes de Acosta. She was thirty-eight, fiercely proud of her Spanish heritage, and, as always, dressed in a contrasty ensemble of solid black and solid white. That her moods were equally dramatic could be ascertained by the intense expression on her sharp-featured face. For some reason, Garbo instantly took to Acosta. She had Viertel invite her for breakfast the following Sunday, and she danced most of the morning with her in the unoccupied house of Viertel's neighbor, screenwriter Oliver H. P. Garrett. The new acquaintances reconvened that evening at Garbo's house, but her mood had changed. "I am not going to take you into the house and you will have to leave soon," Garbo told a crestfallen Acosta. "I am very tired and I have to shoot again tomorrow very early on that ghastly *Susan Lenox*."

"Aren't you happy about the film?"

"Happy? *Who* is happy? No one making films can be happy."

"I'm sorry," said Acosta. "I hoped you were. You were happy this morning, weren't you, when we were dancing and singing?"

"Yes, thanks to you I had a few minutes' gaiety this morning. But now it is nearly evening. Soon it will be night, and I will not sleep, and then it will be morning, and I will have to go again to that terrible studio. Let's not talk. It is so useless talking and trying to explain things. Let's just sit and not speak at all." The awestruck Acosta eagerly complied.

The *Susan Lenox* script was stuck at Susan's ascendance to kept-woman status, where she is installed in a New York penthouse by a crooked politician, Kelly (Hale Hamilton). Rodney Spencer (Gable), the architect who sheltered her from her vicious uncle, has lost track of her. When he finds her a kept woman, he feels guilty for having abandoned her but is openly contemptuous of her situation. Bern and his squad of writers could not decide where to take the story from there. In one version, Spencer comes to the penthouse at two in the morning to taunt Susan. "Well, you have managed to make your gutter quite attractive," he says. In another, written by the celebrated playwright George Kelly, the unseen voice of her conscience urges her to his shabby hotel room, where he is drunk and defeatist. Albert Lewin reviewed this scene: "Rodney's change too sudden and undramatic. Why should Rodney be in difficulties? I can't believe him a failure."

Hardly anything about the script could be believed. This was the result of trying to turn a thousand-page novel about social evils into a three-act star vehicle. The book would not conform to the M-G-M process. In it, Rodney is not Susan's great love, but one of several. After the recriminations, she leaves him to himself, goes to Europe, finds a mentor, becomes an actress, and then loses her mentor to a senseless killing just as she becomes a star. Then she founds an orphanage, named for her unwed mother. "She never

Clark Gable was shocked when he learned that he had been cast opposite Garbo.

marries," says the synopsis. "Men are mere incidents in her life. Her career now is paramount to all else. It alone is true." For some reason, Bern chose to ignore this part of the story, which would have had some relevance to Garbo's persona. Instead, he tried to squeeze as many different visual aspects out of the character as possible. This was his attempt to show that Garbo could be just as versatile as Dietrich had been in *Dishonored*; various scenes shot for *Susan Lenox* had Garbo as a sideshow dancer, a governess, and a nurse. When all the scenes were assembled, they did not make a character—or a movie. The production was shut down on July 11. Acosta

answered her telephone to hear a famous voice. "My present prison term is over," said Garbo. "I have finished shooting."

With the production on hiatus until the script was fixed, Garbo decided to go on a short vacation trip. Edington brought her the keys to a cabin owned by M-G-M star Wallace Beery. It was located on Silver Lake, a man-made body of water in the Sierra Nevada range. James, Garbo's chauffeur, spent three days driving her and Acosta the four hundred winding miles to the lake. "Absolutely no one is to know where we are," Garbo instructed him. "Not even Whistler [her maid], and certainly not Louis B. Mayer!" The women rowed to the cabin, which was on a small island, and spent a week cut off from 1931 America. When it was time to return to work, Garbo grew sad. "I can't," she cried. "I can't go back to Hollywood and that studio life!"

Garbo dutifully reported to the studio on September 2 and began working from a new script. Lenore Coffee had turned in an effective sequence on August 8, but it was not used. In it, Susan finds Rodney in the lodging house and tells him what she has suffered since he deserted her. She points to a "sordid" tableau outside the window, a prostitute soliciting a man in the street. "Look, Rodney," she says. "I have been that woman. I have known that man. That's what you did to me when you left me. It hurts, doesn't it? You told me how cheaply I could be bought. You don't *know* how cheaply. Once—for a drink of whisky on a cold night."

"Why are you telling me this?" he asks.

"Why shouldn't you know it? I had to *live* it. But what I sold was no more myself than the coat I'd pawned the day before."

Gene Markey had also worked on the script, but since Thalberg had moved the end of the story to Central America, Bern chose to use material written by Leon Gordon, the playwright of *White Cargo* fame. Before it was filmed, Jason Joy had Leonard delete racist epithets such as "greasers" and "cock-eyed Jews," and the following speech by Rodney: "I've changed, too," says Rodney, when he finds Susan working in a tropical dive. "I got over all that sentimental bunk. I play your way. When I see anybody I want—if I can get 'em—I just take 'em. It's a lot of fun. I used to think that black was black and white was white. Now I know they're just a smudgy gray." What remained was still strong stuff, with Rodney insulting Susan in front of a rich man (Ian Keith) who has offered to marry her. "Marry? Say, listen. All you need is the price of the marriage license," he sneers. "Just the price. Not the wedding. Just the price!"

"Did it ever strike you for a second that you might be wrong?" demands the properly outraged Susan. "What right have you to take a stand like this?"

"What right?" asks Rodney, who has spent the last three months in a fever-ridden jungle. "You know why I wallow out there in the swamps? You know why I never draw a sober breath on the waterfront? It's heat! Booze! Insects! Damp rot and sweat! But it eats up the memory of you!" As he turns to go, an insistent prostitute accosts him. He picks her up and then drops her—off the second-story landing, and onto a table full of drunken customers below.

The final scene, as implausible as the rest of the film, has Susan pledging to the embittered Rodney: "I'll make you believe in me." Filming finally ended, after forty-nine days, on September 19. *Susan Lenox: Her Fall and Rise* had racked up a price tag of $573,000. A good part of this was for scenes that were discarded by film editor Margaret Booth as she cut the film to seventy-one minutes. The new version

was previewed less than a week later, and Garbo was in the audience. The film passed muster and was released on October 10.

"Garbo and Gable—the names sound well together, don't they?" asked Harriet Parsons, daughter of Louella, in her review. "And if you don't believe the fans think so, just try to plow your way through waiting multitudes outside the Loew's State Theatre." True enough, the M-G-M publicity department had used the delay in filming to bombard the country with scenes of Garbo kissing Gable and with stunning portraits of her taken by Clarence Bull on July 8. The shimmering images worked their magic, dragging in customers who had to scramble for dimes. They scrambled, and enjoyed the Garbo formula yet again. "In *Susan Lenox*," wrote Parsons, "Garbo runs the gamut from a naive, browbeaten country girl, terrified of life (spelled s-e-x), to a glittering courtesan, established in metropolitan luxury. It presents her in the role in which her adorers love her best, that of a woman, glamorous and desired by many men, but sacrificing everything for one great, undying love. She has, fortunately, a leading man who makes such frantic, self-effacing devotion on the part of the great Garbo conceivable. Such has not always been the case in past Garbo vehicles."

The improvement in casting was not enough for most critics. "It is rather disappointing," wrote Mordaunt Hall, "to find [Garbo] in a production which is directed along the lines of old silent film technique, with halting and often crudely written dialogue and poorly developed episodes." James Agate wrote: "The film is good for its purpose because neither hero nor heroine at any moment behaves like a sentient human being, because any straight answer to any straight question would have brought the film to an end at any moment, because love paid for by degradation is the most enticing of the world's plots, and because there is nothing more comforting than a heroine who is not as black as she has carefully painted herself." If the purpose suggested by Agate was to make money, the film was very good, with an $806,000 domestic gross and a $700,000 foreign gross. The Prince of Wales reportedly saw *Susan Lenox* three times; no one reported how many times (or if) he had seen *Dishonored*. Garbo's stardom was still secure. As she moved into the last year of her contract, she could look forward to *Mata Hari* and to working with Salka Viertel and Mercedes de Acosta, both of whom were taking an active interest in her career.

Opposite: Bull shot his *Susan Lenox* portraits with a sharp commercial lens. Although William Daniels used heavy soft focus in the film, Bull had discontinued its use in the portrait gallery. He did light most of this sitting with silk-covered softlights, much in the same way Daniels lit Garbo's close-ups.

PART VI

THE SUPERSTAR

CHAPTER SIXTEEN
Mata Hari

With the back-to-back successes of *Romance, Inspiration,* and *Susan Lenox,* Greta Garbo edged out even the super-popular Marie Dressler as Metro-Goldwyn-Mayer's top-grossing star. *Min and Bill, Prosperity,* and *Reducing* had made Dressler the queen of domestic grosses at M-G-M, but foreign audiences were willing to watch Garbo's films even without subtitles or dubbing. Since February 1930, Garbo had brought M-G-M nearly $5 million of income and had attained an acclaim known only by a few silent-film stars. The performers who had reached those heights—Mary Pickford, Charlie Chaplin, and Douglas Fairbanks—soon found stardom an empty achievement if a studio could force them to use the same formula over and over. One by one, they broke with the studios and in 1919 joined D. W. Griffith to found United Artists (UA), where, as independent producers, they could choose the vehicles that they felt were best for them. In September 1931, Garbo had six months left on her contract, and there was the possibility that she might leave Metro, but she was undecided, even about her remaining projects. She needed a guiding hand, and she was finding her mountaintop a little lonely.

When she descended, it was both for company and for professional counsel. Salka Viertel was not a filmmaker, but she was a mature woman, she had been on the stage, and she had the Old World elegance that Garbo respected. It was becoming apparent that Garbo considered Americans tasteless, insensitive, and self-aggrandizing. She had no intimate American friends, except perhaps one. After finishing *Susan Lenox,* she had ten days before she was to start her next film, *Mata Hari.* She spent every one of those days with her new friend Mercedes de Acosta, who was American but who emphasized her Spanish heritage. Some of Garbo's friends thought the friendship symbiotic.

Raised in the upper echelons of New York society, Acosta also moved in literary circles, and there was not one theatrical luminary of the early twentieth century whom she did not claim to know—or make it her business to know. Eleanora Duse, Isadora Duncan, and Eva LeGalliene were all described as intimate friends. Her very-much-alive but

Opposite: More people saw Greta Garbo in *Mata Hari* than in any of her other films. Released on New Year's Eve of 1931, the film enjoyed a million-dollar profit.

This Gilbert Adrian costume for *Mata Hari* cost $2,000 to make and weighed fifty pounds. It was inspired by Paul Poiret's creations for the 1909 Ballets Russes. After extricating herself from it and slipping into a turtleneck sweater and jersey skirt, Garbo sighed, "Now I am comfortable." Some of her fans agreed. "In my opinion, *Mata Hari* was Garbo's best as far as acting is concerned," wrote Mrs. Jeanne Florio of New Haven, Connecticut, "but won't someone please tell her to stop wearing such ridiculous clothes and hair arrangements."

oddly absent husband, Abram Poole, was a noted portrait painter. Her late sister, the glamorous socialite Rita de Acosta Lydig, had been a celebrated patron of the arts. Thus Acosta had a formidable pedigree, even if her own accomplishments were a trifle difficult to enumerate. She had two novels and four plays to her credit, none of them successes. Yet the relentlessly aggressive socialite knew everyone and, from Garbo's point of view, knew everything—at least everything that a Stockholm slum girl would like to learn. Garbo knew that her own celebrity would require her to meet literati and royalty, and even if Acosta could not write a hit play, she could certainly write real-life dialogue for Garbo. And for a name-dropper like Acosta, Garbo's was the ultimate name.

It was not long before Acosta's friends were hearing accounts of the wonders she was working with Garbo's diction and literacy. Garbo took to this tutelage almost as she had to Stiller's seven years earlier. But Stiller had been a renowned artist. Acosta was harder to describe. Not that a description would ever be printed; there was no magazine yet devoted to dilettantes. Shamed by the success of her sister and husband, Acosta was an aspiring artist who did more socializing than writing. The circles in which she moved consisted of permanently unmarried celebrities such as actress Alla Nazimova or flamboyant artists such as novelist Carl Van Vechten, dancer Clifton Webb, and director Edmund Goulding. The amount of time Garbo was spending with Acosta began to occasion comment.

"Innocent bystanders gasped in amazement to see Mercedes de Acosta and Greta Garbo striding swiftly down Hollywood Boulevard in men's clothes," stated a shocked photo caption. The trade papers also picked up gossip, running it in the form of blind items such as this: "Recent associations are surely showing, [in] superficial effects at least, upon a beautiful M-G-M star. Noted for her grace and 'softness,' she has been appearing lately to show little concern for her appearance, and is wearing her face 'bare.' Heavy masculine tweeds and slouch hats complete the effect." Garbo had worn pants in *The Single Standard* and Marlene Dietrich had worn pants in *Morocco*, but to startle an audience. Garbo had been seen in pants on the back lot during the filming of *Romance*, but this was excused as a convenience between costume changes. To wear men's clothes in public, as she was reported to have done several times, was something else. M-G-M's publicity department made a stern call, not to Acosta or Garbo, but to the trade papers. Garbo continued to shop at the Army-Navy store; it was not long before Dietrich went her one better and made a campaign of wearing men's apparel—even to the premieres of Garbo's films.

It was said that M-G-M was trying to imitate Dietrich's *Dishonored*, but this was not true. M-G-M had been preparing a female-spy project since the winter of 1930, before Dietrich had arrived at Paramount. Of course, M-G-M could have dropped the idea after *Dishonored* premiered, but a chance to beat Dietrich at her own game may indeed have motivated the elaborate production that became *Mata Hari*. The likely inspiration for both films was the 1930 book *Mata*

Hari: Courtesan and Spy by Major Thomas Coulson of the British Intelligence Service. Paramount's B. P. Schulberg was the first to submit it to the SRC, whose readers found its jingoism as troublesome as its sex scenes. German Consul General Otto von Hentig found it "one of the most contemptible pieces of war propaganda I have ever read." As a result, both Paramount and M-G-M turned to other sources for their spy stories.

Garbo still entertained notions of playing Joan of Arc, especially when she learned that Acosta had written a play on the subject. At one point Garbo asked the German director Ludwig Berger what he thought of the idea. "If you had been born in the fifteenth century," he replied, "*you* would certainly have been burned as a witch!" Perhaps an execution scene appealed to Garbo because she agreed to portray Mata Hari, who had been shot by a French firing squad. More likely what appealed to Garbo was the opportunity to portray a character who was something more than a patchwork product of twenty-two writers. Garbo immediately went to the well-stocked M-G-M research department. "Miss Garbo has shown greater interest in the story of Mata Hari than in anything she has ever done before," said Nathalie Bucknall, department head. "She came to me for all the books our department could supply about the adventures of this noted woman spy. She seemed greatly pleased when I secured four or five books dealing with the subject. These she read in the original German. I never knew of anyone being so painstaking in making preparations for a part in a picture as Miss Garbo was for this role."

Mata Hari was the stage name of a Dutch housewife named Margaretha Zelle McLeod, a somewhat pathetic figure whose only avenue of escape from an abusive husband was to flee to Paris and make her debut as a featured dancer. The word *matahari* means "eye of the dawn" in Malayan. McLeod had spent a great deal of time in Java with her military officer husband and had absorbed enough of the culture to transform herself into an exotic personage. Even in wicked Paris, her dance created a sensation. She performed it in the company of four supporting dancers, wearing several layers of Salome-like shawls over a transparent sarong. No one knew that the bracelets on her biceps, wrists, and calves, and her jeweled belt, were borrowed from a museum, or that her breastplates were stuffed with cotton to enhance her profile. All anyone cared about was her presentation. According to her biographer, Russell Warren Howe, it was slick.

A half life-size carving of Shiva, with four arms, was placed on the improvised stage with a bowl of burning oil at his feet. . . . The diaphanous shawls she wore as the dance began were cast away to tempt the god until finally, as the candelabras were capped and only the flickering oil light gleamed on Shiva's features, the sarong was abandoned and her silhouette, with her back to the audience, writhed with desire toward her supernatural lover. The four dancing girls chanted their jealousy as Mata Hari groaned and worked her loins deliriously. All passion spent, she touched her brow to Shiva's feet; one of the attendant dancers tiptoed delicately forward and threw a gold lamé cloth across the kneeling figure, enabling her to rise and take the applause.

Mata Hari's terpsichorean fame was soon equaled by her notoriety as a kept woman, but like the characters in the Garbo formula, the forty-year-old courtesan threw over her older protectors for the love of a Russian aviator half her age. When he was nearly blinded in action, she vowed to devote herself to his care, once she had taken care of some unfinished business. She believed that by offering herself to powerful German soldiers, she could extract information to give to France and become rich in the process. Sadly, she fooled no one. The Germans exposed her cover, making it appear that she was a double agent. Whatever she was, she was not very clever. She was arrested for spying against France in February 1917 and executed in October.

M-G-M's first script was prepared by contract writers Don Ryan and Dale Van Every in June 1930. It begins with a fertility rite at a Buddhist temple in the Malayan jungle. An orgy follows, where a high priest encounters a white woman. Mata Hari is their offspring. In November, Paramount producer Benjamin "Barney" Glazer rewrote the story, setting it solely in Paris, and Leo Birinski wrote the unconvincing dialogue. "There is no glitter whatever in any of these passages," wrote reader Richard L. Sharpe. "Mata Hari was frankly a poseur. She should not talk like a human being at all, except when she is 'off the set,' as it were. She had a definite public act in the public eye in Paris, and she did everything in her power to make herself as strange, as unreal, and as fabulous as possible." Sharpe also thought that the Lord Shiva was an inappropriate choice for "a dance of cruelty and sin and unrest" because he was a god of nature. "A much better choice of deity," wrote Sharpe, "would be the goddess Kali who is the destroying goddess of Indian mythology, represented as black, multi-armed, terrifying, subtle, spectacular, and fascinating."

By the summer of 1931, *Mata Hari* was turning into another *Susan Lenox*, being worked on by a combination of unknown and well-known writers. The latter group included exotic-locale specialist John Colton (whose script was full of misspellings), veteran scenarist C. Gardner Sullivan, and Leon Gordon, who was at the same time writing the cantina scene for *Susan Lenox*. By late September, Gordon

In her fifteenth M-G-M film, Greta Garbo was the World War I spy Mata Hari. Her dance to the Lord Shiva showed what M-G-M did best, transporting an audience to a glamorous world that never existed. Broadway dancer June Knight doubled for Garbo in the long shots of the dance, which was modeled after the 1905 performance of the real-life Mata Hari.

had finished most of *Mata Hari's* structure, but Thalberg and producer Bernard Fineman brought in still more writers to improve dialogue. There was veteran playwright Bayard Veiller, sometime actor Gilbert Emery, and even the British matinee idol Ivor Novello, who was in town for a role in Paramount's *Once a Lady*. The epicene Novello and his director, Guthrie McClintic, the homosexual husband of lesbian stage star Katharine Cornell, were frequently called on by Mercedes de Acosta. Even these stars wanted to know what Garbo was really like. The final draft of *Mata Hari* came from Emery and a contract writer named Doris Anderson on September 28; the film could begin with a completed script.

With uncharacteristic eagerness, Garbo visited the Whitley Heights home of designer Gilbert Adrian to inspect his *Mata Hari* costume sketches. Acosta came along to add Adrian to her personal Who's Who. "The evening I met Adrian we had a lot of fun," she wrote. "He showed me his sketches for Greta's clothes. I suggested that she wear a long black cape for the scene at the end when she is shot, and that she should brush her hair absolutely straight back. This would give a dramatic effect for the ending. Adrian agreed with me and was delighted with the suggestion." One of the other costumes was a marvel of engineering, a gold-beaded sheath draped over form-fitting leggings made of thousands of bugle beads, and topped with a jewel- and sequin-encrusted bodice. Completing the ensemble was a goldbeaded skullcap, accented with five medallions. According to Hedda Hopper, the costume "took eight Guadalajaran needlewomen nine weeks to complete." The costume for the dance to Shiva was equally elaborate and had to be worn by both Garbo and her dance double, a Broadway dancer named June Knight.

Thalberg and Louis B. Mayer had agreed to give Garbo a star as her leading man. Robert Montgomery, who had barely survived *Inspiration*, was only momentarily considered for the role of the young Russian flier. Of male M-G-M stars, that left Buster Keaton, Wallace Beery, John Gilbert, and Ramon Novarro. They chose Novarro. Even if he was Mexican, he could pass for Russian. He had passed for Jewish in *Ben-Hur*, after all, and he was a major star. There was the problem, though, of his height, which was five feet eight inches. At five seven, Garbo might not be at the right sight line for natural-looking love scenes. There had recently been a problem with Leila Hyams and Norman Foster in *Men Call It Love*; her head photographed bigger than his. A few weeks before filming was to begin, Novarro got a call from Fineman's office. "They said 'We have to make a test,'" recalled Novarro. "I heard that she was so tall that I had boots [made] and I put lifts inside." Garbo knew of Novarro. "I met her when she was doing *The Temptress* with Antonio Moreno," said Novarro. "I would go on the set and watch them. That was before she got a little difficult. Her director Mauritz Stiller was a good friend of mine and a good friend

of F. W. Murnau's. He was a big-headed man. He looked strange." No doubt Garbo also knew that, like Stiller and Murnau, Novarro preferred men to women.

The prospect of working with Garbo made Novarro so anxious that he consulted self-help pamphlets. "I used to read these funny little booklets that said 'You might be better than the man you're talking to.' And I said to myself, 'I might be and I might not. I don't think that I am better than anybody—but I don't think that I am less.'" Still, on the day of the test, he did not know what to expect. "They said that at first she was rather offstandish [*sic*]," recalled Novarro in 1968. "I wasn't afraid or timid, really. So I made up and I went on the set—and she was late. Which was very unusual because [I had heard that usually] when she said three o'clock it was three o'clock! So she came in without makeup. And she just looked at me and said 'It's all right.' No test. Nothing. And I said, 'My God! If I had known, I would not have made up and put on all this costume and everything.' But she just wanted to find out my height."

To secure the role, Novarro had to make some concessions. He had been earning $150,000 per film, but the depression was cutting into box-office receipts, and it was also time for him to negotiate a new contract. In order to work with Garbo, he agreed to share billing and to take a two-thirds pay cut. He got $5,000 on signing and $5,000 a week, which anticipated M-G-M's usual extension of shooting for rewrites and retakes. Filming commenced on September 30, 1931, with a director who was new to Garbo, but by no means new. George Fitzmaurice was a twenty-year Hollywood veteran, with romantic hits such as *The Son of the Sheik* to his credit. He was most likely assigned to *Mata Hari* on the strength of his recent work with Thalberg's wife, Norma Shearer, on *Strangers May Kiss*. To prepare for this assignment, Fitzmaurice collaborated with William Daniels and Alexander Toluboff on a storyboard of 300 drawings. "Each one was marked with a scene number," he told the *New York Times*, "and all steps in the action were indicated, such as: 'Shubin reaches for the telephone,' and 'Mata draws the gun from the drawer.'" In addition, he had two cameras on the set for most scenes: one for the wide shot, and one for an over-the-shoulder close-up of Garbo. He also agreed with Daniels on the frequent use of crane shots on larger sets.

When Garbo arrived at her dressing room the first day of filming, she was greeted by a large bouquet of flowers and a card that read: "I hope the world will be as thrilled to see Mata Hari as I am to work with her—Ramon Novarro." Their first scene together was set in Mata Hari's bedroom, a seductive setting of velvet-upholstered arches, satin curtains, and a statue of Shiva over the bed, which, of course, had satin sheets. The first shots took place at the lacquered door of the bedroom, where Lieutenant Alexis Rosanoff (Novarro) entreats the glamorous star he has just met to let him stay for just a little while. The sound levels gave them

The Hollywood premiere of *Mata Hari* was a prestige affair. "The ermine, the chiffon frocks, and the top hats were more in evidence last night at Grauman's Chinese Theatre than at any time since our chief conversation became stock losses," wrote Louella Parsons. Formal wear did not prevent these first-nighters from applauding wildly at the end of Garbo's dance. "Garbo in scant draperies dancing in a weird ceremony before a huge bronze god is a Garbo the public wants and enjoys," decided Parsons. This scene got cheers at every performance, including the matinee that Garbo entered after the house lights had dimmed.

Art director Alexander Toluboff gave Mata Hari's bedroom two arches covered in velvet.

trouble, and the shot had to be taken several times. "I felt very strange," recalled Novarro, "and I imagine that Miss Garbo also felt some restraint at the time." After an hour on the set, the two professionals relaxed. "She was so very charming, however, that I felt instantly comfortable. There was a total absence of the tension I feared." Then it was time for Milton Brown to make the first scene still of the production.

"As we posed," remembered Novarro, "both of us seemed suddenly self-conscious. In a way it was a test. Perhaps she felt I was watching to see if she would upstage me, a trick to hold the center of the picture. Or possibly she was waiting to see if I would try it on her. It is strange, but little things sometimes mount to enormous proportions. Whatever it was that made me feel tense at that moment, it vanished the second I heard the shutter click. She looked up and laughed at me. We were friends." Interviewers found Novarro the most talkative of Garbo's costars since John Gilbert.

When we began work together, I discovered that Miss Garbo did not care to rehearse. It was her habit to walk into her scenes and go right through with them. She knows the story and the dialogue by heart before production begins. But it is difficult for me to work that way. I need rehearsals to make myself certain I understand exactly how a scene should be played. I like to rehearse with the lights, camera,

This set was also used in a 1932 film, Buster Keaton's *The Passionate Plumber*. It was not as attractive without the masterly lighting effects of William Daniels.

microphone, just as it will be when it is filmed. When Miss Garbo realized my method of working differed from her own, she graciously offered to rehearse. While the new camera angles were being lined up on the set, we would sit in her little portable dressing room and go over the lines together. Other times she would prefer to walk outside and run through the dialogue as we strolled the streets between the stages.

In ten years before the cameras, Novarro had worked with a variety of actresses, but he had rarely seen technical mastery allied to inner conviction. "Her emotional intensity is genuine," he said. "The instant she begins a scene, her whole being seems to change. Her role acts as a complete metamorphosis. At once she is Mata Hari and not Greta Garbo. It is an inspiration to work with her. You find yourself living the role, not merely acting it." What surprised Novarro, too, was that her well-known propensity for assuming the dominant position in her love scenes was not a concept thought up by Clarence Brown or Mauritz Stiller; it was her own. This was why she wanted to rehearse her love scenes without the interference of a new director. "Garbo always wanted to rehearse the love scenes with me in private," recalled Novarro. "She needed to be able to concentrate. She had to convince herself before she could convince anyone else." This preparation also took place on the darkened set. "She and I staged our love scenes before Fitzmaurice came in. She would say, 'Well, in the last one *you* sat . . . and in this one *I* sit.'"

After the confusion and false starts of *Susan Lenox*, Garbo apparently found the making of *Mata Hari* to be pleasurable. Daniels also found her more relaxed and amenable to creative improvisation. "Miss Garbo's understanding of camera technique is remarkable," said Daniels. "She makes every effort to cooperate with the cameraman and she really appreciates the difficulties and different requirements of photographing scenes from various angles. She is the most patient and sympathetic player with whom I have ever been associated in pictures." This was important for Daniels, because in this film—for the first time since his brilliant work on *Flesh and the Devil*, *The Mysterious Lady*, and *The Kiss*—he was unhampered by long passages of stagy dialogue and was truly using light to tell a story.

One scene called for Garbo to seduce Novarro on a rainy night. One of her henchmen waits outside, watching for the lights in the apartment to be dimmed—his signal to break in and steal secret dispatches to Russia while the lovers are in the bedroom. Entranced by Garbo, Novarro dims every light but one, a votive light flickering in front of an icon of the Madonna of Kazan. He has promised his mother never to extinguish this candle. Garbo, needing to signal her henchman, and eager to bed Novarro, demands that he put out the candle. Daniels lights Garbo steeply from above, making her

face a blasphemous mask. He lights Novarro from below with the candle, giving him the face of a frightened child kneeling in church.

Novarro gives in, blows out the candle, and then leads Garbo into the bedroom. While they make love and the rain pounds on a skylight, the operative enters, takes the dispatches, carries them to a copy camera, and then brings them back. The script called for Garbo and Novarro to talk in the bedroom while this espionage was proceeding. Daniels had a more cinematic idea for the scene.

I wanted to illuminate the whole scene with just the glow from his cigarette alone. I put a special window behind their heads so that the smoke would drift up past it and be fully visible. Then I had another idea. I'd been to a doctor and he'd put this tiny tube up my nostrils with a brilliant bulb on the end of it. I had a dummy cigarette made with one of those medical bulbs in it, and I stuck the ashes on with glue. I mounted another cigarette under it to cause the smoke. I had a little rheostat by the camera and each time he raised the cigarette to his lips I'd bring the bulb up bright. And the smoke would go up. All you'd see [in the darkness on the screen] was just one gleam.

Mata Hari was directed by George Fitzmaurice, seen here with Novarro and Garbo.

With its delicate balance of light and dark, the scene required continuous adjustments and tests; it took ten hours to shoot. The scene played like this:

CS—Lighted cigarettes of Mata Hari and Rosanoff—the lights move about—Mata's hand is seen as it reaches toward light—and as she puts cigarettes on ash tray at right—their voices are heard.

ROSANOFF
I wish I could look into your eyes.

MATA HARI
Shall I turn on the light?

ROSANOFF
No, please don't.

MATA HARI
Why not?

ROSANOFF
Well—besides, I could never see into your eyes. You have such ridiculously long lashes.

There were other bravura scenes in *Mata Hari*. The film opens with an execution scene, filmed with a camera crane in the Agoura Hills, that is a marvel of visual economy. Mata Hari's trial, instead of having the flat, two-dimensional approach common to such scenes, is made rich by Daniels's use of giant shadows and unorthodox camera angles. Most sensational, of course, is the dance to Shiva. Obviously storyboarded, the scene is a succession of tantalizing vistas, each breathtakingly composed and lit.

Much as Garbo enjoyed working with Daniels, Fitzmaurice, and Novarro, she did not entirely let down her guard. There was the day when she was filming the casino scene with Novarro and a full complement of extras. Fitzmaurice saw that it was going to go into a second day just for one shot. He approached Novarro in the morning. "We have a scene late in the day with some eighty to one hundred extras," said Fitzmaurice. "If Miss Garbo would work one hour late we could finish the scene and dismiss all those extras. Would you mind asking her? You're such good friends." Novarro visited Garbo's dressing room during a break and proposed the idea to her. To everyone's surprise, she agreed. The next day she arrived two hours late. As usual, Novarro sympathized with her.

She wore that gorgeous costume made of many thousands of beads. I think it weighed something like fifty pounds. Naturally it was very fatiguing, going over the scenes again and again to get the correct camera lines and working out traveling shots. It got to be pretty close to five o'clock, and

Miss Garbo was beginning to look tired. Mr. Fitzmaurice was intending to take the scene from another angle when he looked up and saw Miss Garbo removing the elaborate headdress and shaking the hairpins from her head. She smiled graciously, said good night and said she would see us at nine o'clock in the morning. No word of complaint or apology. That's all there was to it. No "I go home!" as I have heard so much about. Just an independence and a courage to do what she believes is the right thing.

Even so, Novarro found her mysterious. "I wondered how Garbo knew when it was just exactly five o'clock, her quitting time. Then one day I learned. Alma, her colored maid, would raise up her makeup box mirror as a signal. When Garbo saw it, she started taking the pins out of her hair without losing another moment."

Mata Hari finished shooting in the third week of November. Only one scene needed reshooting, the spy's admission that she loves her victim. It takes place outside the general's room. She has just shot him to prevent him from framing the young Russian for collusion in their espionage ring. In a December 4 story conference, Thalberg, Fineman, and Edmund Goulding (who was probably going to reshoot the scene) labored over the oldest problem in the arts: who is this character?

The second seduction scene in *Mata Hari* depended on the interplay of light and shadow.

Opposite: This was the vision that ensnared Novarro's character in the first seduction scene.

The second seduction scene in *Mata Hari* was paraphrased by Milton Brown in an artfully lit scene still.

"Up to this time in the picture," said Thalberg, "she has been a very wicked woman. She sees this young, good-looking man, is attracted to him, throws him off after a slight affair, meets him again, and then finds it her duty to spend the night with him. She finds him believing, sweet, and lovely. However, she still goes through with her job and gives them his dispatches. Now this jealous fiend is preparing to expose her to the police. She doesn't mind being exposed herself but wants to protect the boy." Thalberg wanted some speech outside the dead man's room to make the rest of the story work. "If she says, 'You know all about Shubin?' and he says, 'Whatever you have been, whatever you are, we belong together,' then you've got a reason for that woman to go to the hospital [where the flier later lies blinded] and say to him, 'We'll live together.' Then she isn't whining about some fellow she had an affair with. There's the only thing that is in any way different from the average love scene."

Mata Hari premiered on New Year's Eve in New York. Novarro was visiting the city. Garbo was there too, in part to get away from the demands that Acosta was already making on her time, but she did not attend the premiere. It was a smash, portending what M-G-M wanted to believe, but could not quite, in the darkest depression winter yet. *Mata Hari* was on its way to becoming the most profitable film in Garbo's entire career, with a *profit* of more than $1 million. This was in spite of reviews that said things like "she dances rather badly," "her costumes . . . are cruelly unbecoming," and "Novarro lacks vigor. . . . there is too much Latin softness about him." But no one was reading reviews in January 1932. They were either looking for work or watching *Mata Hari*.

Clarence Bull made Garbo's *Mata Hari* portraits on November 19, 1931, and Adrian's costumes gave him liberty to create even more dramatic images than usual.

Opposite: Garbo used her reflection in the camera lens to adjust her poses after Bull set up the angle and composition.

CHAPTER SEVENTEEN

Grand Hotel

Before *Mata Hari* began earning its impressive profits, M-G-M had to acknowledge that Paramount's answer to Greta Garbo was not doing so badly. Marlene Dietrich's first three films with Josef von Sternberg (*The Blue Angel, Morocco,* and *Dishonored*) had brought Paramount a profit of more than *$2 million.* These exercises in style did have detractors. "I didn't know whether I was looking at a spy drama or a hosiery show," *Photoplay's* Leonard Hall wrote of *Dishonored.* "I couldn't see the genius for the legs." Not surprisingly, Adrian made sure to expose Garbo's legs as often as possible in *Mata Hari.* Rumors of a rivalry brought only studied denials from its principals. Dietrich was riding a train from Berlin to Prague when she was interviewed by a Czechoslovakian reporter. "Where did you learn English?" asked the reporter.

Clarence Bull designed this photomontage to illustrate the concept of Hollywood's first all-star film, M-G-M's *Grand Hotel,* which was released in April 1932. Greta Garbo is at center; clockwise from top are Lionel Barrymore, John Barrymore, Wallace Beery, and Joan Crawford.

"Only in Berlin," answered Dietrich.

"How about Greta Garbo?" asked the reporter. "How is her accent?"

"She has one but it is very charming. She has made a hit of it all the way."

"Did you meet Greta Garbo?" the reporter asked.

"Not even once," replied Marlene, who had apparently been advised by Josef von Sternberg to downplay any connection she might have with the Mercedes de Acosta circle. "She doesn't go any place and I don't go anywhere either. There is no possibility of our meeting."

The reporter sensed something. "Marlene is a lady, but just the same she has something of the real bohemian about her. Of course an artist must have some bohemian characteristics. . . . She glances at her red-colored fingernails, her boyish costume and cloak."

"I suppose you hardly expected me to wear anything like this," said Dietrich. "[People] are always thinking about *The Blue Angel* and cabarets and such. I prefer *Morocco.* That's really the film. And Gary Cooper is a marvelous partner. An excellent actor. And Sternberg is a director in a class by himself. I am going back to Hollywood very soon and I don't know yet what picture I shall act in there. I really don't, and I don't worry about it either."

If Dietrich had hinted that her next film would take place on a train, she might have been met with disbelief, as was Sternberg when he told B. P. Schulberg, Paramount's head of production: "Okay . . . this time I'll put Marlene on a train." What kind of movie could take place entirely on a train? For that matter, what kind of movie could take place solely in a hotel? But Sternberg had been reading the newspapers.

Irving Thalberg was interviewed in New York in May 1931 after seeing a play called *Grand Hotel.* Its claim to fame was that it observed the dramatic unities of time and place in a new fashion: the lives of five unrelated characters are mingled and changed by a twenty-four-hour stay in a luxury hotel. "The swift-moving, episodic character of [this] play will probably serve as a pattern for many films," said Thalberg. "I don't mean that the exact theme of *Grand Hotel* will be copied, though this may happen, but that the form and mood will be followed. For instance, we may have such settings as a train, where all the action happens in a journey from one city to another; or action that takes place during the time a boat sails from one harbor and culminates with the end of a trip. The general idea will be that of drama induced by the chance meeting of a group of conflicting and interesting personalities."

The Fox Film Corporation was the first to use this template. William K. Howard's *Transatlantic*, released in August 1931, had a group of characters working out their intertwined destinies on an ocean voyage. It was reviewed as an "aquatic *Grand Hotel*." At Paramount, Sternberg was preparing his multicharacter train story. It remained for Thalberg and M-G-M to make the definitive *Grand Hotel*. They needed to; they owned a stake in it.

In November 1930 there appeared an item by Elizabeth Yeaman in the *Hollywood Citizen-News*:

> There is a new play on Broadway that is one of the hits of the season. Although Herman Shumlin is said to be the producer, it is generally known on Broadway that M-G-M advanced two thirds of the capital to stage the production. The play calls for such a large cast and elaborate settings that several New York producers decided it was just too expensive to stage. Now *Grand Hotel* seems to have justified the faith and money that went into it. According to current rumors, M-G-M has an option on the picture rights of the play, and they are planning to buy it as a future Greta Garbo vehicle.

Yeaman was accurate except for two things: (1) M-G-M had invested $13,500 for a one-half interest in the play; and (2) it spent $35,000 for screen rights to the novel on which the play was based, Vicki Baum's *Menschen im Hotel* (*People in a Hotel*). The German author researched her story by working as a chambermaid in two Berlin hotels, where she observed a scandal involving a ballerina, a businessman, and a call girl. She wove these incidents into a multi-pointed narrative. The businessman needs to effect a merger in the hotel to save his textile firm. His fatally ill bookkeeper has come to the hotel to spend his life savings. A stenographer hired by the businessman needs to supplement her meager earnings with prostitution. A fading ballerina staying in the hotel contemplates suicide. A baron comes to the hotel to steal the ballerina's pearls. Instead, he ends up befriending the bookkeeper, enchanting the stenographer, falling in love with the ballerina, and running afoul of the vicious businessman. The average feature film was a vehicle designed to carry one star; this film would accommodate five, and each of them would have standout scenes.

Baum went to M-G-M to work on the script with Thalberg, but there was not much for her to do, since William A. Drake's playscript had done an almost cinematic translation of her story. Thalberg's most pressing concern was to properly cast the film. Samuel Marx became M-G-M's story edi-

tor in mid-1930 and saw *Grand Hotel* evolve from a stage hit to a project that Thalberg hoped would signal a new narrative form, revitalize some careers, and, of course, stave off depression worries. Both movie theaters and banks were still closing at an alarming rate. As Marx recalled: "An immense amount of soul-searching went on in meetings between

Marlene Dietrich's first 1932 film, *Shanghai Express*, bore a structural resemblance to *Grand Hotel*. No one could accuse Dietrich of copying Garbo. Dietrich understood and used the art of lighting to create character. Lionel Barrymore once said that a cameraman "made love to his light." Dietrich enjoyed a similar relation with her key light, as illustrated by this Don English photo.

Cinematographer Lee Garmes discovered that a certain angle of light, the so-called north light, made Marlene Dietrich look like no one else. Her Hollywood career began with a series of films in which that lighting scheme was used by her Svengali-like director, Josef von Sternberg, to mythologize her. Photograph by Eugene Robert Richee

Greta Garbo's face was as marvelous a canvas for photographers as Dietrich's. Angles of lighting that would be unflattering for another subject only emphasized her beauty. Photograph by Clarence Bull

Thalberg and [Paul] Bern over the actor who was to portray the dissolute gambler, Baron von Gaigern. John Gilbert, struggling with a career that had plummeted with the coming of talkies, told his friends at the studio that he was born for it, that many nights of drinking and carousing had been done in the company of Thalberg and Bern. They knew that he could act the part without rehearsal." The dying bookkeeper could be played by Buster Keaton, whose career was also in trouble. The ruthless industrialist could be played by Clark Gable. Norma Shearer had first choice of every important female role, but fan mail persuaded her not to play the stenographer. Thalberg called Joan Crawford into his office; she was not interested. "I don't want to do *Grand Hotel*, Irving."

"Are you crazy? It's the best opportunity you've ever had," said Thalberg, who reminded her that she had been persistently asking for a prestige picture. Thalberg implied that if Crawford turned down the role, it could go to Shearer.

"Yes, but why must I look shabby, with only one dress?" asked Crawford.

"All right. Adrian will make you two dresses—and a peignoir."

With Crawford settled, all that remained was to secure Garbo. Her contract was due to expire on January 1, 1932. There had been, however, those vacations and absences in 1928 and 1929. Louis B. Mayer added them to the end of her contract, extending it to April 24. After that, who could tell

what she would do? More important than second-guessing her was getting the most from her while she was still agreeable (and accountable). She had been unhappy—and rightly so—with the scripts of *Inspiration* and *Susan Lenox*. *Grand Hotel* would be a welcome change. She would be playing not only a ballerina but also a star, and for the first time she would be portraying a mature woman. On the other hand, this would be the first film since *The Atonement of Gösta Berling* in which she was not the center of attention; for all his vaunted status, Ramon Novarro functioned merely as a leading man in *Mata Hari*. Since *Grand Hotel* would have five stars, Garbo would be appearing in less than ten of its thirty scenes. This brought up another question: how could Garbo costar with Crawford and the others? Her contract stipulated top billing.

A special agreement was drawn up. In it, Greta Garbo would grant M-G-M permission to bill her as "Garbo." The change of name would wriggle around the contract and make it possible for her to appear with other stars in *Grand Hotel*. Harry Edington took the document to his client's new residence on North Rockingham Drive in the Brentwood district of Los Angeles. "I took this up with Miss G.," wrote Harry Edington, "and she tells me as follows. That the billing is all right as far as she is concerned and [she] doesn't care anything about it. However, I could not get her to sign in the space specified by you. There is no reason for her not to sign, except for the reason, she simply doesn't sign papers." The M-G-M legal department accepted this idiosyncrasy and gave Thalberg the go-ahead. He next needed to cast a director. Instead of assigning an in-house veteran like Clarence Brown or Sidney Franklin, he interviewed Edmund Goulding, who had directed Garbo in *Love* four years earlier. According to Sam Marx: "Thalberg was influenced by a belief that Goulding's homosexuality would bring new dimensions to the performances of Greta Garbo and Joan Crawford."

"Eddie thinks like a woman," Thalberg told Marx. "He'll bring out their femininity. I want them to stand out [from] the men." Thalberg offered Goulding, who had just had a flop with the Paramount Nancy Carroll film *Night Angel*, a generous contract for $1,000 a week, which would include preparation and direction of two films. Thalberg got more than his money's worth, since the creative and conscientious Goulding, even while preparing *Grand Hotel*, was constantly offering Thalberg ideas for new projects as well as attending story conferences for existing projects. And he drafted the first complete script for *Grand Hotel*.

Vicki Baum's story made the baron the pivotal character, but it probed most deeply into the mind of Elisaveta Grusinskaya, the ballerina whose stardom is being eroded by the ineluctable approach of middle age.

Opposite: Garbo's suicidal character in *Grand Hotel* was a departure from the self-determining temptresses she usually played.

In John Barrymore, Garbo had her strongest and most charismatic leading man since John Gilbert—and, according to his brother, Lionel, "He was a damned fine actor."

Turning on the light over the center of the mirror, she grasped its frame with both hands and pressed her face close up to the glass, as though she meant to plunge right into it. The attention with which she then studied her face had something probing, greedy, and gruesome about it. . . . Grusinskaya fixed her eyes on her face as though on the face of an enemy. With horror she saw the tell-tale years, the wrinkles, the flabbiness, the fatigue, the withering; her temples were smooth no longer, the corners of her mouth were disfigured, her eyelids, under the blue paint, were as creased as crumpled tissue paper.

Drake's adaptation used dialogue to convey Grusinskaya's well-founded fears. In the same scene, Baron von Gaigern, hiding in her room with her pearls in his pocket, sees her mixing a fatal dose of sleeping powder into her tea. Instead of letting her continue (so that he can escape undetected), he stops her from swallowing it and asks her what would drive a world-famous star to such an act. "Nobody has loved me for a long time," she tells him. "I have been left to freeze with loneliness. It is so ice-cold to be famous. Success perches you up as ice-cold, as lonely, as if you were sitting on the North Pole. . . . One isn't a personality any more, not a woman! One is just a dried-out piece of responsibility that is driven round and round the world. On the day success

ceases, on the day one ceases to think one is self-important, life ceases."

Grand Hotel was the first Garbo film to be personally supervised by Thalberg since *Anna Christie*, and, as much as he admired both Baum's book and Drake's play, he knew that the film could not be a photographed stage play. It had to be that unique amalgam of image and sound that is true cinema. To that end, he embarked on a series of intensive story conferences. Meeting with Goulding, Bern, and Hungarian playwright Frank Partos, Thalberg dissected, probed, and analyzed *Grand Hotel*, continually referring to the excitement of the Broadway production and citing the need to engage the film audience in the same way—with believable characters. "The thing that is so important to an audience is this: by this time they love our *personal* character. They say 'Aha! This is like *my* life.' They understand why it's not a bit important to the hotel night clerk that 'Somebody was killed up there.'" Whether it was the character of the head porter, who was less concerned with a murder than with his wife's difficulties in the maternity ward, or the neurotic ballerina, Thalberg wanted the authenticity that would make this complex story work.

By December 26, 1931, it was obvious that the important scene between Grusinskaya and the baron was not working. Goulding, a former novelist, was writing speeches that were

Instead of retreating to her dressing room between camera setups, Garbo visited with the genial and witty John Barrymore. "She is a fine lady and a great actress," said Barrymore. "'And the rest is silence.'"

too long. "You have two pages of protestation of love," Thalberg said to him. "You're overstressing the man's lovemaking. He says: 'I love you.' She bursts into tears. He comforts her. He would *not* say, 'No, let me stay.' This is sex! You don't want tenderness until morning." Goulding was sent off to rewrite the scene. The final draft took into account the star who would be saying the lines. She could make the word "alone" sound like an entire line of dialogue. And it resonated with as much of her real life as her fans knew. The long lines were shortened, and the word "alone" was emphasized. The novel and playscript both had Grusinskaya say, "I wish to be alone." Goulding changed that to "I want to be alone," which sounded like something that Garbo would really say. And he had her say it not once, but three times.

Solitude was also being espoused by John Gilbert, whose casting (along with Gable and Keaton) had recently been confirmed in the trades. As the start of filming approached, Thalberg began to have second thoughts about casting Gilbert. Sam Marx recalled: "His sunny personality had disappeared, he was morose, his nights filled with imagined dangers. He slept with a revolver nearby." When Thalberg had made the initial announcement, Gilbert had only experienced the failure of three films. M-G-M had then pushed him into three medium-budget projects: *Gentleman's Fate*, *The Phantom of Paris*, and *West of Broadway*. There was little to recommend any of them—not scripts, direction, or leading ladies. What they had in common was a grim, dark, doomed quality, as if someone had put a hex on Gilbert. His voice sounded good in some scenes but metallic in others, especially if he had a solo speech. He appeared to be strug-

gling with the inferior material and looked increasingly dispirited. The three films flopped.

Rumors spread through the sound and editing departments. According to assistant film editor Chester W. Schaeffer: "The sound mixers were told to fix the equalization so that Gilbert's voice sounded queer." Clarence Brown later confirmed the rumors to Gilbert's daughter, Leatrice Gilbert Fountain. "I know what happened," said Brown in 1973. "I was there. Douglas Shearer [head of the sound department] told me himself. He said, 'We never turned up the bass when Gilbert spoke. All you heard was treble.'" Was this corporate intrigue intended to break the expensive contract that Nicholas Schenck had foisted on the company? "Louis B. Mayer was my best friend in pictures," said Brown. "I'm not going to say anything about anyone who is not here to defend himself." Mayer's daughter, though, recalled Mayer returning from the studio one night and commenting on Gilbert's disastrous reviews. "That should take care of *Mr. Gilbert*," said Mayer. Whether he had sabotaged Gilbert or whether the actor was simply the victim of a fickle public, the fact remained that his three 1931 films had failed and that he was increasingly unstable.

Marx overheard Thalberg talking about John Barrymore for the role of Baron von Gaigern. Barrymore had just finished filming the detective thriller *Arsene Lupin* with his brother, Lionel, at M-G-M. John Barrymore also had a hard-drinking reputation, but the prospect of teaming this matinee idol with Garbo made Gilbert look dull by comparison. "Thalberg decided that he had no choice and broke the news to Gilbert personally," wrote Marx. "They would continue to communicate thereafter—it was necessary in order to do business—but their friendship was finished." The new cast lineup also eliminated Buster Keaton, who was falling out of favor because of his drinking. He was replaced in the role of

"You are the most entrancing woman in the world," John Barrymore said to Garbo on the set one day.

the bookkeeper Kringelein by Lionel Barrymore. Gable was also removed from the lineup. He was replaced by Wallace Beery, who did not want the role of the industrialist: "I shot my mouth off to everybody in power," he later said, "but it didn't do a bit of good." Gable could not feel too bad; he was moved to the studio's other prestige film, *Strange Interlude*.

"Greta Garbo was my favorite actress in the world," said Crawford. "For three years I'd come out of my dressing room every day, run past hers, and call 'Good morning!' I could hear her deep voice talking to her maid but she never did speak to me. I'd see her occasionally on the lot. Never a word. Then one morning there was a rush call. Someone was ill and couldn't show up for still art in the gallery. Wouldn't I come and pose in their place? I went sprinting past Garbo's dressing room in such a hurry I forgot to yell 'Good morning.' An instant later I heard her door open, then a resonant 'Allooooo!'"

Now Crawford was not only going to meet her idol; she was going to costar with her. "At last I get to work with Garbo!" she crowed. Goulding spoke with Garbo about

Fred Archer was engaged to shoot poster art of Garbo and John Barrymore on January 27, because Garbo refused to work with George Hurrell again.

scheduling. She told Goulding that she did not want to attend group rehearsals. "I rehearse at home," she stated flatly, and there was not much he could do about it, other than to invite her to a get-acquainted meeting before she left for Christmas vacation in New York. "Greta did agree to attend the first conference," recalled Goulding, "where Louis B. Mayer and Irving Thalberg would be present." The conference was scheduled for 9:00 A.M. Everyone was present except one.

"'Where the hell is that Swede?' Wallace Beery asked.

"The next moment the door opened and Greta entered the room," recalled Goulding. "Everyone knew each other except Greta and Joan. Greta extended her hand and sat next to Joan. [Greta] was amiable, charming and she chatted with everyone present. Yes, even Joan. Mostly with Joan."

After taking the scripts home, both actresses called Goulding. "Eddie, there are no scenes between Miss Crawford and me," said Garbo. "Why is this?"

"I explained to them that *Grand Hotel*, when you take a hard look at it, is two films in one," said Goulding. The central character in each of the films was a woman in crisis, and the two films were linked by the character of the baron. Crawford was further disappointed when she attended the first rehearsal on December 28. Unlike Wallace Beery, Purnell Pratt, and Tully Marshall, Crawford was on time. "Her habit of punctuality cheated her of a good entrance," recalled Goulding. After all were accounted for, Goulding signaled the beginning of the session. "But Miss Garbo has not arrived," said Crawford.

"Miss Garbo has been excused from all rehearsals," explained Goulding.

Filming commenced on January 4, 1932, in a conference-room set with Crawford and Beery. Both were a little stiff, possibly because Beery had walked out of a rehearsal, saying that he would return when Crawford learned how to act. When columnist Dorothy Manners visited the set, she could sense the tension. "Here was a Joan I hardly recognized," she said later. "There was something almost desperate about her . . . a feverish determination not to be swamped by the glamour of Garbo, by the illustriousness of the Barrymores, by the hit-you-in-the-eye personality of Wallace Beery." Goulding was patient and persuasive, and soon he had tamed his first cinematic lions. Next came John Barrymore. Cameraman William Daniels approached the formidable star and asked him, "How do they light you?"

"I have no more idea how they light me than I have how they light a firefly's tail," replied Barrymore. "But I know how I want to look. I'm fifty years old and I want to look like Jackie Cooper's grandson." There was more to it than that, since Barrymore was in truth partial to his left side and concerned that his dewlaps not register on film. Daniels took the appropriate care, even in tracking shots, of which there were many, since Goulding wanted to use the camera as a "walking personality" among the characters.

On January 14 there was snow in Los Angeles, and John Barrymore was waiting on the set at nine for Garbo to arrive for their first day of work together. After waiting for more than twenty minutes, he was growing a bit irritated. Suddenly a prop boy approached him. "I didn't know you were here, Mr. Barrymore," said the boy. "Miss Garbo has been waiting outside the door since nine o'clock to escort you onto the set. It was an honor she wanted to pay you." Barrymore followed him to the door of the soundstage, where he greeted Garbo with the salutation: "My wife and I think you the loveliest person in the world."

"This is a great day for me," Garbo responded. "How I have looked forward to working with John Barrymore!" Filming went well on the first day, and then they had no scenes together for a week. The production was scheduled in double shifts. Goulding would work until five with Garbo and then work with Crawford from six until whenever they ran out of steam. Crawford still did not see Garbo. "One evening," wrote Crawford, "I was just starting to the set when she came up the stairs to her dressing room. I was with [my publicist] Jerry Asher. I literally shoved him into a corner and followed him into it so we would both be out of her way. She'd just finished working. She'd be tired and wouldn't want to be greeted. Just then, the vibrant voice said 'Alloooo!'

"I murmured hello and bolted for the stairs from which she'd just emerged. She caught me in passing. There suddenly above me was that beautiful face with those compelling eyes, and the woman I'd thought was so aloof was saying: 'I'm so sorry we are not working together. What a pity, eh? Our first picture together and not one scene.'"

This behind-the-scenes photo shows Edmund Goulding directing Garbo's first shot in *Grand Hotel*.

To help Garbo film her solo scenes in the hotel bedroom, a technician named Dominic McBride stood by with a gramophone and an assortment of records. For tense scenes, Garbo had him play the *Peer Gynt Suite, Tristan und Isolde,* or *Prelude to the Afternoon of a Faun*; for sad scenes there was the Swedish folk song "O Vermland," or "The Last Spring" by Grieg; and for love scenes there would be the waltzes from *Der Rosenkavalier* by Richard Straus, "On Wings of Song" by Mendelssohn, "Albumblatt" by Richard Wagner, or "Vienna, City of My Dreams" by Rudolf Sieczynski (which was also destined for the film's sound track). One day while Garbo was filming, Louis B. Mayer came onto the soundstage and went into the sound booth with John Barrymore to watch the filming from high above the stage, thinking that she would not see them. Before long Garbo sensed that someone was watching her, and little by little, she lost her concentration. Finally, she stopped and said to Goulding: "I'm sorry, but I can't go on any more today."

John Barrymore exercised caution in his next scenes with Garbo, which took place in the bedroom on Monday, January 25. Sitting across from her as Daniels lined up a two-shot, he said, "You are the most entrancing woman in the world." The subsequent scene played with exquisite timing. Suddenly Garbo leaned forward and kissed him.

"You have no idea what it means to me to play opposite so perfect an artist," she said.

For their scene the next day, Garbo showed a rare concern for a costar. She spent her lunch break rearranging the plush silk-upholstered chairs so that Barrymore could play the scene with his left profile to the camera. "I was touched to think she would make that generous effort so the camera could wander up and down my left—or money-making—profile," said Barrymore.

The honeymoon was jarred by the arrival on the set of Barrymore's friend Arthur Brisbane, editor of the *New York*

Garbo is flanked by Ferdinand Gottschalk, Greta Meyer, and Rafaela Ottiano. The versatile Ottiano also appeared in the Broadway production of *Grand Hotel*. "Rafaela was an artist," said Goulding later.

Journal. Garbo got up quickly and said that she would return when the stranger had left. "If he wants to see me, he can see me in the theater." she told Barrymore after she had returned. "Do you know him?"

"Know him? I used to work for him."

"What?" said Garbo. "You? A newspaperman?"

"Oh, I was just a cartoonist."

"Ah, that's better," she smiled. "Much better."

"I wasn't there when Brisbane came on the set and she walked off," said Lionel Barrymore in 1952, "but it would have been the same if it had been Jesus Christ. She didn't do it to be snotty. She was frightened. She was like a cat that went under the bed when a stranger came into the room. When only the family was around," he explained, "she bounded around, playing with different-colored yarn." Even though the 1927 *Anna Karenina* had been scrapped, and Kringelein shared no scenes with Grusinskaya, Lionel Barrymore counted this as his fourth film with Garbo; he was by now well acquainted with her habits. "She wasn't afraid of the staff, the electricians, or the cameraman. She respected his work. He was always doing something. He made love to his light, was always adjusting it. He didn't care whether Garbo was there or whoever. He was as stuck on that light as [he would be] on some floozy."

John Barrymore was also in awe of the technician that Garbo was. In fact, he was frightened of her, as he confided to Mercedes de Acosta. "Not because she is difficult," he said. "Far from it. But just because she is so perfect as an artist and as a woman. Why has no one ever said that she has such a sense of humor? Do you know, she is always telling me some funny joke on the set and she sees little things to laugh at. Little things most people wouldn't notice. She's really most amusing." She even managed to be cheerful and solicitous when he arrived on the set with a hangover. She brought him to her dressing room and served him an herbal drink. John Barrymore agreed with his brother about Garbo's privacy requirements.

"There is no reason in the world why Garbo should be expected to work in front of visitors," he said. "It isn't like being on the stage, where one is prepared for an audience. On a motion-picture set, one is creating a role, not simply repeating a performance. What would some portrait artist think if his studio door suddenly were opened and a crowd of strangers trooped in and started to watch over his shoulder?" On one of their last days together on the set, Garbo remarked that she thought a certain Hollywood actor was very good. "There are no good actors," said John. "There are only bad ones who try to make themselves and others think they are good. Some can bring it off. Others can't." Although he appeared to be napping, Lionel was watching from the sidelines. "She was nice to Jack," said Lionel. "He was a damned fine actor. That counted. She was concerned with art with a capital A."

After Goulding finished Garbo's intimate scenes with John, there remained the scenes in which she walked regally through the lobby of the hotel. "Now, Miss Garbo," said Goulding from his perch atop a camera crane, "all you want to do is get away from these people. You go through them like a frightened deer pursued by bloodhounds. Now, do you want to rehearse this scene?"

"No. I rehearsed it at the St. Moritz Hotel in New York last month."

Garbo's wry remark was much appreciated but, according to Sam Marx, she had indeed been rehearsing her singular stride. "One afternoon," recalled Marx, "I heard footsteps outside my office window, a pacing back and forth, back and forth. It varied each time, in the speed and rhythm of the steps. Finally I got up to look, and there was Garbo in the alleyway, deep in concentration. She would do a length, put her hand on her chin and puzzle there for a while, then go at it again. I realized that she was working, figuring out how her character would move."

Filming was completed on February 19, and by mid-March Thalberg and Goulding were reviewing a rough cut. On March 17 it was loaded into three suitcases and flown to a sneak preview in Monterey, California. The preview cards said that Garbo was just a little too dour for their liking. Some wanted more Crawford; some wanted more Garbo. Thalberg ordered retakes in which Garbo had to walk through the lobby yet again. A Los Angeles woman named Mona Rogers managed to get onto the set without alerting Garbo. "Not once did I hear the famous 'I t'ank I go home,'" Rogers wrote *Photoplay*. "Not once were the other members of the cast hurled into abject silence to mollify the tempestuous *artiste*. She is a tall, slender girl in a simple black dressing gown, working earnestly and courteously." Goulding used a double to impersonate Garbo in long shot, but she did not do Garbo's walk correctly. Goulding took her fur coat and showed her how it should be done. Garbo, meanwhile, had shown up and was watching this exhibition. "When Mr. Goulding relieved the tedium by strutting across the stage foppishly with a woman's coat wrapped around him," recounted Rogers, "Garbo laughed as heartily and unaffectedly as anyone on the set."

Retakes were completed on March 29, which did not leave much time for editing, scoring, negative cutting, and printing for the April 12 New York premiere at the Astor Theatre. Meanwhile, Marlene Dietrich's train movie had opened. *Shanghai Express* was getting extraordinary reviews, as well it should have, because it was a cinematic accomplishment, a love poem to Dietrich written in light, shadow, smoke, and feathers. The money started rolling in, but too late to prevent Paramount from going into receivership.

Opposite: This portrait was made on April 13, 1932. Garbo, the greatest star in Hollywood, had eleven days left on her contract.

Clarence Bull's portraits of Garbo showed a more contemplative artist with each sitting.

Shanghai Express was called "a *Grand Hotel* on wheels," but it had only one star. On April 12, New York saw the real thing.

"Worshipers of the stars of the Hollywood firmament choked the sidewalk outside the Astor and also the theater lobby, while policemen afoot and on horse urged the throng to keep moving," wrote Mordaunt Hall in his April 13 *New York Times* review. "And from across Broadway blinding beams of light added to the general excitement. Inside the theater it was for a time difficult to move but very slowly, for many of those who had tickets pressed into the aisles and behind the orchestra seats with the evident hope of catching a glimpse of one or another cinema celebrity." After he finished his account of the opening, Hall got down to the business of telling Manhattan what to expect on the screen. "It is a production thoroughly worthy of all the talk it has created," wrote Hall, "and the several motion-picture luminaries deserve to feel very proud of their performances, particularly Greta Garbo and Lionel Barrymore. So far as the direction is concerned, Edmund Goulding has done an excellent piece of work but occasionally it seems as though he relies too much on close-ups."

Grand Hotel, including the close-ups that the country's most important critic thought gratuitous, cost a total of $695,341.20, much of which obviously went to star salaries.

Making the film had been a risky proposition, given the country's dismal economic condition, but it was a scant week before it became obvious that the risk was paying off, at least in New York. The film opened in Hollywood later in the month. As in New York, audiences cheered at the shots of the hotel lobby taken from the soundstage roof, and at the first appearance of each star, both in the innovative credits and in each scene. The glamour of an imaginary hotel in newly troubled Germany brought cheer to Americans beset with their own problems. In the end, the film grossed $2,594,000 and made a profit of $947,000, although these figures may well have been softened for the sake of the Internal Revenue Service; like movie close-ups, movie accounting was often diffused. What was important to Garbo was that she had finally gotten a fine script, a fine director, and a regal costar. For once she had made a film without the obligatory formula, and she was getting the best reviews of her seven-year career. Even the author of *Grand Hotel* (whom she had asked to leave the set of the film one day) was enthusiastic. Writing in *Modern Screen*, Vicki Baum had this to say:

> Here Greta Garbo has achieved something which few people expected of her. She has fitted herself into a play and into a cast and has rendered a great performance exactly at that point where the role was contrary to her own being. The twittering, laughing, hopping about in the tarlatan of a ballet skirt is certainly not what Greta would have sought out as her role. But she has accomplished it. She's gone the whole way from her first words, "I have never been so tired in my life," to the last words, "It will be sunny in Tremezzo. We'll have a guest, Suzette." That dead-tired face in the beginning—where did Greta get those small, sad lines around her mouth and forehead? Then that face in which—between laughter and tears—love awakens. That face full of wanton joy when she is happy. That face full of fear when she waits for her beloved in vain. Unforgettable! Thank you, Greta Garbo!

Grand Hotel was more than a hit for M-G-M and for Garbo; it was a triumph. There was little time to savor it, though, as the days ran out on Garbo's contract. Instead of going to the portrait gallery after the completion of filming, Garbo put it off until she was almost finished with her next film, *As You Desire Me*. She posed for Clarence Bull in the costumes from both films in one all-day sitting on April 13. Bull wondered (but dared not ask) if this was the last time he would ever photograph his favorite subject. No one knew what Garbo would do when her contract expired—not M-G-M, not Harry Edington, not Salka Viertel, not Mercedes de Acosta—not even Greta Garbo.

CHAPTER EIGHTEEN

As You Desire Me

In the spring of 1932, the cultural phenomenon known as Garbomania reached its peak. Greta Garbo had two blockbuster hits in simultaneous release, two 1931 films still making the rounds, and a new film—rumored to be her last—in production. Her films were enjoying long runs for a simple reason: people were paying to see them more than once. This was indeed phenomenal when eight major studios were offering a new film every week. "One sitting at a motion picture is usually a great plenty for your ordinary screen fan at your ordinary picture," wrote columnist Jim Crow. "Two sittings are usually too exacting a call upon a fan's patience. Three sittings are cause for hysteria. But *Mata Hari* stands up to the test, like a good book read again and again." After seeing *Grand Hotel*, another reviewer wrote, "It will be hard to refuse Garbo whatever she wants—even ten thousand a week—after such a performance." Playwright Robert Sherwood, a fan since *The Torrent*, wrote that Garbo was "the finest actress that the screen has ever known."

In response to this adulation, Garbo remained resolutely unavailable for autographs, interviews, or social functions. She was receiving more than 5,000 fan letters a week, but by this time she no longer bothered to sample even a few. She had M-G-M burn most of them. "I [didn't] feel any responsibility for what I didn't ask for," she said later. "In some strange way I never felt that any of it was personal. It scared me as well, because there were people who wrote really smutty letters. Obviously I had to have help with it, to make sure nothing valuable was discarded, but I spent very little time on it myself." In a renewed effort to elude the mail that reached her home, not to mention the increasing number of fans who staked out her driveway, she moved again, this time to Cliffwood Drive in Brentwood, not far from her *Grand Hotel* costar Joan Crawford. None of Garbo's neighbors ever saw her, especially after she put a canvas cover on the fence around her tennis court. It was a newsworthy event when Salka Viertel took her to lunch one day on the roof garden of the Hotel Roosevelt in Hollywood. "An electrical thrill ran through the guests," wrote Molly Merrick in the *Hollywood Citizen-News*.

My waiter whispered excitedly: "Look at her, Madame! She is as dramatic at the luncheon table as she is on the screen."

True enough, the pale girl in the marine blue beret moved her hands as eloquently in relating some incident to her companion as she has in any of her screen parts. She is more animated sometimes offscreen than on, and those two oversized front teeth that are the trademark of the Garbo countenance and that thwart all would-be imitators are unusually attractive in her sculptured countenance.

Time was running out for Garbo's contract. On December 27, 1931, *Variety* printed an article entitled "Garbo

In her seventeenth American film, *As You Desire Me*, Greta Garbo portrayed a cabaret singer who looked suspiciously like her rival at Paramount Pictures. The silent-cinema genius Erich von Stroheim portrayed her sadistic protector.

A lapsed contract implied that Garbo would return to Sweden after completing *As You Desire Me. Photoplay* wrote: "If this must be her last picture, we are glad it is such a fitting swan song."

Asking for More Money in New Deal." It said that she was "desirous of increasing her weekly check to $10,000 if she enters into another agreement." On December 31, Harry Edington's own contract with M-G-M expired. The studio's accounting would no longer compete with Garbo for his attention. Now he could devote all his time to personal management, beginning with the negotiation of a new contract. That contract was the subject of excited speculation. "It looks very, very much as if Greta Garbo's annual threat, 'I go home to Sweden,' is serious this time," said one article. "Greta's contract is up June 1 and she hasn't indicated in any way that she intends to re-sign." Some reporters were mistakenly calculating the expiration date from the 1927 signing date; in fact, the contract had been made retroactive to January 1, 1927. It should have expired January 1, 1932, but Garbo's absences had extended it to April 24, 1932. Even so, its unresolved status had all of M-G-M worried.

Numerous articles claimed to know Garbo's plans. One said that she was planning to remake both *The Torrent* and *The Temptress*. Another said that Thalberg was preparing *Black Oxen*, the Gertrude Atherton best seller about a fifty-year-old woman whose aging process is reversed by a mysterious ray aimed at her ovaries. Other rumors had Garbo demanding $14,000 a week, producing her own version of *Salome*, or moving to Warner Bros. Edington denied that

Garbo was planning to marry Wilhelm Sörenson, but there was no denying that she was putting her immigration papers and passport in order.

Paramount Pictures, still facing bankruptcy, sought to capitalize on the Garbo situation with more Marlene Dietrich films, but the German star was not cooperating. She wanted to film her own screenplay about a mother and her child in depression-torn America. She had been paid $12,000 for it and was determined to make it, in spite of resistance from executives such as Emmanuel Cohen, who wrote: "We fail to see this type of mysterious and glamorous personality obtaining the sympathy of the audience as the mother of a child rather than as a sensual lover." While Paramount went back and forth with Dietrich, M-G-M looked for a Garbo project that could start immediately after *Grand Hotel*.

Mercedes de Acosta, the woman Garbo called a "crazy mystic Spaniard," found herself suddenly without work or prospects after her *East River* (which she wrote with John Colton) was shelved by RKO-Pathé Pictures. She sank into one of her periodic depressions. One day during the making of *Mata Hari*, Garbo came directly from the studio to Acosta's house. "After trying to make me guess what she had up her sleeve," wrote Acosta, "she finally told me that she had talked to Irving Thalberg about my writing a story for her.

She said he wanted to see me the next morning and that if I could think of an idea he would surely put me under contract. All that night I tossed around in bed trying to invent a story that would be right for her. Toward morning I hit on an idea and a title, which was *Desperate*."

Drawing on her own family history, she pitched Thalberg the story of Erik Chanler, a high-strung girl whose mother jumps off a cliff. (Acosta's father had committed suicide in this fashion.) To recover from this trauma, Erik adopts Nietzsche's philosophy. "One must learn to live desperately," she declares, embarking on a series of adventures that recall the jaunty Iris March of *The Green Hat*. Thalberg liked what he heard and installed Acosta in the writers department, where she spent the winter developing her ambiguous heroine. "One feels in her," wrote Acosta, "sadness and gayety [*sic*], sanity and neuroticism, vitality and listlessness, shyness and daring—all of these mixed in a mad contradiction that spends her own strength and throws her back upon herself—that makes her forever a mystery to the ordinary mortal. In her eyes one already sees the doom that comes from the soul rather than [from] outward events."

Erik's ambiguity is not only internal. After her friend Toto is killed in a Harlem nightclub, she disguises herself as a boy in order to hide from the police and spends a disproportionate length of the story in drag, attracting feminine attentions. "Each woman feels there is some unfathomable mystery in this beautiful, pale, Shelley-like boy—that no one can move to talk . . . who has never been seen to smile—who is indifferent and disinterested in the life around him. Everyone wonders about him."

Thalberg began to wonder about Acosta, too, about her influence over Garbo, and about the effect of such a role on Garbo's career. "Do you want to put all America and all the women's clubs against her?" he asked Acosta. "You must be out of your mind."

Acosta told him that Garbo liked the idea of masquerading as a boy.

"She must be out of her mind, too," said Thalberg. "I simply won't have that sequence in. I am in this business to make money on films and I won't have this one ruined." There was also the issue of Garbo's waning contract. Her last film had to be a strong one, and this was no time to abandon the formula. "We have been building Garbo up for years as a great glamorous actress," he said angrily, "and you come along and try to put her into pants and make a monkey out of her."

Not surprisingly, Thalberg dumped *Desperate* in favor of Luigi Pirandello's play *As You Desire Me*, the story of an amnesiac survivor of a wartime abduction. Elma is a Berlin dancer who must choose between the familiar and the unknown. The familiar is a decadent rut with a sadistic novelist; the unknown is a fresh start with an idealistic nobleman who believes that she is Cia, the wife he lost ten years

earlier to invading troops. *As You Desire Me*, with its older man–younger man triangle, conformed superficially to Thalberg's formula for a successful Garbo film, so he assigned the script to Gene Markey, the production to Paul Bern, and direction to George Fitzmaurice. As Bruno, the Italian nobleman, Bern cast Melvyn Douglas, who had just made a successful screen debut in Gloria Swanson's *Tonight or Never*. Casting Carl Salter, the sadistic novelist, was more difficult. A suggestion came from an unexpected source. Garbo had recently seen a lurid RKO film called *Friends and Lovers*, which starred Adolphe Menjou, Laurence Olivier, and Lili Damita. What impressed Garbo was seeing Erich von Stroheim in it, whipping Damita. While Menjou would make a suave Salter, Stroheim would be vividly depraved.

Only three years earlier, Stroheim had been an esteemed filmmaker, directing Gloria Swanson in a Joseph Kennedy super-production called *Queen Kelly*. Garbo had heard Mauritz Stiller say many times that Stroheim was the most important man in American films. "I would like to do something all the other people are not doing," she told the *New York Times* in 1929. "If I could get von Stroheim! Isn't he

Like most M-G-M films of 1932, *As You Desire Me* was a patchwork quilt of rewritten and reshot scenes. This scene with Melvyn Douglas was one of the discarded patches.

During this portrait session, Bull's assistant tuned the radio to classical music. Without moving her head, Garbo quipped: "Oh, is that the way we feel today, Mr. Bull?"

Stroheim, however, Fitzmaurice did not explain the characters to his actors. "He was unable to muster a single additional comment about characterization throughout the making of the picture," recalled Douglas. The actor's first scene with Garbo took place at a train station in which he had to embrace and kiss her in front of dozens of extras. As soon as he began working with her, he was entranced. "Garbo had an extraordinary face, plastic and luminous, the kind of subject sculptors adore. When she began to play, it acquired an astonishing animation. While rehearsing or even shooting with her I could not help thinking, 'My God,

how astoundingly beautiful! This is really happening, somehow, right here in my arms.'"

Their work was interrupted on March 27, when Garbo had to report to the still-standing *Grand Hotel* bedroom set for retakes with John Barrymore and Edmund Goulding. After work, Garbo sometimes visited the British director and his wife, dancer Marjorie Moss, trusting them to keep unexpected visitors away. On one occasion, it was not possible, since they had a houseguest from England, the society photographer Cecil Beaton. Meeting Garbo was for Beaton the culmination of a two-year quest.

In December 1929, he had been in the film capital shooting portraits for his forthcoming *Book of Beauty* when he decided that Paramount stars Gary Cooper, Kay Francis, and Dolores Del Rio were not enough. He importuned M-G-M publicity chief Howard Strickling and got a few M-G-M stars to pose for watercolor portraits. Garbo was not one of them. Before long, he became obsessed with the idea of photographing her. "She is the only person with glamour," he wrote in his diary. Failing to reach her through the usual channels, he wangled Garbo's telephone number out of someone but, upon reaching her, heard only: "Mees Garbo away for weekend." He tried Strickling again. This time Strickling managed to get a direct reply from Garbo. "Oh, I don't know about it," she said. "Oh, well . . ."

Strickling described the unusual quality of Beaton's portraits to her, trying to tempt her with the possibility that they would run in *Vogue*, would be printed in *The Book of Beauty*, and might be the best ever taken of her.

"What difference does it make if the photographs are the best I'll ever have taken?" she asked.

Strickling quit while he was ahead. She had not said no. There was still hope, he told Beaton, who was due to leave Hollywood in a few days. While Garbo was visiting the studio, Strickling again proposed the idea of a special portrait session with this dazzling new talent from London. Beaton's diary entry for January 6, 1930, read in part: "I at last got through to Strickling, and, after having my hopes raised so high yesterday in answer to my 'What about getting Garbo?' there was the deadly 'Not a chance.' Hell. Damn. Blast the bitch. I almost wept with fury, exhaustion, pique. Hell . . . she's got nothing else to do."

By March 1932, Beaton was calmer but no less determined. Fortunately for him, the socially adept Acosta thought Garbo should meet him. When Garbo arrived at the Gouldings' home one evening after retakes on *Grand Hotel*, she allowed Goulding to introduce her to the tall, fey Beaton. He was no less thrilled with her that evening than Douglas was by day. "I could now drink in every detail of her beauty," he confided to his diary. "This marvelous gay creature had the sadness of Debureau the clown—a resemblance accentuated by her pale face, her deep-set darkened eyelids, and skullcap. There was an incredible sensitivity about the modeling of the nose, as if she were able to savor exquisite perfumes too subtle for other human beings to enjoy. Her lips, bereft of lipstick, were like polished shells, and when she gave her big, generous smile, her teeth showed square and shining."

Beaton's interest in Garbo was no longer to photograph her. Like Acosta, he hoped to add her to his gallery of notable intimates. Garbo knew that he was returning to Europe the next day, so she encouraged this fantasy. "You're so beautiful," she told him, complimenting even his hands. When he returned the compliment, she laughed, "I play the most sophisticated women without a manicure." Moss poured mimosas from a pitcher, and the evening gained a glamour glow. "Garbo was inspired to hop about the room gesticulating and giving spontaneous impersonations of grandiose actresses," wrote Beaton, "quoting snatches of poetry or prose that came into her head." Before the party broke up, Garbo asked Beaton a pointed question. "Are you happy?"

"Yes," he answered.

"It's so easy to say 'Yes.'"

"And you?" he asked.

"Tomorrow I go to work with a lot of people who are dead," she sighed. "It's so sad. I'm an onlooker. I've passed being active in life. It's not a question of time and age—but it's just what you are yourself. One doesn't do the things one doesn't want to do." Beaton eagerly transcribed Garbo's non sequiturs—as did all her friends—without trying to make sense of them.

Back on the set of *As You Desire Me*, Garbo was not as passive as she made out. Stroheim was having trouble, and she was contemplating action. "I had looked forward to meeting [Stroheim]," said Douglas, "regarding him as a true genius for his *Foolish Wives* and *Greed*. But he was rude and common, and had such a hopeless stutter that his scenes had to be shot over and over again—angle by angle, phrase by phrase. I was very surprised that a man who had shown such gifts had no subtlety, no savoir-faire." Hopper, who had a solo scene with Stroheim, also recalled his problem. "Erich von Stroheim had trouble remembering his lines and held us up for days," she later wrote. "Garbo was on the set each morning, letter-perfect in her dialogue. Her first rehearsal could have been a final take. But she never lost patience with Stroheim." In fact, Garbo had learned that Stroheim was ill.

Years later he told historian Thomas Quinn Curtiss the truth. "Stroheim was very uncomfortable on his return to M-G-M," related Curtiss. "He distrusted everyone, he was recuperating from a painful operation caused by a fall, and on several occasions he was so ill that he was unable to work. His repeated absences might ordinarily have ended in his being dismissed. Yet Greta Garbo was so protective of him that . . . she told him to telephone her when he felt he could not report for shooting, so that she could then inform the studio that *she* was indisposed."

As filming continued into April, it became obvious that Garbo and Douglas were filming scenes that were subsequently rejected by Bern and Thalberg, not because they were poorly acted, but because the transition from Zara to Bruno's wife, now called Maria, was not explained well enough in the script or directed well enough by Fitzmaurice. "I never knew at any moment what I was supposed to be doing," remembered Douglas. "It was beyond the understanding of any of us." Hopper recalled Garbo doing "a scene that was badly written. She knew and we knew that it couldn't remain in the film. But she gave it the best she had

PART VII

THE CORPORATION

CHAPTER NINETEEN
Queen Christina

Greta Garbo's 1925 arrival in Hollywood had been announced in a perfunctory Los Angeles newspaper item. Her 1932 departure was carried by newspapers all over the world. "Miss Garbo has not made any definite plans as to her future in motion pictures," Harry Edington told reporters on July 21. "When she leaves, she will do so without having signed with any Hollywood company. She affixed her signature to no contract of any nature or sort." To a world of Garbo fans, Edington's statement offered neither hope nor information. Garbo's motives remained as mysterious as her acting technique, but there was no denying her plans. If Edington was to be believed, the inner voices that told her to create were telling her to stop. In fact, Edington was telling a lie. Garbo had most definitely signed a contract. The only truth was that she had not intended to. In April she had made her mind up to leave Hollywood, perhaps permanently. The swirl of circumstances that changed her mind began the previous December when she was preparing for *Grand Hotel*.

At that time, Salka Viertel, whose growing influence on Garbo was not yet apparent, was pondering Garbo's suggestion that she try creative writing. One way to enter this new vocation would be to write a screenplay for Garbo. Anyone who knew Garbo had heard her complaints about the films that M-G-M gave her. "At the beginning of her histrionic career Garbo had the highest of ideals," Cecil Beaton later recounted. "To find herself under contract to appear in a succession of rubbishy screenplays as oversexed, underdressed houris came as a prison sentence."

Garbo never failed to recount the terror she had felt when the studio separated her from Mauritz Stiller. She told screenwriter S. N. Behrman several times that she hated Louis B. Mayer more for pushing Stiller out of Hollywood than for subjecting her to peonage. She clarified this resentment for Beaton in 1947. "I don't hate Hollywood any more than I hate Louis B. Mayer," Garbo told him. "I don't hate anyone, of course, but I don't like Mr. Mayer—although I see

his point and I don't blame him for doing what he did to me. He made me sign a long contract—five years—and I was terrified and very unhappy, for it seemed like a life term." According to Garbo, that term consisted of a cycle of broken promises, usually made at intimidating meetings. "I used to quake at the knees when the studio called me up," she recalled, "and once inside those gates I was so sad. I would be called for a conference, and they'd sit around the table, cigars in their mouths, and they'd growl and bark: 'Now, Garbo, we've got the script and we think you'd do it well. Now read it, but, first of all, imagine how different it will be.' Then they talked by the hour, and we wouldn't get anywhere." All the friends Garbo made after the silent era believed that she had been exploited by a crass, unfeeling company. "Those long years Garbo spent making her silent pictures," wrote Beaton, "were a living nightmare." In December 1931, without considering that there might be two sides to the story, Viertel set herself to the task of improving Garbo's life and, by implication, her own. She could not foresee how far-reaching her efforts would prove.

A biography had just been published of the seventeenth-century Swedish monarch Kristina (usually Anglicized to Christina). Faith Compton Mackenzie's *Sibyl of the North* was not the first in print about Queen Christina. Alexandre Dumas père and the Swedish playwright August Strindberg had also written about her, but this was the first serious biography of the homely woman who had been raised as a man so that she could rule as a king. Viertel later wrote: "The preposterous child of the heroic Gustav Adolph, she was eccentric, brilliant; and her masculine education and complicated sexuality made her an almost contemporary character. Also her escapism, her longing for a world outside puritanical Protestant Sweden, to which she was chained by her crown, fascinated me."

Not coincidentally, Mercedes de Acosta had a similar vision for Garbo. "I had for some time," wrote Acosta, "an idea for a film for her—the role of Queen Christina of Sweden. I had made many notes about it and had written an outline of a story." After five months of Acosta's determined attentions, Garbo was beginning to avoid her, turning instead to Viertel's quiet companionship. Consequently, Acosta had fewer opportunities to present ideas to Garbo.

Opposite: "Bernhardt and Duse were great figures whose fame will endure," wrote Julia Shawell in 1933, "but this woman is something more and strangely different. She seems not so much the artist as the medium through which forgotten things of a far past find expression." Photograph by Clarence Bull

challenge. Garbo would be forced to deal with an entirely new set of executives and technicians, a fearsome prospect. "Somebody joked that Mr. Mayer had made my bank fail so that he could get me back," Garbo later said.

Acosta tried to insulate her from this sudden insecurity by moving her into a less expensive house, but Garbo continued to fret. Acosta's nervous ministrations were irritating in the best of times; with Garbo trying to make a decision, they were maddening. In an Aesop's fable, the wind and the sun have a contest to see who can make a man remove his coat first. The wind blows and blusters, but the man does not remove his coat. The sun exudes its gentle warmth and patiently waits until the man removes his coat. In much the same way, Salka Viertel's serene confidence succeeded where Acosta's jumpy intensity failed. When Garbo needed a friend the most, Viertel was waiting—with a finished treatment called *Christina*.

On July 8, 1932, in an appropriately secret ceremony, Garbo signed a two-picture contract with M-G-M. If the provisions of the twenty-two-page document had been made public, many a star would have thrown a fit. The contract gave Garbo what UA had dangled in front of her: her own production company. Canyon Films would function within M-G-M, and Garbo would be paid $250,000 for each film it delivered. Her weekly salary (in case of delay or retakes) had been $6,000; the contract raised it to $15,000. The first film, which was specified as *Christina*, could be filmed in Europe or at the Culver City studios; the second would be filmed at the studios. She had until May 6, 1933, to give sixty days' notice that she was ready to begin work on the first film. For the second, she would have to reach an agreement with the studio on a choice of property. Possible titles included *Congai*, *Three Weeks*, *Thais*, *Joan of Arc*, and *The Painted Veil*. The contract also gave her approval of the director and four actors for each film.

For a studio other than UA to give an actor so much contractual power was unheard-of. Garbo not only had survived a calamity but also had won far more concessions than she had expected. "I had to sign another contract with Mr. Mayer," she told Beaton later, "but I told him to do pictures that I'd like. He agreed to pay me for half my next picture in advance. He wrote out the highest check I had ever seen. But I had nowhere to put it—no pocket, no bag—so I tucked it into my open shirt." The check was for $100,000. She would receive another $30,000 when reporting for work on the first film, and then $15,000 a week for the next four weeks of production. The remaining $60,000 would be held in escrow and paid (with interest) on completion of the film. With the check pressed close to her heart, Garbo set the first film in motion.

Walking along the Santa Monica beach one afternoon, Garbo pointed out a beachfront estate to Mercedes de Acosta. "That's Ernst Lubitsch's house," said Garbo. "He is the only great director out here. I would like you to meet him."

"*Gott*, such a surprise," exclaimed Lubitsch when he encountered her in his living room. "Greta, Greta, sit down and never go away." After meeting Acosta, Lubitsch said to Garbo: "Greta, why don't you tell those idiots in your studio to let us do a picture together? *Gott*, how I would love to direct a picture for you."

"Ernst, you tell them. I am far too tired to have a conversation with any studio executive."

"What fools they are," he laughed. "How wonderful Greta and I would be together. We would make a wonderful picture."

"We must go now," said Garbo, satisfied that the seed had been planted. "It's after six and nearly my bedtime."

A week later, Garbo took Salka Viertel to another Santa Monica beach house, the large half-timbered one at 707 Ocean Front. They were welcomed by Norma Shearer and Irving Thalberg. "I did not know that she had shown him the manuscript of *Christina*," wrote Viertel. "Although he 'did not believe in historical films and the story was far from perfect,' Mr. Thalberg was interested." Viertel suspected that Thalberg had not read the manuscript when he was vague about its contents. "There are several things I like [in it]," he said. "I would not produce it if I did not think it would make a great picture."

"Calmly Greta said that she had great faith in the story," recalled Viertel. Shearer invited the two women to stay for lunch, but Garbo was in a hurry to leave. The meeting ended on an odd note when Thalberg said: "I will be in touch with Mrs. Viertel and get her an experienced collaborator."

Viertel, who had grown accustomed to working with "Peg" Le Vino, did not want a new collaborator.

"I know Mrs. Le Vino," Thalberg interrupted her. "She is a fine woman but not the person I want on this screenplay." Thalberg may have seen the reader's report prepared by Jessie Burns, which warned of "dull political content" and dialogue that was "merely fair." For the most part, though, Burns liked it. "The story 'moves,'" she wrote, "and is daring in implication without once becoming distasteful. Even in the inference of Christina's passion for a woman the scenes are delicately handled so that only the 'wise' may get the idea." Her main reservation was that Christina's abdication was not sufficiently motivated. "The love that inspires her finally to abdicate should be a tremendous thing and should possess elements that we feel to be new in her life, as Robert Montgomery's freshness was new to Garbo in *Inspiration*, for example."

Acosta was working off and on in the M-G-M writers department; even so, she learned that a Queen Christina script was being developed for her friend. Her proprietary attitude toward both caused her to feel betrayed. "As things often go in the film world of Hollywood," she later wrote, "the

This Milton Brown photo shows director Rouben Mamoulian and cameraman William Daniels shooting Garbo and John Gilbert for *Queen Christina*. Garbo tried to boost Gilbert's self-confidence during filming. "She knew that I was nervous, raw, almost sick with excitement and the thrill of the thing," said Gilbert. "And never once did she fail in consideration of me."

idea was taken from me. Before I knew it, two other people were working on the same story. Their scenario had no relation to the actual historical life of Queen Christina." In late July, just a few days before Garbo's departure, Acosta confronted her about the Christina story. The resulting arguments were so acrimonious that even M-G-M writer Anita Loos thought them worth repeating. "The Garbo-Mercedes business has been too amazing," she wrote to Beaton. "They had terrific battles, and Garbo left without saying goodbye. Then Mercedes flew to New York to see her and Garbo wouldn't. Mercedes flew back despondent." Before boarding the Swedish-American liner *Gripsholm* on July 29, Garbo cabled Viertel: "Auf wiedersehen liebe Salka. Hope to God you had a chance to pay Black and White." The cryptic cable may have referred to some sort of hush money, not to keep Acosta from claiming plagiarism—she had no grounds—but to keep her from bad-mouthing Viertel to everyone within earshot. Years later, Acosta wrote about Garbo's departure: "After she left, Hollywood seemed empty to me."

On August 2, Viertel went to M-G-M with Harry Edington, as Garbo had instructed, and Thalberg offered her a screenwriting contract. Viertel could not understand why Thalberg was bypassing her treatment. "As you know," she said to him, "I have collaborated with Mrs. Le Vino. The studio should first make a deal with both of us and buy the story!"

"But there is nothing to buy," said Thalberg. "You have no copyright. Anybody can come and write a story on a histor-

ical subject." Viertel was stunned by his high-handedness. He continued: "You told me yourself that you intended to make changes. Still, I want to be fair. We will pay you a thousand dollars now and four thousand when the script is finished."

"No, Mr. Thalberg," said Viertel, rising. "You know very well that this is not adequate compensation for a story which demanded a great deal of work and research." Viertel's husband was in Europe, so she could not consult with him, but after speaking with Edington, Le Vino, and a lawyer, she sent word to Thalberg that $10,000 would be a fair price for the treatment. "He had waited until Garbo was gone to tell me that I did not have a copyright," she wrote her husband. Three days later, she and Le Vino accepted Thalberg's counteroffer of $7,500.

On August 7, Viertel attended her first M-G-M story conference, where she met Bess Meredyth, Albert Lewin, and Paul Bern, who had recently married Jean Harlow. She also saw Thalberg's amiable side. "You had a very bad entrée," he said to her, "but if I were not sure that you will be an asset to the studio I would not make you an offer. We need talent, but talent needs us too. You have no experience and I want you to work with Bess Meredyth. She has written great films." Meredyth, married to Warner Bros. director Michael Curtiz, had written three Garbo hits. Viertel knew her as a "jolly blonde, pink-faced, all dimples and curves. . . . She was one of the most highly paid writers at Metro, the author of the much-praised screenplay for *Ben-Hur*, which I was ashamed to admit I had never seen." Nonetheless Meredyth listened respectfully to Viertel's ideas for new scenes. "Christina was not an ordinary woman," said Viertel. "She was besieged by many difficult problems."

"That's fine," said Thalberg, "but how will you dramatize that without making it talkative and dull?"

Viertel was afraid that her new colleagues might recognize her ideas from the script, so she drew on her acting experience to make them sound new.

> My suggestions were pure theater, and as Thalberg was a showman, he listened, attentive and amused. . . . Then abruptly he asked if I had seen the German film *Mädchen in Uniform*, a great success in Europe and New York. It had been directed by a woman, my former colleague at the Neue Wiener Buhne, Leontine Sagan, and dealt with a lesbian relationship. "Does not Christina's affection for her lady-in-waiting indicate something like that?" He wanted me to "keep it in mind," and perhaps if "handled with taste it would give us some very interesting scenes." Pleasantly surprised by his broadmindedness, I began to like him very much.

Garbo arrived in Sweden on August 8 and allowed herself to be interviewed. "What I do in the studios may be important," she told a group of reporters in the ship's smoking room, "but surely the world doesn't care what soap I use to wash myself. I am tired of picking up English, French, German, and other newspapers sent to me in Hollywood and reading my alleged views on love, cosmetics, and health. I have never written a word in my life. I used to be amused over reading these alleged memoirs but now it has become tiresome." The reporters wanted to know if she was going to make films in Europe. "Can't I make it clear that I have no plans?" she asked edgily. "I hope I have convinced you that I am not here as an advertising stunt. I hate publicity. I am very much in earnest about that." Having run her first gauntlet, Garbo proceeded with her long-awaited vacation, which, except for time spent with her brother, began mostly in solitude.

At the writing department, Acosta was still researching unscheduled projects as Meredyth and Viertel finished the first draft of *Christina*. In mid-August, Dietrich's *Blonde Venus* opened to hostile reviews and sparse attendance. Beaton was in town shooting portraits again, and Dietrich was one of his subjects. When Acosta accompanied Beaton to a Harald Kreutzberg dance recital, he introduced her to Dietrich. Acosta and Dietrich had another encounter at an end-of-summer fete. "Thalberg had one of those very grand parties," Dietrich wrote her husband, Rudolph Sieber. "I met a writer, Spanish, very attractive, named Mercedes de Acosta. They say Garbo's crazy about her. For me she was a

Screenwriter S. N. Behrman said that Garbo "identified with the character of Queen Christina. . . . Maybe it was Garbo's idea that as a queen she could do anything she wanted."

relief from this narrow Hollywood mentality." According to Maria Riva, this meeting was characterized by Acosta's flair for melodrama: "My mother told me she found her sobbing in the kitchen during a party at Thalberg's house. Garbo had once again been cruel to this suffering Latin lady and so, what could Dietrich do but comfort and console? This kitchen meeting had many versions but always ended with the 'cruel Swede' being replaced by the 'luminous German aristocrat.'" Garbo's rival for screen supremacy was now her rival for Mercedes de Acosta.

On September 2, 1932, just days after Thalberg's party, his right-hand man Paul Bern was found dead, an apparent suicide. Thalberg was grief-stricken, and for the first time since his 1925 heart attack, he was reminded of his own mortality; Bern was forty-two, Thalberg thirty-three. Mayer mobilized studio manager Eddie Mannix and publicist Howard Strickling to protect the nascent stardom of Bern's widow, Jean Harlow. She was working with Clark Gable on *Red Dust*, a film that had originally been planned for Garbo and Gilbert.

"I was working on another picture [*Kongo*] when Irving Thalberg took Jack out of *Red Dust* and put Clark Gable in," recalled Virginia Bruce. "It nearly killed him. Of course Jack had been driven half crazy by the time I married him but I didn't know that. I loved him madly." The twenty-one-year-old Bruce had married thirty-three-year-old Gilbert on an M-G-M soundstage August 10. The marriage appeared to rejuvenate Gilbert and to restore his hopes for a comeback. His contract was still in force because he owed M-G-M one more film. "They weren't in any hurry to do it," said Bruce. "and he was determined to live out that damned contract. There was some clause in it saying that he could not be seen drunk in public or otherwise disgrace himself, so he drank at home."

When Thalberg returned to work after the grueling inquest into Bern's death, his most taxing project was *Rasputin*, the first film to costar John, Ethel, and Lionel Barrymore. Acosta had done preliminary research on it and was no doubt aware that Diana Wynyard (the young British actress portraying Natasha, the empress's lady-in-waiting) had been signed by M-G-M as a backup to both Garbo and Shearer. Acosta was friendly with Wynyard and her female roommate, novelist G. B. Stern, and learned from them that *Rasputin* had a scene in which the mad monk rapes Natasha. Deducing that Natasha was based on the real-life Princess Irene Youssoupoff, Acosta took it upon herself to contact the exiled princess and her husband, foolishly exposing M-G-M to the threat of a libel suit. When Thalberg found out what she had done, he was furious and fired her. Acosta found solace in Dietrich. "It will be hard to leave Hollywood now that I know you," Dietrich wrote Acosta in a September 15 letter. "Please come," Dietrich wrote to Acosta from her beach house in October. "The ocean is more beautiful than ever, the sun is waiting for you and I am waiting."

Garbo's letters to Viertel were pragmatic. "I know that I am an impossible human being but I cannot make *Christina* in Europe," she wrote on September 12. "When you have trafficked as much in film as I have then you [will] understand." Viertel was understandably let down. "We had always planned that the film would be made in Europe—I had ardently hoped for it. . . . Greta tried to comfort me, saying that after all, Metro was the best studio, Thalberg was the most capable producer to deal with, and that for technical reasons, it would be difficult to make *Christina* in Europe. She was sure that my 'talent and enthusiasm' could defeat Metro's commercialism." Garbo's vacation took her to the sixteenth-century Tistad Castle, where she gamboled in the snow with Countess Hörke Wachtmeister. She also visited the Royal Library in Stockholm and Queen Christina's castle at Uppsala, surprising everyone with her diligent research, which included note-taking and drawing. "Always clever with a pencil, the sketches she made at that time proved invaluable to our research department," recalled Strickling.

Viertel and Meredyth worked on their script through November and December without a producer and without any idea when Garbo would return. "We plodded along, doubtful that the film would ever be made," wrote Viertel. "I had become very fond of Bess, a warm-hearted woman. *Queen Christina* was not exactly her cup of tea but she was interested, and raved about me to the front office where I had first encountered distrust and antagonism. Thalberg emphatically expressed his satisfaction with my work." On December 21, Thalberg signed Walter Wanger, the former production head at Paramount's Astoria studios in New York, as an associate producer. In spite of the depression, M-G-M was ending a banner year and expansion was in order. On December 25, before Thalberg had even settled down to enjoy the Christmas holidays with his wife and two-year-old son, he suffered another heart attack. Although he recovered fairly quickly, it was obvious that he could no longer oversee fifty-two films a year. Mayer waited until Thalberg had left on an extended vacation and then made radical changes in the studio structure. He removed Thalberg as vice-president in charge of production and in his place established a group of producers that included David O. Selznick, the RKO producer who had recently made a star of Katharine Hepburn, and who happened to be his son-in-law. The impact of this change would surely be felt by Garbo, who would now have to deal directly with Mayer, and by Salka Viertel, who had been a Thalberg recruit.

In January 1933, Acosta's affair with Dietrich was still going strong. The liberal star had not yet found Acosta's effusiveness wearing, but when Dietrich met Brian Aherne, the British leading man in her new film *The Song of Songs*, Acosta was relegated to a waiting list. Dietrich's film was getting a lot of press, partly because it was her first American film without her Svengali-like mentor. Her new director was the Russian-born Armenian Rouben Mamoulian, a Broadway import who had taken Paramount by storm with his cinematically inventive hits *Applause* and *Dr. Jekyll and Mr. Hyde*. "Rouben Mamoulian was not your Hollywood-type director," recalled Maria Riva. "No von Stroheim boots and riding crop, not even Cecil B. DeMille pomposity. He was East Coast Ivy League Gray Flannel Suit. His jacket even matched his pants, complete with Brooks Brothers shirt and understated tie. And he was quiet. Mamoulian wasn't just calm, he seemed becalmed." His most recent film, *Love Me Tonight*, was a brilliant, effervescent musical, but not even Jeanette MacDonald, Maurice Chevalier, and tunes by Rodgers and Hart could make it the hit it deserved to be; Paramount had lost too many theaters to the depression. When M-G-M producer Harry Rapf saw the attention that Dietrich was getting, he ordered a progress report on *Christina*.

"Finally the studio appointed a producer for *Christina*," wrote Viertel. "He was Walter Wanger, a handsome man in his early forties, college-educated, with excellent manners, liberal opinions, but evasive and 'diplomatic.' It was easier to talk to Thalberg, who could be blunt and arrogant, but who was seriously involved in filmmaking." On January 24, M-G-M announced that Garbo would be returning to the studio with a new contract and that her first film would be called *Queen Christina*. Wanger immediately made Viertel suspicious by assigning two new collaborators. "Mr. Ernest Vajda was a Hungarian whose faulty English and preposterous personality were softened by the perfect syntax and great gentleness of an Englishwoman, Mrs. Claudine West." Vajda had worked successfully on numerous Lubitsch films. In view of the turgid script that Meredyth and Viertel had written, he and West were a sensible choice for the project.

Meredyth's draft of January 9 ended with Count Magnus arrested and Christina happily reunited with Antonio. This was the kind of Hollywood ending that Viertel deplored, yet because of her lack of writing ability she had allowed it. The story department moved Meredyth to another project and took Viertel off the script. "I was promoted to Wanger's 'assistant and artistic advisor,'" she recalled tartly. "Vajda's screenplay was filled with so-called 'Lubitsch touches,' and the drama turned into a comedy. Of course it no longer had the slightest resemblance to the original story." This was not the worst thing, since the original story lacked both suspense and a sympathetic Christina. Vajda and West attempted to make the proud monarch human, giving her delightfully sharp exchanges with her cousin, who expects to marry her. "You think nothing of fidelity?" asks Charles.

"I admire it," replies Christina. "But I cannot practice it."

"Everyone wants this marriage," insists Charles. "The people want it."

"But it is *I* who have to do the marrying."

"It is not a matter for jesting," says Charles. "Marriage is serious."

"So serious that it is only tolerable as a jest. . . . Stick to your army, Charles. They are used to being ordered around. I am not. I was born free. I shall die free."

Viertel objected to this approach, feeling that Christina's uniqueness was being eroded. "The *Christina* script was shaping into the very Hollywood vehicle Garbo was trying to escape," she later wrote. She argued strenuously against it, but she was quite obviously not a seasoned writer; in fact, she was not a writer at all. No one would speak it aloud, but she was there only because of her influence with Garbo. Her uninformed opinions were questioned at every turn by Vajda. "He was unbearably arrogant, personal, and provoking," wrote Viertel. "Wanger comforted me by saying that he wanted to give Vajda a chance to express his viewpoint and that a British writer, Mr. H. M. Harwood, was en route from London to give 'class' to the dialogue." Harwood did more than that; he gave a much-needed identity to the main character.

"It sounds all psychological and difficult," Harwood wrote in a March 23 review of the script. "I would try to keep it in as light a vein as possible. We must get an impression of a pretty hard, brittle personality (semi-hard-boiled) in the early scenes if we are to get any contrast after she meets *the* man." In keeping with the sexually adventurous films of 1933—*She Done Him Wrong*, *The Story of Temple Drake*, and *The Sign of the Cross*—as well as the spate of films with emancipated heroines—*Christopher Strong*, *Cocktail Hour*, *Female*, *The Warrior's Husband*, and *Ex-Lady*—Harwood made pointed suggestions about Christina's private life. "Sex was to her a relaxation only," he wrote, "an amusement, not a serious matter that could be allowed to interfere with her liberty in any way. If possible, one should show her as the prototype of a modern woman, who resents any of the feminine functions that tend to remind her of her dependence . . . [she] shrinks from both marriage and maternity. Unconsciously she resents the fact that she is not a man."

On March 26, 1933, Garbo boarded a freighter, the *Annie Johnson*, for a thirty-four-day trip through the Panama Canal. Dressed in shapeless sweaters and pants, she ate her meals in a different lifeboat each day in order to avoid the three other passengers aboard. She cabled M-G-M that she wanted Lubitsch to direct *Queen Christina*. When she discovered that his commitments at Paramount made him unavailable, she approved Edmund Goulding, who also turned out to be busy.

Viertel's duties as artistic consultant did not preclude looking at the latest drafts by Vajda, West, and Harwood. "The most important thing in the picture," she wrote in an April 22 critique, "is the scene between Christina and Antonio in her room." This is the scene in which the Spanish

"They warmed and ripened in the Spanish sun," Antonio tells Christina. "My hacienda's overrun with them. In the season of the grape harvest, the air smells purple. Purple grapes." This celebrated scene was criticized by a historical adviser, attacked by censors, and endured by Garbo. "If you're going to eat grapes," she later said, "you shouldn't be lying on the floor on your back."

envoy realizes that he has made a terrible mistake. He has traveled to the Swedish court to present an offer of marriage from King Philip to Queen Christina. Before arriving at the court, he has met a young man—who turns out to be a woman. He has made love to her—and she has turned out to be Queen Christina. He feels that he has been used and tricked. Viertel thought that when Antonio confronts the queen about her deception, she should be nonchalant.

> Christina starts the scene very victoriously: "Well, didn't I promise you we will see each other soon?" She is so convinced that being a queen and having an irresistible personality is only an asset and an advantage in her relation to Antonio. She doesn't consider the marriage business [to King Philip] for a moment seriously. Her attitude toward marriage is not changed for a second. . . . "Who cares about the King of Spain? I wouldn't have married him anyhow. I am young, beautiful, [and] until now I have lived for my country. But I am free to love whom I want! I have the right to live like a man because I work like a man!"

On April 30, Viertel met Garbo at the dock in San Diego and brought her to Mabery Road. Viertel had the sad duty of informing Garbo that her hairdresser, Ruby Neely, had been killed in a car accident some months earlier. Garbo wept openly at the news. "We used to do the shapes together," said Garbo of Neely. "We'd look at pictures [of hairstyles] and see if they would suit my face." Garbo also heard about the new regime at M-G-M; Thalberg was still in Europe, recovering from both his attack and Mayer's coup. In a few days, Wanger visited Garbo at Viertel's home. After giving her the latest script and making small talk, he asked her if she could report to M-G-M on May 15. Garbo rose suddenly, stalked to the door, opened it, and said to Wanger: "Anyone who wants me to work so soon couldn't possibly be my friend." She was more genial when Gilbert Adrian brought costume sketches for her approval. "And here's one for Dietrich!" wrote a fan magazine. "Fully half of Garbo's costumes will be men's attire, mostly uniforms. . . . Adrian says that Garbo waxed most enthusiastic over the masculine attire and merely shrugged at the pretty pretties any girl might wear." Garbo later called Wanger to apologize; she was feeling better. Other reports were not as cheerful.

According to the trade papers, "Garbo didn't like the treatment of *Queen Christina* handed her and she flatly refused to make the picture until there were certain specific changes made in the scenario." Surprisingly, this announcement did not emanate from Garbo's usual spokesman, Harry

"We photograph Miss Garbo more sharply than other stars," said William Daniels. "There is less need, thanks to her complexion and fine Norse skin texture, to make the focus diffused or hazy in order to secure beauty. This sharper focus is very useful because it catches little facets of facial expression a more diffused picture would miss. And that is very important with Miss Garbo, for if you will notice on the screen, some of her finest acting is done very subtly, by means of slight changes of expression."

Edington. After marrying Barbara Kent (who had appeared with Garbo in *Flesh and the Devil* and subsequently helped her with correspondence), he had gone into business as a personal manager. One of his first clients was none other than Marlene Dietrich. Maria Riva remembered him as "a slight man with one of those obligatory cashmere polo coats, complete with trailing belt. He was sharp, quick-witted, with a sense of humor and New York savvy." It was he who had negotiated with Paramount when Dietrich at first refused to make *The Song of Songs*.

"Greta and Harry Edington have now parted company," read a smirking news item, "and Greta talks for herself, assisted by Mrs. Berthold Viertel. The report is that Mrs. Viertel will manage the amazing Swede's fortunes, and those who know the lady say she will be a match for anyone." She was obviously a match for the screenwriters who had tampered with her concept of Christina. Vajda and West were out. Harwood, who had maintained the script's lesbian undertones and restored the tragic ending, was in. The distinguished playwright S. N. ("Sam") Behrman was assigned to the major rewrites. "Contrary to all the gossip, I have never been Garbo's 'advisor,'" wrote Viertel in 1969. "I had no mind whatsoever for business and what I could grasp of it either horrified me or bored me." Yet she had sold an unsolicited script to Hollywood's most powerful studio and outmaneuvered two powerful veteran writers. Partly because of her, *Queen Christina* would be the turning point in Garbo's career.

Perhaps wary of her influence, Wanger strove to isolate Viertel. "I learned from Mr. Harwood," she wrote, "that

Behrman had arrived but that I was to be kept away from him because of my disparaging remarks about the Vajda script." Behrman's latest hit was *Biography*, which was restoring Ina Claire to the Broadway stardom she had forsaken for Hollywood and John Gilbert. Behrman's dramas were funny and full of heart. He was also known as a specialist in star vehicles, having crafted a number of plays for Lynn Fontanne and Alfred Lunt. He was officially under contract to Fox Film, where Viertel had first met him, but M-G-M's largesse took care of all outstanding obligations. "Sam Behrman was about forty," recalled Viertel, "of middle height and weight; his domed forehead was bald, his features distinguished, the brown eyes looked at one with humorous interest and warmth, but they could change rapidly and become absent when he was bored. Boredom was unbearable to Sam; he blamed it on his 'low vitality' and 'terrible temperament.'" Behrman was just right for this job, then, because except for a few of Harwood's scenes, *Christina* was a bore.

"I think that taking so-called dramatic liberties with a historical script is a very natural and inescapable process," said Behrman. "In the case of Christina, so little is known about the Queen's private affairs and personal biases that the picture is probably as close an approximation of the facts as anything could be. The main point at issue, of course, is: Does the characterization emerge as a warm, living human being? If this is answered in the affirmative, your historical play has succeeded." The warmth of Behrman's characters came from humor. Viertel described him as "brilliant, witty, with a weightless sense of humor and a rare gift to uplift, stimulate, and exhilarate." He applied this gift to the script of *Queen Christina*, and by mid-May of 1933, a breathing, smiling woman was emerging from the impassive sheaves of onionskin paper in the M-G-M writers department.

With the script finally taking shape, Wanger turned to the consideration of a director. None of Garbo's options were available except for Mamoulian. Wanger brought him to meet Louis B. Mayer. With Thalberg temporarily out of the picture, "L. B." was attending to more creative functions. Mamoulian was used to working with producers like Wanger or Jesse Lasky, who let him innovate without interference. M-G-M did not cater to directors; few participated in the editing process. It was a producer's studio, where filmmakers like Hunt Stromberg customarily decided on final cuts. "I can't work that way," Mamoulian told Mayer point-blank. "At Paramount I was producer-director. I never had any interference. I had the final say. I would like Walter Wanger's name in my contract."

"We can't do that," said Mayer. "Suppose he dies?"

"Well, if he dies, then I become the producer. I will not do it with another producer."

Mayer was not happy about this, but Mamoulian had directed Fredric March to an Academy Award as Dr. Jekyll and Mr. Hyde, so he acceded. Then there was the issue of Garbo's reluctance to work with new people.

"Why don't you ask her if she would like to see the first cut of *The Song of Songs*, which I just finished with Dietrich," said Mamoulian. Word was sent to Garbo's new home at 1201 San Vicente Boulevard, and she ventured onto the Paramount lot to watch the woman who had bedazzled Mercedes de Acosta. Even at Hollywood's "Continental" studio, Garbo was a must-see. "On her way out to the gate, everybody was spying to get a look at her," recalled Mamoulian, "but she liked the film." If Garbo had heard gossip that Mamoulian had romanced Dietrich during the filming, she paid no attention; she sent word to Mannix that she wanted Mamoulian to direct her.

Wanger and Mamoulian got down to the business of finding an actor to play Antonio, a character who could almost be a throwback to the Latin lovers of ten years earlier. "I read the manuscript and was delighted with the whole idea," John Barrymore wrote to Garbo on May 17. "I had a distinct feeling that in the scenes between us, with your help and your artistry, we could evolve something whimsical, touching, and very lovely in the first part of the play, and something most significant and tragic in the latter part of it." Barrymore had just finished *Dinner at Eight* for Selznick, in which he had given a painfully detailed performance as a faded silent-film star. "Barrymore was very anxious to do [*Christina*]," recalled Mamoulian, "but on second thought it seemed that he would be a little too old." Mamoulian began shooting screen tests of everyone who was anyone: Bruce Cabot of *King Kong*, Franchot Tone of the Group Theater, and even Ricardo Cortez of *The Torrent*. Leslie Howard, whom Garbo admired from *Berkeley Square*, refused to consider working with Garbo because "added to the terrific competition of her personality—which no man has equaled—the film would naturally be cut to her advantage. And where would I be?"

Garbo also liked the young British actor Laurence Olivier, whom she had seen in RKO's *Friends and Lovers*, the same film that yielded Erich von Stroheim. "I raved about [Olivier] to Wanger and Mamoulian," said Viertel, and she arranged for Garbo to see another of his films. "My performances were precious, lacking in vitality, charmless," recalled Olivier in 1986. "But I felt comparatively at ease in my last film for RKO—*Westward Passage* with Ann Harding—and Greta Garbo liked my performance." She liked it enough to approve him without a test, and on June 28, M-G-M announced that Olivier would play Antonio.

Filming was scheduled to commence on August 7, so Wanger and Mamoulian went into high gear, gaining press for trivialities such as a 1630 globe from Stockholm. After looking all over the world, they found the original in the Huntington Library in nearby San Marino. Not surprisingly, the script was still being reworked. Even after Behrman's

excellent work, Mamoulian felt that its plot points needed to be more visual, so he hired a freelance screenwriter named Harvey Gates to think up a more clever meeting for Christina and Antonio. Gates had to devise a way for Antonio to discover that the androgynous young count he has met at a country inn is a woman.

Antonio and the count are of necessity sharing a room and must now get ready for bed. Antonio decides to bathe, but the bathtub is occupied by a cat and her kittens. The count (Christina) picks up one of the kittens as Antonio begins to undress. "Christina turns to leave with the kitten, cuddling it in the nape of her neck and against her cheek—a purely feminine, maternal gesture—forgetting herself for the moment. Antonio watches her, struck by her action with the kitten." The willing suspension of disbelief necessary to accept this ambisexual masquerade was apparently taken for granted by everyone preparing *Queen Christina*. Were her fans so eager to see Garbo on the screen again that they would accept her in any bizarre scenario? What about Thalberg's edict about not making a monkey out of Garbo? Was her popularity unassailable?

Dietrich was in Europe when *The Song of Songs* was released on July 19. It won an enthusiastic review from the *Times*'s new critic, André Sennwald. "Marlene Dietrich floats through it," he wrote, "with the lyric grace of that apparition which was sent by Heaven to be a moment's ornament. For Mr. Mamoulian has the eye of a poet, and his cameraman Victor Milner has the poet's skill." In a *Pictorial Review* article entitled "Garbo or Dietrich?" Julia Shawell decried "an era that has no French kings, when palaces on the Nile have lost their romantic meaning, and there are no more ships for a Trojan siren." But that could be excused because there were movie close-ups and two uniquely glamorous stars. "Each has that something that makes a name last long after a face is dust, an intangible and rare power of fascination." Dietrich possessed the maternal, convivial qualities that Garbo lacked, but both stars had "that certain thing." Shawell believed that Dietrich's effectiveness was due to her cooperation (and collaboration) with directors, cameramen, and costars, as if glamour was something that could be created from the outside in. Garbo's glamour, on the other hand, came from the inside out. "She seems not so much the artist," wrote Shawell, "as the medium through which forgotten things of a far past find expression. Phantom memories, partly comprehended emotions pass through her figure on the screen, leaving a large film public of placid realities in awe and adulation."

Leslie Howard did not plan to act opposite either star, so he could speak his mind to an interviewer. "From a critical standpoint, neither Dietrich nor Garbo is a great actress," he said. "Dietrich has been the more fortunate in having been trained carefully by a director who understands her perfectly. He taught her to be alluring and she has attained her peak in becoming a pictorial triumph. Garbo has succeeded because of her marvelous personality. She might reach true greatness if she corrected some bad mannerisms. It is her own fault that she has been handicapped by inadequate direction, for she has scared everybody so badly that they don't dare to supervise her—to advise her when she is mistaken."

Garbo reported to M-G-M on July 24 and found that the hooks on her dressing-room walls were the wrong height. On the same day, Laurence Olivier arrived from London to essay the most important role in his career thus far; perhaps Garbo would also find fault with *his* height. In a few days, Rouben Mamoulian and William Daniels shot his costume and makeup tests. A few days later they shot the first film of Garbo as Queen Christina. Screenwriter Dewitt Bodeen saw the decaying nitrate film in the late 1960s. "It was a silent wardrobe test," he recalled, "mostly of Garbo in the costumes she wore when she masqueraded as the young man, since these Adrian-designed clothes had to be exactly right. Garbo turned obligingly, putting on and taking off hats with just the right swagger or trying on capes, while that amused smile lighted her eyes."

Mamoulian the poet was also curious to see what could be done with Garbo's face. "I made a rather longish test," he recalled, "and discovered that no matter how you lit Garbo the result was beautiful. I finally decided to experiment with Daniels and see if we could spoil that magnificent face. We put a light overhead, under her face, sideways, every imaginable way, and the final test revealed nothing but beauty. It is an incredibly photogenic face. Nothing could spoil it." Garbo tried a new makeup effect for these tests. She used eyeliner to extend the contours of her eyelids and make them meet outside her eyes. The result gave the impression of oversize eyes, almost like those in a primitive mask. "I never had anyone touch my face," she exaggerated to Beaton years later. "I did it myself. And no tests, except for lighting. I hate tests. What looks good to the eye looks well on the screen. If a dress doesn't seem right in life, then the screen isn't going to make an ugly duckling into a swan." Garbo was cooperative during the making of the tests. Mamoulian had heard all the stories; then, too, she was not acting in these tests, and the soundstage was empty except for a skeleton crew. Mamoulian thought it best to establish ground rules. "I understand," he said to Garbo, "that when you are doing an intimate scene with an actor, everybody has to leave the stage, including the director."

"Yes," answered Garbo. "Clarence Brown used to go and have a sandwich."

"I can't work that way. I am there every second."

"Well, all right," said Garbo after some hesitation. "I will agree to that."

On August 2, 1933, a baby girl was born to Virginia Bruce and John Gilbert. The event occasioned little comment.

Gilbert had finished his contract several months earlier with a pathetic Tod Browning movie called *Fast Workers*. In the minds of most M-G-M employees, he had also finished his career. *Queen Christina* moved forward with a letter of approval from James Wingate, the new head of the SRC, who advised caution in the scenes between Christina and Ebba, her lady-in-waiting. "We assume," he wrote, "that you will be careful to avoid anything in the portrayal of this scene which might be construed as lesbianism."

Filming commenced on August 7, and Mamoulian ran up against Garbo's resistance again. He was on the set of the queen's study for a scene with Reginald Owen, Lewis Stone, and Garbo. "So let's have a rehearsal before we start," he said.

"Oh, I don't rehearse," said Garbo, shaking her head solemnly. "If I rehearse, I become stale. If you take more than one take, I become empty inside." Mamoulian listened calmly, nodded and smiled, and planned his next move. "I never rehearsed with the director," Garbo later told Beaton. "I used to see him going through the script with the other actors, but I couldn't do it if I had to rehearse. It frightened me."

"Well, Miss Garbo, this is incredible," said Mamoulian. "Let's make a deal. I'll do it your way. If that works out, it will be marvelous because I will earn the reputation as the fastest-shooting director in Hollywood. I'll get through the picture in four weeks instead of eight. But if it doesn't work out, you will try to do it my way."

"It will work out," said Garbo.

Mamoulian rehearsed Owen and Stone and then filmed the scene, in which Owen, playing Prince Charles, says to Christina, "You cannot be insensible to the natural feelings of your sex. You are a woman."

"So they tell me," answers Christina.

Mamoulian called "Cut!" The gaffer waited for a signal from Daniels. Garbo was already walking to her dressing room. "Well, how do you feel about it?" Mamoulian asked her.

"Fine! Fine!" She continued to walk past him, then stopped and turned to him. "Well, how do *you* feel about it?"

"No good," he answered. "It's all wrong." He paused and looked at her over the rims of his round black spectacles. "We made a deal. We'll have to rehearse now."

"Believe me, I'll get worse," Garbo frowned. They rehearsed for an hour. "I'm getting worse," she said. After another hour, she groaned. "I am completely empty. There's nothing there at all."

"That's all right," said Mamoulian. "Now we will make Take Two." Then came Take Three, Take Four, and so on, until he said: "Print Take Eight. And print Take One." He turned to Garbo, who was once again on the way to her dressing room. "Now, Miss Garbo, tomorrow morning Take One—yours—and Take Eight—the one I like—will be in the projection room. You go in there alone. You see these two takes and then you tell me which one I should use in the picture, and I promise to abide by your judgment."

Garbo gave a tight-lipped smile of assent, then walked up to Mamoulian and whispered in his ear: "Please do not print Take One." As it turned out, Wanger eventually decided that the scene slowed the film's first act and decided not to use it.

The next day Wanger called Behrman back to M-G-M to do more work on the script. "Mamoulian had already begun the filming," wrote Behrman in 1972. "The set, the queen's palace in Stockholm, was up. Snow had been piled up around it. I was to keep a day ahead of the shooting." It was time to introduce Laurence Olivier to Garbo. She was not interested. "I didn't want to know the people I was acting with," she said later. "I couldn't go out to dinner with my leading man and hear about his wife and family. I just wanted to meet [actors] as strangers on a set." She was properly diffident when Olivier appeared early one morning. He saw her sitting on an antique chest near the edge of the set, "wearing loose lounging pajamas, a cigarette between her slender fingers, a script of the picture carried under her arm. I realized at once that she was going to be difficult to know," recalled Olivier. "She was as shy as an antelope." Olivier, knowing that she had requested him as her leading man, told himself that there was nothing to fear. "I went boldly up to her and said the three or four sentences that I had made up and practiced; but no utterance came from her. I began to flounder and grab at anything that came into my head; some sayings of Will Rogers, of Noël Coward— anybody—anything at all, until I came to a wretched end and stopped, pale and panting. After a breathless pause, she slid herself off the chest sideways, saying, 'Oh, well, life's a pain anyway.'"

After this embarrassing initiation, Olivier had to play a love scene with Garbo. Garbo agreed to a limited rehearsal. "The stage was set for our most important scene when, as Don Antonio, I meet Garbo in her boudoir at the inn and there discover the warm, tender woman beneath the boyish masquerade." Mamoulian gave Olivier his first directions. "I was to come forward," said Olivier, "grasp Garbo's slender body tenderly, look into her eyes and, in that gesture, awaken passion within her, that passion for which she is later willing to give up the Swedish throne. I went into my role giving it everything I had, but at the touch of my hand Garbo became frigid. I could feel the sudden tautness of her, her eyes as stony and expressionless as if she were marble."

This was more unsettling for the cast and crew than Garbo's first day on *Anna Christie*. She had not shown this kind of resistance since her timid days on a set in Sweden. Mamoulian spoke to her softly, according to Olivier.

He asked her to warm up to me, to try to bring some fire into her eyes, some expression of tenderness into the lovely curves of her rich, warm mouth. We tried it again, but

This is the scene that originally ended *Queen Christina*. To avoid depressing the audience, Mamoulian completely rewrote it, removing Ian Keith and reviving John Gilbert.

Garbo was unmoved. She, the great actress, whom everyone expected to go into this tender scene with convincing abandon, was as frigid to my embrace as if she were a woman of stone. Mamoulian came over again. He asked me to talk to Garbo off the set, to try to break down this intangible barrier which had risen between us, these cross currents of magnetism completely out of harmony with each other. We walked a little, smoked together, tried to talk small talk. Then we came back and went into the scene again. Garbo froze up as before.

There was a great deal at stake on this tense set—a very expensive production; the contract of an up-and-coming foreign actor; the first film at M-G-M for both an influential producer and a celebrated young director; and the first film in eighteen months of Hollywood's biggest star. Then Garbo dropped a bomb: she did not want to work with Olivier. She wanted to work with . . . John Gilbert.

"So she simply marched into Mayer's office and said it would be Jack or nobody," according to Gilbert's friend Colleen Moore. "Mayer went through the roof, of course. They'd just gotten rid of Jack a few months before. They certainly didn't want him back again. Mayer screamed and ranted, and Garbo, as always, said nothing until he was finished. Mayer knew it was useless to argue with her." If Mayer was surprised, Gilbert was in a state of shock. His life had gone from a war of nerves at the studio to a war of attrition at Tower Grove Road. "I stayed home waiting," he told an interviewer, "hoping I would be offered work somewhere. Had it not been for my wife, who understood, and my friends, I probably would have lost my mind. Then one day, while I was leaving the house, the telephone rang." Gilbert was being summoned to join Garbo on an M-G-M set.

The resulting screen test was watched with great interest by both Mamoulian and Olivier. "Garbo's face softened," said Olivier. "Into her eyes came a strange, beautiful light. Something seemed to be happening deep down inside her." Then they ran Olivier's first test. Olivier did not spare himself. "Here I am, supposed to be one of the greatest actors in the world, and this fading Jack Gilbert's test was infinitely better than mine." Recalled Mamoulian: "I looked at the screen and the fellow wasn't there." Within days he was in Wanger's office. "Larry, I want you to know something," Wanger said to him. "We're crazy about you here at Metro and we want to put you under contract. But it's just that in this particular part—"

Olivier cut him off and asked for a settlement.

"Why, yes, of course," said Wanger. "Glad to get on to money terms. So much easier than other things." When Wanger mentioned a screen test for Thalberg's upcoming production of *Marie Antoinette*, Olivier said that he was going back to England—for good. Wanger's next call was to Gilbert. "Get down here," Wanger told the skeptical actor. "Mayer's already approved." Gilbert had to agree to a seven-year contract at a very nominal $20,000 per film in order to do *Queen Christina*. On August 11, after signing, he visited the set of *Queen Christina*, where Garbo was filming a scene in bed. When she asked him how he felt, he answered: "Why, it's colossal!" On leaving the soundstage, Gilbert was ambushed by reporters who wanted to know all about his meeting with Garbo. "She was exactly the same today as six years ago," he said, "and she will always be the same—just as bewildering. Three years ago, I could have sworn that she would never look at me again, and now she has fought to get me this part, when I am down and most need encouragement. Incredible." Gilbert later confided to Adela Rogers St. Johns: "There's never been a day since Flicka and I parted that I haven't been lonely for her. I think that she has always been lonely for me."

"Garbo had a long memory," Moore explained years later. "She remembered all the times he'd helped her career." Even so, Gilbert had slid so far so fast that Garbo's gesture was hard to believe. "You know what started all this," said Gilbert, "my so-called decline, was the terribly unfortunate role in which I broke into talkies. *His Glorious Night*. I played a passionate scene à la silent film stuff. You know, all gushing, *blahh*. My God, the people just laughed. I couldn't blame them." Mamoulian began coaching Gilbert and consulting the M-G-M sound engineers, determined not to have any "accidents" ruin his voice in this movie. "I asked Gilbert to speak very quietly," Mamoulian recalled, "and the sound technician did a superb job."

Filming resumed on August 17 with the outdoor scenes where Christina first meets Antonio. "I have been struggling mightily with *Christina*," Garbo wrote to Countess Wachtmeister, "but the worst is yet to come." Mamoulian wanted Garbo to laugh out loud upon seeing Gilbert stuck in the snow. "I can't laugh," said Garbo.

"I hear you laughing in real life like a little girl," Mamoulian contradicted her.

"Yes, but not on the screen," explained Garbo. "I can cry, I can smile, I can go hysterical, I can get angry, but I cannot laugh."

"Go rest and don't worry about it," said the sly director. As soon as she was out of sight, he gathered Gilbert, Akim Tamiroff, and some bit players around him. He instructed them to ignore Garbo when the camera started rolling on her close-up and then to surprise her. "Turn around and make funny faces, the way kids do." His trick worked; Garbo exploded into her very natural guffaw.

On August 19, Irving Thalberg returned to M-G-M and settled into a new office. Because he was now heading an independent production unit, he would no longer be available to shepherd productions such as *Queen Christina*. When Garbo chose *The Painted Veil* as her next film, Mayer assigned it to Hunt Stromberg. In late August, Behrman was still rewriting one of the most important sequences in *Queen Christina*, the romantic scene in the bedroom of the snowbound inn. (The other big scene, Christina's discovery of Antonio's death, was also unresolved.) "Col. [Jason] Joy and I conferred with Walter Wanger on a forthcoming production, *Christina*," wrote John V. Wilson, an SRC official. "Col. Joy advised him to shoot [the scene in the inn] several ways and let us take a look at the resulting shots, to which he agreed." Although Wanger agreed, Mamoulian did not feel in conscience bound to follow the dictates of the censorship office, especially if it would spoil a unique scene. In Behrman's August 22 draft, Christina says, "I have imagined happiness, but happiness you cannot imagine, happiness you must feel, joy you must feel. All my thoughts have been prisons, all my dreams. In this great joy I feel now, Antonio . . . This is how the Lord must have felt when He first beheld the finished world—with all His creatures, breathing, living."

An indication of Viertel's growing influence at M-G-M was her attempt to improve the same scene in an August 28 draft. The improvement amounted to no more than an arbitrary rearrangement of various lines of dialogue; Mamoulian ignored her draft but could not ignore Garbo when she occasionally did the same thing on the set. "That scene I have changed slightly from the script scene because I do not believe *I* would do it so" was her standard explanation of an attack with an invisible blue pencil. "I would not speak these lines as they were, so I have learned them differently. The change is only a little one but it makes them *feel* natural."

The excitement of working on Garbo's first film in so long did not translate into the usual soundstage hubbub, according to Daniels. "You know how noisy most motion-picture

Before shooting the rewritten ending of *Queen Christina*, Garbo asked Mamoulian: "What do I express in this last shot?" He answered: "Nothing. Absolutely nothing. You must make your mind and your heart a complete blank. Make your face into a mask."

"No one could have been less like the actual Queen Christina than Garbo," wrote Behrman in 1972. "But she was thrilling as a symbol." Photograph by Clarence Bull

sets are," he told an interviewer. "Well, an actor accustomed to this sort of picture-making is instantly struck by the hush that greets him on the whole soundstage used by Miss Garbo. He is impelled to talk in a low voice, as though he were in a public library reading room." Much of the keenness in the air came from the anticipation of what would happen when Garbo and Gilbert played their first love scene since *A Woman of Affairs*. Garbo nipped the gossip in the bud. "Mr. Gilbert is a married man now, with a wife and a baby," she said when he began to play the scene too passionately for her liking.

"Backward, turn backward, O Time, in your flight," quipped Gilbert.

Mamoulian's visualization of the postcoital scene required Garbo, dressed in a clinging robe, to walk slowly around the room, touching all the artifacts in it so that Christina will retain the memory of their tryst forever. Mamoulian shot the scene on September 2. To prepare Garbo, he told her: "This has to be sheer poetry and feeling. The movement must be like a dance. Treat it the way you would

music." Instead of playing a phonograph on the set, Mamoulian used another device. "It was done to a metronome," he later revealed. The rhythm of Garbo's cadence would have a counterpoint in the cutting of the shots. "It was a graphic poem," said Mamoulian. Each part of the room was captured in a lovingly framed vignette, and Garbo had a different expression for each. "You did not have to tell Garbo to look like this or that, for this reason or that," said Mamoulian. "No, you just had to tell her which emotion you wanted her to have produced for the scene in question. 'I understand,' said Garbo. And she did understand. She produced the emotion on her face. She produced it in her bodily movements, which is more than you can say about many actors. What was absolutely extraordinary about Garbo was that she was both photogenic *and* intuitive."

Much of the scene's astonishing power was due to the photographic effects achieved by William Daniels, who more than ever was using light to tell the story. Instead of revealing Christina as a woman by having her nuzzle a kitten, Daniels used crosslighting to outline her womanly form when she removes her coat. In the scene where she is "memorizing" the room, the warmth of the hearth is palpable because of the quality of light in each shot. Daniels did this with strategic placement of fresnel spotlights in the fireplace. "All the light in the room came from the fire—or seemed to," said Daniels. "Of course we had to cheat a little by using special small spotlights that illuminated the bedposts, the furniture, in such a way that they seemed to be the kind of light that flickering flames would make. The problem was that the scene had to be done in a very subdued, natural light and still be practical for theater display. I think I learned the realism in this scene, the way of achieving it, from von Stroheim."

The realism of the scene was not total, according to M-G-M's Swedish historical adviser, Colonel Einhornung, whose job was to stay on the set and check for accuracy in props, costumes, and business.

"During most of these scenes, the set was 'fenced in,' so I did not know what was done," reported Einhornung. "However, when I saw apples, oranges, and grapes carried in, I pointed out the impossibility of having them served at the inn, even if it was suggested that [Antonio] brought them from Spain. He had been traveling for weeks, and, besides, no fruit could be kept edible in the very cold winter climate of Sweden." Garbo would not have minded if he had eliminated fruit from the scene. "I did learn one thing," she reminisced about the scene fifty years later. "If you're going to eat grapes, you shouldn't be lying on the floor on your back."

Einhornung was also disturbed by the moral tone of the film. "As for the bedroom scene, it is a gross insult to Swedish history and royalty and Swedish womankind to picture the Queen as a 'light woman' who goes to bed with a complete stranger after having known him for a few hours." Days after the shooting was completed, the SRC wrote M-G-M, asking that they not shoot certain lines of dialogue. "We have received and read your revised version of scene 220," wrote Wingate. "We would recommend further toning down this scene by eliminating the lines 'Do you think the old saints would approve of us? Will we have their blessing?' and 'This is how the Lord must have felt when He first beheld the finished world.'" Mamoulian had shot the lines and fully expected to have them in the final cut.

While Garbo was lost in a romantic fantasy, her friend Acosta was feeling neglected and depressed. Driving toward an intersection in the San Fernando Valley with her maid, she said to herself: "I wish to God a car would hit us and kill me." Within seconds, a car flew through the intersection and crashed into hers, throwing both her and her maid onto the road. They survived, but Acosta had to have plastic surgery, which Dietrich underwrote, even though she was in Europe. While Acosta was recovering, Garbo took time off from *Queen Christina* to visit her.

Gilbert was also hospitalized briefly during the production. The trouble began in mid-September. "I was nervous and gun-shy," said Gilbert. "The executives were looking at me with the old-time, too-familiar suspicion and hostility. I felt that only Garbo really wanted me there." Gilbert would come home from the studio to his wife, Virginia, and baby, Susan, but was so wrought up that he could not enjoy their company. "When Jack was feeling himself, he was the most charming, exciting, intelligent man I've ever known," recalled Bruce. "He had a beautiful body and he was a tender and considerate lover." But Gilbert was preoccupied with what he thought would be his last chance to save his career. "I was sick over the way I was playing my part in *Christina*," he said later. "I was afraid of giving a bad performance. I was working under terrific pressure. I felt the conditions around me were unfriendly. The whole thing kept twisting around in me like a knife." Inevitably Gilbert turned to the whisky bottle. "Sometimes he'd be awake drinking all night," recalled Bruce. "Then in the morning he'd get me to throw him in the pool so he could clear his head. I'm sure the shock must have been bad for him. He had bleeding ulcers. He used to throw up blood in the morning until he fainted."

Garbo sensed that Gilbert was struggling to survive. "She knew that I was nervous, raw, almost sick with excitement and the thrill of the thing," said Gilbert. "And never once did she fail in consideration of me, in tact, in saying and doing the right thing at the right moment. She was gracious and friendly. She sensed every one of my feelings and was tender toward them." Crew members could not help but notice that Garbo was extending herself in an effort to help her former lover. "To illuminate his moodiness, she knocked herself out trying to be gay," said a coworker years later. "Often we saw her watching him, when he didn't realize her eyes were upon him. There was pain and pity in her eyes, as though a bitter-sweet memory was taunting her. Gilbert never reacted to her efforts. He was like a man who had been floored by life, and was too tired to make the effort to get up from the canvas and continue the fight." Bruce also tried to bolster Gilbert's confidence, but she found him harder and harder to reach. "There was no one like Jack when his spirits were up. But when he was down, he was . . . oh, you can't describe it. It was like death." In late September, the combination of anxiety and alcohol made Gilbert too ill to work. The *Hollywood Reporter* snidely attributed Gilbert's weeklong absence to "hysteria."

"The delays were tremendously costly," said Behrman, whom Garbo and Viertel had begun to visit regularly.

> One day when Garbo couldn't work because her leading man had not shown up, my guests were in a state. I complained to Garbo: "How could you ever have got mixed up with a fellow like that?" It was a rhetorical question; I expected no answer. But I got one. Garbo meditated; it was a considered reply, as if she were making an effort to explain it to herself. Very slowly, in her cello voice, she said: "I was lonely—and I couldn't speak English."

While Behrman continued to rewrite scenes for *Queen Christina*, Viertel was attending story conferences for *The Painted Veil* with producer Hunt Stromberg and director Victor Fleming. "I had to spend long hours at the studio," she said, "then many evenings with the indefatigable and painstaking Mamoulian who, after a hard day's work on the set and in the projection room, rushed through dinner to come to my house and go over new problems, prodding, correcting again and again, saying *No* to every suggestion, sure that only he himself could find the solution." Mamoulian had been rewriting scenes after Behrman finished them, because he felt that they did not play correctly. Scenes were reshot. Garbo's ennui returned. "It's been a difficult time," she wrote to Wachtmeister. "It all went wrong. I'm half-done with Christina now and half-done is what she's going to be when she's finished. It's impossible to try and achieve anything out of the ordinary here. This is the last time I'm going to try."

On September 30, the *New York Times* reported that Dietrich was returning from Europe to work once more with Sternberg. Their next film would be *Her Regiment of Lovers*, a story of Catherine the Great. Other proposed historical epics included Norma Shearer as Marie Antoinette and Katharine Hepburn as Elizabeth I.

On October 9, Mamoulian shot the film's final scene, which had been written by Harvey Gates on July 28. In it, Christina goes to meet Antonio on a ship called *The Star of Hope* so that they can leave Sweden together. When she comes on board, she sees Count Magnus standing next to a corpse that is covered with a cape. "Where is Don Antonio?" she asks.

"He is there," says Magnus, nodding to the corpse.

"He is there?" she asks in disbelief.

"It was in fair fight, Your Majesty," says Magnus. "He wanted a duel. It was either he or I. Well—I won. Though it is a sorry victory if you do not forgive me for it. I implore you—"

"Leave the ship, Magnus," Christina says quietly.

"I'm glad I did it. I am glad it happened. In this world there was not room for both of us."

"Leave the ship, Magnus," Christina says again.

Magnus turns and walks off. Christina moves to the bier. She sinks to her knees and slowly lifts the cloth from the face of the corpse. "Antonio, is this you?" she asks. "This is not you, Antonio." She covers the face and stands up, then touches the inert body through the cloth as if she is praying. "To you I cannot speak. But to that Antonio who was, to whom I did speak endlessly of love, I say again, I love you— I love you now and will always love you."

Queen Christina decides to sail with the tide and the scene dissolves to:

"Ext. Bow of Ship. Medium Shot of Christina wind-blown, stalwart as she faces the sunset. Long Shot of the *Star*

"People don't really want to see me in real life," Garbo told reporters. "They go to cinemas to forget their ordinary everyday existence." Photograph by Clarence Bull

of Hope riding before the wind in the far distance. FADE OUT: THE END."

"I had quite an argument with L. B. Mayer on the ending of the film," said Mamoulian. "He wanted a happy ending. This, to me, was unthinkable. Mr. Mayer and his associates felt that the tragic ending would be depressing to the audience. I told him that I was as much against depressing audiences as he was but that tragedy in the theatre does not produce depression." After viewing the rough cut of Gates's scene, both Wanger and Mamoulian thought it could be more uplifting. The first change was to eliminate Count Magnus (Ian Keith) from the scene. Then Antonio was allowed to live long enough for Christina to say good-bye to him. But there was still a letdown at the fade-out.

Wanger had been at Columbia Pictures earlier in the year, where Frank Capra was making *The Bitter Tea of General Yen*. The last image in his film was a close-up of Barbara Stanwyck on the deck of a ship with the wind blowing into her expressionless face. Knowing what Daniels could accomplish with a close-up of Garbo, Mamoulian applied Capra's idea to the ending of *Queen Christina*, envisioning "a rhythmic progression of graphic images—ship sails, faces, pantomimic action, ending with a final close-up of Garbo's face—which began with a long view and ended with an enormous close-up that ran for eighty-five feet. I was sure that the dramatic effect of this silent sequence would produce a feeling of exhilaration, the classical catharsis."

The enormous close-up posed technical problems. Close-ups were traditionally shot with a long lens, usually a 75mm. To move the camera from a wide view of Garbo standing at the ship's prow to a "choker" close-up (forehead to chin) had never been done before, because a long lens would not encompass the wide angle of the prow, nor would a 25mm lens work for a close-up. When brought up close to Garbo's face, a short lens would distort it, making her nose protrude. There was also the problem of diffusion, or "soft focus." The wide angle would require very little, but a very close close-up would require a lot. Daniels thought that the lens problem could be solved simply by using a focal length that was somewhere between normal and long; he was not sure about the diffusion. "We needed a device which would progressively modify the degrees of diffusion as the camera rolled in," said Mamoulian. "We were stuck. Suddenly an early childhood memory popped into my mind—when my parents gave me a magic lantern for Christmas. I thought of that long glass slide on which there were four separate pictures that could be projected on a white sheet or a wall by gradually moving the glass slide in front of the lens. That was it. All we needed was a similar piece of glass on which, instead of pictures, there would be graduated diffusion."

On October 24, the last day of filming, the camera department worked all day to make the diffusion filter. By 4:00 P.M. every other shot of the sequence had been made, and the filter was still not ready for the dramatic final shot. Garbo was in her dressing room, playing a phonograph record of the song "None but the Lonely Heart" over and over, waiting for Mamoulian's directions. If her face was to fill the screen for almost a minute, what expression should it have? Mamoulian later explained how he made his choice.

> With a tragic ending like this, no matter what feelings are portrayed by the actress—and they could range from hysterical sobs to a smile—some of the audience would disagree, would find them wrong. This was one of those marvelous spots where a film could turn every spectator into a creator. If the face is blank, just like John Locke's *Tabula Rasa*, then every member of the audience inevitably will write in his own emotions. Thus, the "expression" would be true for every spectator because it is created by him.

"Garbo always stopped shooting at five," recalled Mamoulian. The filter was delivered to the set at 5:00 P.M. Garbo agreed to work until the shot was completed. "What do I express in this last shot?" she asked Mamoulian.

"Nothing," he replied. "Absolutely nothing. You must make your mind and your heart a complete blank. Make your face into a mask. Do not even blink your eyes while the camera is on you." The M-G-M wind machine blowing in Garbo's face was daunting, but she agreed. "She stayed until seven," Mamoulian recalled. "We made two takes. One was no good. The other was perfect." The new ending was reviewed a few days later. "When Mr. Mayer and the assembled brass were shown the film in the projection room, nary a one of them mentioned depression. In fact, they were all exhilarated."

Neither Garbo nor Gilbert was happy to be called back for retakes in late November, but Mamoulian was a perfectionist. "I feel I've almost never been as tired as I am now," Garbo wrote Wachtmeister. "If only those who dream about Hollywood knew how difficult it all is. The end result seems to be the only thing that counts. I long to get away—the Wandering Jew in me longs to get away, far away." In mid-December, Garbo was able to travel as far as Santa Barbara for the first preview of *Queen Christina*. On December 22, she went to a preview in Hollywood, but the film broke and people in the audience recognized her when the house lights came up, so she darted out of the theater. The New York Astor Theatre premiere was scheduled for December 26, but the film first had to be cut to appease New York state censor Irwin Esmond, who was offended by Christina's line in the bedroom scene: "Do you think the old saints would approve of us? Will we have their blessing?" An around-the-clock editing crew made the requested changes and rushed reels five through seven into the M-G-M lab. A print was flown to New York in time for the first premiere of a Garbo film in eighteen months.

"Soon after entering the Astor Theatre last night," wrote Mordaunt Hall in the *New York Times*, "spectators were transported by the evanescent shadows from the snow of New York in 1933 to the snows of Sweden in 1650. The current offering, known as *Queen Christina*, is a skillful blend of history and fiction in which the Nordic star, looking as alluring as ever, gives a performance which merits nothing but the highest praise. She appears every inch a queen." Hall's review was one of many that acknowledged Garbo's return to the screen was in something more than a vehicle. *Queen Christina* was an achievement, a bold, thoughtful, stylish showcase. Some observers found it a little too bold.

Elizabeth Yeaman of the *Hollywood Citizen-News* wrote: "There are two scenes which I found distinctly offensive: that in which Garbo is helped into her trousers by a slovenly old valet [C. Aubrey Smith], and that in which orders for a morning chocolate are issued from behind the drawn curtains of a bed in the inn. However, last night's audience roared gustily over both the episodes, which I resented and felt might have been handled with subtlety. It remains to be seen what censorship boards think." The New York board had allowed *Queen Christina* to open there, but Joseph I. Breen, who became the new head of the SRC on January 1, 1934, felt that the scene in the inn should be deleted before the film's general release on January 9. He was not the only one. Martin Quigley, editor of the *Motion Picture Herald*, wrote that the scene in the inn "registers with voluminous and unnecessary detail the fact of a sex affair. The sequence is emphasized and dwelt upon beyond all purposes legitimate to the telling of the story, thereby assuming a pornographic character." And as predicted, astute viewers recognized the bisexuality of Garbo's Christina. A Catholic newspaper in Detroit called her "a perverted creature."

"It is quite apparent from our examination of the files that Mr. Wanger paid very little attention to our several letters," Breen wrote to Wingate on January 9, outlining cuts for the bedroom scene. "I think Miss Garbo should be kept away from the bed entirely. The scene should be cut from the action at the spinning wheel, at least, and the business of lying across the bed fondling the pillow is, in my considered judgment, very offensive." The newly appointed Breen had the power to enforce these cuts. He wrote to Mayer, asking that they be made before the release. Mayer told Wanger to take care of them. Unwilling to tamper with Mamoulian's brilliant work, Wanger refused. He reminded Mayer that the Production Code allowed them to appeal Breen's decision to a jury of producers. The film was screened for a hastily convened jury on January 10. A day later, the verdict was sent to M-G-M: "This jury, consisting of Messrs. B. B. Kahane [of RKO-Radio], Jesse L. Lasky [of Fox Film], and Carl Laemmle Jr. [of Universal], saw this picture in your projection room yesterday afternoon and decided unanimously that the picture be approved as exhibited." Wanger's resolve had saved a work of art from being butchered.

Garbo was pleased with Mamoulian—so pleased, in fact, that she accompanied him on a road trip to Arizona. Yet a letter to Wachtmeister in late January indicated otherwise. Garbo wrote:

> I am so ashamed of *Christina*. I often wake up and think with horror about the film coming to Sweden. It's really bad in every respect but the worst thing is they'll think I don't know any better. Just imagine Christina abdicating for the sake of a little Spaniard. I managed to believe for ages that it would look as though she did it because she was weary of it all and from a boundless desire to be free. But I'm not strong enough to get anything done so I end up being a poor prophet. . . . You know I hardly ever mention my films but I feel I have to prepare you.

Garbo had espoused this project, had researched it, and had exercised more creative control over it than over any of her previous films. She felt responsible for its integrity, which reflected on her own. "I tried to be Swedish but it's difficult in Hollywood to be allowed to try anything," she said later. "It's all a terrible compromise. There is no time for art. All that matters is what they call box office." Yet her misgivings were not realized. Swedish moviegoers accepted her portrayal of Christina wholeheartedly. They knew full well that the real queen was ugly and fickle and were happy to have Garbo rewrite history. She would have done better to prepare the Americans she saw on her trip through Arizona.

American small towns appeared to have lost interest in her. "It is a great disappointment that the Garbo picture is not going over in several sections of the country," said the *Hollywood Reporter* on February 13. "The failure of audiences to grab that attraction in the big numbers we feel it deserved sort of twists things up a bit." When the final receipts were tallied, *Queen Christina* could not be called an unqualified triumph. For the first time, a Garbo film had earned less in America than it did overseas. *Queen Christina*'s domestic receipts were $767,000; its foreign grosses were $1.843 million. This kind of money justified Garbo's amazing contract, but it put M-G-M on notice. Something had changed. What was it?

First of all, eighteen months was a long time for Garbo—or anyone—to be absent from the screen. Hollywood functioned on an assembly-line basis. The public expected a regular offering of Joan Crawford, Gary Cooper, or Janet Gaynor. If Garbo said that she was leaving movies, and Edington confirmed it, what could her fans do but grieve and then find another idol? While Garbo was away, Americans had turned their attention to Katharine Hepburn, Mae West, and, most importantly, Franklin D. Roosevelt, the new president. Furthermore, Dietrich's two flops in the same period, as well as the public's rejection of numerous foreign actresses, suggested that the exotic glamour vogue was passing.

Queen Christina's less-than-feverish reception in America was also due to Garbo. The twenty-eight-year-old woman who returned to the screen in this film was a different person from the sexy girl-woman who had set the heartland afire in her silent films. Garbo's attitudes, fears, and beliefs had crystallized while she was away. Unwilling to play the Hollywood game in so many ways, unwilling to share herself with her intimates, she was now withholding something from her fans. The reviews could not pinpoint it, but they felt it. Irving Thalberg's formula had been replaced by Salka Viertel's influence. This was the first film in which Garbo was not offered as someone to be desired, but as something to be revered, a jewel in a grand setting.

"There are times when *Queen Christina* becomes dull in its magnificence," wrote one critic. Another referred to the "clammy *Queen Christina*." The *New Yorker* review said that Garbo did "handsomely, though the story of old Sweden sags a bit." No critic would have described the Garbo of *Mata Hari* as handsome. American men were ready to fall in love with Garbo again, but taking a bisexual queen to bed was a perplexing prospect. Even with the controversial bedroom scene, Garbo was no longer the frankly sexual character of her earlier films, one who appealed to both men and women. Viertel's influence and Garbo's own maturing had changed her on-screen persona. Audiences sensed coldness, remoteness, sadness. *Queen Christina* was the turning point in Garbo's career. After 1933, she would reach the heights of her artistry, but she would never again reach the average movie fan.

Once Garbo got over her dissatisfaction with *Queen Christina*, she accepted it for the remarkable film that it was. "She identified with the character of Queen Christina," recalled S. N. Behrman in 1962. "She said that she came closer personally to the character of Christina than any other [she played]. Maybe it was the idea that as a queen she could do anything she wanted, didn't have inhibitions, and had a sexual mystery too." Behrman's collaboration with Garbo would not be his last. As he learned more about her, he compared her to both the character he had written and the eccentric original. "No one could have been less like the actual Queen Christina than Garbo," wrote Behrman. "But she was thrilling as a symbol: a queen, and beautiful, and she spoke for peace. She was a modest queen; the aristocracy Garbo brought to all her performances was lambent in this one."

Opposite: "Thanks to my playing Queen Christina," said Garbo fifty years later, "the whole world knows who she is." Photograph by Clarence Bull

CHAPTER TWENTY

The Painted Veil

The reflected glory of *Queen Christina* was warm and bright in January 1934. The first to bask in it was Rouben Mamoulian. Coaching Greta Garbo had not immunized him to her allure; he followed eight months of work with three months of courtship. A whirlwind trip to Arizona in January gave rise to rumors of elopement, but when cornered by the press both parties denied a romance. They also took a trip to Yosemite. Garbo had originally planned it with Mercedes de Acosta, who was an expert on reflected glory, then changed her mind without telling Acosta, who paid for hiking clothes at the Army-Navy store and waited in vain for Garbo to show up. "Finally Acosta went to Garbo's house," said Marlene Dietrich. "And there she found that Garbo had gone away with Mamoulian instead of her. Acosta was crying, so, of course, I took her in and fed her."

Acosta was unemployed, at loose ends, and although she had divested herself of suicidal thoughts by visiting a Hindu holy man, she had not overcome her need to monopolize Garbo's time. If every friendship has a contract, both parties must read its terms—and the fine print. Garbo was happy to have Acosta run errands for her but rankled at unexpected visits and betrayed confidences. By the same token, hikes in the woods and walks on the beach with Garbo were never enough for the needy Acosta. "She drove Garbo nuts," said Mary Anita Loos, niece of the screenwriter. One morning, recalled Loos, Mamoulian and Garbo spied Acosta outside Garbo's house. "Mercedes was pacing up and down the sidewalk out front, waiting for him to leave."

"Get me out of here," said Garbo through clenched teeth. "Get me out of here. Mercedes is there!"

Mamoulian escorted Garbo into his car. Garbo went limp and slid down the seat, intent on hiding in the wheel well.

"You sit up, damn it!" said Mamoulian. "And we'll drive out. I will not let you crouch in my car because of this." Garbo reluctantly straightened up and looked straight ahead as Mamoulian drove the car past the humiliated Acosta. Dietrich, who was still friendly to Acosta, listened to her Garbo stories, whether in person or in lugubrious letters. Acosta wrote:

> I have built up in my emotions a person that does not exist.
> My mind sees the real person—a Swedish servant girl with

a face touched by God—only interested in money, her health, sex, food, and sleep. And yet her face tricks my mind, and my spirit builds her up into something that fights with my brain. I do love her but I only love the person I have created and not the person who is real. . . . Until I was seventeen I was a real religious fanatic. Then I met Duse, and until I met Greta, gave her that same fanaticism—until I transferred it to Greta.

Dietrich regarded Acosta's declamations with amusement. "Oh, she was always dramatic," Dietrich later said. At the time she had drama of her own. *The Song of Songs* was not performing as well as hoped, and her work with Josef von Sternberg on *Catherine the Great* was, as always, a love-hate rollercoaster. If anyone was basking in reflected glory, it was Sternberg, who had chosen to put Dietrich in a role that could only be compared to Queen Christina. *Catherine*

Greta Garbo and John Gilbert hoped that the brilliant *Queen Christina* would revive his career, but the film's uneven reception worried even Garbo.

the Great was scheduled for a May release. Garbo's film would still be circulating. Then came the news that London Films was also making a movie about Catherine the Great. Rather than have Sternberg accelerate the pace of his meticulously planned production, Paramount delayed its release until the British film could play its limited engagements. Publicity photos of Dietrich as Catherine were recalled, and new slugs were glued to them: "The title of this film has been changed to *The Scarlet Empress*." Some photos showed Dietrich in a furry Travis Banton costume that bore a striking resemblance to one of Garbo's in *Queen Christina*. Sternberg may have resented Mamoulian. Sternberg had first been approached to direct *Queen Christina*, and Garbo had approved him, but a delay in starting the film prevented what could have been a fascinating collaboration. Would Garbo have submitted to Sternberg's methods? Or would Sternberg have agreed to her requirements in order to give her a Paramount glow?

The person who most deserved to benefit from Garbo's M-G-M glow was John Gilbert. No less a Hollywood personage than Marion Davies expressed concern for him when she said, "If he comes back as a success—and one good picture could do it—Jack will continue as a favorite. Everyone is pulling for him." Louella Parsons saw him on the *Queen Christina* set one day. "The restless look, the suggestion of suppressed bitterness were gone," noted Parsons. "He was exactly like the old lovable Jack, the debonair, devil-may-care lad whose following as a screen actor had not yet been surpassed." Of course Gilbert, with a failing marriage and compromised health, was not the same person he was in 1927, but he did have hope. It led to an ill-advised call to Louis B. Mayer. "I was feeling on top of the world," Gilbert explained later. "I thought I'd call up just to say thank you for the part, for the chance, for everything. I got him on the phone. I started to say thank you to him. I'd hardly opened my mouth before he opened up on me and let me have it— foul abuse, threats, damnation—and all hell broke loose. I tried to scream into the phone that I was just trying to say thanks—I didn't want any more dough."

Far from opening lines of communication, Gilbert's call reminded Mayer that his nemesis was within arm's reach. Mayer called publicity to find out how prominent Gilbert's name was in *Queen Christina* advertising. "Metro is chastising John Gilbert again," wrote *Variety* a short time later. "The *Queen Christina* trailers mention all the featured male support but Gilbert." Gilbert's reviews also indicated his fall from grace. "Mr. Gilbert's makeup may be more than slightly extravagant," wrote a typically ironic reviewer, "but there are scenes in which he acts very well. Ian Keith is highly satisfactory as the villain, Magnus. It is, indeed, almost a pity that Mr. Gilbert was not put in the Magnus role and Mr. Keith into that of the Spaniard." Gilbert read the reviews with a glass of whisky in his hand and a gun nearby. His friend

Adela Rogers St. Johns encountered a disgruntled Gilbert in his driveway one day in January 1934. "Where are you going?" she asked, putting her hand on his arm.

"I'm going to kill Louis B. Mayer," he answered.

"They'll hang you."

"No," he answered resolutely. "I'll kill him and then myself."

"Take me with you," she said. "You shouldn't be alone on a mission like this. Besides, you can't drive in your condition. You've been drinking." Fortunately St. Johns was able to calm Gilbert and dissuade him from carrying out his plan. By April he had been divorced from Virginia Bruce and dropped by M-G-M. "Word had gotten around that his health was precarious," said Colleen Moore. "He'd lost a lot of time during the Garbo movie."

Gilbert retreated to Tower Grove Road, where he occasionally entertained visitors such as actor Ronald Colman, who introduced him to Hollywood's British colony. One of its members was Herbert Marshall, who was now working with Constance Bennett on a remake of Gilbert's *Woman of Affairs*. This time it was called *Outcast Lady*; even with relaxed censorship, the film could not be titled *The Green Hat*. Another visitor to Gilbert's house was an aspiring actor named David Niven, who later recalled:

> In his mid-thirties [Gilbert] was a man of sparkling good looks, but his good humor and laughter seemed dredged up with great effort. Often he did not appear at all, and

Marlene Dietrich's rivalry with Garbo was only one element of Josef von Sternberg's 1934 production, *The Scarlet Empress*, a film of such advanced cinematic technique that even reviewers failed to grasp the enormity of its accomplishment. Photograph by Eugene Robert Richee

Colman and I would take a swim in his sad, leaf-filled pool. Once or twice I caught a glimpse of a beautiful face watching us from a window, and on one occasion, as we were climbing into Colman's car, a figure in a man's shirt, slacks, and a big floppy hat approached from the scrub-covered hills and, with head down, hurried past us into the house. "When Jack's drinking, she goes walking," said Colman phlegmatically.

Some of the garments Garbo wore on her visits to Gilbert came from the salon of couturier Howard Greer. "We were talking one day between fittings," said Greer.

"I suppose nearly everyone who is famous comes into this shop," said Garbo. "Don't they ever frighten you? People always frighten me."

Numerous fan magazine articles tried to analyze Garbo's passion for privacy. The term *agoraphobia* was used in several of them. For whatever reason, Garbo continued to hide and continued to use acolytes such as Acosta as buffers. After the grand reception accorded *Queen Christina* in Europe, the recipient of the most reflected glory was Salka Viertel. With her name engraved in credits and reviews, she assumed the enviable role of gatekeeper to Greta Garbo. Hollywood was baffled; she had come from nowhere. People speculated about the relationship. "Salka was AC/DC," Irene Selznick said in 1990. "Lots of people knew about that. She was quite masculine, I thought—overweight and unappetizing, but charming." Was her influence with Garbo due to a romantic involvement? To all appearances, Viertel was involved not with Garbo but with a neighbor, screenwriter Oliver H. P. Garrett. She did write of her initial entrance-

Beulah Bondi and Garbo have an unpleasant mother-and-daughter talk in the opening scene of *The Painted Veil*. Because of negative preview comments, the scene was cut and the wedding-day sequence was reshot with a different actress playing the mother.

ment by Garbo's beauty, but so did her children and everyone else who encountered Garbo; to be affected by Garbo's appearance was inescapable. Viertel, seated at the center of a literary salon, had her eye on the same thing her guests did—Hollywood money. The studios, notably M-G-M, hired writers on the basis of one theatrical success, put them in little wooden offices, and left them there to daydream and collect handsome salaries. Acosta's tiny résumé was large compared to Viertel's. Frances Marion's list of credits was impressive but did not get her access to Garbo. Viertel had access, and, in 1934, that was what mattered. "She was no more self-seeking than anyone else," said Selznick. "Just a little more successful."

Acosta's estrangement from M-G-M came to an end in early 1934. Lawyer Fanny Holtzmann asked her to testify in a British court that she had warned Irving Thalberg about the libelous rape scene in *Rasputin and the Empress*. While deciding how to respond, Acosta received an invitation to return to the writers department. She called Harry Edington, who said, "We'll make them pay through the nose for keeping you so many months out of a job." When the salary offer grew large enough, Acosta accepted, and Holtzmann lost a witness.

"When I returned to the studio," Acosta wrote Dietrich, "they assigned me *Camille*. I told them I was sure Greta would not do it. Thalberg then asked if I knew what she would like. I suggested *Jehanne d'Arc* [her preferred spelling] and spoke the truth in saying she has many times told me she wished to do it." *Jehanne d'Arc*, the play that Acosta had written for her then-lover Eva Le Gallienne, could be adapted to the screen, but Acosta was worried about competition. *King Kong* producer Merian C. Cooper was making Technicolor tests of Katharine Hepburn at RKO-Radio Pictures for a possible Joan of Arc project. Acosta wrote Dietrich: "Greta for three and a half years has told me that she longed to do *Jehanne d'Arc* and wanted me to write it. When we were in Carmel she again said she would rather do it than anything and lamented the fact that Hepburn was going to do it."

"What stupidity!" exclaimed Dietrich to her husband and daughter upon reading the letter. "Can't you just see Garbo—hearing voices? Being ever so religious à la Swede?" By this time, Acosta's studied intensity was growing tiresome, according to Maria Riva. "My mother had had enough of 'Greta this' and 'Greta that.'"

Thalberg inaugurated his independent production unit with *Riptide* for Shearer and *Outcast Lady* for Bennett. He could get Garbo with the right script. Knowing that Selznick and Hunt Stromberg wanted her too, he asked Acosta if she had any ideas. "I believed that Greta was worth much more than all the glamour and sex films she had been forced to play in," said Acosta. She was perhaps aware of the outcry from grassroots organizations against "wicked" films such as

Milton Brown portraits of Garbo on the set of *The Painted Veil* are all that remain of a transitional scene in which she wanders around her house thinking. She wrote a friend what she thought of *The Painted Veil*: "Rubbish."

Riptide. "I had always wanted," wrote Acosta, "to see her in a peasant role in which she could brush her hair straight back off her face and wear simple clothes instead of the grand ones she had always been seen in. I wanted her for once to portray a role where beautiful clothes would not stand between her and her great acting." This was a disingenuous statement. The majority of Garbo's audience was female. Glamorous gowns sold movie tickets.

"I wanted her to do a picture close to the soil where nature would play a part. Nature is Greta's element and in no picture had she been allowed to express it. I told Thalberg this. I also told him that I thought Greta should play the roles of saints."

"What saints?" Thalberg asked.

"Of course Jehanne d'Arc. She is a natural for this. All the scenes should be shot in France and in all the places where Jehanne d'Arc lived and fought." M-G-M had shot no film overseas since the near-disaster of *Ben-Hur* in 1924; even Garbo, while campaigning for *Queen Christina*, had admitted the unlikeliness of such a trek. Thalberg, however, expressed interest and commissioned a script. Acosta began work on it and did not show it to Garbo, but she could not resist boasting about it to others. In early March she went to see Le Gallienne in a Los Angeles staging of *Hedda Gabler*, where, to Le Gallienne's annoyance, "She talked a great deal about 'Greta this' and 'Greta that.'"

Viertel was too busy looking out for Garbo's interests to talk about her. She was working with Hunt Stromberg, who had beaten Selznick and Thalberg to get Garbo's approval for *The Painted Veil* as the second of the two films in her two-film deal. Fresh from sexy hits such as *Red Dust*, *Bombshell*, and *The Thin Man*, Stromberg was a good prospect for Garbo's career. Coincidentally, the 1925 Somerset Maugham novel had been threatened with a libel suit by a man named Walter Lane, who said that Maugham's character of the same name would disturb his privacy. Changing the character's name to Walter Fane (and a not-so-simple cutting and gluing of pages) had saved it. Its title derived from a line in a Percy Shelley sonnet: "Lift not the painted veil which those who live / Call Life: though unreal shapes be pictured there / And it but mimic all we would believe." Maugham's story charted the emotional and spiritual growth of a girl named Kitty who marries a stuffy older man to escape an aimless social life in London. She goes with him to China, where an affair with a breezy diplomat causes her heartbroken husband to wish her dead in a cholera epidemic. But it is he, the selfless scientist, who dies, leaving Kitty to face her future and herself.

At story conferences with Stromberg, Edith Fitzgerald, and John Meehan, Viertel turned Kitty into an Austrian girl named Katrin. In the process, most of the story's depth fell off the conference table, and *The Painted Veil* became a conventional triangle. It was not quite the older man–younger man formula of yore, but it was nothing original either. "I have repressed the memories of *The Painted Veil*," wrote Viertel. "I only recall that the producer, wanting to stress the Chinese background, insisted on scenes with a statue of Confucius under a tree. For some strange reason he always called him 'Vesuvius.'"

The first script was submitted to Joseph Breen in April 1934. He responded gruffly that it contained "pretty strong sex situations." There was no reason for worry. Even though Breen was growing confrontational with producers, they could probably get around him. After his rout by the *Queen Christina* jury, major cuts to that film had been made by only one censor board. The call for "clean pictures" was coming from fringe groups who had no power to influence the studios, and federal censorship was a boogeyman who was waning, along with the worst of the depression. In the year since Franklin D. Roosevelt had taken office, the national economy had improved to the point where weekly movie attendance had risen to 70 million. America's sixth-largest industry was doing fine and needed no advice.

The director chosen to helm *The Painted Veil* was Richard Boleslavsky, a former Polish lancer, an alumnus of the Moscow Art Theatre, and the author of a book called *Acting: The First Six Lessons*. Respected by his colleagues for both his handling of actors and his use of creative cutting, he had recently directed Clark Gable in the medical drama *Men in White* and Marion Davies in the lavish Civil War drama *Operator 13*. In late May, while Garbo's new script was being worked over by unlikely writers such as Vicki Baum (of *Grand Hotel*) and Dorothy Farnum (of *The Divine Woman*), political changes were brewing that would affect both *The Painted Veil* and Garbo's future films.

Catholic bishops, feeling deceived by the industry with whom they had drafted the Production Code in 1930, were rallying huge numbers of Catholics against what they considered sinful movies. Among those listed in Catholic publications as "condemned" were *Riptide*, *Men in White*, and

This cut scene was also part of the wedding-day sequence in *The Painted Veil*. In it, Garbo encounters a middle-aged British doctor whom she marries on impulse. Herbert Marshall was enjoying a banner year as a Hollywood leading man.

In this Milton Brown photo, Richard Boleslawski (a.k.a. Boleslavsky) directs Soo Yong and Garbo while seated on the floor with William Daniels. Boleslawski said that Garbo "was so completely thorough in her art that one found her almost as marvelous as the camera itself."

Queen Christina. What had started as isolated protests were spreading across the country, mobilized by a Catholic organization called the Legion of Decency. When studio executives saw that the Legion had its strongest constituency in the cities where theater chains had their largest holdings, they started to sweat. Day after day they read the invective leveled at them by high-ranking clergymen. On June 7, Bishop Joseph Schrembs of Cleveland wrote a letter that was read at all masses in his diocese. "If the sale of black children produced abolitionists," he said, "then the sight of children's souls sold to the devil by Hollywood must produce a new wave of abolitionists—who will destroy this spiritual bondage." On June 8, Denis Cardinal Dougherty of Philadelphia voiced the first threat against Hollywood. "A vicious and insidious attack is being made on the very foundation of our Christian civilization," said Dougherty. "Perhaps the greatest menace to faith and morals in America today is the motion-picture theater. Nothing is left for us but to boycott." A week later, the Legion of Decency, by then 3 million strong, held a rally of 50,000 people. Bishop Schrembs roared at them: "Purify Hollywood or destroy Hollywood!" Within a week, a Catholic boycott emptied theaters in virtually every major Midwest city. Within two weeks, studio revenues had dropped so sharply that production budgets were in jeopardy. The *Los Angeles Times* declared: "Hollywood is in the most serious crisis of its history."

At a June 13 meeting of the MPPDA in New York, Joseph Breen, acting on behalf of its Hollywood office (and on behalf of the Catholic bishops whom he had secretly incited against them), presented a pamphlet titled: "A Code to Govern the Making of Motion and Talking Pictures." The architect of the Catholic boycott now had the means of controlling the content of Hollywood films. His new Production Code featured "Compensating Moral Values," a requirement that

evil be identified as such by a major character in every film, and that it be punished by the end of the last reel. The Code also centralized absolute authority in Breen. A film could not be produced if he didn't approve its script. It could not be released if he didn't give it a special seal. If a company tried to release it without a seal, no MPPDA theater could play it. The jury that had approved *Queen Christina* was abolished and replaced by a disinterested board of directors in New York. On July 15, the *New York Times* solemnly reported the scene in Hollywood as the Studio Relations Committee was replaced by the Production Code Administration (PCA).

> With the new purification regulations going into effect, the motion-picture industry scurried about this week trying to salvage some films, revise others already produced, change those before the cameras that are thought to be questionable, and rewrite stories that may not meet with the new conception of things. . . . Metro has suffered most heavily of all the studios. Greta Garbo's *Painted Veil* was given a scouring; *The Green Hat* has had several days of retakes made . . . and the $25,000 paid for *The Postman Always Rings Twice* has been written off as a loss.

The effect of the reconstituted Code on Greta Garbo's career was considerable. *The Painted Veil*'s transgressions were made less explicit and their punishments more severe. Equally important, Garbo's earlier films, which were still playing all over the country, were withdrawn from circulation. All of them, except for *Grand Hotel* and *Mata Hari* (which was severely cut), were declared unfit for reissue. *Queen Christina* was soon pulled from circulation. If this was how Breen treated the earlier manifestations of Garbo's uniquely adult persona, what would he do to her future projects? Her contract negotiations were only a few months way. What would she be worth to M-G-M if Breen would not permit her to make adult films? Who would pay to see Greta Garbo in *Rebecca of Sunnybrook Farm*? Or, more to the point, as Joan of Arc?

In June, Garbo moved to a house on Carmelina Drive in Brentwood. Not long after, the ever-watchful *Hollywood Reporter* noted that Acosta had also moved to that street. By this time Acosta was totally absorbed in her *Jehanne d'Arc* screenplay. As evidenced by her letters, her conversations, and her behavior, Acosta's preoccupation with Garbo had advanced to the point of obsession. In the process of modifying the Le Gallienne vehicle for Garbo, Acosta began transferring Garbo's traits to the saint and vice versa. "She and Jehanne d'Arc became inseparable in my consciousness," wrote Acosta. "I arrived at a point where I could not tell which was Greta and which was Jehanne. So complete was this transference in my mind that when I walked with her in the hills or on the beach I often saw her in medieval costumes or in armor."

Before descending the stairs for a two-second crane shot directed by Boleslawski (below, with script), Garbo prepared herself. When W. S. Van Dyke reshot the scene, he asked Garbo: "Listen, honey, how many ways are there of coming down a staircase?"

art," he said, "that one found her almost as marvelous as the camera itself."

The Painted Veil had dialogue that was far more literate than was heard in Garbo's previous films. She still arrived on the set letter-perfect, but sometimes she had to be corrected on her pronunciation of polysyllabic words. She was used to cutting out such stumbling blocks, but on this film she could not. "I could only do something when it was strange [and new] to me," said Garbo years later. "I didn't even know what it was all about. I didn't like to know what the lines meant. Sometimes I would cross them out. Whenever the script said 'Listen,' 'Listen to me,' or 'So then,' I would shuffle over to the next thing. I did anything that came into my head and made a kind of fantasy of it, but I never knew what I was doing."

On this film, she could not get away with capricious cutting, and this made her, according to Marshall, "anxious and straightforward. When occasions arise, such as scenes, dialogue problems or wardrobe, she does not condemn or disapprove. She will only tell you that she is anxious about it." In a letter to Countess Wachtmeister, Garbo expressed her real opinion of *The Painted Veil*: "Rubbish—the film, I mean."

She was, as usual, unhappy with her assignment, well paid though it was. "I am still not rich enough," she wrote. "The only natural thing for me to do right now would be to disappear from films and get people to forget totally that I ever existed—I mean so that no one would look at me on the street." In late July, Garbo missed several days due to illness.

When she returned, she was hoarse. Boleslavsky shot around her as much as possible, and the sound engineer compensated the rest of the time. Her voice was noticeably richer, an aftereffect of her passing illness. This helped in her scenes with Marshall, who possessed a mellifluous speaking voice.

The elegant Marshall, often described as the consummate English gentleman, saw qualities in Garbo that his manner no doubt elicited. "I have never met a more natural woman than Greta Garbo," stated Marshall. "I would say, as an outsider, that much of the coldness that is ascribed to her is because she does not extend herself." Her other leading man in *The Painted Veil* was the thirty-five-year-old George Brent, a popular Warner Bros. player who had recently dissolved his marriage to stage and screen star Ruth Chatterton. In the colorful, unaffected Irishman, Garbo found something to enliven her days on the set. Brent lived on the shores of Toluca Lake, a private community in the rustic, undeveloped San Fernando Valley. Like Marshall, who had lost a leg in World War I, and Boleslavsky, who had been wounded as a lancer, Brent had seen action. He had been a young courier during the Irish Rebellion and had escaped arrest and execution only by sailing to America. Garbo visited his home for boxing lessons and, seeing that he was not part of the Hollywood social scene, started to spend time with him. Rumors of a romance began to spread.

In early August, while Brent and Garbo were enacting an adulterous affair before the cameras and engaging in a casual one after hours, Acosta presented *Jehanne d'Arc* to Thalberg. "He praised it extravagantly," wrote Acosta, "and said it was the best 'one-man job' he had ever seen. After reading it he actually came out of his office and with his arm around me walked me to my car. Even his secretary was astonished by this. I was extremely pleased and touched. He said he was going to discuss the film with Greta that day."

This was an opportune moment, since Garbo's contract would expire with the completion of her current film; her intramural corporation, Canyon Productions, was also closing down. Persuading her to sign a new contract was in great measure contingent upon an attractive property. *Jehanne d'Arc* was surely it. To Wachtmeister, though, Garbo confided indifference. "I'm lying on a table in my so-called garden," she wrote. "I say so-called because it is extremely small and has nothing in common with what a 'star' would call a garden. . . . Oh, it's such a pity that I'm not home. I think about it and long for it every moment. But prostitutes are never very happy. I've already been back here for more than two and a half years now [*sic*] and have only made two films. It's that awful contract I signed. I can do nothing about it."

About the same time, an article appeared in *Variety*, quoting an executive in M-G-M's New York office that "Garbo's European standing has not been impaired by *Queen Christina* and that for prestige, if nothing else, she

will continue to be a goodwill asset to the company." There was speculation that Harry Edington would relieve Salka Viertel as Garbo's de facto manager. And Acosta was talking behind the scenes. Items mentioning *Jehanne d'Arc* began appearing in local newspapers. "For the life of me," wrote Elizabeth Yeaman, "I can't figure out why anyone would want to visualize Garbo as Joan of Arc. Garbo is Swedish, guttural, and deliberate. She does not look French and certainly has not the volatile tongue of a French girl."

Acosta was in bed one night when the telephone rang. She was startled to hear the voice of Irving Thalberg. He sounded uncharacteristically dour. "Garbo does not want to do this film," he said, referring to *Jehanne d'Arc*. Acosta was too shocked to speak. "Have you discussed this with her?" She mumbled the halting answer that she had of course not talked to her about it—at all. "I'm as disappointed as you," said Thalberg. "She may change her mind. Come and see me tomorrow and we will talk about it."

Acosta saw Garbo the next morning but hesitated to broach the subject. Garbo avoided it too. Later that day, Acosta was ushered into Thalberg's office. The news was worse than she expected. "Greta is being influenced by someone," said Thalberg. "She would not make this decision on her own. But don't be discouraged. She may still do it, and if she does not I will find someone else who will. She is not the only pebble on the beach."

"I wish I thought so," said Acosta, holding back tears. "But in spite of what you say," she stammered, "I know damn well that she is the only pebble that can play Jehanne d'Arc."

"Don't worry," said Thalberg, trying to console her. "Your script will be done. Such good work cannot be wasted."

Acosta left Thalberg's office a devastated woman. Someone, most likely Salka Viertel, had sabotaged her efforts in an attempt to sever her tenuous connection with Garbo. Acosta, pathologically afraid of that very possibility, never brought up the stillborn script of *Jehanne d'Arc* to Garbo.

On September 13, Garbo filmed a scene with Brent in which they are the only Caucasian witnesses to a Chinese festival. In an outsize pageant, the sun marries the moon after a fiery altercation with a dragon. The sequence was choreographed by the famed "Orientalist" painter and dancer Hubert Stowitts, who also portrayed the sun god, stripped to the waist and painted with nut brown makeup. More than one hundred spectators—including Helen Hayes, Dorothy Arzner, Billie Burke, and Anna May Wong— watched the filming from bleachers and burst into applause at its conclusion. The exotic diversion was an obvious attempt to open up a stuffy story. No matter how grand the star, her film could not be sold without a trailer showing expensive scenes.

Dietrich's own new film promised a surfeit of spectacle, a lavish re-creation of the eighteenth-century Russian court. Would it help her career? The stakes were high. On

September 15, Paramount released *The Scarlet Empress* to hostile reviews. *Time* magazine wrote: "Sternberg has achieved the improbable feat of burying Marlene Dietrich in a welter of plaster-of-Paris gargoyles and galloping Cossacks." Richard Watts in the *New York Herald Tribune* wrote: "Under [Sternberg's] tutelage Miss Dietrich has become a hapless sort of automaton." The insightful André Sennwald wrote in the *New York Times*: "A ponderous, strangely beautiful, lengthy, and frequently wearying production, his new work is not a dramatic photoplay at all, but a succession of overelaborated scenes, dramatized emotional moods, and gaudily plotted visual excitements." Perhaps what Sennwald was trying to say was that Sternberg had made a film so advanced in cinematic grammar that it was beyond the grasp of film viewers used to standard "wide shot–medium shot–close shot" filmmaking. Most filmgoers did not read such reviews; all they needed was word of mouth to know that *The Scarlet Empress* was not for them. The extraordinary film was seen by no one. Mae West called it "an arty disaster." Paramount wondered how many more flops Dietrich could survive.

Edington, who now represented both Dietrich and Garbo, asked M-G-M if Garbo could be billed in her nineteenth film by her last name only. This would put her in the same category as stars such as Duse and Bernhardt. M-G-M liked the idea and designed the credits so that the titles would float over a panel of tall letters: GARBO. (The other change was that Richard Boleslavsky was billed as Boleslawski, a spelling he retained; he had been born Boleslaw Ryszard Srzednicki.)

The first screening of *The Painted Veil*, held in Glendale, was not a success. "The star's clothes," wrote Douglas Churchill in the *New York Times*, "were so—well, distinctive—that at one of the most tragic points in the film the audience burst into gales of laughter upon her entrance." The outfit in question was her nunlike nurse's uniform. "No star," wrote Louella Parsons, "not even a Garbo, can afford to be laughed at." Other laughs had come because of a pillbox hat Garbo was wearing in a nondramatic scene. She complained to Stromberg, who in turn spoke with an offended Adrian. Garbo did not help matters by asking if someone else could design for her in the future. After smoothing the ruffled feathers of all parties, Stromberg decided on retakes, but not of scenes with the hat; it remained, and eventually it started a fashion trend.

Trade reviews did not like the film's opening. *Variety* described a "slow, confused start," going on to say that "Boleslawski's direction is slow and often seems uncertain of its objective, although his detail is well handled and the emotional scenes with Garbo and Marshall achieve a poignant quality." *Motion Picture Daily* complained of the "heavy treatment" but thought that the film was "photographed with such artistry by William Daniels that those

appreciative of art will overlook certain weaknesses of the story." Stromberg assigned contract writer Rowland Leigh to evaluate the film. "The wedding of the younger sister," wrote Leigh, "is a good occasion on which to start the story. But the characters of the mother and the father are wrongly drawn. The mother's hardness is exaggerated almost to the point of farce."

While new scenes were being written, M-G-M and Edington entered into contract negotiations. On October 23, Garbo signed a one-picture contract for $275,000, and shortly thereafter she notified Selznick that she was ready to hear suggestions for her next film. Thalberg was absorbed in *Mutiny on the Bounty*, so Selznick proposed a remake of *Love—Anna Karenina*—to be directed by George Cukor. Garbo expressed interest. On November 8, she returned to the Austrian set to retake the first four scenes of *The Painted Veil*. The severe Beulah Bondi was replaced by the apple-faced Bodil Rosing, who bore a slight resemblance to Garbo's own mother. The argument between Frau Koerber and Katrin about the latter's unwillingness to marry became a sweet exchange about waiting for the right man. Taking a cue from the *Motion Picture Daily* review, the scene was written so that the camera could rest on a beautifully composed and lit close-up of Garbo throughout.

Boleslawski was unavailable for retakes because he had gone to Darryl F. Zanuck's Twentieth Century Pictures to direct Ronald Colman in *Clive of India*. The man Stromberg assigned was as unlikely a director for Garbo as Bondi was a mother. W. S. Van Dyke II was the hard-drinking, no-nonsense contract director who had taken Myrna Loy from a series of Eurasian temptress roles to leading-lady status in *Penthouse* and *The Prizefighter and the Lady*. Her standout performance in *The Thin Man* vindicated him, as did the film's outstanding grosses. No one expected him to make a career of directing Garbo, but he could give her retakes the energy they needed.

On the first day of shooting, Garbo and the company reported to the set to find that Van Dyke was not yet there. The lanky, handsome director breezed in shortly after nine. "Hi, honey," he said by way of introduction, taking a startled Garbo by the arm and walking her through her first scene. Then he hollered to Daniels: "Okay, kid, turn 'em over!" Before Garbo had a chance to comprehend, Van Dyke was setting up the next shot. There had been no rehearsal to speak of, and he was apparently satisfied with the first take.

Cecilia Parker was on the set with Garbo, since their opening scene also had to be reshot. "Garbo and I did have one conversation," Parker said. "It was about mountains. I happened to be saying that I have a little cabin up in the hills

Opposite: Garbo's portraits for *The Painted Veil* reflected a new screen persona. Sexy languor was giving way to melancholy contemplation. The change was effected by meddlesome advisers and the powerful Production Code. Photograph by Clarence Bull

The *New York Times* critic André Sennwald called Garbo "the most miraculous blend of personality and sheer dramatic talent that the screen has ever known."

added to Acosta's emotional turmoil. Garbo kept her at a safe distance while availing herself of her services; Dietrich could no longer be bothered. M-G-M retained Acosta, but she produced no usable writing for some time.

The Painted Veil premiered in New York on December 6, 1934. Reviews still faulted a dull script, insubstantial characters, and Hollywood chinoiserie but raved about Garbo's newly expanded range. "Again Greta Garbo triumphs by the sheer beauty of herself and her spirit over a picture that is only tolerable because what she gives to it," wrote Norbert Lusk in *Picture Play*. "Magically, she makes her heroine sensitive, poetic, and soulful as only Garbo can." André Sennwald's *New York Times* review said:

> It is the height of dishwater diplomacy to affect a temperate attitude toward this cool and lovely lady with the sad white face and the throaty voice. She is the most miraculous blend of personality and sheer dramatic talent that the screen has ever known, and her presence in *The Painted Veil* immediately makes it one of the season's cinema events. Watch her stalking about with long and nervous steps, while she waits to be told if her husband will die from the coolie's dagger thrust. It is as if all this had never been done before. Watch the veiled terror in her face as she sits at dinner with her husband, not knowing if he is aware of her infidelity; or her superb gallantry as she informs him of what it was that drove her into the arms of his friend; or her restlessness on the bamboo porch in Mei-Tain-Fu with the tinny phonograph, the heat, and her conscience. She shrouds all this with dignity, making it precious and memorable.

Within weeks, box-office receipts confirmed trade-review predictions. *The Painted Veil*'s domestic profit was a mere $146,000. The film was too heavy for American audiences, not because it had the confusing brilliance of Sternberg's work but because it had confusing characters. Whose fault was this? Had Maugham's novel been ruined by the Production Code? The PCA was a redoubtable presence, but the flaws in this film could not be laid at its doorstep. Garbo had too much control over every other element of the project; more correctly stated, she had delegated too much control. Her reliance on Salka Viertel, who was not qualified to judge literary properties or dramatic values, was undermining the best efforts of producers like Stromberg, directors like Boleslawski, and even visual artists like Daniels. *The Painted Veil* made a profit only because of its popularity in Europe, where visually sophisticated audiences were content to float from one compelling close-up of Garbo to the next, unbothered by inconsistent characters. American audiences wanted believable characters in a good story, not an image of Garbo filtered through a dilettante's sensibilities. Until—and unless—Garbo understood that, her career was headed for the same downward spiral as Dietrich's.

where I like to go off by myself. Garbo overheard me and said that she loves mountains too. She told me what they mean to her—grandeur and everlasting patience and a dwarfing of the silly frets and fevers of little human beings."

Before Garbo could expound further on the subject of topography, Van Dyke was beckoning her. "The script says you come through that door and you go out *that* door," he said, indicating the passage from the kitchen to the library, where she would collide with Marshall. Once again, Van Dyke filmed her without a rehearsal.

"How was that?" Garbo asked warily.

"Swell," answered Van Dyke. "Now the script says you have a change of costume and you come in that door and come down the staircase."

"Mister Van Dyke," asked Garbo, "don't you ever rehearse?"

"Listen, honey, how many ways are there of coming down a staircase?"

Garbo completed her six days of retakes in a very good mood, Edington told M-G-M.

While the film was being edited, a tragic episode occurred. Mercedes de Acosta, driving her new car, struck and killed a pedestrian. Before long, the victim's family learned that Acosta worked for a film company and sued her for $50,000. The case, which was not settled for three years,

CHAPTER TWENTY-ONE

Anna Karenina

Choosing David O. Selznick as a producer was a wise move for Greta Garbo in 1935. Her career needed expert guidance, and Selznick was qualified. Before joining M-G-M in early 1933, he had filled the coffers and heightened the prestige of both Paramount and RKO. The resistance that greeted his arrival at M-G-M in 1933 turned to grudging respect as he produced glittering, literate films such as *Dinner at Eight*, *Manhattan Melodrama*, and *David Copperfield*. Katharine Hepburn owed her stardom to his production of *A Bill of Divorcement*, and Joan Crawford climbed out of a career slump with his super-hit *Dancing Lady*. If anyone could pull Garbo out of the doldrums, it was Selznick. Why, then, was he developing a project that sounded so uncommercial?

Garbo had already done a film based on Count Leo Tolstoy's *Anna Karenina*. It had been her most profitable silent

"Miss Garbo, the first lady of the screen, sins, suffers, and perishes illustriously in the new, ably produced, and comparatively mature version of the Tolstoy classic," wrote the *New York Times* critic André Sennwald in his review of Garbo's twentieth American film, *Anna Karenina*. Photograph by Clarence Bull

film, but that was partly because it capitalized on her romance with John Gilbert. In late 1934, it was obvious that the Production Code was sending studio story departments to library shelves in search of classics that would not, in the phraseology of Joseph Breen, "offend against common decency." Universal was filming *Great Expectations*, RKO was filming *Vanity Fair*, and United Artists was releasing *The Count of Monte Cristo*. Yet there was no guarantee that a great book would make a popular movie. Samuel Goldwyn used literary classics to launch the Soviet actress Anna Sten, but he found that Emile Zola's *Nana* and Tolstoy's *Resurrection* (filmed as *We Live Again* by Rouben Mamoulian) made unwieldy star vehicles. Both failed miserably at

"Not even Garbo in the Orient has approached, for spectacular effects, Dietrich in Spain," wrote *Variety*'s Cecelia Ager of the 1935 film *The Devil Is a Woman*. Photograph by Josef von Sternberg

The unrelieved sadness of *Anna Karenina* was as much a function of the Production Code as of Tolstoy's writing.

you? They are so god-damned noble, simple, and splendid. I'm so glad you're not one any longer." The subtext was that both Cukor and Walpole were successfully integrated show-business homosexuals.

Not so successfully integrated was Mercedes de Acosta. Pushed to the sidelines by the flurry of activity around Garbo's new project, Acosta sought spiritual counsel from Sri Meher Baba, who recommended that she write a screenplay about him; perhaps then she would find the right formula for Garbo, both aesthetically and personally. Acosta had no ideas and no money, so she went to New York to see her husband, Abram Poole. While there, she made the mistake of bringing a woman to the bedroom of his apartment. He walked in on them and decided it was time to end their marriage of inconvenience. When Acosta made a hasty exit, one columnist wrote: "Mercedes d' Acosta [*sic*] is in Europe divorcing her husband, Abram Poole—or didn't you know she had one?"

In January 1935, Garbo was vacationing with George Brent at a Coachella Valley resort called La Quinta. Selznick was consulting with Cukor about the Dane-Viertel script. "Selznick found the screenplay we delivered much too long, the scenes Victorian, the dialogue too stilted, and he wanted changes," wrote Viertel. "But Winifred in her impatience to leave thought it was perfect. She had a play in rehearsal in London." Selznick let Dane go; he had other plans. On January 7, he dispatched Viertel to La Quinta with a letter for Garbo. Selznick was already known in Hollywood for his lengthy memoranda. This was no exception.

We have lost our enthusiasm for a production of *Anna Karenina* as your next picture. I personally feel that your audiences are waiting to see you in a smart, modern picture and that to do a heavy Russian drama on the heels of so many ponderous similar films, in which they have seen you and other stars recently, would prove to be a mistake. I still think *Karenina* can be a magnificent film and I would be willing to do it with you later, but to do it now, following the disappointment of *Queen Christina* and *The Painted Veil*, is something I dislike contemplating greatly.

Mr. Cukor shares my feeling and it seems a pity that we must start our first joint venture with you with such a feeling of dread for the outcome. If we make the picture, Mr. Cukor and I will put our very best efforts into it and I am sure we could make a fine film, one excellent enough to dissipate the obvious pitfalls of the subject from the viewpoint of your millions of admirers. But I do hope that you will not force us to proceed.

We have spent some time in searching for a comedy and although several have been brought to me, there are none I feel sufficiently important enough to justify the jump into comedy; to say nothing of the difficulty of preparing a comedy in the limited time left to us. Therefore, since you feel you must leave the end of May and cannot give us additional time, we have been faced with the task of finding a subject that could be prepared in time and which might inspire us with a feeling that we could make a picture comparable to your former sensations and one that would, at the same time, meet my very strong feeling that you should do a modern subject at this time in your career. The odds against our finding such a subject were very remote and I was very distressed and felt that there was no alternative left to us but to proceed with *Karenina*.

Now, however, I find that I can purchase *Dark Victory*, the owners of which have resisted offers from several companies for many months. The play is at the top of the list of several studios, and if we do not purchase it, the likelihood is that it will be purchased at once for Katharine Hepburn. . . . I have asked Salka to see you and to bring you this letter and to tell you the story—which I consider the best modern woman's vehicle, potentially, since *A Bill of Divorcement* and which I think has the makings of a strikingly fine film. . . .

Fredric March will only do *Anna Karenina* if he is forced to by his employers, Twentieth Century Pictures. He has told me repeatedly that he is fed up on doing costume pictures; that he thinks it is a mistake to do another; that he knows he is much better in modern subjects and that all these reasons are aggravated by the fact that *Anna Karenina* would come close on the heels of the Anna Sten-

Mamoulian-Goldwyn picture, *We Live Again*, from *Resurrection*, a picture which has been a failure. . . . I have asked Salka to telephone me as soon as she has discussed the matter thoroughly with you.

The result of Viertel's journey was that Garbo agreed to do *Dark Victory*. When Selznick set about securing playwright Philip Barry to adapt it, however, the plan hit some snags: Barry might not be available in time, and he might also be too costly for a project already burdened with Garbo's salary. Whitney's asking price for the play was also quite high. By late January, *Anna Karenina* was reinstated, with a familiar—and much-needed—collaborator. "Sam Behrman was between plays," recalled Viertel. "David asked him to write the final script. It was wonderful to have Sam back, intense, moody, and chain-smoking." Recalled Behrman: "I became, in some sort, a Garbo specialist, as I had the reputation of being, in some sort, a Lunt specialist."

To all appearances, the real Garbo specialist was Salka Viertel. And she did not limit her influence to scripts; she was stage-managing Garbo's social life. On January 26, Garbo surprised all of Hollywood, and, by way of wire services, all of America, by showing up at an exclusive nightclub, the Café Trocadero. When she appeared in the foyer at 11:30 P.M., patrons gaped in disbelief. The orchestra stopped playing. It just could not be. But there she was, wearing a tailored suit and a tie, accompanied by French director Marcel Archard, Salka Viertel, Gottfried Reinhardt, and his father, Max Reinhardt, who was codirecting *A Midsummer Night's Dream* for Warner Bros. The club's owner, Billy Wilkerson, signaled to the conductor to resume playing. The headwaiter rushed over and whispered: "I can give you a table in a corner where no one will see you." Garbo said that she would prefer to sit at a table adjoining the dance floor with Princess Natalie Paley and Felixe Rollo, a purported Egyptian prince. Nearby tables in the nightclub were occupied by Hollywood notables such as Ernst Lubitsch, Louis B. Mayer, Lili Damita, Walter Wanger, Fritz Lang, and Marlene Dietrich. "You never saw so many women in severely tailored suits," wrote Harrison Carroll in the *Evening Herald-Express*. Mayer smiled across the room at Garbo. Lubitsch came to her table to say hello. Damita's date, arriving late, mistook Garbo for Damita and slapped her on the back, saying, "Hello, Toots." Garbo took it in stride. Wanger asked Garbo for the first dance.

"No, not tonight, Walter," she replied. "This is all new. Let me get used to it first."

Garbo sipped champagne and talked with her friends while everyone in the club discreetly craned his or her neck to see if she would look at or talk to Dietrich. "The reported snubs between the Swedish actress and Marlene Dietrich were not apparent to this observer, who kept a pretty close watch," wrote Carroll. "Marlene said afterward that she did nod to Garbo. But she did chide photographers for chasing her rival."

"That wasn't nice," said Dietrich. "Why didn't you let her enjoy herself for the evening?"

"They are trying to renew the old Garbo-Dietrich feud for publicity purposes," wrote columnist Sidney Skolsky in the *Hollywood Citizen-News*. Dietrich was not a regular at Viertel's salon but knew everyone who was. She had the same manager, Harry Edington, as Garbo. *The Scarlet Empress* and *The Painted Veil* had both been box-office disappointments. This nightclub "act," which got a great deal of press coverage, was in all likelihood an Edington-Viertel brainstorm meant to gild two birds with one story. It worked.

There was one person who did not curry favor with Viertel. Although Behrman had Viertel dictate her ideas to a secretary in their writing cubicle, he did not take her seriously. "Walking up and down," recalled Viertel, "I described the night train approaching relentlessly—the lights from the carriage windows on Anna's face—her running down an embankment and throwing herself between the cars, then—a prostrated figure on the rails—the train disappearing in darkness—and last, a woman's handbag on the embankment. 'And that's what's left of a human being,' I concluded, almost in tears. I turned to Sam. He burst into roars of laughter." Behrman later said: "Her relation with Garbo was strange."

A candid photograph taken by William Grimes from a catwalk shows (at left) Gyles Isham and Maureen O'Sullivan concentrating on their lines while Garbo and Fredric March laugh over a mazurka step.

Garbo was determined to leave for Europe in May, so every department at M-G-M began working from the pages that Behrman had completed in order to start shooting on March 1. Cukor, intrigued by a Katharine Hepburn project at RKO, backed out of *Anna Karenina*. Garbo asked for Clarence Brown. "I really did like Mr. Brown," she said years later. Adrian began designing ultra-feminine gowns. "*Anna Karenina* is the first time in a while that I've been able to costume Miss Garbo in this manner," he said. "The picture transpires in the frothiest, most beribboned and beruffled era in history." Garbo cooperated by coming to the studio for fittings. One organdy gown made its designer so happy that he gushed: "If you weren't Garbo, I should be down on the street with my camera, making a record of this dress." Garbo said, "Get your little camera."

Skolsky reported in his column that she was heard playing a record of Cole Porter's "You're the Top" in her dressing room. She kept resetting the needle to the verse that said "You're the National Gallery / You're Garbo's salary."

In late February, the film was ready to roll. Breen had approved the latest incomplete script, so Selznick thought it safe to proceed. Since gaining his powerful post, Breen had become almost as sociable as the habitués of the "Troc." Martin Quigley, the contentious publisher of the *Motion Picture Herald*, was keeping tabs on Breen's public appearances. He visited Breen in late February and brought him to task for his extravagant lifestyle, telling him that he had "gone Hollywood." Quigley had already caused Breen problems. He had griped to Will Hays about the insufficient censorship of Lubitsch's *Merry Widow* the previous October. Breen had fixed it in a hurry. Disapproving of Breen's new image, Quigley wrote the influential priest Father Wilfred Parsons. Breen saw that *Anna Karenina* could turn into another *Merry Widow*.

On March 5, Breen demanded changes in Vronsky's character. "As we see it," wrote Breen, "he is a seducer who lives openly with an adulterous woman who he finally deserts to return to his former military and social life. There is no clear indication that he is condemned or punished for his behavior. We feel that the present treatment leaves the picture open to the accusation that it sets up a double standard of morals." This was a shock to Selznick, who had already made all the concessions Breen had sought. There was more. Breen wanted all physical contact between the lovers cut. "We realize that the deletion of all scenes showing Vronsky and Anna tender and affectionate and kissing each other may somewhat affect the quality of the story," said Breen, "but the cumulative effect of such scenes, if retained in the picture, is likely to prove highly dangerous from the point of view both of public reaction and political censorship." He further required that a scene of the lovers living together in Venice be cut and that a scene be added in which Vronsky is forced to resign his commission.

Two days later Selznick sent an outraged reply. "I am distressed," he wrote, "because your comments come too late to do anything but give us the alternative of making a completely vitiated and emasculated adaptation of Tolstoy's famous classic. Miss Garbo leaves for Europe, willy-nilly, the middle of May, which gives us just enough time to make the picture, allowing leeway for scoring and preview. Had you, in December, the same objections as now to the script, I would most certainly have abandoned the whole project." Garbo had recently expressed interest in a comedy called *Tovarich*, but it was far too late to shut down *Anna Karenina*.

Selznick continued: "*Anna Karenina* is solely and simply a love story—and an adulterous love story. To try and make it anything else is utterly impossible. As to the physical contact between Anna and Vronsky, I don't know how love scenes can be played, particularly in a story of this kind, without physical contact. . . . If we eliminate these and any such references, I challenge anyone to demonstrate to me how the picture of *Anna Karenina* can be made at all. If anyone can do this, he is much more competent than I."

Selznick concluded by agreeing to Breen's request for changes in Vronsky's scenes "even though it is in violation of Tolstoy; even though it surprised me that at this late date you should make additional criticisms; even though the writers of the script are violently opposed to it; and even though it is very harmful to the story point of Vronsky's voluntary sacrifice for Anna." Preproduction was momentarily halted for rewriting. Fortunately, Garbo chose that moment to request a two-week postponement of the start date, most likely for reasons of health; her "old trouble" was still very much in evidence. On March 12, Selznick worked on the script in a conference with Viertel and Behrman. His notes read: "Lengthen this scene [105] between Dolly and Anna—Dolly's desperation—she makes the point that she can't leave Stiva because of the children; she can't live with him. Her hysteria, her tears—also her reaction as Anna gets her to weaken: 'Yes, but he has kissed her!'—visualizing the physical relation between the governess and Stiva. Refer to dialogue in Chapter XIX of the book."

On the next day, Selznick received a letter from Breen in which he acknowledged Selznick's willingness to cooperate and withdrew many of his objections with the understanding that Selznick would "avoid shooting these scenes in a manner that would tend to glorify Anna's sin while at the same time ridiculing those who condemn her for it." Breen later reported to Hays that he had approved *Anna Karenina* because "the sin of Anna and Vronsky is not presented as attractive or alluring. As soon as the relationship with Vronsky has begun, there is not a single hour of unalloyed bliss for Anna, while trouble is brewing for Vronsky, too. Anna, in her most mirthful moment, is melancholy. When she says 'I am happy!' we know that she is deceiving herself." With this strange interpretation of Tolstoy imposed on them,

Production Code administrator Joseph Breen tried to have this romantic scene in Venice eliminated from the script of *Anna Karenina*.

Behrman and Selznick worked feverishly to ready the script. Viertel showed Garbo the latest draft, telling her how hard she was working to maintain its authenticity. Garbo perused it with her usual misgivings, but she found it very different from what she had expected. "When I read the script it was the first time that I was a little thrilled," she later told Cecil Beaton. By March 18, Behrman was frantically writing in pencil over existing versions of scenes.

One case was the scene in which Anna tells the debutante Kitty to enjoy her youth. In the book the speech read: "Oh! What a happy time you are at. I remember, and I know that blue haze like the mist on the mountains in Switzerland. That mist which covers everything in that blissful time when childhood is just ending, and out of that vast circle, happy and gay, there is a path growing narrower and narrower, and it is delightful and alarming to enter the ballroom, bright and splendid as it is. Who has not been through it?"

Behrman's version, after the penciled corrections, was: "You are at such a happy time in your life, Kitty—that blissful time when childhood is just ending and the future is so warm and inviting. I remember—one swims in a mysterious

blue haze like the mist on the mountains in Switzerland. That mist covers everything and from it may rise at any moment the shape of the beloved one—only half imagined, half dreamed."

Garbo took her blue pencil to it so she could more easily enunciate the words: "*That's such* a happy time in your life. *A* blissful time, when childhood is just ending, and the *future's all* warm and inviting. I remember. One swims in a mysterious blue haze—like the mist on the mountains in Switzerland. That mist covers everything and *out of it* may rise at any moment the shape of the beloved one—only half imagined, half dreamed."

Selznick applied this minute attention to every page of the script and to every aspect of the production. "Mr. Selznick drove with a passionate intensity, drove himself and everyone else," recalled Rathbone. "Perfection for David was not the ultimate, but only the penultimate." Rathbone also strove for excellence. He sent memos to Selznick with suggestions from Tolstoy's text. One memo read: "In Chapter Twelve, Part IV [Karenin] says: 'I would give a great deal for doubt to be still possible. When I doubted I was miserable,

Hollywood trade papers thought *Anna Karenina* too sad for the average audience. "It may be argued that the picture is art," wrote *Variety*, "but with an investment of the magnitude of this picture, if healthy returns are expected, art is a secondary consideration."

but it was still better than now. When I doubted, I had hope, but now there is no hope, and still I doubt everything. . . . ' Could a place be found for this speech or a part of it. It is such a tragic exposé of his inability to face life—the human side of life—with any understanding." Selznick forwarded the memo to Viertel, but it was not used.

On March 25, *Anna Karenina* finally went into production. Clarence Brown immediately noticed a difference in Garbo. "Formerly it disturbed her to have me sit in front of the camera," he said. "Now it doesn't distract her." Fredric March, whose love scenes were few and restrained, noticed that when he put any vigor into his embraces, Garbo found a bit of garlic to chew on. One day, after his angles were completed, he started for his dressing room, and then decided to watch Garbo working on her own close-up. Impressed by her technique, he walked over to her and complimented her.

"Do you mean you watched me acting?" she asked.

"Why, yes—"

"You should not have done that," said Garbo, and she walked off in a huff.

Garbo eventually warmed to March. "We would bounce a medicine ball back and forth, and one day she stripped to

the waist to take the sun. Then she caught herself and asked if it embarrassed me. It did not. I was not overwhelmed by Garbo's beauty. I think at the time women were more attracted to her than men."

Rathbone's experience with Garbo was not quite so cordial, especially as he had met her before. "I used to go along to visit John Gilbert quite a lot [in 1928], and Garbo and I were introduced at one of his parties. There was a jolly crowd present. Most of them were good-looking Hollywood stars. But there was no one there so radiantly beautiful as Garbo. . . . There was nothing languorous about her. She was a great sport and great fun. She played tennis energetically and really well." Seven years later, when Rathbone was introduced to Garbo on the set, she gave no sign that she remembered him. "She had changed," said Rathbone. "I got the impression of someone in distress. All that jolliness had disappeared completely. Talking to her I felt somehow that I was intruding. She seemed to be tired." Freddie Bartholomew, who was playing their son, said to Rathbone: "I have never met Miss Garbo, and I really am so frightened." Rathbone introduced the eleven-year-old boy to her, but she remained formal to both of them. "If her attitude had related to me alone I think I might have understood, for it could have been that her growing hatred of me (as Karenin) might have been more difficult to simulate had we become good friends. It troubled me at first, but I soon dismissed it in my tremendous admiration for her consummate ability as an actress, perhaps the greatest I have ever played with."

Maureen O'Sullivan played intimate scenes with Garbo and felt that Garbo was barely there. "As an actress she gave you very little," recalled O'Sullivan. "When working with her one felt that she was doing nothing, really, that she wasn't even very good. I thought: 'If that's what the studio is so excited about, well, they must be mad.' I thought she was terrible—not doing a thing while the rest of us acted up a storm around her. But then I saw the rushes, and Garbo had made fools of all of us. She was the only one who stood out and who made the scenes believable." As before, Brown gave Garbo very few directions. "She knew just what she had to do and how she expected to do it," he said. "If the director suggested changes, she listened respectfully, sometimes arguing quietly but never angrily. She always wanted to give the best she had. Everything was for the picture's sake."

"She made tiny movements," said Rathbone, "minute changes of expression which I didn't notice at the time, but when I saw the scene on the screen I was amazed. There was the scene where I had to tell her while we were out driving in a carriage that she was seeing too much of this other man, Vronsky. She said nothing and seemed to do nothing. But on the screen I found that she had made a tiny movement, the slightest possible drawing away from me, so that she did not touch me as she sat. That little gesture could not have been more effective. With it she conveyed an impression of utter loathing." Whether it was the concentration that made such mastery possible or her innate fear of people, Garbo spent most of her time in her dressing room, conferring with the veteran actress Constance Collier, who was another Viertel salon regular.

Garbo's maternal scenes were a pivotal part of the film. "I told her one day," March recalled, "how wonderful she had been with the boy in the silent version of *Anna Karenina*, letting him really take over their scenes together." In this film, Garbo was having trouble with the awesomely talented Freddie Bartholomew. "Imagine a production with Garbo and Shirley Temple," Selznick had quipped at one point, but it was not funny to Garbo; her passive manipulation did not subdue the little dynamo. Rathbone succeeded by telling him that his aunt was dying. Bartholomew grew teary-eyed and behaved long enough to make the scene. Garbo had no such ploy. "I did see her cry once," recalled Behrman. "That was on the set of *Anna Karenina*. She was having trouble in the scene with her son." Garbo later referred to Bartholomew as "a monster."

Garbo's few light moments on the set were reserved for William Daniels, whom she spooked by sneaking up behind him and honking the bicycle horn attached to his camera dolly. He appeared to be the only coworker of whom she was truly fond, as well she should have been. He was once again innovating ways to showcase her beauty, even though Brown did not stop the movie for each breathtaking close-up, as did the directors of *Queen Christina* and *The Painted Veil*. From her first shot in the film, in which a blast of steam melts to reveal her face, to the last, in which the lights of the passing train flash on her face in a syncopated rhythm as she steels herself for a death plunge, every cinematic portrait advanced the plot and was essential to it.

Daniels felt that the art he was capturing with his camera was mostly intuitive. "I don't think she is conscious of movement, voice, or expression," he said. "She just seems to think her part, and everything about it expresses it to perfection. That is why we use so many close-ups. She can tell so much with the subtlest glance of an eye and put so much meaning into a fleeting expression. In a more distant shot these subtleties would be lost." Daniels did as much for Garbo as Sternberg did for Dietrich—without exacting an egotistical toll.

On May 3, Paramount released *The Devil Is a Woman*, the last film that Sternberg would make with Dietrich. Always controversial, Sternberg had ended the collaboration with a bang. "Miss Dietrich and I have progressed as far as possible together," he announced to the press before telling her. "My being with her in the future will not help her or me." In spite of this declaration or perhaps because of it, his superb movie was given an even nastier reception than *The Scarlet Empress*. "It is not hard to understand why Hollywood expressed such violent distaste for Josef von Sternberg's new film," wrote André Sennwald in the *New York Times*. "For the talented director-photographer, in *The Devil Is a Woman*, makes a cruel and mocking assault upon the romantic sex motif which Hollywood has been gravely celebrating all these years. . . . A story which is deceptively conventional on the surface becomes a heartless parable of man's eternal humiliation in the sex struggle." Sennwald went on to predict that the film would be totally rejected by American audiences, even though it was the best of the seven Sternberg-Dietrich films, perhaps the most sophisticated film ever made in Hollywood—and it was gorgeous. "Always a master of light and shadow, Mr. von Sternberg achieves a delicate and sinister beauty." *The Devil Is a Woman*, if nothing else, was one of the greatest achievements in black-and-white photography Hollywood had ever seen. After five years of glamorizing Dietrich, Sternberg had at last transformed her into the most glamorous *thing* ever seen on film.

Variety's Cecelia Ager wrote: "Not even Garbo in the Orient has approached, for spectacular effects, Dietrich in Spain. With fringe, lace, sequins, carnations, chenille, nets, embroideries and shawls, Miss Dietrich is hung, wrapped,

In this portrait, Clarence Bull used candles and a long exposure to illuminate Garbo's face.

draped, swathed, and festooned. . . . Her costumes are completely incredible, but completely fascinating and suitable to *The Devil Is a Woman*. They reek with glamour." But this glamour did nothing to endear Dietrich to the public, for she played a capricious creature, an inscrutable destroyer of men. What had possessed Sternberg to make such a labor of hate? Insiders commented that the masochistic character of Don Pasqual as played by Lionel Atwill looked and acted exactly like Sternberg. Dietrich's on-screen treatment of him was likened to her treatment of the besotted genius in real life. When she snatches money and a cigarette from him to bestow on her new lover, a slick toreador dressed in black and white, it was a replay of the times she dumped him for Mercedes de Acosta. In Robert Z. Leonard and Mae Murray there was a precedent for a jealous director and a flirtatious star, but there was no precedent for playing out a private obsession on the screen. If Dietrich's last three flops had not extinguished her stardom, this film would. Garbo had a clear field.

On his last day of work with Garbo, Rathbone sat next to her just off the set. Garbo sat silent, priming herself for her next emotional release. Rathbone surprised himself by breaking the silence with a respectful request. "Miss Garbo," he said with exquisite restraint, "I wonder if you would grant me a very great favor. When I work with anyone I admire as much as I admire you I ask for the privilege of a signed photograph. I have one here that will help me remember the wonderful experience in playing opposite you. Would you sign it for me?"

"I never give picture," answered Garbo after a pause. Then it was time to do their scene. On Garbo's last day with Bartholomew, she had her revenge on the "monster." Bartholomew's aunt handed him a freshly printed portrait of Garbo and aimed him toward her dressing room, saying, "Greta Garbo loves you."

"I knocked on her dressing-room door," Bartholomew recalled. "She came, and I said, 'Would you sign this for me?' And she said, 'No,' and closed the door."

The last scene to be shot was Garbo's suicide scene at the train station. Knowing that the scene was scheduled for May 14, syndicated columnist Sidney Skolsky disguised himself as an extra and crept onto the soundstage where a section of the station had been built. "I managed to sneak around and under the elevated platform," wrote Skolsky. "I was completely out of sight. Garbo arrived, and director Clarence Brown did a run-through of the scene. Garbo stood on the platform." In the first shot, Garbo was to rise from a bench and walk along the tracks as the train was readied for departure. "I was under Garbo, looking straight at her through the cracks in the platform," wrote Skolsky. "The customary chalk marks were made to mark the spots where Garbo was to start and walk into camera range. Instead, Garbo paced the platform. She returned to the starting chalk marks." She looked like a woman contemplating suicide, but she also looked like an actress who sensed something was amiss.

"Let's try one," said Brown.

Garbo did not respond to her cue. In a firm voice she said, "I'm not doing anything until the stranger leaves the set."

"She hadn't seen me," wrote Skolsky. "No one had seen me. How did she know? Then all hell started to break loose. Assistant directors, second cameramen, prop men, makeup ladies were on a noisy manhunt, in all directions. Grips stood on their high flywalks as if they were prison guards ready to shoot. The soundstage door opened, and a bulky member of the M-G-M police force stamped in, his fat hand on his holster. . . . Soon they'd be looking under the platform."

Deciding that his time was up, Skolsky made a break for the emergency exit and ran into an open door on the next soundstage, where he buttonholed dance director Seymour Felix and pretended to be interviewing him. Skolsky's pursuers came through the door. Recognizing him as a prominent member of the press, they stopped in their tracks and decided to leave him there.

The first cut of *Anna Karenina* was previewed in Riverside on Tuesday, May 21. "I drove out with Mr. and Mrs. Selznick, Mrs. Viertel, and Miss Garbo to Riverside," wrote Behrman. "The delicacy and distinction of Garbo's performance affected me as it did the audience. I felt as I always did watching her that she is the most patrician artist in the

Opposite: Garbo as Anna Karenina, the heroine who is "doomed to bliss—and despair." Photograph by Clarence Bull

world. Mr. and Mrs. Selznick were pleased. But on the way home in the car, Garbo sat silent. She spoke once, in reply to a query from Selznick as to how she felt.

"Oh, if once, if only once, I could see a preview and come home feeling satisfied!" The limousine brought the group back to Selznick's house, where Garbo drove her hostess crazy searching for tennis shoes. "Nothing mattered to Garbo but the tennis," recalled Irene Selznick. "Everybody got a drink and we turned the outside lights on and went down to the court." Garbo beat both Cedric Gibbons and Selznick. "Never before or since have I seen her in such high spirits," said Irene.

Behrman was scheduled to leave the following Sunday. Early that morning the phone rang. It was David Selznick. "He said he had been talking to Miss Garbo," wrote Behrman. "She was unhappy about several points in the film. She insisted that I remain to fix them. He was sorry but he could not let me go for at least another week. It was like being told, after weeks in a hospital, that you could leave on a certain day and then at the last minute having the promise revoked." He spent the next week preparing scenes for Garbo to shoot so she could be on time for her train.

On Thursday, Garbo signed a contract for two more films at $250,000 each. First she would do *Marie Walewska*, but if the studio did not have that prepared by the time she returned, she had the choice of *A Woman of Spain* or *Camille*. New terms provided that Garbo be paid $10,000 a week while retakes were being written. Garbo left Hollywood on Friday, May 31. "The picture looks excellent," Selznick wrote in a memo to both publicity directors: Howard Strickling in Culver City and Howard Dietz in New York. "Garbo herself thinks it's far and away her best work, so I hope you are not going to dish it out as if it were another *Christina* or *Painted Veil*."

On June 27, the PCA granted *Anna Karenina* a certificate. That did not stop the Chicago branch of the Legion of Decency from putting the film on its "Condemned" list. Selznick appealed to Breen, who arranged for a group of Catholic clergy, including the influential Archbishop John Cantwell of Los Angeles, to see the film. Cantwell was satisfied that the film observed the dictates of the Code and wrote to the Midwest priests, who removed the film from their list.

When *Anna Karenina* premiered on August 30, the audience applauded at the sight of Garbo materializing from behind a cloud of steam. There was a feeling in the air that Garbo's fortunes had improved. "Greta Garbo, after several years of miscasting, is back at last in her own particular province of glamour and heartbreak, of tragic lovely ladies and handsome ruthless men," wrote Eileen Creelman in the *New York Sun*. "She has even discarded those extraordinary costumes that made her look like a theatrical dressmaker's advertisement, and, happily aided by excellent photography and becoming gowns, reclaimed her own unique beauty." The most important review was also the most laudatory. Writing in the *New York Times*, André Sennwald thought the film was "a dignified and effective drama because of that tragic, lonely, and glamorous blend which is the Garbo personality." Sennwald did not distinguish Garbo's own melancholy from the fatalism imposed by the Production Code. "Miss Garbo, always the apex of the drama, suggests the inevitability of her doom from the beginning, streaking her first happiness with undertones of anguish, later trying futilely to mend the broken pieces, and at last standing regally alone as she approaches the end."

Trade- and fan-magazine reviews found the film overly long, overproduced, and oddly unromantic. Breen had been more successful than the hypocritical Russian society that Tolstoy decried; he had kept Anna and Vronsky from expressing their passion, and some reviewers felt cheated. "This is a weak and dull picture," wrote a reviewer in *Photoplay*, "yet the persuasive genius of Garbo raises it into the class of art. What should be moving seems dated, though the production is magnificent, and Garbo, exquisitely photographed, has more fire than in her last several pictures." All reviews saw Garbo as the perfect Anna and hoped, like *Variety*, that the film's box-office receipts would "come close to establishing modern-day highs."

Anna Karenina did not do as well as *China Seas*, which had Clark Gable and Jean Harlow, or *Top Hat*, which had Fred Astaire, Ginger Rogers, and Irving Berlin, but it did better than expected outside the big cities, selling the most tickets to a Garbo film since *Anna Christie*. The film grossed $865,000 domestically and $1,439,000 abroad, but its net profit was reported as only $320,000, because Garbo's salary really was "the top."

"Garbo asked me to produce all her pictures," recalled Selznick, "but by that time I was getting ready to leave M-G-M and in spite of the honor, I had my own ambitions." With backing from Whitney, Thalberg, and several others, Selznick started his own company, Selznick International Pictures. Thalberg was now the only independent producer at M-G-M, with first call on Garbo's services. Though she was not nominated for an Academy Award, her performance in *Anna Karenina* received the New York Film Critics Award for best feminine performance of the year. Just thirty and at the height of her powers, Garbo was ready for a truly great role. Even in the shadow of the Code, it was possible to craft films that were literate and mature, if not frankly adult. In late 1935, Thalberg looked forward to a season that would include his first Garbo film since *As You Desire Me*.

CHAPTER TWENTY-TWO
Camille

Metro-Goldwyn-Mayer, the most lavish studio in Hollywood, had a parsimonious side that publicists never mentioned. Although most stars and writers were kept on salary through fallow periods, the studio cut costs in every other area. When shooting on a set was completed, the set was taken apart and put in storage. Unlike the Fox Film Corporation, which built new sets for nearly every film, M-G-M reused sets constantly. The gleaming foyer and staircase of Greta Garbo's home in *Anna Karenina* turned up a short while later in Robert Z. Leonard's *Escapade*, the lovely film that introduced Luise Rainer to American audiences. By the same token, space was not wasted. When Thalberg hired RKO producer David Lewis in the summer of 1935, he walked him to an empty second-floor suite at the far end of a long wooden building. "Greta Garbo is in Europe," said Thalberg, "and for the time being we're giving you her dressing room." Lewis was surprised at its starkness. "When I walked in," recalled Lewis, "I saw a tiny outer room. There was a low table and a couple of wicker chairs and a narrow wicker sofa. In the dressing room part, off the small bathroom, there were wall-sized mirrors

Marlene Dietrich's first foray into romantic comedy was Ernst Lubitsch's production of Frank Borzage's *Desire*.

on three of the walls. . . . It was the most simple suite imaginable, and there was not a picture on the wall." Thalberg showed an uncanny prescience by placing Lewis in Garbo's suite. Though none of them knew it, Lewis would be Thalberg's associate producer on Garbo's next film, a project redolent of illness and death.

Louis B. Mayer's disposition to both Thalberg and Garbo was favorable in 1935. Thalberg's production unit had been turning out hit after hit—*Mutiny on the Bounty*, *China Seas*, *Riffraff*—proving that he had lost nothing since his health crisis but the vice-presidency. Garbo continued to be the most talked-about star in the world. With Selznick's departure from M-G-M, it made sense for Thalberg to mount a production for the star whose career he had done so much to shape. To that end, he made sure that Garbo's special friends were readily available. Before Mercedes de Acosta departed for Europe, he told her: "When you return we will talk about *Jehanne d'Arc* again. I have not given up the idea of doing it or the hope that I will be able to persuade Garbo to change her mind." Thalberg also made sure that Salka Viertel was accommodated. "As I was considered a Garbo specialist," recalled Viertel, "I moved to the newly built Thalberg bungalow." Viertel wasted no time in reminding Thalberg of her influence with Garbo. "I told him of an idea which I had for Garbo," wrote Viertel, "Marie Walewska's love for Napoleon. He thought the political background too complicated for American audiences, but became interested after I had suggested Charles Boyer to play Napoleon." Thalberg got tentative agreements from both Garbo and the PCA that the story was acceptable, and before Viertel left on her own trip to Europe, he assigned her to it.

Garbo's career was back on track, but what about her rival's? After the spectacular, disastrous end of her seven-film, five-year collaboration with Josef von Sternberg, Marlene Dietrich was both literally and figuratively in need of direction. Her plight was such a conversation piece that the Broadway play *Boy Meets Girl* had a line in which a studio offers young writers "two thousand a week to save Dietrich!" The consensus was that she had been ruined by her own discoverer, that she had lost her hold on American audiences. Garbo was sometimes described as remote, but at least she was human. Critics charged that Sternberg's heavily stylized films had transformed Dietrich into an ivory icon. Though Ernst Lubitsch was production head at Paramount Pictures, this did not preclude his making a film with Dietrich. "Lubitsch was an ambitious man, a manipulator," recalled Maria Riva. "He was very clever, with a lot of qualities von Sternberg would have liked to have had." Lubitsch made sure that Sternberg's contract was not renewed, and then prepared a romantic comedy for Dietrich. In *The Pearl Necklace*, Dietrich would play a jewel thief—still glamorous, but imbued with humanity.

The brightest aspect of this project was Dietrich's costar, Gary Cooper. The oddest aspect was her insistence that the second male lead be John Gilbert. Since *Queen Christina*, Gilbert had made only one film, a minor Columbia Pictures comedy called *The Captain Hates the Sea*. He had given up his acting career and was rarely seen in Hollywood society. One exception was a dinner at the palatial beach house of loyal Marion Davies. "I had to go to that dinner at the Hearsts," Dietrich told her husband. "Absolutely awful! Only one interesting man—one of Garbo's lovers. I don't understand how she gets them. He was drunk the whole evening, but if you go to bed with Garbo, you *have* to drink." Perhaps Dietrich was amused by the idea of rescuing another of Garbo's cast-off lovers. Perhaps she responded to the charm that Gilbert still possessed. For whatever reason, she made the steadfastly alcoholic actor her new project. Her attention worked wonders. Gilbert stopped drinking and regained a modicum of his ebullience. Looking very much in love, he and Dietrich were seen at numerous social functions in the fall of 1935, including the one at which actress Elizabeth Allan sensed that his claims of recovery might be premature. "I was dancing with him and I smelled a peculiar sort of medicinal odor on his breath," recalled Allan in 1987. "I thought it might be dope. His eyes looked rather odd and he acted strangely. Marlene insisted on taking care of him." Allan, who was becoming a Metro star with films like *A Tale of Two Cities*, was warned by the studio that her friendship with Dietrich might make her a lesbian by association.

Gilbert's regained health led Dietrich to suggest him for *The Pearl Necklace*; Lubitsch made a Technicolor test of Gilbert, Dietrich, and Cooper. Unfortunately for Gilbert, Cooper's test impressed Dietrich more than Gilbert's did. "Marlene was unable to resist Gary Cooper," said Leatrice Gilbert Fountain. "The moment Father found out, he went to pieces again." Gilbert's return to the whisky bottle caused a heart attack while he was swimming with Dietrich one day. Wary of insurance problems, Paramount dropped him from the cast list of *The Pearl Necklace*, which was retitled *Desire* and assigned to Frank Borzage. Yet Gilbert persisted in his declarations of love for Dietrich. "One day, Marlene went over to play tennis with him at his house," said Fountain. "He fell down in front of her with some kind of seizure. The real shock was that much of his hair fell out. His hair lay on the court. I think she really panicked then and realized what she had done. Her guilt was terrible to see."

Garbo had her own health concerns in the fall of 1935. Vacationing in Sweden, she began to suffer a recurrence of her ovarian problems. Then she was notified that Thalberg wanted to reverse the order of the films specified in her contract. One reason was the unavailability of Salka Viertel, who was traveling. The other was the availability of George Cukor, who had a decided preference. "Thalberg was going to do two pictures with Garbo, and he offered me the choice between them," said Cukor. "One was *Marie Walewska*, with Napoleon as the leading man. Well, Napoleon absolutely stumps me! He's fascinating to read about, but he's a Great Man—and they all come out like waxworks in the movies, even American patriots. So I chose *Camille*. I'd seen the play, and I felt it would be the perfect meeting of the actress and the role." Garbo was not happy about the change in plans. She wanted to work with Viertel and Clarence Brown first, she was coping with health concerns, and she was burdened with a sudden, unavoidable visit from Acosta.

In late November, Garbo wrote Viertel for support, albeit long-distance. In her letter she made a reference to Viertel's "troubles." Forty-six-year-old Viertel was having an affair with twenty-three-year-old Gottfried Reinhardt. Garbo also made a veiled reference to abortions performed years earlier.

> I waited almost too late [tonight] to write. But I am in bed most of the time and so stupefied that I can't even bring myself to write! I have been in bed for years, I feel. So you have had troubles too. I have no lovers but I have troubles just the same. Maybe it is from the wrong done to my poor body.
>
> Mercedes has been here as you know by now. I took her to Tistad as I didn't know what else to do. She is more quiet than before but otherwise the same. She didn't see much of Stockholm as I was afraid to let her stay there. I was a wreck after she went and I told her she must not write me. We had a sad farewell and I don't think she will write. I miss you terribly Salka as I am very fond of you to put it very mildly.
>
> To talk of movies, I do not understand why they are not going to do Walewska first. And are you not doing anything on *Camille*? God help me if Thalberg does it alone. Will you answer me on that? I could write Mayer otherwise and perhaps he could let Selznick do *Camille* instead of Thalberg. . . . Please ask Thalberg to think very carefully about Camille. It's so like *Anna* [*Karenina*] that I am afraid. Why don't you ask him to read the Spain story? I don't know if Brown is the man to do it. As a matter of fact he isn't. But if a really suited director could be found and you ask him to read it and then try and see if you two together can get Thalberg interested. God knows if it is done the way I see, it's no loss. And it's devastating to do the same story again.

Anyway, if at least it was the Walewska story I came back to, it's a newer thing because [Napoleon] isn't [the] usual figure on the screen—like my other fifty thousand lovers. Will you talk to him and please write me? Is Sam Behrman around the lot now? I hope you and Sam will be on *Camille*. Time goes so quickly and I will be back and the story will be in a horrible shape. I shall otherwise have to write and ask if you can wait with Walewska and start on *Camille*. I am very nervous, as you see in this silly letter, but every time the studio goes through the same mistakes and one's heart goes fluttering again.

Just as Viertel had gotten her young boyfriend a job as assistant to M-G-M producer Bernard Hyman, Garbo asked Laudy L. Lawrence, the head of M-G-M's Paris office, to give her brother Sven a job. In so doing, she opened a small can of worms. A standard interview with Sven disclosed that "his health is very bad. Incidentally the entire family is in bad health, including Garbo. I believe her sister died from TB long ago," Lawrence wrote Mayer, "and Sven is in bed a whole lot more than out of it." Confirming rumors that were surfacing in the international press, Lawrence finished his letter with unsettling news. "Garbo is rather seriously ill," Lawrence wrote on December 3. Less than a week later, Garbo wrote to Mayer herself, saying that she had been sick since September and was now confined to her bed, awaiting surgery. She respectfully requested that he give her time to recover; Mayer cabled his consent.

On New Year's Day 1936, John Gilbert was so ill that he had to forgo a visit from his daughter, but he continued to receive Dietrich. The next day he suffered another heart attack. A week later, in the wee hours of the morning, Gilbert had another seizure. A doctor was called to the house by an unknown party. "My mother admitted to me being in his house that night," wrote Maria Riva. After Dietrich had fled the premises, the doctor declared Gilbert dead; he was thirty-six years old. Garbo was standing in the lobby of a Stockholm theater when reporters rushed her with the news. She made no comment but quickly left the building and secluded herself for several days. Thalberg took time off from his production of *Romeo and Juliet* to attend Gilbert's funeral, which he lamented for Dietrich's tasteless display of grief. "She behaves like *she's* his widow," agreed Virginia Bruce, Gilbert's last ex-wife. Thalberg's associates noted that the funeral did not affect him as visibly as had Paul Bern's, but mortality must have been on his mind. Most of the films he was planning—*Romeo and Juliet, Camille, Maytime, The Good Earth*, and *Marie Antoinette*—had death scenes.

The production of *Camille* began, as did every M-G-M film, with research by studio writers of low rank. It was with a "ditchdigging" assignment that Thalberg secured his connection with Garbo. "On my first day back in Hollywood," wrote Acosta, "I went to the studio to report to Thalberg. He told me he was planning to produce *Camille* for Greta and asked me what I thought of the idea. I answered that I thought she would be magnificent in the role, surpassed possibly only by Duse. He seemed pleased and relieved and asked me to reread the play in French and make notes. He asked me to describe how Bernhardt had acted the part. I left the studio excited and stimulated that Greta was to play what seemed to me a perfect role for her, and one that had been done by two such great actresses as Duse and Bernhardt." Following this interview, which took place in mid-November 1935, Thalberg hired Frances Marion to prepare the actual screenplay. Since her work on *Anna Christie*, Marion had been busy with Marie Dressler and Mary Pickford films. She was qualified to write *Camille*, having written a 1915 version for Clara Kimball Young. Other productions of the Alexandre Dumas fils play included Metro Pictures' 1921 film with Alla Nazimova, and First National's 1926 film with Norma Talmadge. In December, Thalberg hired British novelist James Hilton, author of the best-selling *Goodbye, Mr. Chips*, to collaborate with Marion.

The handsome red-haired woman of forty-seven, who had been single for four years, took a second look at the

This is how Greta Garbo looked in her own clothes and hairstyle at the time she made her twenty-first Hollywood film, George Cukor's *Camille*. Photograph by Clarence Bull

thirty-three-year-old man with the flawless complexion. Hilton was married, but he had an air of availability. And Marion was lonely. Her cowboy-star husband, Fred Thomson, had died suddenly in 1928, leaving her with two small sons. Her ex-husband, director George Hill, had committed suicide in 1934. She had hoped for a liaison with David Lewis, but learned that he was living with homosexual director James Whale. In a highly unconventional arrangement, Marion embarked on an affair with Hilton while he and his wife were her houseguests, and the passionate new couple somehow found time to work on *Camille.*

Marion regarded *Camille* as a tired, wrinkled old property. While she taught Hilton the craft of screenwriting, Marion tried to "iron out all the old creases" in the story. The 1848 novel *La Dame aux camélias* (*The Lady of the Camellias,* but incorrectly popularized as *Camille*) was Dumas's fictionalized account of his ill-fated romance with the notorious courtesan Marie Duplessis, a high-spirited, good-natured country girl who came to Paris to promote her fragile beauty. Self-educated, extravagant, and generous, Duplessis was kept by a count but had affairs with numerous rich and titled men. She also gave a year of her life to the young, penniless Dumas. She would have faded into memory if it were not for her bad luck in contracting tuberculosis, then known as consumption. Her lingering death was as picturesque as her life had been. Forced to sell her jewelry and many of her possessions, she retained a velvet-covered prayer bench and a little dog. She would linger in the window of her apartment, wrapped in a red shawl, holding the dog, too weak to do anything but watch the passing parade below. She died in 1847 at the age of twenty-three. A year later she was immortalized as Marguerite Gautier in *La Dame aux camélias.*

The tragic novel made Dumas, who was himself not yet twenty-three, rich and renowned. In four years, he turned it into a play that both attracted stars and made them. "I have lived for love and now I am dying of it" was a line that never failed to move an audience. By 1936, though, the story was showing its age. "The play presented some enormous problems," said Cukor, "because you had to make a modern audience understand its conventions. It came from a time when a woman's reputation, her virtue, was a terribly important thing and a big bonanza for drama." Thalberg assumed that Marion and Hilton would find a balance between sentiment and cynicism. "Frances and Jimmy Hilton continued to work away at *Camille,*" said Lewis. "They wanted to finish before letting me see what they were up to; they thought they were writing the Bible. They wanted to do a full script. Thalberg knew that if it wasn't any good, he could throw it out." Thalberg's practice was, of course, to have numerous writers working on the same script. Tess Slesinger and Ernest Vajda were also preparing scenes, but their approach was nothing like Marion's. "Frances was having fun," wrote

Lewis. "She was dramatizing her current 'love affair' with Jimmy Hilton. She was the pale, frail Marguerite and he was the charming, delightful young Armand."

Acosta, meanwhile, realized that working on a Garbo film was not bringing Garbo any closer, and everyone in Thalberg's bungalow seemed to know more about Garbo's activities than she did. In desperation she sought counsel from an Italian mystic named Sorella Maria. "I'm worried about you," Maria answered Acosta. "Not only because of your loneliness and your difficulties, which pain me. But because of the state of slavery in which you live. Since she scorns all you've done for her out of the extreme generosity of your heart; since she acts so indifferent and obstinate in her silence; one must respect her way of being and what she wants. You in turn must become absolutely reserved." Too distraught to assimilate these words of wisdom, Acosta focused on Garbo's return.

Garbo arrived in New York on May 4, where she surprised the press by granting a short interview in which she dismissed her illness as "something like the grippe." She traveled across country with Berthold Viertel, who watched closely as she granted a spontaneous interview to Kay Proctor, an enterprising reporter who had staked out Garbo's train in the desert town of Barstow. "Please, you will not mind if we are brief?" asked Garbo. "It has been a difficult trip. No peace. No rest. And I am not well. I am coming back here to get well in the lovely sunshine. Now what is it you want to know? What can I tell you?" Proctor wanted to know why Garbo appeared to be terrified of people.

"It is not that I do not like people," answered Garbo. "I do. Believe me. But it does frighten me when hordes of strangers rush at me, pull at me, stare at me. It is a dreadful feeling. It is . . . it is humiliating! I do not want to be ungracious but they make it impossible for me to do anything but shut myself away where they cannot reach and tear at me." The desert heat was affecting Garbo. She raised her hand to catch a bead of perspiration on her forehead. "Next?"

Proctor was curious why Garbo refused (most) interviews. "I have a whole lifetime to talk to people," Garbo smiled. "Now it is my work that must have all my attention. When I make a picture, I give everything of myself to it." In a statement that must have given M-G-M pause, Garbo expressed uncertainty about *Camille.* "She is such a tragic figure. I do not know. I have not yet read the script. It may please me very much."

Of greatest interest to Kay Proctor was Garbo's private life. Garbo admitted, wrote Proctor, that John Gilbert "occupied a place in her heart, a dear place. His passing brought deep grief to her." Standing nearby, Berthold frowned and Garbo became sententious: "All life is a romance." Then she became introspective: "I am a peculiar woman. I cannot do too much at once, think of too many different things. My health now. Next the picture. Then maybe [a] house. Maybe."

In Cukor, Garbo found a collaborator of equal stature. "After I saw how she wanted to play a scene," said Cukor, "I talked it over with her and made a suggestion from my mental picture of the scene. But at the same time I made it clear that I respected her conception, and that she had given me fresh ideas which I was more than willing to blend with my own."

While an energized Acosta helped Garbo look for a new house in Brentwood, Joseph Breen expressed his own objections to *Camille*. "You have put too much emphasis on the point that living as a mistress is a highly profitable enterprise," he wrote M-G-M, suggesting various changes that would allow him to pass the script: Marguerite should not be so calculating in her pursuit of a wealthy protector; she should not live with Armand; she should not even visit his apartment at midnight; she should declare her intention to end her life as a kept woman; and last but not least, she should repent. The censor's reaction to the Marion-Hilton script was nothing compared to Lewis's. "I read it with horror," he wrote. "It was ludicrous—flowery, overblown, and just badly conceived and overwritten. It was almost comic opera. I remember Armand's pet name for Marguerite was *ma petite choux* ("my little cabbage") . . . even in the death scene."

As Lewis had anticipated, Thalberg hired another writer. His choice was playwright Zoë Akins, whose screenplays for Ruth Chatterton had made her an early talkie star. Akins's most recent job for M-G-M was on Thalberg's *Outcast Lady*. "She was on the stout side," wrote Lewis, "an ugly woman with a sort of pig face, but with a personality so enchanting I remember her as beautiful." What was crucial to this project was objectivity, something Marion had lost to her own romantic glow. Akins was currently married to a younger British man with a title. She was lavishing gifts on him and had not worked for two years. Lewis told Cukor and Thalberg that she needed a job—and could give the script a picaresque flavor. "She had a tender understanding of life. She had lived all over the world and had known fascinating people."

June saw a series of story conferences with Lewis, Cukor, Akins, and Thalberg. "We have a problem," said Thalberg. "Audiences must forget within the first five minutes that this is a costume picture. It must be contemporary in its feeling, but one thing mitigates against that: the point that a girl's past can ruin her marriage. That problem doesn't exist any more. Whores can make good wives; that has been proven." Thalberg's perception was based on the somewhat isolated morality of Hollywood, but his point was well taken: the play was a museum piece. Akins mulled over the problem; Thalberg brought it up at succeeding conferences, but no one had a solution. One night, when driving home from the studio, Lewis got an idea. He pulled into a gas station on Overland Avenue in Westwood and called Thalberg from a public telephone.

"Instead of the story being based only on the boy's life being ruined," he asked, "suppose we have a case of a very jealous boy? It isn't a question of his life being ruined by her past. It's a question of his *jealousy* ruining his life."

With this insight, the problem was solved, and *Camille* moved forward. Cukor had to take time off when his mother fell ill and suddenly died. Garbo returned to the studio in mid-June and surprised studio manager Eddie Mannix by declining the dressing room he had furnished for her in a streamlined new building that had been completed in her absence. She was superstitious and insisted on her dressing room in the old wooden building, so Lewis moved out of it and over to Thalberg's bungalow. Garbo also threw M-G-M into a tizzy by asking if she could start costume fittings early. She had visited Adrian at his home and seen his costume sketches, which were inspired by Constantin Guy's drawings of Marie Duplessis. Garbo liked the sketches and was eager to begin.

According to her contract, the studio was required to begin her weekly paycheck of $10,000 two weeks before shooting began. The M-G-M legal department worried that her visiting Adrian would signal the beginning of the two-week period. If so, it would mean that production would have to begin prematurely. If it did not, the studio would face the possibility of (1) paying Garbo for sitting idle; or (2) paying Garbo for retakes that might be necessitated by an insufficiently prepared film. That Garbo wanted to come in for fittings, which she did not enjoy, and early, was in itself noteworthy. The studio took precautions before deciding.

An unsigned memo recorded corporate anxiety. "We discussed this with [lawyer] George Cohen, who advised against permitting Miss G. to appear for fitting unless an agreement was signed by her under the terms of which she agreed that the two weeks period would not commence." With due haste, the studio traced the circuitous path to Garbo. "Went to Mr. Hyman, who phoned Salka Viertel, who confirmed Garbo's view. Discussed this with [casting executive Benny] Thau, who spoke with Mr. Hyman, who confirmed his understanding of Garbo's agreement. Permission to attend Adrian was granted." Garbo attended a fitting on July 7. Next she met with art department head Cedric Gibbons, who happened to be a close friend of Dietrich's. Garbo then met with Cukor.

"I sensed that she was a little distrustful of me," recalled Cukor. "Having her own very clear idea of how *La Dame aux camélias* ought to be played on the screen, she was not unnaturally afraid that I, too, would have ideas on the subject, and that a clash would develop when we faced each other . . . on the studio stage." Playing Armand to Garbo's Marguerite would be the fresh new star Robert Taylor. M-G-M had been grooming the former Spangler Arlington Brugh for two years when a loan-out to Universal for Irene Dunne's *Magnificent Obsession* made him an "overnight" sensation. "Police had to rescue [costar] Barbara Stanwyck

"Don't drop me this time," Garbo said to Robert Taylor (off-scene) as they rehearsed a tricky scene.

and Robert Taylor from the fans at the preview of *His Brother's Wife*," reported a Los Angeles newspaper as *Camille* went into production, and Thalberg enthused to Frances Marion about the pairing of Garbo and Taylor: "We can't miss with these two!" With only three years' experience in front of the camera, the twenty-four-year-old Taylor was not so sure. "I was scared to death at the thought of appearing with Garbo in *Camille*," Taylor recalled. With similar sentiments, much of the *Camille* company braced for Monday, July 29, their first day on the set with Garbo.

The momentous day was reported by the British magazine *Picturegoer*: "Stage 23 at M-G-M had been transformed into the Théâtre des Variétés, 1847 vintage. Several hundred costumed extras swarmed the stage. At one end, cameraman Bill Daniels and his crew were lining up the first shot, the initial meeting of Garbo and Taylor on the foyer steps. George Cukor was in a huddle a short distance away with members of his staff. Taylor was resting in the shadows. An hour sped by before a lithe figure in black silk pajamas came on the stage. She paused to scan the setup. Eventually she detected Daniels. She tiptoed up behind Daniels, and playfully poked him in the back. It was Greta Garbo."

Akins and Lewis were also on the set, hiding in the shadows, when Garbo's voice boomed over a loudspeaker. "Miss Akins and Mr. Lewis," said Garbo, "you will please come on the set." The nervous couple approached Garbo, who was now dressed in a white moiré taffeta gown. "Miss Akins, thank you for your beautiful script," said Garbo, who then looked at Lewis, sizing him up. "I expected you to be a little older and a little uglier, but," she paused, "all right. You are welcome on my set any time."

Also visiting the set was the author of the discarded script. Frances Marion looked at Garbo with a critical eye, not having seen her for six years. "She gave no impression of having aged," recalled Marion, "but she had lost that darkly brooding look in her eyes which was so unfathomable when she was young." Marion took the occasion to wish Garbo well; Garbo fielded the salutation. "If you spoke to her, even a casual greeting, she gave you a look at once watchful and shrewd," wrote Marion. "Curiously, it was never a direct look, but seemed to bypass you and focus on some distant object. This was Garbo's way of rejecting you; she did not want to be burdened with too many friends." Everyone had a different experience with Garbo. "I was one of the few women ever allowed on a Garbo set," recalled Margaret Booth, who sat behind Daniels at the edge of the set. "I was the film editor on *The Mysterious Lady*, *Susan Lenox*, and *Camille*. One day I was at Bullock's Wilshire inspecting some yard goods and there was Garbo. She was wearing her large floppy hat and I thought she probably didn't want to be recognized, so I said nothing. The next day at the studio she came over to me and said, 'Margaret, why didn't you speak to me yesterday?'"

One of Cukor's first scenes with Garbo was the medium shot where she moves through her most familiar environment. Cukor said:

> I wanted to show that Marguerite was a public woman, that she went to the theater to be seen. She had to walk through a crowded lobby of men wearing hats (which they always did at the theater in those days—you can see it in contemporary prints). I wanted her to walk through to show herself, as if on parade for clients. At first Garbo walked through rather quickly, as if she didn't want to be seen. I might have said, "Walk through a little more brazenly, a little more slowly," but I didn't. I realized she was right. She could slip through, and you knew damn well the men would look at her anyway.

Cukor had a habit of sitting under the camera as the scene played, mouthing dialogue with the actors, mimicking their gestures as if going through it for them. His silent accompaniment sometimes caused him to make strange, exaggerated facial expressions. It did not take Garbo long to let him know that he was distracting her. She was more gentle with Taylor. "Of course I was nervous," he said. "Miss G's first thoughts were not so much on the picture as they were of putting me at ease." When Taylor asked her how she managed her enviable poise, she said that her motto was "Nothing matters very much—but everything matters just a little." Taylor was surprised to see that Garbo wore a very old pair of bedroom slippers under her expensive costumes. When she didn't know how wide the shot was, she would ask Daniels: "Is the feet in?"

Garbo appeared to be at ease with Taylor, even though she maintained her reserve. "Garbo didn't talk much to Robert Taylor," recalled Cukor. "She was polite but distant. She had to tell herself that he was the ideal young man, and she knew if they became friendly she'd learn he was just another nice kid." On the whole, though, Garbo's coworkers saw her lower her guard. "During the first few days of shooting," reported Sidney Skolsky, "the extras were asked to get off the stage when they weren't in the scene with Garbo, but recently she has permitted them to stand by and watch, provided they don't gape." On other days, it was two steps forward, one step backward. "In an apparent effort to be like other stars," wrote Harrison Carroll in the *Evening Herald-Express*, "the temperamental Swede started the picture minus the black screens that usually shield her from fellow players and set workers while she emotes before the camera. At the end of the day, though, La Garbo appealed to director George Cukor. 'I am so nervous seeing so many new faces.' So now the screens are up again."

Cukor felt comfortable enough with Garbo to ask her why she minded people watching. "She said that when she was acting she had some kind of ideal picture in her mind—something she was creating. . . . She could imagine certain things [but] if she saw people off the set staring at her, she felt like an ass, like somebody with a lot of paint on her face making faces. It stopped her imagination." One evening, Thalberg and Cukor were watching the rushes of Garbo's first scenes in the theater.

"George, she's awfully good," said Thalberg. "I don't think I've ever seen her so good."

"But Irving, she's just sitting in an opera box," said Cukor.

"She's relaxed," said Thalberg. "She's open. She seems unguarded for once." He pondered this new image in story conferences with Akins, who was still writing scenes for the film. "She is a fascinating artist, but she is limited," Thalberg told her and Lewis. "She must never create situations. She must be thrust into them. The drama comes in how she rides them out." Elsewhere in the Thalberg bungalow, Viertel was working on the Walewska script. "While I was explaining to the best M-G-M minds the partition of Poland and what Napoleon was doing in Warsaw in the year 1807," wrote Viertel, "George Cukor was directing Garbo in *Camille*. Not often have I see her as happy, glowing and inspired. I had told her what a profound impression Sarah Bernhardt had made upon me when I was a young girl, and she could not hear enough about it."

Not having worked with Garbo before, Cukor did not appreciate his effect on her. "On the set she was not only very amenable but really very comic," said Cukor. "One day we were doing a particularly dry scene. I heard her refer to it as 'government business.' When I asked her what she meant, she replied, 'That is what I call dull scenes. They are like government business!'" By late August, the change in Garbo was marked. "Greta Garbo has been making comical faces at cameraman Bill Daniels," reported Jimmy Starr in the *Evening Herald-Express*. "What's come over her anyway?" In a rollicking polka scene with actor Rex O'Malley, Garbo lost her balance. "She started giving way, and over she went," recalled O'Malley. "I fell, too, as gently as possible, right on top of her. She burst into laughter. 'It's my little feet,' she said. Perhaps the funniest incident took place on Lot 3 in front of the newly constructed "Camille house." Taylor alighted from the carriage in which he and Garbo were arriving, came around, and picked Garbo up so he could carry her into the stone cottage. Suddenly he realized that he had not positioned himself correctly for the weight of her costume, and he unceremoniously dropped her on the ground. No one laughed harder than Garbo.

In late August, Cukor was directing the intimate scene in which Armand discovers Marguerite alone in her bedroom after a coughing spell interrupts her polka and she takes leave of her vulgar friends, who were splendidly played by Lenore Ulric and Laura Hope Crews. "Armand comes in and he's revolted by the coarseness he's just heard," said Cukor. "I'll never forget how beautifully Garbo played that next moment. She has a line that Zoë Akins wrote—'These are the only friends I have and I'm no better than they are.'—as if to warn him not to put her on a pedestal." Armand is so in love with her that her warning is pointless. His sincerity wins her, and she agrees to meet him later. Before sending him off, she says good-bye in an unusual way. Garbo thought of a technical approach to the scene. "She did this memorable, erotic thing," recalled Cukor. "She didn't touch Armand, but she kissed him lightly all over his face, barely brushing him. . . . Garbo had rapport with an audience, could let them know she was thinking things, and thinking them uncensored. There was no body contact in that scene, which didn't matter. Garbo had that other quality in her character, and without it you can't generate a real love scene. She was rather cool, but seething underneath. You know that she's reckless and nothing will stop her."

Thalberg was increasingly enthusiastic over the rushes. "I think we have caught Garbo as she should be caught," he told Lewis one day at a conference. "She will be the most memorable Camille of our time." Story editor Sam Marx asked Thalberg how the production was going. "If only they were all like this," answered Thalberg, referring obliquely to troubled productions such as *Rasputin and the Empress*. In the last week of August, the bloom came off the camellia.

"So weighty and heat-preserving are Garbo's costumes that she nearly fainted after being under the lights for less than an hour," reported Jimmy Starr. "In order that Garbo might work with ease, a special icebox and wind machine, eight feet square, was constructed." In all probability, heat was not the only cause of Garbo's discomfort. Her manner grew formal, and she became unaccountably rude, even to Thalberg. Noticing him on the sidelines, she sent word that his presence was making her nervous and that she wished him to leave. "I've been put off better sets than this one," he said to Lewis before leaving for a Labor Day vacation.

On Friday, September 11, Garbo complained of feeling ill and went home early. Viertel was in Berkeley, depositing her son at the university. She returned on Monday, and before she had time to find out how Garbo was feeling, she got a shock. "We were having coffee in a drugstore," recalled Viertel, "and we saw a newspaper with the headline: 'Irving Thalberg Dies at 37.'" Incredible though it sounded, a head cold that Thalberg had caught two weeks earlier had taken a deadly turn toward pneumonia, and though his heart had been diagnosed as weak, it held up while a vicious infection disabled his lungs. He died on Monday, September 14. The studio that he had cofounded a mere twelve years earlier was stunned and disbelieving. Lewis heard the news in a meeting and stumbled out, numb and disoriented. "I went into the anteroom," he wrote. "Everyone there was weeping. Nobody seemed to know what to do."

In the days and weeks following Thalberg's funeral (which Garbo did attend), people wondered what effect his

death would have on every project and career at M-G-M. "Only a few days before, Sam [Behrman] and I had finished our Walewska screenplay and we had talked to him," said Viertel. "He was in a good mood, very pleased with the rushes of *Camille*. In the last months Greta and I had often mentioned how much happier he seemed. After my first clash with him about *Queen Christina* we had got along well and he had always been very cordial to me. I felt terribly sad."

"There was no one to take his place," wrote Acosta, "and I knew that no one could take his place as far as producing for Greta was concerned. She was very much affected by his death." Garbo later told Sven Broman: "I liked him. But he died much too early. The best die young." Acosta saw more misfortune coming: "I felt that there would be many changes in the studio and that a number of people, including myself, would lose their jobs. I was right about this. A great many people who worked for Thalberg were taken off the payroll, and I was one of them."

Garbo returned to the *Camille* set in a different frame of mind, as did the entire company. Within a week, they were filming Marguerite's death scene. Taylor brought his phonograph to Garbo's dressing room so that she could play Paul Robeson records to put her in the mood. "My mother had just died," recalled Cukor, "and I had been there during her last conscious moments. I suppose I had a special awareness. I may have passed something on to Garbo without realizing it." Garbo later praised Cukor's sensitivity. "Cukor gave me direction as to how to hold my hands," said Garbo. "He had seen how, when his mother lay dying, she folded her hands and just fell asleep."

About this time, as if there had not been enough sadness, Daniels's father died. Overcome with grief, Daniels went on a drinking binge. Three days later he woke up in Chicago, not remembering how he had gotten there. In March he had disappeared while shooting *Romeo and Juliet*, but Norma Shearer had gotten him reinstated. This time Mayer put him on suspension. Hal Rosson replaced him temporarily for the outdoor wedding scenes on Lot 3. The film was finished by the distinguished Karl Freund, who was returning to cinematography after three years as a director. Freund changed the lighting scheme on Garbo's close-ups. He moved the key light from Daniels's "Rembrandt" position to a position on axis with Garbo's nose, something approaching the lighting used on Dietrich. Freund did this because the Rembrandt was beginning to show how tired and drawn Garbo's face was.

After the success of *Desire*, Dietrich had signed with Garbo's former producer, David Selznick, for his second independent production, *The Garden of Allah*, a Technicolor romance set in the desert. She told dialogue director Joshua Logan what she thought of the script. "Garbo wouldn't play this part," said Dietrich. "They offered it to Garbo and she said she didn't believe the girl would send the boy back to the monastery. She is a very clever woman, Garbo! She has the primitive instincts those peasants have, you know."

Garbo's instincts were still creating wondrous effects on the set of *Camille*, according to Lewis. "Everything in the film depended on the magic of Garbo," he wrote. "Cukor and she became very close. He understood and brought out the best that was in her." On October 20, Sidney Skolsky was again spying on a closed set.

Garbo wore a black evening gown with silver stars on it. Taylor was attired in a typical Armand costume. Garbo's face looked pale. She had on a pallor makeup to be the sickly Camille, but her back was tanned from sunbaths. Garbo's favorite cameraman, Bill Daniels, was not filming the scene. Karl Freund was at the camera. Later, I learned that Daniels was ill.

The sequence is at a card table and the dialogue is brief. Garbo talks about the other woman that Armand has been with. George Cukor rehearses with Garbo and Taylor many times before he decides to take the scene. Cukor then shoots eight takes and orders three printed.

Lewis marveled at Cukor's technique. "He was so fascinated with her," wrote Lewis, "that if he had a closeup of her, he would often say, without stopping the camera, 'One more, Greta.' And, by God, she would give him something different and exquisite every time. In fact, he might get eight or ten takes with her before he exhausted all that she had to give. You could have made ten films from the outtakes of *Camille*, each with a wonderfully different shading of Garbo."

Cukor pressed Garbo for more variations because he knew her resources. "She often did unexpected things," he recalled. "In the gambling casino scene, when she drops her fan and De Varville makes her pick it up, she made a remarkable movement, almost like something in a dance, like Isadora. She didn't kneel to pick it up; she bent sideways in the most beautiful way." Garbo did not improvise these effects but came to the set with them formulated and rehearsed. "Another scene that was very tricky is when Armand's father comes to see her, and she agrees to give Armand up. It's when the conventions of the play show through most nakedly, but Garbo humanized it. After the father left, she sank slowly to her knees and put her arms on

"I was scared to death at the thought of appearing with Garbo in *Camille*," recalled Robert Taylor. "Needlessly. She was a fantastic human being. She loved acting and the people she worked with."

Clarence Bull used lace, tulle, and net to partially mask Garbo's face in these *Camille* portraits.

the table." That Garbo acceded to additional rehearsals and multiple takes in front of Cukor showed the respect he engendered.

"If I hadn't been so out of sorts," Garbo wrote Countess Wachtmeister, "*Camille* would have been one of my most entertaining memories, thanks to the director. He really is extraordinarily nice. He looks so funny with his huge hips and his woman's breasts. I'll soon be finished with the whole thing and blessed be the memory. There you are. That proves that I'm not always ungrateful." Garbo was curious to know about her friends in Sweden, where she had recently purchased property. "You never tell me anything about what is happening to people at home," she wrote. "But then nothing does happen—as we always said in the film of *Grand Hotel*: 'People come and go, but nothing happens at the Grand Hotel.'"

Filming ended on October 27, but there was a feeling of unease in the air. Mayer asked Lewis to bring Garbo to see him. Garbo said, "Sure," not knowing quite what to expect. "I walked her up to his office," recalled Lewis, "and he slammed the door in my face. I'm sure he made a pass at her. Two minutes later she emerged and said, 'That was an experience!'" Garbo did not disclose the nature of the experience to Lewis, but a few days later the "other shoe dropped." Lewis

was informed by Benny Thau, a casting executive, that *Camille* had just been assigned to Bernard Hyman. "It's finished and there's very little to do," said Thau mysteriously. "Hyman was a dear friend of Irving's. He might help it. He definitely won't hurt it." Of course Hyman was also the boss of Viertel's boyfriend, Gottfried Reinhardt. A round of retakes began as Hyman (and Viertel) tried to improve something that needed no improvement.

A familiar face was increasingly in evidence, that of Reinhardt, who admittedly had no use for Cukor. "He always seemed to be 'on,'" said Reinhardt. "He was always aflutter. Always. Some people liked that. It stimulated them. Not me." Anita Loos saw studio politics at work. "[Cukor] had that taste that, aside from Thalberg, nobody at the studio understood. And after Thalberg died, I think he was more or less thrown to the wolves," said Loos. To many of the men who had worked with him, Thalberg's legacy was a reminder of their debt to him, and they were determined to bury it. Hyman had just made a huge success with *San Francisco*, not because of his own talent but because of Loos's airtight script and W. S. Van Dyke's direction. It was Hyman's tampering that had ultimately caused the *Rasputin and the Empress* libel suit. (The Youssoupoffs would not have had a case had he not added a title card that read: "This film concerns the destruction of an empire brought about by the mad ambition of one man. A few of the characters *are still alive*. The rest met death by violence.") His compulsive tampering with *Camille* gratified his ego but maddened Garbo.

"I have never worked under conditions like these before," she wrote Wachtmeister. "I sometimes start crying from tiredness. I leave home at about 8:00 A.M. and don't get home before 8:00 P.M. I've been feeling out of sorts the whole last month and still had to work. I have been getting treatments after my hours at the studio but don't know if it's helped or made it worse. . . . My writing's a bit confused but what can you expect from a lady of the camellias?" Acosta, though persona non grata at M-G-M, was privy to Garbo's suffering on *Camille*.

"It was a great physical effort for her to make it," wrote Acosta. "Many times when she was on the set or before the camera she was in such pain that she could barely stand on her feet. Often she came directly from the studio to my house, looking deadly white and sometimes unable to drag herself up the stairs." It was at this time that Garbo confided to assistant director Eddie Woehler that her illness was caused by a flare-up of her ovarian problem. "There is no doubt that at this time she really was ill," wrote Acosta, "but there was a psychological factor involved. She had so much identified herself with the character of Marguerite that even off the set and out of the studio she was conscious of the illness of this tubercular woman. Sometimes when we walked in the hills or on the beach she would stop and put her hand to her heart as though her breath was coming too fast."

One scene that was reshot, although not because of Hyman, was the death scene. "We had to make two different endings to the film," Garbo recalled. "Well, actually, there were three. In one version, I got to say more on my deathbed. In another, I had to be quieter and just slowly slip away. They plumped for the latter version and we were all in agreement on that point. It didn't really feel very natural talking that much when you've just about given up the ghost." The retakes were Cukor's doing. "The screen is just too realistic for a long aria when someone's dying," he said. "It seemed unreal for a dying woman to talk so much." Rex O'Malley recalled the stress of the process. "After three times, as she lay there dying in bed," he said, "Garbo suddenly became hysterical with laughter."

Salka Viertel later took credit for the best version of the scene, according to Christopher Isherwood. "Garbo was so inadequate in the last scene of *Camille* that Salka had them give all the lines to Robert Taylor," Isherwood wrote in his diary. "Garbo only had to say 'Yes' and 'No,' and it came out great." Given the circumstances of the retakes, it was unlikely that Viertel could override Cukor. It was highly likely that she would overstate her influence. "Salka Viertel said Garbo was not an actress but a personality," wrote Lewis. "I disagree completely. It was as though [Garbo] had a direct pipeline to the power of inspiration. She was a fascinating actress." Cukor recalled Garbo's painstaking preparation, the hallmark of a true actor. "Garbo always went through a great deal to get a scene right, and I said to her once that she seemed to act a role so easily. She laughed and said that she would kill me for saying such a thing!" At her own expense, Garbo later quipped: "If you're going to die on the screen, you've got to be strong and in good health." Many years later she admitted to a friend that she had watched the rushes of her best version of the death scene and could not believe what she saw. "She told me," said David Diamond, "that she was baffled by what she'd done and by the peak she'd reached. She couldn't explain it."

After $100,000 of new material was edited into the film, it was previewed in Santa Barbara and poorly received. Lewis attended a late November preview at the Golden Gate Theatre in Whittier. "Hyman's new beginning was interminable," wrote Lewis. "It set up the characters too well. Anything they did from there on out was pure boredom. *Camille* had suddenly become a heavy-handed costume picture." Thalberg's insistence on making the conflict a timeless one had been ignored. Long, pointless scenes (much like the scenes Viertel had cowritten for *Queen Christina* and *Anna Karenina*) had taken the place of the precise, neatly interlocking ones of the first version. Motivations were changed too. "The scenes showing the jealousy of the boy were cut," said Lewis. "He was now the same old dreary Armand Duval from the novel. What Thalberg had striven for in those months of preparation was gone. The [preview] was a

disaster. Garbo was there, and the audience applauded when the Baron slapped her! They hated her. She shuddered and was gone when the preview ended."

Fortunately for Garbo, Akins and Lewis were not content to let Hyman have his way with *Camille*. The next morning, they went over his head and paid a visit to Eddie Mannix, whom they asked to authorize changes. He told them that there was no time to shoot any additional scenes. There was another preview scheduled, and the film was supposed to open a new theater in two weeks. Heading for the typewriter in an adjoining office, Akins said, "I'll have a new scene ready in twenty minutes." She did, and the next day Garbo was back on the set, making a touching speech that began: "Once I had a little dog." She wrote to Wachtmeister: "*Camille* never ends. We have to shoot retake after retake and are going to do more in a couple of days. It's not exactly a masterpiece either. . . . Nothing new has happened apart from Mercedes wanting me to ring. But I am going to have to think about the matter first. Poor Mercedes. She has got an extraordinary ability to make people nervous. Even people who are not quite as unkind as me."

A preview of the reassembled film was held at the Four Star Theatre on Wilshire Boulevard in Los Angeles. Significantly, Lewis was not invited, but he did hear reports. "It's great!" exclaimed Margaret Booth, putting her arms around him. Lewis also saw Garbo, who was going home to rest up for her next cinematic exertion. "I ran into Garbo on the lot," recalled Lewis. "She was getting into her Packard. I waved and said, 'Hi, Greta!' She saw me, put her hood over her head, rushed into the car without speaking, and quickly drove away."

Heralded by an ad campaign that cried "Garbo Loves Taylor in *Camille*," the film was released in late December but was not reviewed until it premiered on both coasts in late January 1937. Even after the excellence and emotional power of *Anna Karenina*, no one expected *Camille* to be so fine—or so moving. "When illness and tragedy overtake the heroine," wrote Harrison Carroll, "she invokes pathos so deep that many in the audience were openly weeping." Louella Parsons wrote: "Perhaps it is the unexpected humor injected into her characterization that gives her warmth and a human touch noticeably missing from many of her previous performances. Even the always hectically dramatic

death scene has been treated with pathetic appeal, and if you can watch it without a tear in your eye, you have more fortitude than the crowds that poured into Grauman's Chinese yesterday." *Variety* reported that Garbo's erotic play was effective. "It's a brief moment, scarcely an eye flash, but audiences will giggle. They did here." Garbo's first review by Frank S. Nugent, the new film critic of the *New York Times*, was an exceptional one: "Greta Garbo's performance . . . is in the finest tradition: eloquent, tragic, yet restrained. She is as incomparable as legend tells us that Bernhardt was. Through the perfect artistry of her portrayal, a hackneyed theme is made new again, poignantly sad, hauntingly lovely."

Garbo was again nominated for an Academy Award but lost to M-G-M's new star Luise Rainer for her performance in *The Good Earth*, another posthumous Thalberg project. For the second year in a row, Garbo did win the New York Film Critics award for the best feminine performance of the year. Even more auspiciously, she was awarded the "Littris et Artibus" decoration by King Gustav of Sweden, an honor previously bestowed on Jenny Lind and Sarah Bernhardt. If *Camille* had to be judged only by its box-office receipts, there was also good news there. Because of retakes, its budget had risen to $1,486,000. Even so, it managed a profit of $388,000. Beyond this there was the unanimous agreement that Garbo's performance as Marguerite was touched by something indefinable, perhaps genius, perhaps inspiration, perhaps white magic. Garbo herself was unable to explain it. Whatever it was, it elevated her above every other performance of the year. For all her quirks, foibles, and demands, she had delivered a unique commodity to the world, a work of art created by an artist at the height of her powers.

While her intimates congratulated themselves on their proximity to such greatness, David Lewis glimpsed its future. One day during the filming, he was walking by the long wooden building. As he later wrote: "I heard a plaintive cry, 'David! David!' It was Garbo. I went upstairs. She was sitting in front of a magnifying mirror. With a tragic look on her face, she said, 'These lines around my mouth . . . I'm getting old.'

"I laughed and said, 'Greta, you've had them ever since I can remember. It's the way you hold your mouth.'

"But she kept repeating, 'I'm getting old. *I'm getting old.*'"

Opposite: "I wouldn't have thought of doing *Camille* without Garbo," said George Cukor. "Somehow that ill-starred, tainted creature is something that she has in her face."

THE EXPENSIVE LEGEND

CHAPTER TWENTY-THREE
Conquest

If Greta Garbo had reached a Hollywood pinnacle after eleven years and twenty-one films, where were her cinematic peers? There were only two M-G-M stars who had lasted as long as Garbo: Joan Crawford and Norma Shearer. For silent-film stars who survived the talkies, stardom depended on roles like Marguerite Gautier, and with the Production Code withholding the best literary and theatrical properties, finding such a role was not easy. Crawford was given empty comedies like *Love on the Run*. Shearer was waiting for the role that Thalberg had planned for her, Marie Antoinette. As the 1930s waned, both stars found themselves fighting for primacy. At Paramount, Marlene Dietrich was winning her battles and, after her post-Sternberg slump, was again running neck and neck with her rival.

Cinematographer Karl Freund adjusts Greta Garbo's hat in this behind-the-scenes shot from the 1937 film *Conquest*. Photograph by William Grimes

Marlene Dietrich rarely posed for a photograph that was not lit with her trademark Paramount north light, but after she was labeled "box-office poison," she allowed something different.

Opposite: Clarence Bull's portraits of Greta Garbo for *Conquest* had a regal dignity.

While Garbo was earning laurels for *Camille*, Marlene Dietrich was gracing the covers of both *Time* and *Newsweek*. The reason? There were several. Dietrich had made a comeback with *Desire*. She had quit a film called *I Loved a Soldier* because it was unglamorous. She had gotten extensive publicity for her Technicolor debut in *The Garden of Allah*. Most significantly, she had been hired for a British film, *Knight without Armor*, at a salary of $450,000, the highest ever paid a motion-picture star.

Garbo would be earning only $250,000 for her next film, unless there were delays or retakes. Since it was based on historical figures, it would be a larger production than *Camille*, but producer Bernie Hyman had made *San Francisco* without retakes, so there was cause for optimism.

Conquest was director Clarence Brown's seventh and last film with Garbo. It was her twenty-second M-G-M film. Photograph by William Grimes

There was also cause for concern, given the overproduced movies M-G-M was making since Thalberg's death. *New York Times* critic Frank S. Nugent wrote:

> Metro makes the most beautiful bores in the world. They are designed by Cedric Gibbons, gowned by Adrian, and have dollar signs all over them. No other studio in Hollywood can build such ballrooms and fill them with such lovely, lacy ladies. No other studio makes such enchanting beer gardens, with the moonlight just right and the dance floor perfection. No other studio can make such a big picture out of such a small script. Some day, we fear, Metro will make so great a production that cast, script, director and all will be engulfed in it, swallowed up like Jonah by the whale.

Nugent's warning had not yet sounded when Hyman proclaimed to Salka Viertel that he wanted his film about Marie Walewska to be "the best Garbo ever made." If not the best, it would certainly be the biggest, the longest, and the costliest.

The Marie Walewska saga began, of course, back in 1935 with Viertel's research in Thalberg's bungalow. It continued with the adaptation of a 1904 novel by Waclaw Gasiorowski called *Pani Walewska.* As George Cukor had observed, this was an unlikely role for the "Duse of the screen." Marie was the eighteen-year-old wife of an elderly Polish count. He and the nobility wanted her to sleep with Napoleon Bonaparte in the hope that he would liberate Poland from Russian domination. "There are times when all splendors become

oppressive," he wrote, cataloguing her charms. "Your country will be dearer to me when you take pity on my poor heart. N." Marie gave herself to Napoleon, fell in love with him, and bore him a child. Though he did not keep his promise to free her country, she loved him until her dying day, and his name was the last she spoke.

Hers was a touching story, to be sure, but it did not resemble the Garbo formula; *Camille*, through all its permutations, did. Garbo was a glamorous figure who inspired romantic triangles. Marie Walewska was a colorless girl who followed a soldier around Europe, waiting for him to toss her a few crumbs. How would such a character be played by an actress best known for fatalistic languor? The story was more Napoleon's than Marie's. Nevertheless, Viertel thought she knew best and persisted. Garbo never questioned Viertel. M-G-M never questioned either of them. The only question Garbo had for Viertel was a kinky one. "I was thinking," Garbo wrote Viertel, "about the Napoleon story, and was going to ask you something that you probably will not like. I have a great longing for trousers. If I ask you in time maybe you can put in a little sequence with trousers, maybe Marie Walewska dressed as a soldier going to Napoleon's tent at night or something." (This was a scene that Frances Marion had to write into every Marion Davies film, since William Randolph Hearst had a fetish for Davies in male attire.) Before Viertel could gratify Garbo's request, she had to have the basic plot approved by the PCA, which found more to object to than trousers.

"The story deals with adultery not only condoned but urged upon Marie by her elderly husband and the Polish statesmen," wrote PCA officer Charles R. Metzger in December 1935. "It deals with diplomacy in which women's favors are used as pawns for securing advantage, nothing new, but a bit unsavory for the average middle-class motion-picture audience." The story was not a Tolstoy piece that could be bowdlerized at will, warned Metzger: "The characters and the events represented in this story are all historical facts and this illegitimate child survived and became a rather important person in France. . . . It is not possible to 'clean this story up' under the Code and have no intimate relationships between Marie Walewska and Napoleon or the industry makes itself somewhat a laughing stock by its treatment of historic facts." Once Joseph Breen reviewed the story, he saw that there was ample opportunity to make Marie suffer for her sins, and, better yet, the script did not linger on them. "We are particularly pleased to observe," wrote Breen, "that there is little physical contact suggested between the illegitimate lovers and, likewise, a conspicuous absence of bedroom scenes, scenes of illicit fondling, etc. This, in our judgment, is going to add much to the worthwhile flavor of the story."

With a yellow light from the PCA in January 1936, Viertel crept ahead. She was not competent to complete a screenplay, so she relied on whatever collaborator Thalberg assigned her. "I began to work with a writer who liked only westerns and was utterly uninformed about anything that had ever happened in the world," recalled the politically keen Viertel. "It became obvious to Thalberg that our collaboration was a failure, and he chose his favorite writer and one of the most talented and expensive on the lot to work with me. Donald Ogden Stewart was brilliant and delightfully amusing, but he, too, had a deep dislike for Napoleon and soon wriggled out of the assignment." Anyone else would have seen the departure of two writers as a sign that Napoleon was not movie material, but not Salka. "I cannot bear any longer explaining to people why Napoleon did not marry Marie Walewska," she wrote to Berthold Viertel in a fit of intellectual snobbery. "Gottfried says I am dramatizing myself. I know I have to pull myself together."

In mid-1936, Thalberg still saw potential in Marie Walewska and brought in the clever S. N. Behrman to shore up Viertel. Even Behrman did not warm to the material. "I wished to convey my personal feeling that the existence of Napoleon, 'the archaic little man,' as H. G. Wells called him, was a disaster for the human race," recalled Behrman. "But it was not easy to get sympathy for this point of view from a group of men who had busts of Napoleon in their offices, since he represented their secret wish-dreams of conquest." The project got a boost when an appealing actor was found to play Napoleon. Charles Boyer had been kicking around Hollywood for five years, but had only recently won audiences with a series of films for Walter Wanger, who agreed to loan the thoughtful Frenchman to M-G-M. "I was fearful that to the French people, no performance of Napoleon Bonaparte, not even a perfect one, would be satisfactory," said Boyer.

Viertel and Behrman had just completed their first draft when Thalberg died. Unlike Mercedes de Acosta, Viertel was not affected by the mass firing of Thalberg loyalists in October 1936. It was tacitly understood that Garbo's Cerberus was immune to pink slips. "It seemed likely," wrote Viertel, "that one of Thalberg's close associates would take over the production of *Marie Walewska*, and the heads of M-G-M wanted Greta to express her preference." This was when David Lewis escorted Garbo to Mayer's new office. The meeting was short, not because Mayer made a pass at her but because she did not know (or care) whom to suggest. "She left the decision to L. B. Mayer and Mannix, who could not see eye to eye in the matter," said Viertel. "Mannix suggested Bernie Hyman. Gottfried had often told me that there was no nicer and more decent person on the M-G-M lot than Bernie, a close friend of Thalberg. Greta and I had lunch with him and found him pleasant and sympathetic, but the question of whether he was the right producer for our film remained unanswered." Still, with her boyfriend stationed in Hyman's office, Viertel could both monitor and influence Garbo's next project.

In fact, the mistress of her own literary salon found the semiliterate producer in the loud plaid jacket less malleable than she had expected. "Bernie Hyman was a very amiable fellow—with a streak of stubbornness," said Behrman. "He would read a scene and say it lacked 'zip.' Sam Hoffenstein said of him that he was like a glass of water without the glass. He also said that he was like Dr. Jekyll in the uncapturable moment before he merged into Mr. Hyde." Viertel expected that the combination of Garbo's importance and Reinhardt's influence would bring Hyman around to her way of thinking. "He was very sentimental, extremely kind, and rather endearing," wrote Viertel. "If it had not been for that, I could not have survived his indecision and endless procrastination. To some extent, because Hyman listened to him, Gottfried was helpful in preventing a disaster."

The disaster Viertel feared was the subversion of her project. This would have been a blessing, for even with Behrman's polished dialogue, the script was a lifeless portrayal of a lackluster character. Hyman read it and could not find much to like in it; it had "no heart, was sophisticated and cold. It did not make you cry." Reinhardt tried to explain his boss to Viertel. "Hyman was an important producer," she recalled, "who only approved screenplays he himself had supervised, and he disliked ours heartily." Worse than that, he wanted her to rewrite it, with or without Behrman, who by this time had happily departed. "There was no use resisting," Viertel was advised. "The script would be rewritten even if William Shakespeare had been its author. It was imperative for Bernie's ego to start from scratch because that way he could get used to the story and the characters. This always took a long time."

Marie Walewska (Garbo) is dominated by Napoleon (Charles Boyer) throughout *Conquest*, which was historically sound but dramatically disappointing.

Taking the time to compose and light an on-the-set portrait of cast and crew such as this was considered too costly by the late 1930s. *Conquest* was the last Garbo film to enjoy this luxury. Photograph by William Grimes

Viertel went to Hyman's office, where he was enjoying a simultaneous scalp massage and manicure. She explained to him "that what we wanted to show was Napoleon's growing megalomania, his ruthless use of the Polish legions without any intention of restituting their country, and Marie's disillusionment with the man she worshiped, her realization that he was an egotistical monster whom she could not cease loving." An egotistical monster was something that a producer could visualize; the image of Garbo cowering before it was titillating. "I want this to be the best Garbo ever made," said Hyman again, sitting up enthusiastically.

Reinhardt later joined the dismayed Viertel over drinks and tried to encourage her. "I am sure that you can save many scenes from the Behrman script," said Reinhardt, "as in the course of time Bernie will become convinced that everything has been invented under his guidance. On the other hand, if you refuse the assignment, somebody else, much less scrupulous, will tear down [your] script, and suggest another story—which Garbo will reject—and we'll have to start all over again." When Viertel questioned the exasperating procedure, Reinhardt said, "This may seem cynical to you and a waste of money, but that's not your responsibility. The more Bernie spends, the closer he is to becoming an executive."

The first money Hyman spent was to bring back Behrman. By November, there were enough scenes to get the art and wardrobe departments started, and production was scheduled for January 1937. "I'm afraid this last film isn't going to be much fun," Garbo wrote Countess Wachtmeister. "When Adrian, who does my clothes, read the script, he said, 'Who cares about Napoleon?' And I'm afraid he's right." Boyer was unavailable in January, so production was pushed to March, which gave Hyman the opportunity to hire Zoë Akins for rewrites. When Garbo read the script, she told Acosta that she did not have "the slightest idea what this story is all about or who the hell Marie Walewska is."

In February, Garbo ventured to the Santa Monica beach house of Anita Loos for a small party. It was there that she met fifty-four-year-old Leopold Stokowski, the white-maned Philadelphia Orchestra conductor who had gained a wider celebrity since appearing as himself in Paramount's *Big Broadcast of 1937*. Loos watched the leonine Stokowski corner Garbo. "Stoki didn't waste much time on the overture," recalled Loos. "He got straight down to business, laying on the charm. He told Garbo they were destined to have a history-making romance, like Wagner's with Cosima. It was written in the stars. There was no use in their trying to escape it. The gods had made their decision. Mere mortals could only obey. It was a direct attack mixed with a little mystical stuff." Loos, who was one of Garbo's few American friends, was aware of her new leanings. "Any kind of mystical stuff made quite a hit with Greta in those days," recalled Loos in 1955. Garbo's interest in mysticism was partly due to Acosta, who was then dabbling in Eastern religion. Acosta also introduced Garbo to Bieler's Broth, the health food concocted by Dr. Harold Bieler of Pasadena.

Garbo was also seeing a psychologist. "My latest physician is a little hunchbacked man who I am dragging down into the abyss of pessimism," Garbo wrote Wachtmeister. "He sees me as an interesting case of depression. He says he is a psychologist and wants to help me in that way. He keeps me for an hour and a half every time. We sit there fencing with words and keeping a watchful eye on one another. One day, when I was very tired, I said, 'Everything is futile.'

"'Yes, that's true,' he said. But then he realized that that's not the way to treat a depression so he gave me a piercing look and said one had to look at life with a sense of humor."

As the starting date of *Marie Walewska* approached, there was little cause for humor. Ten writers had already labored on the script, but it was nowhere near completion. The most recent was the poet and screenwriter Samuel Hoffenstein, who had cowritten Dietrich's *Desire*. "Often I wondered how this Chassidic soul landed in Hollywood, but he made a lot of money," wrote Viertel. "Expressing himself in exquisite English, slightly tinged by an Irish brogue, he would surprise one by bursting into a Yiddish song [and] when intoxicated, he would improvise for hours in verse which, unfortunately, he forgot the next day." His influence on the script was limited to outlines of Viertel's thoughts; none of his witty scenes was approved by Hyman.

Filming commenced on March 3, 1937. "Even when Garbo was in a strong enough position to dictate to the management, she was miserably unhappy," wrote Cecil Beaton. "When Mercedes drove her to the studio for the opening day's work on *Marie Walewska*, Greta was in tears all the way to Culver City, crying 'This is prostitution.'" Cukor had heard Garbo express such sentiments. "You know, I don't think acting is all that wonderful," she told him. "I am not proud to be an actress." To her friends in Sweden she wrote how much she wanted to be with them, roaming their estate and hunting. "My last hunt was at Tistad," she said. "But that time it was a fox that was shot. There are only lions here at M-G-M so I'm not interested." She did not mention Stokowski, whom she was converting from hunter to prey.

The atmosphere on the set was more congenial than Garbo would have her friends believe. Boyer was as respectful and conscientious as Garbo could want, Akins was still working on the script, and Clarence Brown was directing. This was his seventh film with Garbo. Sidney Skolsky reported that Garbo spent her time "chatting away about the diet she is on." She occasionally joined in baseball games, as she had on the *Camille* set. She was in a good humor, as actor Leif Erickson found out one day. "In one scene I was supposed to take hold of Garbo," said Erickson. "When I did, her gown got caught on a button of my uniform and ripped. There was Garbo in the altogether! Well, I fell back and looked at her in amazement. Instead of getting angry, she smiled. 'I thought that would inspire you,' she said." Garbo also resorted to practical jokes on the set of *Marie*

While Garbo waited for her cue, William Grimes snapped this candid photo of her.

Walewska, although they were not as well received as they had been by Cukor and Daniels. When Garbo crept up to the playback machine and switched it on, startling everyone, Brown yelled: "What dope put that on?"

"I did," answered Garbo meekly, and the entire set broke up in laughter.

"During the whole of *Anna Karenina*," wrote Viertel, "Clarence Brown could not have been nicer to work with. Although not the most sensitive judge of a script, he was inventive on the stage, an excellent technician and competent in handling the actors. But Napoleon and Marie went against his grain and we had to fight his disgruntled obstructionism." In fairness to Brown, the script, arriving piecemeal as it did, was almost impossible to integrate into a logical whole. It may not have been Napoleon and Marie that irked him, but the inability of Hoffenstein, Behrman, and Akins to make the story plausible. (In fact, a total of seventeen writers finally worked on it.) Who could believe that this powerful-looking woman would simper after a blustering midget for an entire movie? Filming one pompous, wordy, preposterous scene after another in the winter, spring, and summer of 1937 made the cast and crew feel as if they were stuck in Napoleon's Russian campaign, or worse, as if they were pushing elephants across a river of tar. Garbo passed the tedious months mixing Bieler's Broth in a blender and conversing with Karl Freund, who was again her cameraman; Bill Daniels had been forgiven for his absences but was booked solid on Jean Harlow and William Powell films.

"*Conquest* is of road show magnitude and caliber," wrote *Variety*. There was no question about the magnitude. "The money M-G-M spent on it socks you in the face with every change of scene," wrote the *Literary Digest*.

"G. G., what do you do when you go home?" Freund asked.

"I rest a bit," answered Garbo, "the maid brings me dinner, then I study the next day's script and go to bed. I've been in my new house three months—and would you believe it—I've never seen the living room. I eat, study, and sleep."

"And what else do you do?"

"I sometimes play checkers," said Garbo. "With myself."

"And what do you do about sex?"

"Once in a while I go out, when I meet a man who enjoys me. When he arrives, I peek out at him to see what he's wearing and then I dress accordingly. Many of the men who ask me out go crazy about my Swedish maid, who is very pretty. They pat her on the cheek and flirt with her, but for me, at the end of the evening they say, 'Thank you, Miss Garbo,' and they tell me how wonderful it was, but not one ever says, 'Let's go to bed.'"

It was known that Garbo was seeing Stokowski, who insisted on dates in restaurants and nightclubs. As usual, photographers and fans pursued her. "I give them everything I've got on the screen," she would tell Brown the next day. "Why do they try to usurp my privacy?" Viertel was nonplussed by Garbo's involvement with Stokowski, Acosta was jealous, and the public was enthralled. For the first time

since John Gilbert, Garbo was involved with a star. Judging from her letters, she disdained the glamorous life. "I am incredibly tired of being a 'star,' tired of the films they offer me here, just *tired* in a word," she wrote. "But I am not satisfied with what I've got in the way of money, so I'll have to keep working for a while longer."

At Paramount, Dietrich was working on an elegant new film with Garbo's friend Ernst Lubitsch, who had been removed from the post of production head and was now solely directing. Acting with Dietrich in *Angel* were Herbert Marshall and Melvyn Douglas. "She was tremendously meticulous," remembered Douglas, "about her hair, makeup, lighting, jewelry, and costumes. I'd never been so impressed. She knew exactly where the lights were to be set for her." Cameraman Charles Lang, a master in his own right, had to defer to her lighting scheme. "Lee Garmes had laid down the pattern of lighting for Dietrich, with a spot, high, very high above the camera," said Lang. "I simply followed this. At night she would watch the rushes and say, 'No, this isn't right, that isn't right.' She'd criticize or praise, assessing herself as a painter would his own painting. It was extraordinary how objective she was about herself. It was as though she were not herself—that she saw herself at one remove."

Norma Shearer and Carole Lombard were also expert at analyzing the lighting of their close-ups. In contrast, Garbo did not look at the rushes during the making of *Marie Walewska*. She was as technically expert as the others, but she was not objective. She could not bear to see anything other than what she had imagined during a scene.

After eleven years, Brown was still fascinated by Garbo. "Greta Garbo had something that nobody ever had on the screen," Brown told Kevin Brownlow in 1967. "Nobody. I don't know whether she even knew she had it, but she did. And I can explain it in a few words. I would take a scene with Garbo—pretty good. I would take it three or four times. It was pretty good, but I was never quite satisfied. When I saw that same scene on the screen, however, it had something that it just didn't have on the set. Garbo had something behind the eyes that you couldn't see until you photographed it in close-up. You could see thought."

In early July, the production passed the four-month mark, and it was still not completed. Viertel had managed to get a few of Behrman's scenes reinstated, but she could not prevent Hyman from discarding the farewell scene that she and Hoffenstein had written. Hyman thought the scene should be "heartbreaking." They had not provided the "uplifting lines" it needed. He hired Charles MacArthur to write a new ending. As Napoleon was rowed to a waiting ship, Garbo watched sadly from a window, holding back tears, clutching her illegitimate son (Scotty Beckett). Clarence Brown remarked to her afterward: "You look tired, Miss Garbo. You'd better go home. You must be dead."

Louella Parsons thought that *Conquest*'s hairstyles and costumes were unflattering to Garbo.

"Dead?" she asked, looking up from her canvas-back chair. "Dead? I have been dead many years."

Filming ended on July 16, but there were the inevitable retakes. When the negative of *Marie Walewska* finally went to the laboratory—retitled *Conquest*—the production had logged 127 days of shooting; Garbo had been ill for nineteen of them, but her misery was well compensated. Her total earnings for the film came to a record $472,499. She had beaten Dietrich again.

Before *Conquest* was released, Dietrich's three films hit the theaters. *Garden of Allah*, which had cost $1.4 million, made none of it back. *Knight without Armor* became "a night without an audience." *Angel* fared worse, if possible. Unfavorable previews and PCA scolding brought months of editing. When *Angel* was finally released in late October, Dietrich's carefully constructed countenance got sarcastic reviews. "She is wearing eyelashes you could hang your hat on," wrote *Variety*. "When she blinks them, monstrous and sinister shadows flap bat-like across her curiously ascetic features," wrote Basil Wright in the *Spectator*. *Angel* fell to earth with a thud. On December 22, Paramount Pictures terminated Marlene Dietrich's contract.

Conquest premiered in New York on November 4. As Napoleon said, "There are times when all splendors become oppressive." Many critics agreed. Writing in the *New York Times*, Frank S. Nugent said:

If *Conquest* cost the $3,800,000 that Metro-Goldwyn-Mayer says it did, the company was overcharged. For the new film at the Capitol, with all the munificence of its

Clarence Bull's portraits of Garbo for *Conquest* used hard light to make stately images.

Clarence Brown said in 1967: "Greta Garbo had something that nobody ever had on the screen. Nobody. I don't know whether she even knew she had it, but she did."

production, with all the starring strength of a Greta Garbo and a Charles Boyer, is merely a surface show. It goes no deeper than the images its screen reflects. One can watch it and study it as academically as we would watch a procession of ants underneath a magnifying glass. Mr. Boyer's Napoleon does not fire the imagination or encourage respect. Miss Garbo's Marie Walewska is a creature built upon illogic. We view the destinies of both with interest but not with compassion; and compassion is all-important in a romantic tragedy.

Variety was sanguine about the film's potential: "*Conquest* is of road show magnitude and caliber. Here Metro has an offering in which to sell Garbo to every kind of audience, a Garbo who in a new and less exotic guise will have tremendous appeal to the smaller communities as well as in the key spots where she has heretofore appealed primarily." In Hollywood, Louella Parsons was quick to spot the film's structural problem, and she had no qualms about disclosing it: "Garbo is completely overshadowed by Charles Boyer, who takes the picture, wraps it up, and walks away with it." Par-

sons also had some pointed comments about the effects of Garbo's health-food regimen. "The clothes of the Napoleonic era are not particularly becoming to her, nor is the coiffure which accents her painful thinness. She has lost so much weight that there are certain scenes where she is almost emaciated-looking. It was all very well in *Camille*, but in *Conquest* it is very unbecoming." However, reviews like this were in the minority. Most critics exhorted every man, woman, child, and pet to see it. Perhaps in gratitude for the advertising money M-G-M had pumped into their publications, editors told critics to rave—or else.

The New Yorker felt no such obligation. "Madame Garbo's elegant anemia, I fear, can pall a little," wrote John Mosher. "Her performance seems static, though the story covers a period of years. Beautiful, fragile, and tired, she stands in the first scene among the Cossacks invading her husband's house; and quite unchanged, fragile and tired still, she waves her last farewell to Napoleon, as though she would assert and try to prove that loyalty is but a symptom of exhaustion."

It soon became obvious that *Conquest*'s massive ad campaign had interested few in Napoleon's peccadilloes. In January, the *Motion Picture Herald* printed a letter from an exhibitor in Columbia City, Indiana. "The costliest picture Metro has produced, and I credit that they poured the jack into this epic. But the film did not do any business here. It died here, and the bankers will be moving in on Metro. It is a super colossal magnifico—but a dog at the box office."

When the figures were finally tallied, they were enough to make strong men faint. *Conquest* had cost $2.732 million—more than any sound film so far. What was jaw-dropping was that it lost *$1.39 million*. M-G-M could no longer refer to Garbo as a goodwill asset. M-G-M could say nothing. The exhibitors could. On May 3, 1938, the Independent Theater Owners of America took out full-page ads in numerous trade papers stating: "The following stars are Box-Office Poison: Joan Crawford, Bette Davis, Marlene Dietrich, Greta Garbo, Katharine Hepburn, Mae West, Edward Arnold, and Fred Astaire." What did this mean to Garbo? She was in Europe with Stokowski at the time. "I have been away [from you] far too long," she told Wachtmeister. "One thing is clear. I have to stop making films. I cannot go on this way." If she was serious about quitting Hollywood, she was doing everything to make that possible. Her indolence, her fear, and her recalcitrance had tried the patience of her coworkers. Worst of all, her passive reliance on Salka Viertel was alienating both her colleagues and her fans. One badly managed movie showed how tenuous stardom was. One more might put Garbo in worse disfavor than Dietrich. A unique talent and an entire career were at stake. Who or what could save Greta Garbo?

CHAPTER TWENTY-FOUR

Ninotchka

The star system was nearly twenty-five years old in 1938. What Hollywood had learned about a star's life span in that time was not encouraging: it was less than ten years. Mary Pickford was fortunate. After becoming a star in 1914, she survived a divorce, a limited variety of roles, and the advent of talking pictures. Then, in 1929, approaching forty, she began to make films that veered too sharply from her image as America's Sweetheart. The films failed, and she retired in 1934. The length of her career was unusual, but its pattern was not. Numerous silent-film stars—Gloria Swanson, Ramon Novarro, Colleen Moore, Clara Bow, and Marion Davies—made happy transitions to talkies, only to fade by the mid-1930s because they had not found a new persona or adapted the old one. Of the dozen stars created by M-G-M in the booming twenties, only Norma Shearer was secure in 1938. The stigma of box-office poison stayed with Joan Crawford and Greta Garbo.

Marlene Dietrich made a marvelous comeback in the 1939 Universal film *Destry Rides Again*. Photograph by John Engstead

There was a precedent for comebacks. Crawford had slipped badly in 1932 with two flops, *Rain* and *Today We Live*, but she bounced back. M-G-M added her "dancing daughter" persona to her "shopgirl on the rise" formula and made one of the most commercial films of the decade, *Dancing Lady*. This was what Garbo needed, and a smart producer could do it. He simply needed to repackage her old formula. There was every reason to try. Garbo was the most celebrated star in the world. Her potential as an actor was unrealized. The studio had all the resources necessary to launch a major comeback, but as the 1930s drew to a close and Garbo approached thirty-five, there were three obstacles.

The first obstacle was Salka Viertel, who had become both the sole avenue to Garbo and the arbiter of her projects. If *Conquest* was any indication, Viertel was driving a wedge between Garbo and her public. It was hard for audiences to care about a star who was increasingly remote. Viertel's relationship with Garbo was different from Mercedes de Acosta's, but her concept of Garbo was just as unrealistic. For some weird reason, both women disapproved of the sensuality of Garbo's earlier films. Acosta wanted to "unsex" Garbo, making her mannish and aggressive. Viertel wanted to make her sexless, an intellectual abstraction. When Garbo was grudgingly allowed her to express her sexual self, both Viertel and the Production Code punished her. Some people liked this. "Garbo was the only one we could kill off," recalled M-G-M executive J. Robert Rubin. "The Shearer and Crawford pictures had to end with a clinch, but the women seemed to enjoy watching Garbo die." For Garbo to be universally popular, she had to be alive, healthy, and sexy. Her films had to appeal to everyone, not just the intelligentsia that passed through Viertel's living room. No M-G-M producer dared say this to Viertel; she might deny him access to Garbo.

The second obstacle was Garbo herself. Even when communicating through Viertel, she was difficult and mercurial. She offered the studio no help. She dealt with the issue of roles only when pushed to it, and then she deferred to Viertel. It took forever to find a property that she would approve, and longer to get her to the studio. How could she revive her career when she made so few films? In 1938, neither she nor Dietrich made one. "It never pleased me to act all the time,"

Greta Garbo's 1939 comeback in *Ninotchka* was as dramatic as Dietrich's, if not as deliberately glamorous. Photograph by Milton Brown

Garbo told Cecil Beaton later. "In fact, I tried to make only one picture every two years so that for months on end I could go to Sweden, or walk in the mountains, and not think about motion pictures." She seemed to forget that the public had a short attention span. If she took her sweet time returning, she might not be welcomed back with open arms. She might be ignored. In short, she was a liability to her own career.

The third obstacle to a comeback was the instability of the market. As the self-absorbed Garbo traveled through Europe with Leopold Stokowski in 1938, even she had to acknowledge the unrest that was everywhere. In mid-March, while the couple was staying in the Italian village of Ravello, Austria was annexed by Nazi Germany. If war broke out in Europe, M-G-M would be unable to exhibit films there, which meant losing two-thirds of Garbo's audience. "Garbo was a money star only in Europe," said Gottfried Reinhardt, who watched his boss, Bernie Hyman, assume the blame for *Conquest*'s domestic failure. Clarence Brown, its director, had also seen the shift. "She had a fanatical following in the United States," said Brown, "but unfortunately all those fans were not enough. Her pictures opened to bigger grosses than any other pictures we handled, but they didn't hold the extended run. Once the fanaticism was over, the box-office takings went way down. On the other hand, in Europe, Garbo was queen. Over there, Garbo was first, second, third, and fourth." If that market was diminished by border problems or lost to an all-out war, a Garbo comeback would be impossible.

This had occurred to Garbo's colleagues and advisers as early as mid-1937, and they tried to think of some way to win back her American audience. "After *Conquest* was previewed," wrote Viertel, "Bernie told me to think about another story for Garbo." Reinhardt, who had Viertel's ear in a way that Hyman did not, tried to warn her. "Only keep away from historical topics," said Reinhardt. "Convince Garbo to do a comedy for once." True to form, Viertel kept her own counsel and proposed that the studio purchase *Madame Curie*, Eve Curie's biography of her scientist mother. "You are incorrigible!" Reinhardt told Viertel after the story editor demurred.

One day in mid-1937, Viertel was sitting in the Brown Derby restaurant when she recognized Melchior Lengyel, the Hungarian writer whose plays had been the basis for two recent Marlene Dietrich disasters, the aborted *I Loved a Soldier* and *Angel*. Viertel knew him from the M-G-M writers department. "Always smiling, Lengyel would come to the studio with ideas and stories which he told very amusingly, in an absurdly concocted Hungarian English," recalled Viertel, who was fluent in five languages. "You don't happen to have a story up your sleeve that could be advertised with the slogan 'Garbo Laughs,' do you?" Viertel asked him.

Lengyel was pleased to be asked but could not recall one while standing over her table. "Over the years I had jotted down rambling thoughts for possible later stories and plays," he recalled in 1948. "A few days later, looking through several years of entries in my notebooks, I came across a memo I had made two years before in Europe." Lengyel called Viertel and a meeting was arranged, with Garbo no less.

"When I arrived," recalled Lengyel, "Miss Garbo was in the swimming pool. I was introduced to her at the edge of the pool."

"You have a comedy for me?" Garbo asked as she emerged from the water.

Lengyel opened his well-thumbed notebook and read aloud: "Russian girl saturated with Bolshevist ideals goes to Paris. She meets romance and has an uproarious good time. Capitalism not so bad after all." Lengyel enumerated the various directions in which he could take the story. Garbo listened intently, chuckled, and then laughed out loud.

"I like it," she announced. "I will do it." Then she turned away from Lengyel and Viertel and dived gracefully into the pool. Within a week, Lengyel had collected $15,000 for his idea. Producer Sidney Franklin, who was a Thalberg alumnus, could see that the story was a variation of the original Garbo formula. Instead of having Garbo rescued from an older man by a younger man, Lengyel would have Garbo rescued from communism by a young sophisticate. It might just work. By late August, Lengyel had finished a treatment entitled *Ninotchka: (Love Is Not So Simple)*. In a typically funny scene, Ninotchka, the humorless Communist envoy, is being wooed by Leon, a worldly Parisian. She is willing to look at his etchings but cannot understand his elaborate seduction technique; she wants him to get down to business. He points to a chorus of alley cats outside his window. "There is no reason for them to complicate things," says Leon. "The male has no need of prowling about roofs at night and meowing so heartbreakingly to be heard by the female. And do you know that even snails, than which no slower, more frigid animal could be imagined, walk around each other for two full days at an increasing pace in the season of love, before they embrace? The whole drama of love, in fact, is nothing but a game—pursuit and flight." Ninotchka has no intention of fleeing—until she discovers that Leon is a member of the nobility, anathema to her ideals.

For some reason, Viertel was not able to persuade the studio to assign her to *Ninotchka*. Perhaps it was because Lengyel was a self-sufficient writer, or because Hyman turned the project over to Franklin, who preferred to use seasoned writers like Claudine West. Franklin was also preparing to direct *Marie Antoinette*, a Thalberg project recently reactivated by Louis B. Mayer for Norma Shearer. The only way Viertel could keep her finger in the pie was to have Reinhardt assigned to *Ninotchka*; she went to work on it. The deliberate Franklin took too long to prepare *Marie*, so in January 1938, Mayer gave it to W. S. Van Dyke, leaving Franklin free to supervise Lengyel.

"Love, my dear young lady, is not so simple, even among cats," says Leon in the new draft. "Else why this unearthly concert at this time of night? Mr. Puss is courting Miss Pussycat—a very complex procedure—among cats as among all other creatures. Why do doves bill and coo? Why do snails, coldest of all creatures, circle interminably around each other? Why do moths fly hundreds of miles to find each other? Why do flowers open their petals?"

The actor suggested for Leon was William Powell, but he was on sick leave. While grieving for Jean Harlow, who had died the previous June, Powell had been diagnosed with colon cancer. There was no rush to cast the film; Garbo was in Sweden. In February, she joined Stokowski in Rome, and then in late March she brought him back to Sweden, dodging reporters all the way. The political situation in Europe was worsening since the German annexation of Austria, where Nazis started to carry out Adolf Hitler's program of anti-Semitic persecution. More than 70,000 Austrians were arrested, but some escaped, following refugees from Germany and France to Los Angeles. Viertel's salon had already been graced by the presence of distinguished refugees such as Thomas Mann, Lotte Lenya, and Igor Stravinsky. "With the influx of the refugees in the thirties," wrote S. N. Behrman, "Hollywood became a kind of Athens. It was as crowded with artists as Renaissance Florence."

Film director Robert Parrish, who was playing juveniles in M-G-M films in 1938, recalled one visit to 165 Mabery Road. "I walked in the back door one day and there was a guy

with short hair cooking at the stove. In the living room, Arthur Rubinstein was tinkling on the piano. Greta Garbo was lying on the sofa, and Christopher Isherwood was lounging in a chair. 'Who's the guy in the kitchen?' I asked no one in particular. 'Bertolt Brecht,' came the reply." Viertel had been a busy hostess before; she was now helping refugees find lodging and jobs. This elevated her to a unique position in Hollywood society. Reinhardt later wrote:

> The greatest contrasts collided in the salon of Salka Viertel. It was where Greta Garbo elucidated to Max Reinhardt how she intended to play Hamlet; where Chaplin rounded out his universal gifts and recruited his musical ghostwriter, the brilliant sycophant Hanns Eisler; where the happy-go-lucky virtuoso in the grand tradition, Arthur Rubinstein, was polite to the unhappy and unlucky, tradition-trampling Arnold Schoenberg, where the brothers Heinrich and Thomas Mann, estranged for decades, were reconciled . . . where Greta Garbo knelt before Stokowski and listened, enraptured, to such tales as when he spent an entire day—sunrise to sunset—with a native sage on an Indian mountaintop, gazing at the landscape spread out below and discussing the eschatological problems of the world.

While these literary lights scintillated around her, Viertel still found time to look after her own interests. Hyman wanted to have more than one project to offer Garbo when she returned from Europe; she had left without signing a new contract. When she was interviewed in Sweden in January 1938, she was candid about her expectations. "No, I am not going to play Joan of Arc," she told a reporter. "Has

A photograph is worth a thousand words, especially when it contradicts press agentry. Director Ernst Lubitsch claimed that Garbo was totally uninterested in mirrors during the making of *Ninotchka*. Here she is with her favorite cameraman, William Daniels, who was fresh from the triumph of *Marie Antoinette*.

"Compare Garbo's performance with the strenuous if veteran performance of Ina Claire," wrote Otis Ferguson in *New Republic*, "and you will see by contrast something of a natural style in acting which may take hard work to perfect but never looks like it." Claire, who had introduced a naturalistic style of acting to the theater twenty years earlier, was playing a fluttery, artificial woman; Ferguson had obviously missed her hilarious performance as a gold digger in the 1932 film *The Greeks Had a Word for Them*. Melvyn Douglas is the man between Garbo and Claire in this scene from *Ninotchka*.

that silly story got to Europe too? It is so idiotic! I am tired of period pictures and I want to do something modern now. My next film is to be a comedy."

The reporter asked if it would have the usual sad ending of a Garbo film.

"Will I be allowed to keep my lover in it?" Garbo answered one question with another. "Certainly I am hoping so. Don't you think it is high time they let me end a picture happily with a kiss? I do. I seem to have lost so many attractive men in the final scenes."

Viertel was determined to push the Madame Curie project, so she laid the groundwork and then presented it to Hyman. "What makes you think Garbo would be interested in *that*?" he asked.

"I am certain she will," insisted Viertel. "Please let me send her a cable!"

"She's never heard of Marie Curie!" Hyman laughed at Viertel.

A day later, Viertel wore a knowing smile as she handed Hyman a cable from Garbo that read: "Love to play Marie Curie. Could not think of anything better." She also had the satisfaction of pointing out how stupid the M-G-M story editor had been to let the Curie book slip through his fingers. Universal had bought it for Irene Dunne. Now that Garbo was interested in it, M-G-M had to pay Universal an exorbi-

tant sum to get it for her. Hyman assigned Viertel to the script, which only meant that she was doing research. "I began to acquire a great deal of information about Polonium, radium, radioactivity, and the atom." In the spring of 1938, Anita Loos brought Aldous Huxley to M-G-M. After some jockeying by Loos and Viertel, the author of *Brave New World* was put to work on the Curie project at a salary of $2,000 a week.

"Aldous wants it to be done properly and nobly," wrote his wife, Maria. "The great advantage of having Garbo is that she passionately wants to play that part; she admires Aldous and would do a bit more under his direction." In late August, after eight weeks of work, Huxley turned in a 145-page treatment. Loos and Viertel both found it excellent, full of drama and heart, but it got no farther than Hyman's secretary, who read it for the producer and then told him: "It stinks." Huxley did not take the rejection lightly. "Anita couldn't understand why he was so upset," wrote Christopher Isherwood. "She didn't understand that we thought writing something for Greta Garbo . . . was more glamorous than winning a Pulitzer. She had been around Hollywood so long she couldn't understand the magic it held for outsiders like Aldous and me. She thought Hollywood had failed Huxley where I'm pretty sure that Huxley felt he had failed Greta Garbo."

Before Viertel could do anything to save his script, she had to see her family in Europe. Acosta took advantage of her absence to plan a meeting between Huxley and Garbo. Viertel returned in September, doing her best to keep calm after the alarming scenes she had witnessed. "As soon as I entered my hotel room in New York, Bernie's voice from the West Coast welcomed me back to America," wrote Viertel. "He announced that the studio had decided to shelve Marie Curie; and that I should be thinking about a comedy for Garbo." Garbo returned from Europe in October. While passing through New York, she wired Viertel about the advisability of meeting with George Cukor before she signed a contract. She was disappointed to hear that Cukor was set for *Gone with the Wind* and only Edmund Goulding was available. As soon as Garbo arrived in Hollywood, Acosta invited Huxley to meet her. He later described Garbo's eerily quiet house:

> On a very large sofa sat a very small woman, a small but most exquisite woman, both in features and figure, and in the manner of her dress. She was beautiful, very beautiful, but her beauty seemed to me to have that decadence one had seen before in very old and renowned Spanish or Italian families. I was right in at least one respect, as she introduced herself as Mercedes de Acosta. I sat opposite her and we maintained a polite conversation until Miss Garbo entered the room. She was dressed as a boy, a very beautiful boy, I grant you, but I was somewhat startled by the transformation.

Garbo wanted to know if Huxley had any ideas for film roles. He admitted that he had been too busy to do the proper research. Garbo and Acosta were not worried. They had an idea for him. "I want you," said Garbo, "to write me a story about St. Francis of Assisi."

"And do you wish to enact the part of St. Francis himself?" Huxley asked after a shocked pause.

"That is correct," Garbo replied, as Acosta evinced a slight smile of approval.

"What!" Huxley gasped. "Replete with beard?" His indelicate question brought the strange interview to an end, but he eventually established friendships with both women.

At M-G-M, Viertel had managed to get Reinhardt installed in Sidney Franklin's office as an associate producer on *Ninotchka*, which was being expanded from Lengyel's script by Sam Behrman. In the latest draft, the stern young Russian's purpose in visiting Paris is to secure a deal: the French will get the ore in a Siberian nickel mine if the Soviets get food for the starving masses. The desperation of these Russian characters was nothing compared to the terror experienced by German Jews on November 9, the Kristallnacht, when Nazis smashed the windows of Jewish businesses, torched synagogues, and murdered citizens in the streets. These were distant events to Hollywood until Joseph Kaufmann, head of Warner Bros. distribution in Berlin, was beaten to death by Nazi thugs in front of the company office for no other reason than being Jewish. Warner Bros. closed the office and began producing anti-Nazi films like *Confessions of a Nazi Spy*. *Ninotchka* was hardly in the same category; rather than attacking communism, it ridiculed it. Neither studio worried about censorship in Germany or Russia. The two countries were on the verge of signing a nonaggression pact, and Hollywood was no longer sending films to either of them. There was a loss of revenue, but not enough to worry M-G-M or Garbo.

In November, as Garbo's contract negotiations began, Behrman returned to New York to polish his latest play, *No Time for Comedy*, in expectation of the opening with Katharine Cornell and Laurence Olivier. He was joined by Reinhardt, who was there to make sure that he finished *Ninotchka* in a timely fashion. He was slow, but his draft was already as funny as his best theater work.

LEON
Am I repulsive to you?

NINOTCHKA
No. Your skin is good. The whites of your eyes are clear and the cornea is excellent.

LEON
Your cornea is terrific. Tell me, Ninotchka. You're an expert. Can it be that I'm falling in love with you?

NINOTCHKA
No, it cannot. Love is a romantic designation for the most ordinary biological process—a lot of nonsense is talked and written about it.

LEON
Oh, I see. What do you use instead?

NINOTCHKA
I acknowledge the existence of a natural instinct common to all.

LEON
So far, so good. Now then—again I appeal to you as an expert. What can I possibly do to foster such an impulse in you?

NINOTCHKA
You don't have to do anything. Chemically we are already quite sympathetic.

On November 16, Franklin made a call from his M-G-M office to Reinhardt's hotel in New York about the tardiness

Garbo's superbly nuanced deadpan made a huge hit of *Ninotchka*.

"Garbo Laughs!" said the ads for *Ninotchka*. She had laughed in films before, but it was easier to characterize her as humorless. The film did not need spurious claims to revive Garbo's career.

of Behrman's latest draft. "This sort of let us down," said Franklin. "Bernie thought it was foolish of you to go to New York under these circumstances. He thought Sam was writing on his play, too, and that his mind was divided, and that's why he isn't doing his best work."

"You can tell Bernie that [Sam] hasn't got his mind on anything else. . . . Would you want to take somebody else or what?" asked Reinhardt.

"He doesn't really write down-to-earth motion-picture scenes," said Franklin. "But if we could just get fifty percent more value in [those] lines from him, we would have something to patch up. It's hard for me to say. . . . Bernie thought we should get another writer and we work here while you work there. As the stuff comes in. I wanted Claudine [West to stay on], but she's balking. She says she's no comedian. . . . It doesn't sound like [Sam] is going very fast."

"I don't know a much better man," said Reinhardt. "It must be cut down. It must be made clear about the coal mine, but I think basically it isn't bad."

The upshot of this transcontinental conference was that Samuel Hoffenstein and Jacques Deval joined West on the script in Culver City. By late December, though, Behrman had embellished Lengyel's story with two wonderful scenes: one took place in the Eiffel Tower, and one in a working-class restaurant. On December 29, Garbo signed a contract for one film at $125,000, which was a comedown from her last. A day later, director Ernst Lubitsch signed a two-picture deal at $147,500. *Ninotchka* would be first, and then *Shop around the Corner*, but if Garbo decided not to do *Ninotchka*, Lubitsch was still obliged to do *Shop*. The contract allowed no other M-G-M project, not even Hunt Stromberg's all-star production of *The Women*. "The minute Lubitsch took over, I told Behrman we might as well forget the whole thing," recalled Reinhardt. Behrman continued writing, and, after his play opened, he returned to California. Reinhardt dutifully reported the change in management to Viertel. She did not worry; she still had the final say in matters relating to Garbo, Lubitsch notwithstanding.

On February 8, 1939, Lubitsch started work at M-G-M. His first order of business was to tell Sidney Franklin that he did not like the Behrman script. At this point, Lubitsch brought in screenwriter Walter Reisch, whose *Escapade* was responsible for Luise Rainer's stardom. Lubitsch told Reisch that Behrman's dialogue was good but his plotting was not; they went together to Hyman's house to talk it out with Behrman.

"I just want to prove to you that this script will not play," Lubitsch told Behrman as he proceeded to act it out in a highly exaggerated fashion.

"But if the man who owned the Globe Theatre heard you read *Hamlet* like you read my script, Hamlet would never have been produced," said Behrman, aware that he was losing ground. When he said he did not want to work with

Reisch or anyone else, he was asked to leave the project. Lubitsch next wanted to meet with Garbo, but Viertel told him she was not feeling up to it. "I don't like to work for months on the film before shooting," said Garbo. "I don't want to go to the studio except when I'm necessary. I'm not one who must be performing in front a camera in order to feel good. I don't want to be bored, and the only way I can preserve what I've got to give the screen is to save my energies for the cameras." Lubitsch was beginning to lose interest, especially with the real-life drama playing in Europe. In mid-March, Germany invaded Czechoslovakia.

Ninotchka took a new course. It appeared that William Wyler would direct it, with Cary Grant starring opposite Garbo in a script by Ben Hecht and Charles MacArthur. Garbo visited a very nervous Cary Grant, and then vetoed the idea. Lubitsch still wanted to do the film. RKO director Garson Kanin later asked him why he thought the film could ever get off the ground. "Because she was funny," Lubitsch answered. "You couldn't see it? You didn't know it off screen? How funny she was? How she would make certain remarks about some of the producers? . . . She was *funny*. And I knew she could be funny on the screen. Even in some of the serious things she showed humor. You didn't notice how she always had such a light touch? Most of them are heavy. *Heavy*! But she was light, light always, and for comedy, nothing matters more."

As everyone who knew Garbo could attest, she was also unpredictable. That she was funny at Lubitsch's house did not guarantee that she would be funny on a soundstage. Eddie Mannix told Lubitsch that he would have to talk her into doing it. Predictably Garbo got cold feet. She would not consent to meet Lubitsch at the studio or at his home. With some hauteur of his own, he declined to go to her. Viertel stepped in and diplomatically arranged a lunch meeting at the Villa Nova restaurant on the Sunset Strip. According to Reisch, "Garbo arrived, said she was on a diet and would just listen as he discussed the film. Poor Lubitsch had ordered an immense meal—the antipasto, a dozen special dishes, and the Chianti, and the frutti, and the dishes were already on the table."

"I never touch lunch," said Garbo brusquely.

"All right," smiled Lubitsch. "I will eat and you listen."

At that point, said Reisch, Lubitsch became a character in one of his own sequences. "He started telling Garbo the story. He got more excited with each line, and forgot the food. An hour later, when he had finished talking, he looked at the table—it was cleaned out. Garbo had been so carried away by his enthusiasm that she had forgotten her diet and put away the whole meal." Garbo was sated—but was she satisfied with the script? Yes, but did Lubitsch think she could really play comedy?

"In case M-G-M is wondering why Ernst Lubitsch is the only producer with offices in the old scenario building," reported Harrison Carroll, "the entrance is right by the studio gate, making it easy for Greta Garbo to escape notice when she slips in to confer with Lubitsch." Garbo was sitting tensely on the leather sofa in Lubitsch's office. His black eyebrows knit tightly. "Can you laugh?" he asked her with the utmost seriousness.

"I think so," Garbo answered.

"Do you often laugh?"

"Not often," Garbo answered quietly.

"Could you laugh right now?"

"Let me come back tomorrow," Garbo said after a thought-filled pause.

Garbo returned to Lubitsch's office the next day and sat forward on the sofa. "All right," she said. "I'm ready to laugh."

"Go ahead," said Lubitsch.

"And she laughed and it was beautiful," Lubitsch recalled. "And she made *me* laugh! And there we sat in my office like two loonies, laughing for about ten minutes. From that moment on, I knew I had a picture with her." Lubitsch and Garbo began to meet at Perino's restaurant on Wilshire Boulevard, where her culinary quirks soon attracted attention. "Greta likes the cooking there and loves to surprise Lubitsch with the Swedish and European dishes she orders,"

"I feel it is wicked that Billy Wilder and Walter Reisch and I are even mentioned in connection with *Ninotchka*," said writer Charles Brackett. "It was so much Ernst Lubitsch's own baby. He was a director in a creative frenzy at the time, and everything he did was to me wonderful and funny and stimulating." Here Lubitsch acts out a scene for Garbo.

Lubitsch explained how he directed Garbo: "I would go to her with a suggestion, saying, 'This is how I see the scene. Now you go away and think it over.' And she would go into a corner, all by herself, and brood."

wrote Louella Parsons. "For a girl who is so thin, the illusive Greta sets great store by her food and frequently goes into the kitchen and confers with the chef." Lubitsch, having made so much progress with Garbo, began submitting drafts of the script to Joseph Breen at the PCA, who inexplicably wanted M-G-M to refrain from depicting Moscow. Deval, who did the rewriting, also had to make Ninotchka so lady-like that she would resist the Parisian's advances.

Reinhardt was not happy to report to Viertel that Lubitsch had taken Deval, West, and Hoffenstein off the script and put Walter Reisch on it. Reisch and Lubitsch had decided to change the plot point from a nickel mine to a grand duchess's jewelry confiscated by Bolsheviks in 1917. "The nice thing about jewels is that they are photogenic," explained Lubitsch. "You can photograph them sparkling on a woman's tits." Reinhardt reported the tasteless remark to Viertel, who started to wonder what Garbo was getting into.

"We were in Sidney Franklin's office and we started arguing about the jewelry," said Reinhardt. "I thought it cheapened the plot. Well, Lubitsch stopped and asked Franklin if he could take me out and talk to me. Franklin said of course."

"Gottfried," said the diminutive Lubitsch to the towering, bulky Reinhardt, "don't make a mistake. Don't fight me on this. You'll lose."

Urged on by Salka, who did not believe that *she* could lose, Reinhardt complained to Franklin about Lubitsch. In short order, Reinhardt was removed from *Ninotchka*. Viertel's connection to—and control of—the script was terminated. She had underestimated Lubitsch's power, and overestimated her own.

Story conferences moved to Lubitsch's house, where he and Reisch turned the material over to Charles Brackett and Billy Wilder, the team that had worked with Lubitsch on his last film, *Bluebeard's Eighth Wife*. "Brackett, Reisch, and I were working for weeks wondering how to show Greta Garbo, the communist, seduced by capitalism," recalled Wilder. Their script had not improved greatly on Behrman's. His funny lines were still there, but they had encrusted them with exposition. At one point during a fevered conference, in which they were making no progress, Lubitsch got up and went to the bathroom. When he came out, he said: "Boys, I've got it. I've got the answer. It's the hat!" Lubitsch had had an inspiration. Instead of using pages of dialogue to show Ninotchka's change of attitude, he would use a visual cue. Early in the film, walking with the three envoys, Ninotchka stops to look at an expensive, silly hat in a store window. "How can a civilization survive which permits their women to put a thing like that on their heads?" she asks gravely. "It won't be long now, comrades." But after being softened by Leon's influence, she sees the world differently. She shows the three men out of her hotel room after another meeting, locks the door, nervously walks to the bureau, expectantly opens the drawer, and gingerly pulls the hat from where she has hidden it. She puts it on, and then sits down in front of a mirror to admire her new self. "Now *that* is the Lubitsch touch," said Wilder.

The director and his three writers worked happily from early April through late May. "It was so much Ernst Lubitsch's own baby," said Brackett. "He was a director in a creative frenzy at the time, and everything he did was to me wonderful and funny and stimulating." Wilder was in awe of Lubitsch's capacity for invention. "He wasn't just a gagman, he was the best creator of toppers," said Wilder. "You would come up with a funny bit to end a scene, and he would create a better one. I think he thought up the bit where the picture of Lenin smiles back at Garbo. I can't be too sure. He would look at our stuff and go, 'Ho ho, very good,' and scratch out the next line. He'd read a bit more, go 'Ho ho,' and scratch out another line. What he did was purify, and that was what made him a great writer." At one point, Reisch wrote a memo to Franklin, asking that Lubitsch be given a writing credit; it did not happen.

The only rain on this parade came from the PCA. Breen objected to the "use of the word 'biological' . . . as well as the line 'I acknowledge the existence of a natural impulse common to all.' This line and Leon's reply: 'What could I possibly do to encourage such an impulse?' are questionable under the Code. We presume there will be no suggestion of a sexual affair between Leon and Ninotchka." These lines stayed in, because the writers had baited Breen with a flagrant Code violation. "I held my breath," says a character in a party scene. "And then I felt the husband fumbling for his slippers. I pushed them from under the bed—toward him—and what do you think he said? 'Aren't these slippers marvelous? I go away for a ten-day trip, and when I come back, they're just as warm as when I left them.'" Breen cut the slippers speech and left biology alone.

The only other objection to the script came from Garbo. She drove all the way to M-G-M because of a line in which Ninotchka states that the hard wooden third-class benches in the train should be upholstered. "We communists will change this from the bottom up," she declares. Sitting in her car with Lubitsch, Garbo argued that the line was vulgar and insisted that it be changed, because she was not going to say it. Then she went back and forth with him for two hours about the nightclub scene in which she would have to get tipsy on champagne.

"I don't think that I can play it," she said.

"Look here," said Lubitsch firmly. "I'll do anything you want. I'll change the script. I'll change the dialogue. But this can't be changed. Too much depends on it. You must make up your mind that you have to play it."

Garbo reluctantly agreed and left the studio, but the unresolved problem added to her anxiety about appearing on film for the first time in two years. She attended a dinner party given by Cole Porter for newlyweds Carole Lombard and Clark Gable. "Garbo was uncommunicative," said Elsa Maxwell. "No one noticed that she slipped out of the room after dinner. I went to the powder room, opened the door, and stood there transfixed. Garbo was staring so intently in the mirror that she did not hear me enter. I have no idea how long she had been studying her reflection, but she shuddered suddenly and buried her head in her arms."

About the same time, Garbo wrote a typically plaintive letter to Hörke Wachtmeister. "My studio is starting to collapse because everything is in chaos," wrote Garbo. "I should have started work in November but nothing gets finished. It is miserable having to live your life and spend your time in this way, so I have been putting out my plants instead. I have no idea what will happen, but there's a little angel somewhere who is changing my life—I don't know into what!" The angel may have been Lubitsch, who, assisted by some first-rate writing talent, was crafting a script of extraordinary quality. True, the script was still one-third Lengyel and one-third Behrman, but the new third made the other two thirds come to life. Breen approved it on May 24, and a week later the studio braced itself for the return of Garbo.

"On her first day's work before the cameras in two years, Greta Garbo had a beautiful case of jitters," reported Harrison Carroll in the *Evening Herald-Express*. "She came onto the *Ninotchka* set wearing a blue robe over blue pajamas, gave a nervous good morning to Lubitsch and to cameraman Bill Daniels, and said: 'Let's start right away.'" Her first scene showed her unpacking a portable typewriter in the hotel suite and taking depositions from the errant envoys. Between scenes, Garbo retired to her dressing room, where she waited for Daniels to signal that the next setup was ready. He would press a button by his camera that was connected to a red lightbulb over her door. "There never was a harder worker than I," Garbo told Beaton eight years later. "I never entertained or saw visitors. I never gave any trouble. I was just there, waiting for anybody who wanted me." In front of the camera, though, she reverted to form. "I remember going to the M-G-M studios one day and seeing Garbo on the set," said Wilder. "I'd never seen her in the flesh before, and naturally I was very excited. But as soon as she knew I was around she insisted that a large screen be placed around her so that I couldn't see what was going on."

The jewels in the story are being fought over by the Soviets and by their previous owner, the Grand Duchess Swana, an exiled White Russian who claims that the envoys have no

Clarence Bull made certain that he got Garbo to pretend she was laughing in their portrait sitting for *Ninotchka*.

right to barter with them. Cast as the imperious noble was Ina Claire, the stage star whom John Gilbert had married on the rebound in 1929 and divorced two years later. Once she and Garbo got past their initial awkwardness, they got along well—up to a point. Claire insisted on watching Garbo work.

"Are you ready, Miss Garbo?" asked assistant director Charles Dorian one day.

"As soon as Miss Claire gets from behind that curtain, yes."

On another occasion, Garbo had to do a telephone scene in which she grows tearful. Claire found a hiding place and watched Lubitsch film the scene. At its conclusion, Claire emerged from the shadows and walked up to Garbo, who was startled. "I didn't see you."

"Well," said Claire, "I am here to tell you that scene was one of the most extraordinary things I've ever seen. And damn you, I saw you cry."

"Very unmanly of me, wasn't it?" said Garbo, who turned her back on Claire and stalked to her dressing room. It was not long, however, before Garbo was laughing at Claire's chic antics, which included tap-dancing to a recording of "Broadway Rhythm."

Lubitsch watched Garbo carefully. He had heard that she was a vegetarian, and he thought she looked too thin. "Roses I got to have in your cheeks!" he said to her. "One nice, thick, juicy steak is more important to this picture than all the dialogue!" Acosta took Garbo in hand and made sure she went to Perino's more often. One day Garbo was spotted there using a soup spoon to eat spaghetti and ice cream. "Nice pink cheeks! Nice bright eyes! Beautiful!" said Lubitsch when he saw an improvement.

Not far away, Salka Viertel watched with a cynical eye. "Lubitsch came to my office every day, telling me what scenes they had shot and how wonderful Garbo was," said Viertel. "Piled up on my desk were novels and plays which the story department thought 'excellent Garbo material.'" Viertel, more and more engaged in relief work, sifted through the material and waited for a chance to regain control.

Lubitsch had cast Melvyn Douglas, with whom he enjoyed working on *Angel*, as the urbane Leon. "I was frequently at the house of Garbo's friends, Salka and Berthold Viertel," recalled Douglas. "Garbo would drop in, sit on the floor, giggle at this and that, and then be gone without a word. It was not easy to carry on a conversation with her. She talked warmly about music on several occasions, even before she became involved with the conductor, Leopold Stokowski, but she didn't read much and seemed out of touch with the world around her." On the set, though, Garbo was in surprisingly fine fettle, according to a studio publicist. "The most hilarious moment on the set came when Garbo read the line, 'Go to bed, little father. We want to be alone.' The star herself gave vent to a loud laugh and everyone else on the set joined in." Douglas recalled other days, when she lapsed into moodiness. "She didn't show up for work several

times during the filming on *Ninotchka*," said Douglas, "which gave rise to the usual jokes about 'I want to be alone,' but I doubt that that was the problem. My guess is that Garbo was struggling with the part. And couldn't face the cameras until she had settled the difficulty in her mind. There was nothing dishonest about the woman. I thought her less mysterious than insecure."

The filming went well all through June, thanks to a carefully prepared script. Less than three scenes were changed in the course of shooting. They involved changes in Garbo's wardrobe, which looked drab in the rushes. She was given a stylish Russian blouse for the retake of her first scene in Leon's apartment, and a luxuriant off-the-shoulder evening gown made of white tulle for the nightclub scene, which was first shot with a high-necked crepe dress. Garbo was used to retakes, but she was not used to Lubitsch's directing style, which consisted of acting out each scene for every actor. "Lubitsch was clever," wrote Cecil Beaton. "He was so much better as an actor than any of his casts. It was depressing to see him acting every part so well."

"I remember one morning," Garbo told Beaton, "going in and seeing him, cigar in mouth, with my big leading man, running through a scene on the sofa that I was to do. He was being so funny! But underneath he was a vulgar little man, and he made such a noise on the set, always shouting. One day I spoke to him in German: 'Please, when you speak to me, please speak more softly,' and he was so surprised that from then on, whenever he looked at me, he became quieter." On the whole, though, the making of *Ninotchka* was, after *Flesh and the Devil*, Garbo's brightest experience at M-G-M. Acosta saw a good deal of Garbo at this time. She later wrote:

Never since I had known her had she been in such good spirits. She had begun shooting the first gay picture she had ever done, and Lubitsch was directing it. "The first time I have had a great director since I am in Hollywood," she said. Greta was a changed person. She used to come for me usually after shooting, and we walked in the hills. She laughed constantly and she used to repeat the question "Why" as she did in the picture. She would imitate Lubitsch's accent and ask over and over again "Vhy? Vhy?" She acted out scenes for me from the picture, and some days she would really be Ninotchka. It was fascinating to see how by playing a gay role rather than a sad one her whole personality changed.

Lubitsch was happy with Garbo too, especially because of her no-nonsense work habits. "Having worked with many women stars," said Lubitsch, "I have found that one of the difficulties with them is their slavish devotion to the mirror. Some of them take a terribly long time to powder and make up between scenes. They are so much concerned about their looks that they exhaust their vitality. In the eight weeks during which I worked with Greta Garbo she never looked into the mirror once unless I told her to do so." Lubitsch had recently worked with Claudette Colbert, who would not allow her right side to be photographed, and Marlene Dietrich, who kept a full-length mirror next to the camera. Dietrich had sailed to France in June and was staying at the Hôtel du Cap at Eden Roc, in the south of France, with an entourage that included her daughter, her husband, his mistress, Josef von Sternberg, millionaire Jo Carstairs, and Erich Maria Remarque. It was assumed that Dietrich had given up on Hollywood and was considering a French film project with director Pierre Chénal.

Lubitsch accommodated Garbo by scheduling the nightclub scene toward the end of the shooting. She did extremely well in the restaurant scene where Ninotchka laughs for the first time. The scene had caused some anxiety, since the film would be sold with the phrase "Garbo Laughs!" During filming, Garbo laughed quite heartily and uproariously but emitted no sound. "She was unable to articulate so much as a titter," recalled Douglas. The sound department solved the problem in the final mix by raising the volume of the laughter of the people around her. But there was still that nightclub scene to do, and Garbo dreaded it. According to Lubitsch:

> When we finally did get to it she was very—afraid is too strong a word—timid. But finally I got her to relax completely by talking to her and being patient. I would go to her with a suggestion, saying, "This is how I see the scene. Now you go away and think it over." And she would go into a corner, all by herself, and brood. Then she would do the scene again. If it still wasn't right, I'd say—just casually, passing by her, "Very good, but if you could just do—" Then I'd leave her alone again. Thus I gave her confidence, gradually, so when she came to the drinking scene she was completely at ease.

Filming ended on July 28, and news began to spread that Garbo and Lubitsch had made a superlative movie. Garbo could make a comeback if *Ninotchka* played in Europe, but that was up in the air. Germany's advances on Poland were making France nervous and England angry. As talk of war spread, M-G-M looked anxiously to its foreign market.

Over at "major minor" Universal, producer Joe Pasternak and writer Felix Jackson were remaking a low-budget 1932 western, *Destry Rides Again*. Pasternak borrowed James Stewart from M-G-M to play Destry, but he needed to balance the whimsical tale of a nonviolent sheriff with a strong female role. "The girl in the original picture was dull," said Jackson, referring to an actress named Claudia Dell. "The girl was a frail, silly child waiting for her man to come home," said Pasternak. He and Jackson changed the sweetheart to a dance-hall girl with as much star power as the hero, "the equal of Destry in looks, drive, and personality.

She should be more than able to take care of herself . . . but she must be unpredictable underneath, like a cat." Pasternak had tried to sign Dietrich for Universal in 1928. "I knew Marlene was box-office poison," said Pasternak. "I was worried about what Sternberg had done to her. He had turned her into a waxen image. I had met her in Berlin and I knew she wasn't like that. She was tough, down-to-earth, real." Pasternak called Dietrich at the Hôtel du Cap.

"Why do you want me?" she asked without much enthusiasm.

"Because of the wonderful work you have done," answered Pasternak, "I know you'll be great in this picture I have for you."

"Okay," said Dietrich. "What is it?"

"It's a Western."

"Oh, no! You must be crazy!"

"Darling, please trust me," said Pasternak, "It's a marvelous part. You'll be sensational."

"I guess you haven't heard, my friend," said Dietrich. "I'm box-office poison."

"You won't be after this picture is finished."

After ten years of photographing Garbo, Bull was no less fascinated with her face.

For the *Ninotchka* portrait sitting, Garbo wore an evening gown that was not in the film, but Bull shot only head shots of her in it; this part of their sitting was inspired.

Dietrich thought the whole idea far-fetched, but she asked Sternberg and Remarque what they thought. They told her not to hesitate; she should make the film. "I put you on a pedestal, the untouchable goddess," said Sternberg. "He wants to drag you down into the mud, very touchable. A bona fide goddess with feet of clay. Very good salesmanship."

As Universal geared up for Marlene Dietrich, M-G-M prepared to sell the new Garbo. A late-August preview was a little worrisome. "Unless the film is slashed and parts redone," wrote Hedda Hopper, "Ina steals it." Franklin and Lubitsch cut two of Ina Claire's scenes and then brought her back to shoot transitional material. Salka Viertel, increasingly nervous about the situation in Poland, sailed for Europe in late August, leaving Garbo to socialize with Acosta, who used Garbo's newfound food obsession to introduce her to the well-known nutritionist Gayelord Hauser and his male housemate, Frey Brown. At first they made a glamorous foursome, but before long, Acosta was excluded from their outings, and Garbo was seen around town so often with Hauser that items began popping up in the news about "Garbo's New Love." Neither Garbo nor Hauser discouraged the coverage of their friendship, which, given his relationship with Brown, was nothing more than that, but Hauser, like Viertel, derived a thrill from sequestering Garbo. "The lady went through one of her 'depression weeks' and hasn't been able to do a thing," he wrote not too apologetically to Acosta, "which may explain why she has not called you again. I hope that by the time you receive this she has gotten in touch with you. Do take my advice

and not write to her at this address, as that is one of her pet peeves."

This petty intrigue was overshadowed by the events taking place in Europe. On September 1, 1939, while Viertel was still there, her homeland of Poland was attacked by Germany. Two days later, England and France declared war on Germany. Viertel hightailed it back to Los Angeles, where she overlooked her grievance against Lubitsch long enough to work with him on a European Film Fund. For all her power plays, she was genuinely concerned with helping the hundreds of displaced Jewish refugees coming to Hollywood. She gained nothing from her philanthropic work except the gratitude of people who might otherwise have died in Europe or starved in California.

In late September, M-G-M held a second preview of *Ninotchka*. Garbo arrived at the theater in Long Beach early, so she had to stand in line with a group of sailors until the manager recognized her and brought her to a roped-off section inside. This was her first preview since *Camille*, and she was, as ever, uneasy. As the film played, it became obvious that people were really enjoying it; in fact, they were hooting and hollering and clapping. "She was so excited," said Lubitsch. "When people started to laugh, it was the most amazing thing! She looked around like she'd heard thunder claps!" Wilder, Brackett, and Reisch were there, too, and Wilder could not believe the difference between the woman he had seen working at M-G-M and the image on the screen. "The face, that face, what was it about that face?" asked Wilder years later. "You could read into it all the secrets of a woman's soul. You could read Eve, Cleopatra, Mata Hari. She became all women on the screen. Not on the soundstage—the miracle happened on that film emulsion."

After the film, Lubitsch was tremendously curious about Garbo's reaction. "Do you like yourself in it?" he asked. Her answer was surprising. "She didn't know if she was bad or good." When she wrote to Wachtmeister, though, she had made up her mind. "My film is finished," wrote Garbo, "and I'm afraid it doesn't amount to much." Whatever it amounted to, there was the sad fact that it could not be shown in Europe, so Louis B. Mayer, Eddie Mannix, and the rest of M-G-M's upper echelon braced for another Garbo flop. She was not interested in a new contract, so they chose not to force the issue. Perhaps the long-dreaded "last Garbo picture" had finally come to pass. If so, some changes could be made.

Viertel had signed with agent Paul Kohner, who told her that her M-G-M writer's salary of $650 a week was insufficient. "On the day Kohner was supposed to discuss my contract with Eddie Mannix, I came home just as the telephone rang, and picked up the receiver. Steeling himself to firmness, the story editor informed me he was taking me off the payroll." When Viertel finally reached Kohner, she heard the supposed reason for her dismissal: Eddie Mannix was angry that she had dared let an agent represent her. "Let her see if you can get her a better job!" he had yelled at Kohner. Viertel, the power broker, suddenly found herself powerless. Garbo did not lift a finger to help; she was spending most of her time with Hauser.

Ninotchka premiered on October 26, 1939, at Grauman's Chinese Theatre, and two weeks later in New York, vying with war news for attention. "Stalin won't like it. Molotoff may recall his envoy from M-G-M," wrote Frank S. Nugent in the *New York Times*. "We still will say Garbo's *Ninotchka* is one of the sprightliest comedies of the year, a gay and impertinent and malicious show which never pulls the punch lines (no matter how far below the belt they may land) and finds the screen's austere first lady of drama playing deadpan comedy with the assurance of a Buster Keaton." If Garbo read this review, she might have had some satisfaction. "We did not like the 'drunk' scene here," Nugent went on, "but, in disliking it, we knew it was the writer's fault and Mr. Lubitsch's. They made her carry it too far." Howard Barnes in the *New York Herald Tribune* addressed the broader issue. "Now that she has done it," wrote Barnes, "it seems incredible that Greta Garbo has never appeared in a comedy before *Ninotchka*. The great actress reveals a

Bull used "eclipse lighting" to make this portrait of Garbo.

command of comic inflection which fully matches the emotional depth or tragic power of her earlier triumphs. It is a joyous, subtly shaded, and utterly enchanting portrayal which she creates to illuminate a rather slight satire and make it the year's most captivating screen comedy."

The most optimistic note was sounded by a trade magazine, the *Hollywood Spectator*: "Exhibitors who may have shied away from the old Garbo need not be afraid to offer their patrons the new one." The optimism was well founded. On November 22, a *New York Times* item reported that 300,000 people had seen *Ninotchka* in its first two weeks at the Music Hall. In a follow-up to his review, Nugent wrote that he had received "protests and forlorn expressions of regret from the persons who have gone to see *Ninotchka* and couldn't hear half the picture for the audience laughter and applause. That's a terrible state of affairs, of course, because *Ninotchka* is really too good a comedy to be laughed at that way. We had to see it twice, and then we had to read the script (it was labeled 'Temporary Incomplete,' and that's as final as they come in Hollywood) before we were fully satisfied it was as funny as we thought it was." *Ninotchka* would be a tough act to follow—especially for Garbo's longtime rival, whose film opened on November 29.

Destry Rides Again was greeted with skepticism. Dietrich in a Universal western? "Marlene Dietrich returns to the screen after a two-year absence to be hailed once again as one of the great glamour stars of all time," said one of the first reviews. "Here is a Dietrich we have long suspected existed behind that eternal mask of beauty and who now breaks forth with all the fury of an exploding firecracker," wrote another. The all-important *Variety* review called Dietrich "a trouper with a wealth of talent for comedy and character delineation. Her work as the hardened, ever-scrapping gin-mill entertainer serves pretty much as the teeter-board from which the picture flips itself from the level of the ordinary western into a class item." Having made her own sensational comeback, Dietrich signed a two-picture contract with Universal. Would Garbo fare as well without Europe?

A spring 1940 letter to *Box Office* magazine came from an exhibitor in Alberta, Canada. "Surprise picture," wrote the Canadian. "We have been afraid of Garbo for years, but she is human after all! Good business even with weather poor and roads bad." When all the returns were tallied, *Ninotchka* had done very well, grossing $1.187 million domestically and, even without Europe, $1.092 million overseas. It was nominated for a Best Picture Academy Award, and Garbo received her fourth Best Actress nomination. Sad to say, neither received the honor on awards night. This was a minor consideration after the slump from which *Ninotchka* had lifted Garbo. Her twenty-third Hollywood movie proved that she was still a star of the first magnitude, loved by her fans and revered by critics. Everyone at M-G-M was happy—everyone except Garbo.

"I still don't know what I'm going to do about filming," she wrote Wachtmeister in November. "I find working more difficult than ever. I don't know why that's so, but I get so embarrassed when I'm in the studio." Garbo was still plagued by anxiety and moodiness, so she began seeing Dr. Eric Drimmer, a Swedish psychologist who had opened a practice in Los Angeles that year and was treating, among others, Robert Taylor and Clark Gable. Drimmer's initial notation about Garbo was that she was seeking "relief from nervous tension." Six months of treatments followed, underwritten by M-G-M in the hopes that Garbo would feel well enough to make another *Ninotchka*.

"As I became familiar with her problems," Drimmer wrote in 1959, "I grew increasingly convinced that Greta Garbo suffered from a shyness vis-à-vis the world around her that bordered on the pathological. During our many long conversations, I also came to realize that the first step towards a change for the better in her health had to come from within herself. She had to openly reveal her fear, not hide behind it or call it something else."

Drimmer believed that Garbo's celebrity was the true cause of her anxiety, and that she should publicly avow her fear of strangers. "If a normal human being is suddenly faced with a dangerous wild animal, that person will experience intense fear. That is exactly what Garbo felt when faced with a crowd of people. A few strangers pushing forward to get autographs, and even her colleagues on occasion, could fill her with terror. Her sole impulse was to turn and flee." At the conclusion of his work with Garbo, Drimmer held out little hope. "Perhaps the myth of her solitude was too firmly entrenched," he wrote. "Or perhaps she lacked the strength to fight her way out of it."

Garbo had begun the 1930s with "Garbo Talks." She was beginning the 1940s with "Garbo Laughs." In her private life, she was not doing much of either, according to some of her friends. According to others, she was as sprightly as ever. With her film finished, she felt the usual compulsion to escape to Sweden; but the Atlantic Ocean was full of warships, so she contented herself with trips to New York, where she stayed in Sam Behrman's apartment. Away from Salka Viertel and Gayelord Hauser, she appeared to be directionless, unmotivated. Any other star would have been champing at the bit for a film with which to top *Ninotchka*. Garbo passed her time in solitude, not knowing or caring if M-G-M was looking for her next vehicle. Viertel was not at the studio to tell her that M-G-M was too busy grooming the "sweater girl" Lana Turner, the Anglo-Irish Greer Garson, and the Viennese Hedy Lamarr to think about Garbo, comeback or not.

Opposite: Greta Garbo at thirty-four by Clarence Sinclair Bull.

CHAPTER TWENTY-FIVE
Two-Faced Woman

As *Ninotchka* finished its last engagements in far-flung rural theaters, Greta Garbo's next film was of vital interest to Salka Viertel, but Garbo's confidante was momentarily without influence. After Viertel's dismissal from M-G-M, Paul Kohner had found her a position at Warner Bros., where a story editor gave her minor tasks that did not lead to screen credit. Viertel made it known through Gottfried Reinhardt that she would like to return to Metro. She was in her office at Warners when she received a call from Eddie Mannix.

"When are you coming back?" asked the usually tough executive. "Don't you miss me?" Viertel fielded his blandishments and got an appointment. "Determined to stand my ground," she wrote, "I went to Mannix. He embraced me, said he loved me, and that M-G-M was one big family to which we both belonged, and I needed no agent as long as he, Mannix, was taking care of me."

Mannix dazzled Viertel with some fast talk about how much Warners was taking out of her $1,000-a-week salary.

Marlene Dietrich's 1941 film *Manpower* continued the string of hits that followed her comeback in *Destry Rides Again*. Photograph by Bert Six

He offered her $750, but not under the table, so she would be making more than her earlier $650, but less than at Warners. She wisely agreed to go along with it, and Mannix happily rehired her. "And so, much to Greta's pleasure, I returned to the M-G-M fold and to the perennial search for a Garbo story." And to her own pleasure, Viertel was back in control of Garbo's career.

Marlene Dietrich wasted no time in finding a follow-up to *Destry Rides Again*. In *Seven Sinners*, which was released in October 1940, she had another role that made the most of her talent for putting over a song. Her background, after all, was in musical theater, so she was wonderfully convincing as a knowing chanteuse in a smoky cabaret. The success of *Destry* had not been a fluke. Dietrich was still a star, and what was true for her was also true for Garbo: the American public was ready to see her in another lighthearted offering. Even though he had not been part of the team that finished it, Sam Behrman was happy to see how *Ninotchka* turned out. "I was astonished and delighted," wrote Behrman. "I saw Garbo doing what she had never done before—giving a first-rate high-comedy performance." The first thing that occurred to him was to congratulate Lubitsch. "I wired Ernst to tell him my pleasure in it," wrote Behrman. "When I came to California I telephoned him on arrival."

Lubitsch himself was more than pleased with *Ninotchka*. "I wouldn't have done it if Garbo hadn't been cast for it—and without Garbo I don't think it would have meant a thing," he said. Behrman, no doubt aware of Dietrich's newfound comedy bent, was fired with enthusiasm for another Lubitsch-Garbo collaboration. "I went at once to see him," wrote Behrman. "I told him that he had opened a new vista for Garbo. She could play comedy; she must!"

"She made age-old gags seem brand new," Lubitsch agreed. "She understood perfectly what I wanted, and performed exquisitely."

Behrman saw Lubitsch bubbling with comic notions but wondered why he was not developing them. "He said he had several ideas for her," wrote Behrman, "but the difficulty was that he couldn't get her on the telephone." This was strange. Garbo had wanted to work with Lubitsch for ten years, had socialized with him, had respected him. Why would she refuse his calls?

"I spoke to Salka Viertel about this," wrote Behrman. "She told me Garbo had not really been happy on the set with Ernst. There was no *Stimmung* there." Behrman was shocked. How could such a delightful film have been made without a rapport between Garbo and Lubitsch? After a few weeks in Hollywood, Behrman began to hear more stories. One came from Max Reinhardt, who was hoping to mount a production of Maurice Maeterlinck's *Sister Beatrice*. "A pity that we cannot reach Greta Garbo," wrote Reinhardt. "Having to perform almost exclusively in pantomime, she would be perfect as the Madonna." From everyone, Behrman heard the same thing: Garbo was incommunicado to the people who had worked with her on *Ninotchka*. This pattern of disavowal was ultimately revealed for what it really was—Salka Viertel's revenge on the people who had let her be dismissed from M-G-M. She could not punish Garbo, but she could certainly remind everyone else who was in charge, and who was going to stay in charge.

"She was the only one with genuine access," recalled Irene Selznick. "If you were trying to get to Garbo, the shortcut was Salka. She was sort of her broker and had enormous control over her, and she was nobody's fool. She was Miss Fix-It—discreet and shrewd. You could talk to her: 'All right, Salka, come on. Put the cards on the table. What is it you really want?' She could talk Garbo into something she didn't want." But Garbo had wanted to do *Ninotchka*. "She talked quite freely of the experience of working on that particular picture," wrote Cecil Beaton. "She had not enjoyed it and worried that it was vulgar. It did not strike her as being funny." Gottfried Reinhardt was in a position to hear Garbo's impressions of Lubitsch firsthand, given his relationship with Viertel. "Garbo didn't care for him," recalled Reinhardt, who did not care for Lubitsch himself after being bounced off *Ninotchka* by him.

The result of Viertel's proprietary vendetta was a dog-in-the-manger situation. She kept everyone away from Garbo, yet she lacked the creativity to generate projects for her. The best she could do—while maintaining her salon and aiding refugees—was to read socially conscious books and recommend them to Garbo, who admitted to finishing very few of them. Viertel told Bernard Hyman that a book by Los Angeles author Scott O'Dell would make an excellent Garbo vehicle. "The locale was northern California, in the wonderful country around San Jose," wrote Viertel. "When I suggested the book, Bernie seemed interested, mainly because he immediately conceived the slogan: 'Garbo Plays a Western.' But as he preferred to make films in the studio, his addiction to farce and operetta won out. I had no help from Gottfried, always capable of swaying Bernie, because this time he shared his views. What they all would have liked best was a sequel to *Ninotchka*." Reinhardt had become a full-fledged producer at M-G-M while Salka was in exile at Warners. His first project was *Comrade X*, a carbon copy of *Ninotchka*

Two years after her 1939 hit *Ninotchka*, Greta Garbo returned to the screen in another comedy, *Two-Faced Woman*. Photograph by William Grimes

starring Hedy Lamarr as a dour Soviet converted to capitalism by Clark Gable, an American journalist. If M-G-M really wanted another *Ninotchka* for Garbo, Reinhardt had effectively eliminated that possibility. The larger issue was what Garbo wanted.

"I don't know what I'm going to do with myself," she wrote to Countess Wachtmeister in March 1940. "I've kept away from the studio. If peace comes, what I want most is to go home and not to make another film. I don't even want to think about it." But there were many people around her who did want her to think about it, and they kept after her. On November 20, Garbo signed a contract with M-G-M to make a film tentatively titled *I Love Your Sister*. When the terms were released, they caused much comment. "Greta Garbo had the local citizenry gasping on the ropes this week with the disclosure that she had requested a fifty percent cut in salary," reported the *New York Times*. "Quite on her own, Miss Garbo nearly put M-G-M officials in a swoon by suggesting that her salary be cut from the usual $250,000 to $125,000. The reason she gave for her action was that inasmuch as the greatest source of revenue for her films, the foreign market, no longer existed she felt obliged to share in the hard luck." In truth, Garbo signed for $150,000, but the even percentage made for a better story. And a story was all that M-G-M needed, now that Garbo had met the studio halfway. While Viertel continued to sift through literary properties, Garbo amused herself by traveling to Nassau and New York with Gayelord Hauser; her romance with Leopold Stokowski had ended without incident some months earlier.

In early January 1941, Dietrich was preparing for a new film, *The Flame of New Orleans*, when she heard that Erich Maria Remarque had met Garbo at a party in New York. At the end of the month, Hedda Hopper reported that Remarque was seeing Garbo. "Fur will fly if it's true Garbo has taken Marlene Dietrich's latest beau, Erich Remarque, away from her," wrote Hopper. Dietrich was preoccupied with the French actor Jean Gabin in Hollywood. If there was still a rivalry between her and Garbo, Dietrich was ahead, with two comedy hits to Garbo's one. *The Flame of New Orleans* was a period film directed by the French René Clair, whom Viertel no doubt knew. Yet she and her colleagues could not agree on the right vehicle for Garbo. "I gave up arguing," wrote Viertel, "and half-heartedly suggested a comedy by Ludwig Fulda, *The Twin Sister*, an old standby of the Vienna Burgtheater." Hyman had turned his attention elsewhere, so Sidney Franklin was producing. By a coincidence, Franklin had in 1925 directed Constance Talmadge in a silent version of this story. It called for a more-than-willing suspension of disbelief, even for a silent farce.

A woman fears that her unglamorous appearance is cooling her husband's ardor. To test him, she invents a twin sister and disguises herself as this worldly personage. He falls

Roland Young and Garbo worked well together in *Two-Faced Woman*, but we will never know how well they worked in this scene; it was cut to make the film play better.

for the bogus sister, and the usual complications ensue before she unmasks herself. It was a plot that worked only if directed at such an accelerated pace that the characters (and the audience) never had time to ask questions. Franklin thought that George Cukor would be equal to the task, as well as acceptable to Garbo. "I was terribly upset when I heard she was going to do this story," wrote Mercedes de Acosta. "The same plot had already been used twice in the silent films with other actresses in the title role. Why this old chestnut was dug up again for her I will never know."

What Viertel had once referred to as "the best minds at M-G-M" settled on this play because it would showcase two Garbos for the price of one. They blamed the public's loss of interest on her foreignness. The only thing to do was Americanize her. She would no longer be exotic or European. She would be light, bouncy, and domesticated, like a neutered pet. M-G-M had Lana Turner, the "Sweater Girl," and Warner Bros. had Ann Sheridan, the "Oomph Girl." Garbo could be as fresh, athletic, and sexy as any of them. In customizing Garbo to compete with these stars, there was a risk. No one stopped to think that she was almost thirty-six. No one questioned the wisdom of tampering with her image. And no one remembered that Thalberg's Garbo formula also worked in comedy. His observation that she should not create situations was forgotten in the haste to make her over. In this story, Garbo would be a puppet master pulling the strings—on herself. In real life, it was hard to tell who was really pulling the strings.

"The studio made her feel that she should do a film that would appeal to the American market," wrote Acosta, "which meant appealing to a very low standard as far as Greta was concerned." The problem, though, was that she was not concerned; she barely paid attention, preferring to let Viertel make decisions. "The setting of the original play was Renaissance Italy," wrote Viertel. "I shared the task of making it contemporary with the well-known German actor and dramatist Curt Goetz. As he barely spoke English, he was handicapped in adapting his witty lines to American humor, and he was replaced by Walter Reisch." Reisch was known for his ability to find a workable three-act structure for a story; he was not known for comedy dialogue.

In March, while Reisch struggled with this unlikely material, Garbo was embarking on a romance with Dietrich's beau, Erich Maria Remarque. "Garbo picked me up," he wrote in his journal. "Drive to the ocean. Walk the beach. Gentle wind, tender words, soft ocean. Garbo, the barefoot, big-foot beauty." In April, they went to see United Artists' *That Hamilton Woman*, which starred Vivien Leigh as Lady Hamilton and Laurence Olivier as Lord Nelson. The patriotic saga of a fight against a marauding dictator captured Winston Churchill's imagination for obvious reasons. It affected Garbo very curiously: she broke down and sobbed at the unflinching depiction of Lord Nelson's death.

Garbo was spending an increasing amount of time at Remarque's rented house, so it was inevitable that the phone would one day ring with a call from her rival. When it finally happened, Remarque tried to pretend that he was alone. Dietrich wanted him to come to her house; he tried to get out of it without saying why he could not come. Dietrich was too smart for him. Remarque finally admitted that he was with Garbo. Dietrich launched a "bombardment of jealousy" and told him all about Garbo: she could be "arrogant and ugly" and was known to have both breast cancer and syphilis. True to form, Garbo did not deny the ridiculous allegations but disappeared into the night. Remarque joined Dietrich, who suddenly grew "warm and caring."

At M-G-M, Viertel watched with dismay as her Garbo project threatened to jump the tracks. "The conferences with Franklin have become so dreary that Walter Reisch blew his top," Viertel wrote Berthold. "The result is that Franklin does not want to produce the film. Mannix called me to report to him and I supported Walter's outburst." What happened next was not hard to predict. Franklin was replaced by Viertel's "friend," Gottfried Reinhardt, and the studio approved a cost-conscious budget of $316,000 for the project, which was now called *The Twins*. "At the time when each day brought news more horrible than one could bear, it was not easy to manufacture a silly comedy," wrote Viertel. On April 6, German forces invaded Greece and Yugoslavia. On May 31, German airborne troops defeated the British on Crete. Viertel's mother was safe in Moscow, but no one knew for how long. Viertel concentrated on the script, which was still not working. She had Reinhardt get rid of Reisch and bring in Sam Behrman. His office was next to Reinhardt's in the new Thalberg building. Garbo was supposed to join him, Reinhardt, Viertel, and Cukor for a meeting one day. She was late, so Behrman went down the hall to the men's room. As he entered, he saw Garbo, standing at the window. He inquired of her what she was doing there.

"Watching the view," answered Garbo.

"Which view?" Behrman asked carefully.

Garbo told him that this particular window had the best view of the Los Angeles basin from Culver City. "She was not easy to talk to," remembered Behrman. "She was deliberate, guarded. She was a peasant. And an aristocrat. And a royal martinet!"

The all-important script was progressing too slowly for Garbo, who as usual wanted to start right away and then leave town. According to Viertel, "Sam Behrman and I wrote the screenplay with Mr. George Oppenheimer who, having participated in the creation of Marx Brothers comedies, was an expert in the farcical situations to which Bernie was so devotedly attached. As nothing divides people more than the difference in their sense of humor, it was a miracle that my friendship with Gottfried survived the severe test. Sam Behrman's authority and intervention survived many bitter

Another cut scene had Ruth Gordon advising Garbo how to look more glamorous.

Constance Bennett played Garbo's rival in *Two-Faced Woman*; she stole so many scenes from Garbo that one-quarter of the film was reshot.

feuds." As the June starting date for filming of *The Twins* approached, its thin script was being pulled in all directions. Viertel wanted to keep Garbo from being sexy. Behrman tried to keep the sexiness intact with his trademark wit. Oppenheimer wanted more physical humor. Reinhardt, who was distraught about the war, could not control any of them, which infuriated Viertel, who took it out on him in private. Cukor was not very helpful in the story conferences. His main concern was trying to differentiate the twins by what they would wear. The thwarted Reinhardt found Cukor a convenient target. "We certainly didn't get along professionally—at all," said Reinhardt. "He was a type of man that I really didn't go for. His homosexuality—even though I have had many good friends who were homosexuals—his homosexuality bothered me. Perhaps, above all, because he was so ugly, and that made it ludicrous." The hostile atmosphere affected the script, and it would not jell.

Joseph Breen of the PCA warned Reinhardt about a basic problem when he read the treatment. In it, New York magazine editor Lawrence Blake goes to a ski resort for a vacation. During a snowstorm he has a fling with Karin Borg, a clean-cut ski instructor. When he returns to the city, she follows him and, seeing his involvement with the fashionable playwright Griselda Vaughn, masquerades as her nonexistent twin sister, Katherine, who is everything that she is not. The problem was the snowbound interlude, a wistful throwback to *Queen Christina*. "In those days, cinematized sexual intercourse was—well, it just wasn't," wrote Reinhardt. "The script was turned down by the Breen Office on the grounds that it conveyed implications of a premarital carnal relationship. What if the cad marries the girl of high principles and then abandons her? And what if she, through her masquerade stratagem, wins him back? The Breen Office liked that. So the offending scenes were rewritten." Breen found the fragmented rewrites impossible to judge. "Due to the fact that this script is coming in segments," wrote Joseph Breen, "it is very difficult to render any kind of intelligent opinion as to the final acceptability of the various sequences. Such an opinion will probably have to wait until we can judge them in reference to the whole story." Breen then left the PCA to take a job as head of production at RKO-Radio Pictures. In the ensuing shuffle an incomplete script was approved, a decision that would later haunt both the PCA and M-G-M.

Not only Garbo was impatient to start; Reinhardt was told to hurry Cukor along or else. With the script still far from finished, Cukor began casting the film. He wanted Cary Grant for Lawrence Blake, but Benjamin Thau would not give him anyone more important than Melvyn Douglas, who had been criticized in some quarters for espousing liberal causes. Cukor wanted Constance Bennett for Griselda and the much-respected Broadway actress Ruth Gordon for Miss Ellis, Blake's secretary. He had to fight Reinhardt to get

them, not because they were inadequate but because he had to fight Reinhardt for everything. William Daniels was tied up with a Judy Garland movie, so Garbo had to accept Joseph Ruttenberg, who had done a fine job of flattering the entire cast of *The Women*.

Adrian designed a chic wardrobe for Garbo's masquerade as Katherine, but at the last minute Hyman told Reinhardt that it was too glamorous; Garbo needed gowns that were more American-looking. "They wanted to make her a 'sweater girl,'" recalled Adrian, "a real American type. I said 'She has created a type. If you destroy that illusion, you destroy her.'" Adrian was overruled. Claiming that the PCA had objected to one of Adrian's designs, Reinhardt made Garbo go to wardrobe and look at gowns by other designers, some of which had been worn by other actresses. She made tentative choices, but there was time; her ski-lodge scenes would be shot before the nightclub scene.

As Garbo nervously prepared for her first film since 1939, Dietrich began her fourth. She was on loan-out to Warner Bros. for a rough-and-tumble movie with George Raft and Edward G. Robinson called *Manpower*. Raft, whose romance with Norma Shearer had been curtailed by Louis B. Mayer, cast an admiring eye at Dietrich on her first day on the lot; before long, they were a Hedda Hopper item.

Filming of *The Twins* commenced on June 18, 1941. On that morning, Cukor went to Garbo's dressing room, closed the door, and chatted with her while Ruth Gordon and Melvyn Douglas awaited their calls for the first setup. "The camera crew, the assistant director, and the unit manager waited impatiently," wrote an M-G-M publicist. "Why was Cukor wasting so much time? They were even more perturbed when they heard the sound of throaty laughter emanating from Garbo's dressing room. As the laughter died, the star and director appeared on the stage."

"Now!" said Cukor authoritatively, and Garbo took her place on the set. He later explained that he needed that time with Garbo to help her make the transition from her own world to that of the soundstage. "With Garbo," said Cukor, "the problem is to make her forget her shyness, to make her feel that everybody is for her rather than against her. That is done by keeping the atmosphere light and friendly, by laughing, telling jokes, not by standing in awe. After Garbo is loosened up, the rest is easy."

Cukor soon found that with an incomplete script, nothing would be easy. The scenes of Garbo and Douglas in the snowbound lodge were fairly straightforward, but the scenes of her arrival in New York had to be shot twice because the script did not play. Behrman had to rewrite scenes over and over. Oppenheimer was called to the set. Ruth Gordon was in the street scene, which was shot on Lot 3. "This is a distance of a mile from the dressing rooms," said Gordon. "Four times a day, Garbo walked it. As the cars were taking the rest of us back and forth we would wave to Garbo striding down

Constance Bennett and Garbo had little to say to each other between scenes.

the road in the sunshine. If she starts down a street on the shady side she automatically gravitates to the sun." The scene where Karin makes an unexpected appearance at her husband's office had to be rewritten five times. In it, Karin sees a magazine article about Lawrence's old flame. A photo caption reads: "Griselda Vaughn: Youth . . . Beauty . . . Achievement."

"Is that all?" Karin asks.

"The other things you couldn't put into a caption," replies Miss Ellis.

"If this is what's wanted I think I can supply it," says Karin. "Elegance? Well, I'll be elegant. Chic? Well, why shouldn't I be chic? Perhaps I was stupid to try to change *him*. I'll let him change *me*. I'll go Miss Vaughn one better. What did you say her dressmaker's name was? Or didn't you?"

The scene was eventually discarded, further blurring the difference between the "good twin" and the "wicked twin." Other scenes were rewritten on the set without Behrman's knowledge or approval. One of the script's flaws was the misogyny of Lawrence Blake, who treats his new wife with impatient contempt. At bedtime he is mean to her, implying that he married her on a whim. In the morning he tells her: "Your plans don't amount to much." The script is sympathetic to her and yet gives her no reason to take such abuse and then go chasing after him. In the following scenes, her character becomes more and more foolish, losing any resem-

blance to the lovely, sincere woman of the opening. "Behrman did most of the writing and it was witty and graceful," recalled Oppenheimer. "But by the time it had been transmitted to the screen, something had happened to alter it radically. Behrman, a gentle soul with good manners, became almost feral as he watched what was meant to be a sly satire on the earlier Garbo pictures changed into a plodding, dull romantic comedy, played with hammer in hand rather than tongue in cheek." Cukor was after some effect, but no one knew what it was. Arguments ensued. "We had too many fights on that film," Reinhardt recalled. "From the very beginning, from the script, and later because of the way he shot."

"I've started work on a film, which probably won't amount to much," Garbo wrote Wachtmeister on June 23. "In any event, I don't feel too ashamed. But these are such strange times that they are worried that if it isn't a tiny bit vulgar it won't do well. It's strange that I should be writing about films when war is at our doorstep."

Garbo had a difficult time with a scene in which Karin has to endure Blake's arrogance. She is swimming as he tells her that she has to subordinate her life to his and accompany him to New York. Garbo had warned Cukor that she did not want to be shot in a bathing suit. He wrote Katharine Hepburn, asking if she had a suit to lend Garbo. The suit finally came from the New York designer Valentina, whom Garbo had met earlier in the year. Even though the scene required no extras and the set was closed to visitors, Garbo still suffered. "She held up production during the filming . . . but, from her point of view, she may have had reasons for being apprehensive," recalled Melvyn Douglas. "George Cukor insisted on filming her emerging from a pool in a swimming suit and, no great bodily beauty by Hollywood standards, she loathed the scene. Furthermore, the film depended on facility with words, as comedy often does, and she knew this was not her strongest area."

Garbo was letter-perfect if she had time to memorize her dialogue thoroughly. The constant rewrites hampered her. Even so, according to Cukor, her record was impressive. "Only four times during the picture did she 'blow' her lines," said Cukor. "When she did, she usually turned her head away from the camera and said 'I'm sorry.' If she only knew how very often the other girls 'go up' in their lines!"

Garbo so far appeared less nervous than she had on other sets, surprising everyone by allowing Ruth Gordon to watch her. "I refused many invitations because I would much rather watch Garbo work than go swimming or horseback riding," said Gordon. "She minded not at all that anyone in her troupe observed her. For me that was much more of a holiday—watching this fascinating woman who is also such a great actress—than anything else I could have done." Oppenheimer was also surprised by her change in policy. "I had heard that on the set she was particularly withdrawn,

Garbo not only had to memorize lines that were being written as she rehearsed this scene but also had to bounce to the beat of the "Chicachoca."

never greeting anyone, staying in her dressing room until her presence was needed, not mingling with the other actors, and not permitting visitors, including her writers. This was certainly not true," wrote Oppenheimer. "I was called on the set many times, always to be cordially greeted by Garbo. She did spend most of her time in her dressing room, but when she emerged she was always easy and affable." The only friction occurred when Constance Bennett was pointedly rude to newcomer Robert Sterling. Garbo snubbed Bennett and gave a private tea party for Sterling in her dressing room.

Garbo's mood darkened with the filming of the nightclub scene, in which she would have to do an extended rhumba in front of a hundred extras and without a dance double. In preparation, the studio sent choreographer Robert Alton to her home to coach her. He rang the doorbell, knocked, and called out, but he received no welcoming response. When he was about to leave, he looked into the garden and saw Garbo in the branches of a tree. "Go away, rhumba!" she yelled at him. Caught between M-G-M and Garbo, Alton took charge of the situation and Garbo relented. When it came time to film the scene, there were costume problems. "Two days before we were to start shooting the party sequence," recalled Joseph Ruttenberg, "Garbo nixed the dress she was supposed to wear. After being shown dozens more, she picked one—the worst possible choice. It had shoulder pads and was low-cut and she didn't have much of a chest." Cukor and Adrian were also present.

"Isn't that beautiful?" asked Cukor, indicating a sleeveless black gown with a weirdly shaped décolletage.

"Well, it's a beautiful dress, but . . ." Ruttenberg hesitated.

"You don't think it's very good looking for me," said Garbo.

Ruttenberg shook his head.

Garbo pointed to her breasts and said: "Joe, these things here—this is God's. I'm not responsible."

Garbo settled on the black gown. "They tried to put some jewelry on her, but it just didn't look right," recalled Ruttenberg. "You see, she was difficult to photograph. If her clothes were on the severe side, with clean lines, it would simplify things. Unfortunately she had a taste for bulky, ugly clothes that made her look much older than she was. It was like she couldn't stand to look beautiful; she only felt comfortable frumpy." If the gowns weren't bad enough, the hairstyles Garbo had to wear in the guise of the sophisticated twin were totally wrong for the shape of her head and face, with unbecoming clumps of curls that emphasized her age. She looked like her beautiful self in the bedtime scenes; her hair was allowed to fall loose and full, framing and balancing her face. No doubt aware of her disadvantage, Garbo began her work on the nightclub set with a case of nerves. It did not help when three extras from another set attempted to mingle with the nightclub extras. Garbo noticed them staring at her. She walked over to assistant director Charles Dorian and said: "There are some people here who do not belong."

"Persons not working in this company kindly return to their own set," Dorian said over a loudspeaker.

Cukor began to deviate from the still-unfinished script, improvising the dance scene. Garbo was uncomfortable. Oppenheimer was called to the set. "Robert Alton, the choreographer, was showing her the steps and I was required to dance along with them, injecting and shortening the dialogue to the rhythm of the dance," wrote Oppenheimer. Garbo found the process enervating. "If I were to write my own dialogue," she explained years later, "I'd need more time and experience than I have to give to it. Then I'd have to be on the other side of the camera. As it is, I am the one who is in front of it. The others can make their mistakes, but it is I who am being made a fool of." There was a limit to the foolishness of the rhumba scene; a dance double did the more complicated steps in wide shots. But Garbo, if not quite on the beat, was surprisingly graceful in the medium shots and looked as if she was having a good time leading an entire dance floor in a Pan-American dance step.

The rest of the nightclub scene, which involved some sharp repartee with the waspish Constance Bennett, showed how expert Garbo had become after fifteen years in Hollywood. Her intonation, her cadence, her timing—all the hallmarks of a skilled actor—were impeccably attuned to Behrman's droll dialogue. "Outside of love, everything else seems to be a waste of time," says Katherine to some scandalized socialites. "I like *men*. Preferably rich men." In these delicately crafted scenes, Garbo showed no loss of ability for her two years' absence—and, sadly, what the screen had been missing.

Sadder still was the remainder of the script, in which her innate dignity was sacrificed to a series of embarrassingly overwritten scenes. She was made to do a drunk scene in which she gracelessly slides off the edge of a bed. She was made to do a hangover scene in which an icepack is secured to her head with a towel. She was made to do a vamping scene in which she stupidly climbs up on a sofa to push Douglas away from her. At one point she tells him: "I see my future. I'm a flower of evil. A few more burning, flamelike years—and then the end. In this harsh new world, there is no place for me." Then the telephone rings. She slinks to it, unflattering shadows aging her face, and answers in a mock-sepulchral voice: "Hull-llow?" This kind of humor could have worked if the tone had been consistent; it was not.

The title of the film was now *Two-Faced Woman*. It was a misnomer. The woman was not two-faced; she was multi-faced, and none of them matched. Character, mood, and pacing changed from scene to scene. Bereft of her formula and a structured work environment, Garbo was lost. "I must work in my own way," she said later. "If I don't, then I'm sunk. The last film I made was my downfall because I allowed

myself to work differently in many ways." Unfortunately, the woman who could put stray extras and insensitive executives in their place was powerless before Salka Viertel, George Cukor, and Sam Behrman. "She couldn't impose herself on people, even when she knew what they were doing was not good," said Behrman. "She was insecure with cultivated people. She was afraid of being found gauche. She really had an inferiority complex about her lack of education." Afraid to question the intellectuals to whom she had entrusted her career, the most she could do was to whisper to Douglas and Acosta: "They're trying to kill me."

As the misguided film neared completion, Garbo wrote to Wachtmeister: "I'll soon be finished with my latest baby and have no idea what it will be like. Wonder when you'll get to see it. Don't even know if you can see films from here like before. I'm only very sorry that the story has changed so much. Salka had a much better story to begin with. But since I would rather go walking in the country than fight for stories, it will have turned out like it has." Filming ended August 22, but Garbo did not telephone Clarence Bull for her customary end-of-production portrait sitting. She had a feeling that her work on *Two-Faced Woman* was not really finished. "Even while we were doing it, it had a chill, a portent of failure," Cukor said later. Word came that Adrian was leaving M-G-M. "It was because of Garbo that I left M-G-M," said Adrian. "When the glamour ends for Garbo, it also ends for me." Garbo went to his office to say good-bye. Fifteen years later, Adrian was still astonished as he confided to his friend Leonard Stanley what Garbo had told him. "I'm sorry that you're leaving," said Garbo, "but, you know, I never really liked most of the clothes you made me wear."

In short order, Cukor joined Adrian and Lubitsch on Garbo's list of proscribed talents. "Garbo was strange," said Reinhardt. "Many good directors she didn't like. She liked directors who left her alone, like Clarence Brown. She didn't care for directors who directed her. She had some kind of somnambulistic instinct for her effect on the camera. Whoever tried to interfere with that she instinctively fought. You couldn't really direct Garbo." The proof of her discomfort was not long in coming. Producer William Frye wrote in 1999 how she "described in graphic detail the horror of going to the preview in Long Beach and realizing the picture was no good." Oppenheimer was present at that preview and had foreseen a problem. "Someone sold Cukor on the idea that Garbo did not, as the legend went, have big feet," wrote Oppenheimer. "As a result he conceived the notion that Melvyn Douglas should lift one of them up in a bedroom scene. We pleaded with him to abandon the idea, but he was adamant. At the first sneak preview Garbo's bare foot looked even larger than the legend. It elicited one of the loudest and rudest laughs I have ever heard in a theater."

A hasty postmortem revealed that Constance Bennett was doing what Ina Claire had done in *Ninotchka*—stealing the show. All of Bennett's scenes were cut from the third act. No longer did the film end with Griselda being lost in the snow and making Larry realize that he has loved Karin all along. Instead, the film ends with a cartoonish chase on skis. All the personality conflicts and identity confusion remain unresolved in a slapstick finale. A resigned Garbo returned to the studio for two weeks of retakes. "*Two-Faced Woman* was not good and it could never be made good," Garbo said later. After a date with her one night after work, Remarque wrote in his journal: "[Garbo] with curls and red fingernails, came from the studio. Tired, older, a little sad." Cukor had an even more unsettling glimpse of Garbo's inner life when he entered her dressing room one day during the retakes. She was sitting alone in front of the large mirror at her dressing table. She was also holding her magnifying mirror in her hand. She looked despondent. When she sensed Cukor was behind her, she looked up from the mirror and suddenly said: "I am old!"

"No, you are beautiful," replied Cukor, thinking that she was being dramatic.

"No, look!" she said, pointing to her upper lip. Cukor leaned closer. He could not see what she was pointing to. She turned so that the light crossed her face. He squinted. Yes, there were two very fine lines running vertically from her top

Garbo's anxiety about the troubled production of *Two-Faced Woman* was compounded by her fear of aging. Her twenty-fourth American film would be her last.

lip. But they were hardly worth worrying about if they did not show on-screen. Garbo would not be reassured. "Those lines will get deeper," she said darkly. "I must quit."

The retakes were finished on October 2, and Behrman was leaving for New York again. "I went over to the set to say goodbye," he recalled. "I went up to Greta and she kissed me."

"What's this I hear about your going to New York?" she asked playfully. "I thought you were just going to Beverly Hills for a swim."

Like so many of her jokes, it made no sense, but he laughed and said good-bye to her on the set of *Two-Faced Woman*. He later would say that he felt guilty for helping to assassinate her. The next day, Garbo went to Clarence Bull's gallery for a portrait sitting. The photographer also sensed a difference in the woman he had not seen in two and a half years. He shot many poses of her with her head leaning across the arm of a chair or over the edge of a bench. This angle pulled the skin of the face tight, acting as a temporary face-lift. Garbo was not up to shooting as many poses as she had for *Ninotchka*, and she wore only one outfit in the sitting. The sweater and gold bracelet she wore were her own. Bull had a feeling that he might not photograph her again. When she put a scarf on her head to leave, he asked for one last shot. She patiently came back and sat down as he squeezed the bulb and released the shutter in front of Greta Garbo for the last time ever.

Garbo did not attend the preview of the reassembled film, which took place in downtown Los Angeles. One trade review said rather ominously: "Lacking is the smoothness and uproarious humor that were found in *Ninotchka*. The farce is broad and free and definitely not for the kiddies. Some of the sequences may have been passed by the Hays Office because the two principals are married." The worst news was that the laughs came in the wrong places. Another review painted an awful picture: "The parade of Garbo's eye-enticements is so obviously done as to draw unwanted laughs during the early footage, and breaks out at times during the later reels when the vamping antics again brought dubious chuckles from the preview audience, which wasn't sure whether the farce was intended."

Unaware of this fiasco, Garbo went out on the town, patronizing a private nightclub where her rival entertained the gay and lesbian clientele for free. Hedda Hopper reported, "The other night Marlene Dietrich, at the Club Gala, sang her entire repertoire of songs, and who should be there lapping it up but Greta Garbo and Gayelord Hauser?" A few days later, Garbo sent a letter to Wachtmeister. "I have finished with my latest and sadly it's just nothing," she wrote. "Maybe you'll see it soon and then you'll be able to see for yourself what's missing from my art. It was heartbreaking for Salka and me."

What *Two-Faced Woman* lacked in artistry was camouflaged with an ad campaign that made "Garbo Loves Taylor

Like a race-car driver checking his engine before a race, Garbo studied her face in a magnifying mirror.

in *Camille*" sound like a Shakespeare sonnet. "Go gay with Garbo! Garbo is twins and she's double trouble for Melvyn Douglas! Garbo swims! Garbo skis! Garbo originates the new Short Bob! Garbo rhumbas the Chicachoca! Garbo wrestles with her man while clad in filmy finery! Garbo at her gayest!" It was to this accompaniment that the next phalanx of reviewers marched into M-G-M screening rooms and theaters. Seated front and center were twenty-eight members of the Legion of Decency. Twenty-one of them found *Two-Faced Woman* offensive. On November 24, the Reverend John J. McClafferty, executive secretary of the Legion, announced: "*Two-Faced Woman* has been rated as 'C' or 'Condemned' for the following reasons: Immoral and un-Christian attitude toward marriage and its obligations; impudently suggestive scenes, dialogue, and situations; suggestive costumes."

"The defunct Hapsburg monarchy," wrote Viertel, "must have been much more broadminded than the Legion of Decency and the 'Catholic Interest Committee of the Knights of Columbus of Manhattan and the Bronx,' who both maintained that our comedy was glorifying adultery." She may not have taken the censure seriously, but there was no denying its influence. On November 26, the amusement inspector in Providence, Rhode Island, refused *Two-Faced Woman* a seal. Prints were cut in Chicago and Milwaukee. In Omaha, it was reported: "City Welfare Board members termed 'improper' a scene in which Greta Garbo lies languorously on a divan in her husband's apartment, and that portion will be deleted in screenings here." The scene in question had Garbo lying back on a sofa and saying "Come!" to Douglas. Within days, *Two-Faced Woman* was banned in Boston and Buffalo and boycotted by Catholics in Albany, Baltimore, Hartford, Philadelphia, St. Louis, Indianapolis, and Los Angeles. On December 1, New York Congressman Martin J. Kennedy called on Will Hays to prevent the film's general release, saying that it was "a danger to public morality"

Greta Garbo's thirteenth and last portrait sitting with Clarence Bull took place on October 3, 1941. She had turned thirty-six on September 18. This unretouched proof shows what she would have seen before the negative was retouched.

sade—in a world torn by strife, with his own country on the brink of it—against my sinful *Two Faced Woman*." Mayer chided Reinhardt and told him to "flush that filth down the drain where it belongs." Viertel defended her protégé and spoke with Mayer, saying how hurt Garbo was by the controversy. Mayer conveyed this to Spellman and invited him to view the film himself. "After a lunch with the executive," wrote Viertel, "his Eminence had a wonderful time in the projection room. He gave the film his blessing but suggested that we add a scene, showing that the husband knew all along that the twin sister was his one and only wife."

Melvyn Douglas was called in for a day of quick retakes. He had to stand in a phone booth and say: "So my wife left for New York, eh? Three days ago. You're sure. Hm. Two can play this game!" Of course, if this shot indicated that Lawrence knew that Katherine was really Karin all along, his behavior in succeeding scenes would now look not merely silly but downright nutty, but no one at M-G-M cared as long as the changes could get them off the condemned list. Cuts from the negative included the lines:

"No matter how many times you marry, you and I are inevitable."

"You international trollop!"

"I never take money from relatives. Only from strangers. It's my code. 'A poor thing, but mine own.'"

"How does my position affect your position?"

"Let's drink to what's in our minds: I know I'll drink to what's in *my* mind."

"Are you all things to all men?"

"Do you believe in the effect of climate on morals? You must have been born in the tropics!"

The public-telephone scene and the cuts cost nearly $20,000. Reinhardt had to work on Sunday, December 7, to complete them in time for a new shipping date. "I sat in a dubbing room at M-G-M, mixing tracks into a composite that we hoped Heaven's Deputy would reward with his blessing. Between reels I listened," wrote Reinhardt, "as I did every Sunday morning, to the New York Philharmonic broadcast. . . . The concert was abruptly cut off by an emotion-choked voice announcing that Japanese planes had just bombed Pearl Harbor and destroyed three-quarters of the United States fleet." The *Two-Faced Woman* furor was quickly eclipsed by the country's precipitous plunge into the greatest armed conflict in the history of the world.

No one paid attention to the anticlimactic item that ran on December 18: "The Legion of Decency, after review of the revised version, has deemed the revisions sufficient to warrant the removal of the picture from the 'C' or 'Condemned' classification to the 'B' or 'Objectionable in Part' classification." In fact no one was paying attention to anything but World War II; there was no fanfare for Garbo. "Her pictures

and that "the production of this motion picture must be considered an affront to the Congress of the United States." The film was released on December 4, and the Association of Theater Owners in Indiana implored Hays to take action, saying that Catholics were threatening to boycott all theaters. *Two-Faced Woman* was single-handedly bringing back memories of June 1934. When the commotion reached Greta Garbo, she said quietly: "They've dug my grave." On December 6, M-G-M withdrew her film from release.

While this drama was being enacted in the lobbies of various movie theaters, Gottfried Reinhardt was called on the carpet at M-G-M. He defensively reminded Mayer, Mannix, and Hyman that the PCA had passed the film. Articles to this effect were printed in the trades, but the Legion of Decency got bigger ones. "It protested vehemently," wrote Reinhardt, "that it was adulterous for a man to have love relations with his sister-in-law. My counter-argument that his sister-in-law was, in truth, his wife they dismissed as Hollywood sophistry and enlisted no less an authority than Francis Cardinal Spellman, Archbishop of New York, to support their contention." This prince of the Catholic Church happened to be a very close friend of L. B. Mayer's. "He, even more incensed than his minions," wrote Reinhardt, "took time off from shepherding X-million souls to wage a one-man cru-

are so far apart," wrote Hedda Hopper on December 14, "that Metro starts off each publicity campaign with a broadside, as if she'd been buried and dug up for the occasion. We've had 'Garbo Talks,' 'Garbo Sings,' 'Garbo Dances,' and 'Garbo Laughs.' No doubt her ultimate picture will be 'Garbo Retires' and do terrible business from a public expecting a bedroom farce." Hopper failed to mention the noise Garbo made in her hangover scene in *Two-Faced Woman*; it could have been advertised as "Garbo Snorts!" But the loudest, most emphatic snorts came from the critics who caught *Two-Faced Woman* as it crept in the back door of the Capitol Theatre in New York. The *Times* led the pack:

> Don't look now, but there's more than one slip showing in the slightly laundered version of *Two-Faced Woman*. After considerable commotion over its alleged breaches of nice conduct, it is hardly necessary for us to sit in judgment upon such delicate matters of public interest, inasmuch as the film decisively condemns itself by shoddy workmanship. Miss Garbo's current attempt to trip the light fantastic is one of the awkward exhibitions of the season. . . . She is as gauche and stilted as the script when playing the lady of profane love. No doubt her obvious posturings, her appallingly unflattering clothes and makeup were intended as a satire on the vamps of history. Instead, her performance misses the satire and looks like something straight out of the movies of 1922. Mr. Douglas, who probably spends more time in pyjamas than any other leading man in history, continues to look as if a brisk walk in the open air in street clothes would refresh him. Open the windows, Messrs. Cukor, Behrman, Oppenheimer, et al. This is 1942, and Theda Bara's golden age is gone.

The common element of the *Two-Faced Woman* reviews was emotion. Critics used to analyzing cinematic works in purely intellectual terms suddenly found themselves in pain. Cecilia Ager, writing in the newspaper *PM*, was eloquent in her anguish.

> The screen doesn't have an actress to compare with Garbo for loveliness, sensitivity, incandescence. She has the feeling first, and she's acquired the technical proficiency and the knack of timing with which to express it. In *Two-Faced Woman* she reveals still deeper stores of humor and evanescent tenderness than ever before. Her voice has become an instrument that indicates all the emotions in their most subtle gradations. Just on the record of the sound track she's superb. And this is the woman, so unusual in movies that she's no longer a person but a symbol, a legend, whom *Two-Faced Woman* does everything it can to destroy. The wickedness in *Two-Faced Woman* is not in its careless disregard for what are supposed to be public morals [but] in its vandalism. In its story's frenzy to cover up its own empti-

A fully retouched portrait from the *Two-Faced Woman* sitting shows the Garbo that M-G-M was selling in 1942.

> ness, its sterility, its lack of any fine feelings, it makes Garbo a clown, a buffoon, a monkey on a stick. That it is a comedy does not excuse its confused motivation, its repetition, its distasteful heartlessness.

Time magazine was as succinct as usual. "An absurd vehicle for Greta Garbo," it said. "Its embarrassing effect is not unlike seeing Sarah Bernhardt swatted with a bladder. It is almost as shocking as seeing your mother drunk."

Like the voice crying in the wilderness, Mercedes de Acosta still talked about her idol to anyone who would listen. "Garbo was humiliated by the reviews and by the furor created by the women's clubs," said Acosta. "To my way of thinking all this was a tempest in a teacup and as stupid as the picture itself. But I think Greta's regret was more in her soul for having allowed herself to be influenced into lowering her own high standards. She said, 'I will never act in another film.'"

Whether Garbo said this or Acosta decided that it was an attention-grabbing way to end her story is a good question. If *Two-Faced Woman* was a disaster, it was a disaster

This previously unpublished *Two-Faced Woman* portrait was Clarence Bull's interpretation of the title.

somewhat akin to the sinking of the *Titanic*, about which historians for years have been saying: "If only . . . if only the iceberg had been sighted a minute earlier, if only the water-tight compartments had worked as designed, if only there had been enough lifeboats. . . ." These conjectural regrets were echoed in a very minor way in the artistic disaster that allegedly ended Garbo's career; Cukor, Viertel, or Behrman was often named as a fatal element. Was *Two-Faced Woman* a full-fledged disaster? Viewed without critical expectations, the film was more funny than awful. Garbo revealed comic skills beyond even those she had demonstrated in *Ninotchka*. That was part of the problem. There were so many Garbos in *Two-Faced Woman* that it was frustrating to watch, a compendium of outtakes from unrealized Garbo films, all of them tantalizing in their newness. It was this fragmented, incomplete quality that hurt the film most. Years later, audiences could accept a film that was a series of blackouts, but not in 1942. Like the *Titanic*, *Two-Faced Woman* happened to be in the wrong place at the wrong time.

"People often say glibly that the failure of *Two-Faced Woman* finished Garbo's career," said Cukor in 1965. "That's a grotesque oversimplification. If only life were tied up in such neat packages! It certainly threw her, but I think that

what really happened was that she just gave up. She didn't want to go on." Cukor was correct in asserting that the truth was more complex than the legend. But *Two-Faced Woman* was not even as abject a failure as contemporary reports led Garbo to believe, and nowhere near the fabulous flop that legend has made it. The 1941 film with the starting budget of a 1926 film grossed $1.8 million, which was not bad for a market deprived of Europe and Asia. M-G-M reported a loss of $62,000, which was partly the result of Garbo's salary during retakes and the additional work necessitated by the Legion of Decency. If the American public had totally lost interest in Garbo, the loss would have been four times that, especially in the frantic first days of the war.

Garbo had achieved too much in fifteen years and twenty-four movies to be rejected by the country that had made her a star. Even in 1942, she could still continue to work there. Contrary to other legends, Garbo did want to go on. For all her protestations to the contrary, she still believed that her next film would, with the help of God, M-G-M, and Salka Viertel, be worth her while.

Opposite: Because Garbo did not model costumes from *Two-Faced Woman* in this sitting, Bull did not shoot as many portraits as usual, but he still captured a variety of moods.

Epilogue

In the months following the general release of *Two-Faced Woman* in January 1942, Garbo carried on with her eccentric, well-established routine. Travel was curtailed because of the war, and even a jaunt to Mexico was momentarily out of the question, but Garbo had the use of Sam Behrman's apartment in New York, and her mother and brother had settled in suburban New York, so she contented herself with the social life in Manhattan. There was no lack of invitations for someone of her standing, and she cut a swath through society. Mercedes de Acosta had long since exhausted her Hollywood options. Seeing that Garbo was becoming something of a New Yorker, Acosta followed her there. Garbo at first tolerated Acosta's breathless presence, but kept her at bay when she became too intense. Salka Viertel was still at M-G-M, still looking for the next Garbo property. Her fights with Gottfried Reinhardt during the making of *Two-Faced Woman* began an estrangement that eventually ended their relationship; he left her and married a younger woman. Viertel was still in the good graces of Bernie Hyman. She made fun of his sentimentality, but he was the last producer at M-G-M who was actively interested in Garbo.

Gossip columnist Hedda Hopper had never lost interest in Garbo. Since acting with her in *As You Desire Me*, she had become something of a Garbomaniac. After every Garbo portrait sitting, Clarence Bull had to make two complete sets of custom prints. One was for Garbo's family; the other was for Hedda Hopper. In early 1942, she questioned Louis B. Mayer about Garbo's future. "As long as I'm head of this studio," Mayer told her, "Greta Garbo can go on making films here." This statement flew in the face of recent events. One by one, the female stars who had made the company rich were being put out to pasture. First there was Norma Shearer, whose 1942 films—foolish, empty vehicles—had flopped. Then there were Jeanette MacDonald and Myrna Loy, who were also aging. Joan Crawford held on, but her last few films had been as unsuccessful as Shearer's. It was evident that M-G-M was putting its energies into a new group of stars—Greer Garson, Katharine Hepburn, Lana Turner, Hedy Lamarr, and Judy Garland. Instead of working harder for Garbo, the studio borrowed a new Swedish star, Ingrid Bergman, from David O. Selznick. For Garbo and her contemporaries, 1942 was the Twilight of the Goddesses.

In the middle of the year, Viertel glimpsed a ray of hope. "One day Bernie Hyman asked me excitedly to come to the projection room and see a Russian film that a European producer, Mr. Rabinowich, had imported." The film was Viktor Eisymont's *Frontovyye podrugi* (*The Girl from Leningrad*), a straightforward story of a heroic nurse caring for a soldier wounded in the Russian-Finnish war. "I asked Greta to see the film," wrote Viertel, "and she was very impressed." M-G-M bought the rights to the film, and Viertel began developing the script. On September 7, Hyman died suddenly of heart failure. It looked as if Garbo and Viertel had lost their champion, but Mayer honored the late producer's wishes. On December 20, he signed Garbo to do *The Girl from Leningrad*. The one-film contract called for her to be paid $70,000 on signing and $80,000 on completion of the film. A few months into 1943, the project was suddenly abandoned. "Perhaps Garbo's enthusiasm was not emphatic enough," wrote Viertel, "or they did not want to make a film sympathetic to the Soviets, or L. B. Mayer felt compelled to glorify the deeds of the Red armies in his own way." Viertel's suspicion was aroused by another M-G-M project, *Song of Russia*. She was certain that the story of an American conductor and a Soviet girl was based on Garbo's well-publicized romance with Leopold Stokowski, but after six years this was hardly topical stuff. Viertel, like Acosta, was inclined to be Garbocentric.

If Garbo was not going to do *The Girl from Leningrad*, what was she going to do? For a while, there was talk of her doing *The Picture of Dorian Gray*, but it was no more than talk, even though its director was Albert Lewin, a Thalberg colleague who had worked on many of Garbo's silent films. Viertel appealed to Mayer on Garbo's behalf. Mayer protested that it was Garbo, not he, who was holding up progress. Eddie Mannix had told him of his ongoing efforts to please Garbo, but that he and she did not see "eye to eye in the choice of film material." She was as uncooperative as ever. "Even that poor little girl, Judy Garland, she always does what I tell her," said Mayer. "Even Norma listens to me. Only Garbo is difficult. I am her best friend. I want her to be happy. She should come and tell me what she wants." Then he added, with characteristic slyness, "I'd talk her out of it."

This was the last photograph made of Greta Garbo at her last Hollywood portrait sitting.

Viertel went back to Garbo and told her that she should talk to Mayer herself. Clarence Brown heard Mayer's version years later. "Mayer knew that the European market was gone," said Brown, "where Garbo was so strong. And things looked shaky in the American market too. But Garbo's contract still had some time to run. Mayer called her in to explain the market situation. He told her that they did not want to make another picture but that they would pay her as provided by her contract." At this point Mayer brought out a check for the balance of Garbo's *Girl from Leningrad* contract—$80,000. He presented it to her with mock regret.

"No, Mr. Mayer," said Garbo, putting the check on his desk. "I did not earn it."

For years afterward, Mayer would tell this story, saying how much he admired Garbo for what she had done. His admiration did not prevent him from ordering studio employees to go into her dressing room and pack her things in cardboard boxes so that Lana Turner could move in. Joan Crawford got the same send-off when she terminated her contract a few months later. The millions that these stars had brought Mayer did not move him to so much as send flowers when they departed.

Although Garbo made anonymous donations to war relief, she was conspicuously absent from efforts to keep the home fires burning. Marlene Dietrich, even while busy with films in 1942, began working up an act to take overseas to entertain the troops. Melvyn Douglas, who joined the army himself, had worked with (and observed) both Garbo and Dietrich. "She and Garbo were entirely different," said Douglas. "Marlene was and has continued to be much more 'with it' in the sense that she was a part of the actual, day-by-day, growing world. Garbo was quite the opposite. She was off on cloud nine, all by herself, a curiously detached sort of person." Dietrich's tireless and inspiring work with the USO in Europe reminded her how much she enjoyed working in front of an audience. A few years later, she moved from the soundstage to the live stage and began giving the spectacular concerts that would distinguish the rest of her career. Garbo, cut off from protective Metro, knew full well that no other studio could afford the luxury of black flats and closed sets. Not long after she left the studio, her long-standing Cerberus was given walking papers. At fifty-five, Salka Viertel found herself both unemployed and unemployable.

"A few jobs were offered me," Viertel wrote, "but they were always connected with speculations on getting Garbo. An agent told me that it was difficult getting an assignment for me because I had been identified with films like *Queen Christina* and *Anna Karenina*, which had only made money in Europe. *Conquest* especially had been very costly." There was also the problem that Viertel, who was not really a writer, required that she be attached to any Garbo project—as a writer. It was generally assumed that she was responsible for alienating the American public from Garbo, so she was the last person who should have a say in Garbo's new career. Any producer who wanted Garbo would have to deal with this delicate but unavoidable problem, yet there were calls from Walter Wanger, David Selznick, and Dore Schary. Possible projects included *Mourning Becomes Electra*, *The Paradine Case*, and *I Remember Mama*. Clarence Brown and George Cukor told Viertel that they would love to direct Garbo again. "Greta is impatient to work, but on the other side she is afraid of it," Viertel wrote Cukor in 1945. "I understand this very well after all these years of idleness. Work is a habit, and she has lost it."

Having surrounded herself with dilettantes, Garbo was living her life as they did, filling her days with idleness and her nights with parties. Her absence from the screen at first looked like the two-year intervals between *Conquest* and *Ninotchka* and *Two-Faced Woman*. When it stretched to four years, producers and agents wondered what Garbo was up to. Did she want to retire? As usual, she was resolutely irresolute. "I have been considering a film I might try making but I don't know," she wrote to Countess Wachtmeister in 1945. "Time leaves its traces on our small faces and bodies. It's not the same any more, being able to pull it off. So I was wondering whether I should or not. At present, only 'our Father in Heaven' knows whether it will come off."

Joan Crawford returned from a two-year hiatus to make a sensational comeback in *Mildred Pierce* at Warner Bros. in 1945, proving that another studio could do as well for her as M-G-M. Myrna Loy returned to the screen in 1946 in a mother role, which was a sign that times had changed. Jeanette MacDonald waited until 1948 to do the same thing. More significantly for Garbo, Norma Shearer, who had acquired a cinematographer's ability to critique her appearance on film, also toyed with the idea of a comeback, but ultimately surrendered to the reality of her age and appearance. The flattering tricks of light, lenses, and filters could only do so much for a forty-five-year-old face, and she had not been happy with her close-ups since turning forty. For fifteen years she had collaborated with cinematographers to create the illusion of perfect beauty. When that illusion could no longer be maintained, it was time to retire. More than Shearer's, more than anyone's, Garbo's screen persona depended upon that illusion. Her beauty was a tool of expression. If the tool became dulled, could she express herself? Would she have the confidence to try?

"Stars look at themselves and they see that their youth is past, their beauty is gone," said Rouben Mamoulian. "It's a tough experience, and much harder on actresses. Beauty has so much to do with their fame." For someone so self-critical, the thought of facing a camera at forty must have been unnerving. "I know she was fully aware of how beautiful she was," said David Lewis. "She constantly examined her face. That was why she had that magnifying mirror. I don't think it was vanity. She simply knew what her values were."

In May 1949, at the age of forty-three, Garbo submitted to three screen tests in order to help Walter Wanger secure backing for a film based on Honoré de Balzac's *La Duchesse de Langeais*. One test was shot at the Chaplin Studios by James Wong Howe, another at Universal by Joseph Valentine, and a third, also at Universal, by William Daniels. Garbo had to go on her own to these tests, put on her own makeup, and wear her own clothes. "It's so much harder for me now," Garbo told Cecil Beaton. "[At M-G-M] I had it all my own way and did it in my own fashion." The tests were exciting for the cinematographers; the mature Garbo had lost none of her magnetism. "The minute the camera started rolling, she took on, oh, a wonderful feeling," said Howe. "You could see this creature just come alive." To Wanger's surprise, Garbo agreed to look at the tests. She was not displeased, because they caught a new depth of expression in her eyes. But even with precise lighting and heavy diffusion, she could see flaws in her face. Beyond that, there was the inevitability of going to a new studio and facing new people.

"How strange that I got mixed up in that business, but I did!" said Garbo to Beaton when he hesitantly brought up her film career, a topic that her friends knew better than to mention after the 1940s. Beaton felt strongly that Garbo should return to the screen, that to resume her career would give her life some direction. Garbo was pessimistic. "If I disliked it all then, what would I feel about it now?" she asked him. "In those days I didn't have to bother about camera angles or anything. Now I'd feel so forlorn with everybody staring at me. I'd be conscious of the things in my face that weren't there before."

"With a good cameraman you'd be far more beautiful than ever," Beaton ventured.

"That's not the point," said Garbo. "*I* would know the way I look. I'm a perfectionist. It would make me uncomfortable if things weren't as they should be. I'd be humiliated."

Beaton had recently photographed Garbo. She had resisted his entreaties for a portrait sitting for years, but when she needed a passport photo, she gave in. She would not go to a studio, so he was forced to shoot the pictures in a hotel room. He used light from table lamps and from windows to achieve the effects that he usually got with specialized lighting tools. He shot with a Rolleiflex and did not retouch the negatives, which was unusual at the time. Garbo looked stunning, but she also looked older.

"I remember the first time I made a film in Sweden," she told him. "I was with older actors, and they were horribly frank about the things that happened to their faces in front of the camera. They described how their chins would go out *this* way if their heads went *that* way, so they asked that I should walk the other way around a table in order that they could show their best profile. It was horribly tedious! But what would happen to me? Even if the public didn't notice these things, I would! And that would be obnoxious! No. In certain ways I miss that life, but I'm not an actor who must go on in any circumstances. . . . I don't have to do it, so what's the point?"

What could he say to that? She didn't have to work. She didn't really want to. What's more, she was afraid to. Afraid of dealing with people. Afraid of how she would look. Afraid that without the illusion of physical perfection, she would lose her magic. Afraid that she already *had* lost it. In truth, that magic had always made her feel like a child who discovers that she has psychic abilities: she cannot articulate them or control them, but they present an awesome responsibility. Garbo had told David Diamond that she was unable to account for the power of her performance in *Camille*. "She

couldn't explain it," he said. Cukor also acknowledged something in her that was beyond mere acting. "Garbo has a magic that can't be defined," said Cukor. "She is a rare creature who touches the imagination." Brown felt that Garbo's greatest potential was still untapped, but that she needed to apply a technical approach. "If she had understood the English language thoroughly," said Brown, "and had known how to use it dramatically, on top of her great God-given talent, there would have been no limit to what she could have done."

The idea of studying English with a tutor or studying acting with Madame Maria Ouspenskaya was alien to Garbo, who had a limited attention span and inconstant energy. What she chose to do at this crucial point in her career was nothing. Her resolve was frozen by a combination of sloth, dread, and narcissism. She could not go back. She could not go forward. She turned down almost every film offered her. On the few occasions when she did accept, some minor delay frightened her and she bolted, throwing away the chance to renew and expand her gifts. In truth, these gifts had not brought her any great happiness. Unlike Dietrich, who was energized by applause, Garbo did not relate with an audience, glory in her achievements, or view her films with satisfaction. Her gifts had not enriched her emotionally; they had drained her. Now they had become a burden. She could not define them or control them. At last, in an effort to find peace in a world that valued her only for those gifts, she abandoned them.

When Greta Garbo died on April 15, 1990, she left the world a legacy of images: twenty-four American films and thousands of Hollywood portraits. There could have been more. They could have been better. For those of us who treasure this legacy, there are reasons to be happy. The fragile nitrate film that captured her work has survived the passage of decades. Her work has been kept available by its owners. And we know, when looking at a photograph of Garbo or watching her on the screen, that she used her gifts with integrity. She demanded respect for her work, refusing to give anything less than total concentration. It was not merely fear, indolence, and vanity that ended her career. It was her resistance to compromise. As she said, "I had it all my own way and did it in my own fashion." That is what ended her career, and what makes her cinematic legacy the exquisite thing that it is.

Acknowledgments

This book has been gestating since the days in 1964 when I visited the Lockwood Branch of the Oakland Public Library, looking for books and magazines that would tell me more about the Greta Garbo films I had just seen on television. I feel that in many ways this book fulfills the quest I began then. For helping me research and complete *Greta Garbo: A Cinematic Legacy*, I wish to thank the following institutions, archives, and individuals: the library at California State University, Hayward, and the Beverly Hills Public Library. I thank Caroline Sisneros of the American Film Institute. I thank Bob Thomas for granting me access to his Irving Thalberg research files at UCLA. I thank Sue Guldin, Faye Thompson, and Barbara Hall of the Margaret Herrick Library at the Fairbanks Center for Motion Picture Study; thanks also go to the staff of Columbia Printing in Los Angeles. I owe a debt of gratitude to Ned Comstock of the Cinema-Television Library of the University of Southern California for his unfailing resourcefulness and insight. There is hardly a chapter here that does not owe something to his generosity.

The following memorabilia dealers and photographic agencies helped me illustrate the text: Michael Epstein and hurrellphotos.com; Mike Hawks and Pete Bateman at Larry Edmunds Bookstore; the John and Susan Edwards Harvith Collection; Lauretta Dives, Ricky Byrd, and Phil Moad of the Kobal Collection; and my friends Howard Mandelbaum, Rob Milite, and the staff of Photofest. I especially thank John McElwee for the loan of many rare production stills. I thank Ben Carbonetto for being a modern de Medici.

I am grateful to Kurt Bier, Bruce Paddock, and Bronni Stein for many hours of diligent, thorough research.

I thank the following for advice, assistance, and referrals: Anita Bennett, David Bennett, Karie Bible, James Curtis, Gerry Day, Charlotte Del Rose, Kim Hill, Matthew Kennedy, John Koch, Arthur Lucia, Pauli Moss, Connie Parker, Susan Shearer, André Soares, and Karen Swenson.

I thank Carrie Beers and Katherine Evans at Turner Classic Movies. I particularly want to acknowledge George Feltenstein at Warner Bros.; Roger L. Mayer, President and Chief Operating Officer of the Turner Entertainment Company; and Richard P. May, Vice President in Charge of Preservation at Warner Bros. Without these dedicated individuals and the farseeing patronage of Ted Turner, there would be no Garbo legacy. Her films would have gone to nitrate heaven long ago, or, if not, they would now be locked away where no one could see them. Few companies have done as much to preserve and share our American film heritage.

I wish to thank these individuals for taking the time to review the manuscript: Sam Green, Michael Epstein, Bruce Paddock, Howard Mandelbaum, Kevin Brownlow, and Mick La Salle of the *San Francisco Chronicle*.

I thank my literary agent, Alan Nevins of Firm Books, for his splendid work on my behalf. I thank Eric Himmel, Vice-President and Editor-in-Chief of Harry N. Abrams, Inc., for encouraging me to begin this project. I thank Carol Morgan and her staff for working so hard to publicize this and all my previous Abrams books. I thank Miko McGinty for an elegant design job. I thank Richard Slovak for his special editing help. I thank Elisa Urbanelli, my editor, for again helping me achieve the delicate balance between idolatry and scholarship.

I thank my cousin, Michael Chambless, for lending me two dollars to buy *The Films of Greta Garbo* at Holmes Bookstore in Oakland in June 1966. I thank my English teacher, Patrick McCormick, at St. Joseph High School in Alameda, California, for the 1968 film series that gave me and so many other students the opportunity to see and analyze these films. I thank my brother Guy for helping me present the series. I acknowledge the late Porky Calado of the Audio-Visual Department and I thank Robert L. Hillmann, my film teacher at California State University, Hayward, for helping me understand and emulate William Daniels's lighting.

Finally, I thank my father for taking me to the Tower Theatre in Oakland in November 1966 to see *Mata Hari* in 35mm on the big screen. As I learned that day, watching Greta Garbo on TV was a thrill, but seeing her on the big screen was a revelation. After that, I understood why so many people wanted to write books about Garbo. Thank you for encouraging and supporting my writing.

—M. A. V.

Notes

Preface

6 *Her beauty is more . . .* James Agate, *Around Cinemas*, quoted in Durgnat, *Greta Garbo*, p. 16.
the furthest stage . . . Quigly, "Garbo, Garbo, Garbo."
Why should this . . . Balász, *Theory of the Film*, p. 74.
What, when drunk . . . Tynan, *Curtains!*
To see, in these . . . Durgnat, *Garbo*, p. 51.

7 *Have you ever thought . . .* Auriol, "Faire des Films—V—Avec Qui?"

8 *Two Swedish . . .* Kingsley, "Two Swedish Players Now En Route Here," p. A10.

9 *My father was . . .* Paris, *Garbo*, p. 80.
an awesome . . . Selznick, *A Private View*, p. 60.
Stiller frightened . . . Ibid.
Who's that . . . Crowther, *The Lion's Share*, p. 111.
When we stepped . . . Selznick, *A Private View*, p. 60.
Louis B. Mayer . . . Biery, "The Story of Greta Garbo (Part 2)," p. 128.
Tell her that in . . . Crowther, *The Lion's Share*, p. 111. This quote about "fat women" first appeared in Bosley Crowther's 1957 book, *The Lion's Share*, an MGM history that some historians now view as unfair to Mayer. Crowther's uncredited sources were later revealed to include Norma Shearer, Howard Strickling, and Eddie Mannix, all of whom saw Mayer when he returned from Europe in January 1926. Shearer, Strickling, and Mannix customarily declined interviews by biographers and film historians. (One of the few exceptions Shearer and Strickling made was for Samuel Marx's 1974 *Mayer and Thalberg*.) Considering Mayer's self-congratulatory theatricality, it is likely that he embellished the conversation to include the "fat women" quote, and one of the parties listed above related it to Crowther in 1956.

10 *Miss Garbo says . . .* Roberts, "Confidences Off-Screen," p. 53.
He was highly . . . Haworth, "I Loved Garbo," p. 87.

11 *Bye, bye . . .* Laing, *Greta Garbo*, p. 53.
Her shoes were . . . Ibid.
Is it anyone . . . Billquist, *Garbo*, p. 99.
I remember the day . . . Davis, *The Glamour Factory*, p. 99.
I'm going to be . . . Billquist, *Garbo*, p. 20.
As early as . . . Biery, "The Story of Greta Garbo (Part 1)," p. 31.

12 *Stiller's the most . . .* Broman, *Conversations with Greta Garbo*, p. 55.
You know, she . . . Bainbridge, *Garbo*, p. 58.
Moje did have . . . Ibid., 64.
Stiller [expected] to . . . Bainbridge, *Garbo*, p. 100.
They asked me . . . Higham, *Hollywood Cameramen*, p. 67.
Fools, all of them . . . Palmborg, *The Private Life of Greta Garbo*, p. 42.
You are quite right . . . Billquist, *Garbo*, p. 100.

13 *They were a . . .* Bainbridge, *Garbo*, p. 89.
I don't see why . . . Paris, *Garbo*, p. 90.
I often saw the young . . . Gish, *The Movies, Mr. Griffith, and Me*, p. 300. There has been some question as to the clarity of Lillian Gish's recall, since this story is supposed to have taken place on the set of *The Scarlet Letter*. Also impossible is a visit by Garbo and Stiller to that set when they arrived at M-G-M in September 1925; *The Scarlet Letter* was not filming until January 25, 1926. A photograph of Hendrik Sartov aiming his magic lens at Gish on the set of *La Bohème* in October 1925 makes all the stories dovetail.
If you drop me . . . Fountain, *Dark Star*, p. 45.
Go ahead . . . Hopper, "Garbo Romance Meets Approval of Old Friend."

Chapter One

15 *To dramatize . . .* "'The Torrent,' Adaptation by Dorothy Farnum, dated September 19, 1925," *Ibáñez's Torrent* file, M-G-M story file collection, Cinema Television Library, University of Southern California (hereinafter MGM-USC).

These things make . . . Laing, *Greta Garbo*, p. 60.

16 *It was all very strange . . .* Sundborg, "That Gustaffson Girl (Part Two)," p. 42.
There she was . . . Higham, *Hollywood Cameramen*, p. 67.
Oh, Mauritz . . . Borg, "Garbo's Untold Story," p. 20.
Here is a man . . . Swenson, *Greta Garbo*, p. 95.
It was very funny . . . Biery, "The Story of Greta Garbo (Part 3)," p. 65.
Borg, Borg, . . . Borg, "Garbo's Untold Story," p. 20.
Greta is starting . . . Bainbridge, *Garbo*, p. 92.
For once she . . . Borg, "Garbo's Untold Story," p. 20.
A couple of days . . . "William Daniels, September 11, 1967," Bob Thomas interview notes, Bob Thomas Papers, Arts Special Collections, University of California Los Angeles (hereinafter Thomas/UCLA).
Don't pull them . . . Carr, *Four Fabulous Faces*, p. 4.
I didn't learn . . . Paris, *Garbo*, p. 98.
Look at her . . . Laing, *Greta Garbo*, p. 74.
Hey, Borg . . . Borg, "Garbo's Untold Story," p. 21.
Tell that dumb . . . Zierold, *Garbo*, p. 46.
What makes that big . . . Ibid.

17 *And what do . . .* West, "That Stockholm Venus," p. 36.
Cortez resented . . . Borg, "Garbo's Untold Story," p. 20.
She was unknown . . . Paris, *Garbo*, p. 96.
Here! Give me . . . Borg, "Garbo's Untold Story," p. 22.
Let him have . . . Billquist, *Garbo*, p. 110.
In Sweden we . . . Hall, "Hollywood Surprises New Swedish Actress."

18 *One night I . . .* Paris, *Garbo*, p. 98.
I would go home . . . Biery, "The Story of Greta Garbo (Part 3)," p. 65.
Borg, I think I shall . . . Borg, "Garbo's Untold Story," p. 22.
The first time . . . Hopper, "The Garbo I Know."
I've been down . . . Swenson, *Greta Garbo*, p. 96.
We thought her . . . Bainbridge, *Garbo*, p. 76.
Strange quality . . . Paris, *Garbo*, p. 96.
He just said he . . . Biery, "The Story of Greta Garbo (Part 3)," p. 65.
I tried to explain . . . Sundborg, "That Gustaffson Girl (Part Two)," p. 42.
We're spending . . . Zierold, *Garbo*, p. 47.
Who are they . . . Borg, "Garbo's Untold Story," p. 20.
That pumpkin . . . Ibid.
Get that woman . . . Ibid., p. 21.
I called to her . . . Ibid., p. 22.
A rushing flood . . . Daum, *Walking with Garbo*, p. 62.

19 *We all thought . . .* Bainbridge, *Garbo*, p. 93.
She's got it . . . Marion, *Off with Their Heads!*, p. 134.
Stiller was raving . . . Bainbridge, *Garbo*, p. 93.
He was angry . . . Broman, *The Divine Garbo*, p. 76.
That fellow Rafael . . . "'The Torrent.' Preview of Jan. 26, 1926. Dictated by Bela Sekely," *Ibáñez's Torrent* file, MGM-USC.
If time lets . . . Unless otherwise noted, intertitle and dialogue quotations are transcribed from tapes provided by the copyright holder of the film cited.
We are supposed . . . Ibid.
the murmurs of . . . Swenson, *Greta Garbo*, p. 99.
She seems an excellent . . . Conway, *The Films of Greta Garbo*, p. 47.
Greta Garbo, making . . . Unsourced clipping, Greta Garbo core collection microfilm files, Margaret Herrick Library, Fairbanks Center for Motion Picture Study, Academy of Motion Picture Arts and Sciences, Beverly Hills (hereinafter FCMPS).
My first film . . . Billquist, *Garbo*, p. 115.

20 *She is a tall . . .* West, "That Stockholm Venus," p. 36.

Chapter Two

21 *Then came the . . .* Sundborg, "That Gustaffson Girl (Part Two)," p. 42.
With Mauritz . . . Borg, "Garbo's Untold Story," p. 20.

The Torrent? Bah! . . . Bainbridge, *Garbo*, p. 97.
Like another Helen . . . "Cast of Characters for 'The Temptress,'" p. 1, *The Temptress* file, MGM-USC.
bad womens . . . Palmborg, *The Private Life of Greta Garbo*, p. 46.
Some time I would . . . Ibid., p. 50.

22 *That poor girl . . .* Daum, *Walking with Garbo*, p. 57.
I have never . . . Billquist, *Garbo*, p. 101.
No more pictures . . . Zierold, *Garbo*, p. 44.
You must go out . . . "THE TEMPTRESS Incomplete continuity by R. Levan, Mr. Stiller's assistant, January 2, 1926," *The Temptress* file, MGM-USC.
I saw fifty . . . Bainbridge, *Garbo*, p. 99.
When Stiller refused . . . Borg, "Garbo's Untold Story," p. 20.
When he wanted . . . Palmborg, *The Private Life of Greta Garbo*, p. 47.

23 *Metro intended to . . .* Borg, "Garbo's Untold Story," p. 20.
Now: all explode . . . Bainbridge, *Garbo*, p. 99.
I am so unhappy . . . Paris, *Garbo*, p. 106.
Is the man . . . Bainbridge, *Garbo*, p. 100.
He had his own . . . Ibid.
Why should things . . . Billquist, *Garbo*, p. 119.
My father was . . . Paris, *Garbo*, p. 108.
Thalberg talked . . . Bainbridge, *Garbo*, p. 100.
They brought me . . . Ibid.
Ah, that is bad . . . Walker, *Garbo*, p. 46.

24 *I saw Stiller . . .* Borg, "Garbo's Untold Story," p. 20. Then, as now, deaths of celebrities and their relatives were subject to false reporting. Alva Gustaffson's death on April 21, 1926, was variously attributed to tuberculosis, spousal abuse, or cancer. Karen Swenson's *Greta Garbo* points to lymphatic cancer but cites no document.

25 *I was in agony . . .* Sundborg, "That Gustaffson Girl (Part Two)," p. 42.

26 *I couldn't hear . . .* Bainbridge, *Garbo*, p. 101.
I was heartbroken . . . Sundborg, "That Gustaffson Girl (Part Two)," p. 42.
I was frantic . . . Palmborg, *The Private Life of Greta Garbo*, p. 49.
How I was broken . . . Biery, "The Story of Greta Garbo (Part 3)," p. 144.
I never missed . . . Ibid.
She walked the . . . Bainbridge, *Garbo*, p. 102.
You know these Americans . . . Broman, *Conversations with Greta Garbo*, p. 74.
For six months . . . Sundborg, "That Gustaffson Girl (Part Two)," p. 42.
Niblo at last . . . Borg, "Garbo's Untold Story," p. 55.
I could not . . . Biery, "The Story of Greta Garbo (Part 3)," p. 144.
I did not teach . . . Hopper, "The Garbo I Know."

27 *It has made me so very . . .* Broman, *Conversations with Greta Garbo*, p. 74.
Having to be . . . Ibid.
I am so homesick . . . Borg, "Garbo's Untold Story," p. 55.
first tamales . . . Ibid. It was more likely one of the new Mexican restaurants that were all the rage in the mid-1920s, perhaps El Cholo.
Borg, people say . . . Ibid.
On those long . . . Ibid.
I know you are . . . Ibid.
Beautiful lady . . . "The Temptress, Complete continuity by Dorothy Farnum 2/18/26," *The Temptress* file, MGM-USC.

28 *In America you . . .* Palmborg, *The Private Life of Greta Garbo*, p. 50.
I never see anybody . . . Swenson, *Greta Garbo*, p. 114.

29 *the Department of . . .* Walker, *Garbo*, p. 54.
a strange man . . . Borg, "Garbo's Untold Story," p. 55.
I've worked five . . . Broman, *The Divine Garbo*, p. 82.
Es ist ein Skandal . . . Billquist, *Garbo*, p. 99.
When I was at Metro . . . Bainbridge, *Garbo*, p. 103.
Dreadful . . . Broman, *Conversations with Greta Garbo*, p. 72.
I want to go on record . . . Bainbridge, *Garbo*, p. 106.

Chapter Three

31 *If you and I* . . . Billquist, *Garbo*, p. 23.

I do not care . . . Ussher, "A Swedish Siren," p. 48.

She spoke very little . . . Fountain, *Dark Star*, p. 116.

The Swede isn't . . . Marion, *Off with Their Heads!*, p. 132.

Gilbert adds to . . . Fountain, *Dark Star*, p. 105.

I never went . . . Ibid., p. 117.

32 *Not since Rudolph* . . . Ibid., p. 109.

Mr. Gilbert's acting . . . Ibid., p. 120.

Keeping in mind . . . "The Undying Past Cp. (22 pp.) by Frederica Sagor 11/15/25," *Flesh and the Devil* file, MGM-USC.

I did not like . . . Biery, "The Story of Greta Garbo (Part 3)," p. 144.

My sister had . . . Ibid.

Mister Mayer . . . Ibid.

She had developed . . . Bainbridge, *Garbo*, p. 102.

You are now a . . . Borg, "Garbo's Untold Story," p. 20.

She has many . . . Palmborg, *The Private Life of Greta Garbo*, p. 62.

You are hereby . . . Mayer memo to Garbo, August 4, 1926. Fragmentary copy, Photoplay Productions Collection.

33 *I think I will* . . . Marx, *Mayer and Thalberg*, p. 87.

Who the hell . . . Crowther, *The Lion's Share*, p. 113.

Borg, . . . that girl thinks . . . Borg, "Garbo's Untold Story," p. 54.

Hello, Borg! . . . Biery, "The Story of Greta Garbo (Part 3)," p. 144.

I went back . . . Ibid.

To hell with . . . Crowther, *The Lion's Share*, p. 113.

While we were making . . . Broman, *Conversations with Greta Garbo*, p. 62.

Some instant spark . . . "Garbo in Love," King Features, 1937.

John Gilbert was . . . Vidor, *A Tree Is a Tree*, p. 134.

I know the person . . . Carr, *Four Fabulous Faces*, p. 150.

He was so terribly . . . Biery, "The Story of Greta Garbo (Part 3)," p. 144.

the buttons began . . . Crowther, *The Lion's Share*, p. 113.

34 *Mr. Brown had* . . . Ankerich, *The Sound of Silence*, p. 157.

an inventor of detail . . . Higham, *Hollywood Cameramen*, p. 58.

For the arbor . . . Ibid., p. 57.

Flesh and the Devil was advertised . . . (caption) "Letters to the Editor," *Motion Picture* magazine (August 1927), p. 8.

35 *It was the damnedest* . . . Fountain, *Dark Star*, p. 126.

Flesh and the Devil had . . . Billquist, *Garbo*, p. 124.

I had a romance . . . Brownlow, *Hollywood*, p. 199.

Clarence Brown says . . . Markham, "An Idyll or a Tragedy," p. 100.

[Garbo] was kneeling . . . Ibid.

36 *Jack helped her* . . . Fountain, *Dark Star*, p. 126.

If John Gilbert . . . Sundborg, "That Gustaffson Girl (Part Two)," p. 42.

There was a very real . . . Ibid., p. 118.

capricious as the devil . . . Palmborg, *The Private Life of Greta Garbo*, p. 56.

There is something . . . (caption) Smith, "Up Speaks a Gallant Loser," p. 33.

He is a great . . . (caption) Palmborg, *The Private Life of Greta Garbo*, p. 71.

If they don't star . . . (caption) Conway, *The Films of Greta Garbo*, p. 55.

38 *September 8 wedding* . . . Much credence has been given to the story that the September 8 wedding of Eleanor Boardman to King Vidor was also going to be a double wedding for Garbo and Gilbert. This oft-repeated tale has Gilbert waiting impatiently for Garbo, only to encounter Louis B. Mayer in the guest bathroom. Mayer then makes the hateful remark that Gilbert need not marry Garbo, just sleep with her. Gilbert knocks down Mayer, supposedly ensuring the premature end of his own career. Who exactly was the source of this anecdote? It first turns up in Leatrice Gilbert Fountain's 1985 biography of her father, *Dark Star*, where it is related by Boardman, who had also told it to historian Kevin Brownlow. The story is questionable.

Eleanor Boardman claimed to have been outside the guest bathroom. Why would the bride be wandering around the house at her own wedding? And how could she have heard the whole exchange if it took place in the bathroom? Why would Mayer, who was famous for his reluctance to address sexual matters openly, make such a statement? At this time, he already detested Gilbert. That he would speak about intimacies with an employee he hated was out of character for a man concerned with power and propriety. For that matter, why would Mayer care enough to give Gilbert advice, even sarcastically?

"Why would Boardman spin a tale of the second wedding both to Leatrice Jr. and to me?" Kevin Brownlow wrote the author on June 28, 2004. "She was fairly reclusive, not the sort who would invent such dramatic stories for effect. Most peculiar. Do you have a theory, or do you just think she was elaborating to make an effect?"

My theory is that Boardman made up the story in order to kill two birds with one stone. More than Renée Adorée, Pauline Starke, or Aileen Pringle, Boardman was halted in her ascent to stardom at M-G-M by Garbo's arrival. Boardman was not dissimilar in appearance and could conceivably have played in *The Torrent, The Temptress*, and most of the others. She had good reason to resent Garbo and missed no opportunity to diminish her in later interviews. Vidor pushed Boardman's career, but—her performance in *The Crowd* notwithstanding—not even a director of his stature could make her a star if she lacked the requisite charisma or talent. Unlike Garbo, she did not do well in her first talking films. M-G-M dropped her, and she ended up in minor films. She subsequently married Harry D'Abbadie D'Arrast, an unpopular and out-of-step comedy director, and moved far away from Hollywood.

Besides wanting to malign Garbo with her story, Boardman was also eager to get at Mayer, who had never been particularly helpful to her or Vidor. Beyond that, her reasons for inventing such a vicious story would indeed be mysterious—unless one was a silent-film scholar approaching her for an interview in the 1980s. On reaching her by telephone, one would inevitably hear a pointed question about one's surname: "Is that Jewish?" If the answer was in the affirmative, the request for an interview was declined. After further research, these scholars determined that Boardman and D'Arrast had left Hollywood because of their well-known anti-Semitism. This might explain why a long-retired movie actress might have unkind stories to tell about the most successful Jewish executive in show-business history. Irene Mayer Selznick told author Barry Paris in 1990 that he had been at the wedding and that no such incident had taken place.

She is a wonderful . . . Palmborg, *The Private Life of Greta Garbo*, p. 57.

In the end . . . Ussher, "A Swedish Siren," p. 31.

Here is a picture . . . Conway, *The Films of Greta Garbo*, p. 55.

Never before has . . . Bainbridge, *Garbo*, p. 118.

Here is the picture . . . Conway, *The Films of Greta Garbo*, p. 47.

I am disgusted . . . Fragmentary clipping, author's collection.

titters and disrespectful . . . Ibid.

the audience roars . . . Ibid.

It is a pity . . . Billquist, *Garbo*, p. 131.

Oh, I thought . . . Ibid.

Miss Garbo may . . . (caption) Schallert, "*Flesh and the Devil*," p. 5.

Chapter Four

40 *Perhaps it is your* . . . Calhoun, "They Learned about Women from Her," p. 80.

celebrated of two . . . Ardmore, *The Self-Enchanted*, p. 170.

I do not like . . . Biery, "The Story of Greta Garbo (Part 3)," p. 144.

I went to see her . . . Smith, "Up Speaks a Gallant Loser," p. 120.

Gilbert pleaded . . . Bainbridge, *Garbo*, p. 128.

She keeps saying . . . Zierold, *Garbo*, p. 63.

Stiller's attitude . . . Borg, "Garbo's Untold Story," p. 55.

I hope they leave . . . Ussher, "A Swedish Siren," p. 30.

41 *I could not do* . . . Biery, "The Story of Greta Garbo (Part 3)," p. 144.

It was the first time . . . Ibid.

Yesterday you were . . . Letter, Louis B. Mayer to Greta Garbo, November 5, 1926. Fragmentary copy, Photoplay Productions Collection.

Greta met him . . . Smith, "Up Speaks a Gallant Loser," p. 33.

With arms outstretched . . . Borg, "Garbo's Untold Story," p. 55.

I did not talk . . . Biery, "The Story of Greta Garbo (Part 2)," p. 144.

She was devoted . . . Broman, *Conversations with Greta Garbo*, p. 60.

You can say . . . Ibid.

She hates Hollywood . . . Zierold, *Garbo*, p. 63.

I suppose you have . . . Bainbridge, *Garbo*, p. 123.

42 *You cannot imagine* . . . Ibid., p. 122.

All I wanted . . . Biery, "The Story of Greta Garbo (Part 3)," p. 144.

GRETA GARBO SAYS . . . *Variety*, December 15, 1926.

They had a cartoon . . . Biery, "The Story of Greta Garbo (Part 3)," p. 145.

These fools . . . Bainbridge, *Garbo*, p. 119.

The reason that . . . Walker, *Garbo*, p. 68.

If I had granted . . . Billquist, *Garbo*, p. 133.

Miss Garbo is . . . Swenson, *Greta Garbo*, p. 134.

43 *I hope that* . . . Bainbridge, *Garbo*, p. 123.

so worn out . . . Ibid., p. 120.

My first impression . . . Broman, *Garbo on Garbo*, p. 78.

I did not say . . . Biery, "The Story of Greta Garbo (Part 3)," p. 144.

eloped to . . . Unsourced clipping, Garbo microfilm files, FCMPS.

for observation . . . Swenson, *Greta Garbo*, p. 144.

I heard one day . . . (caption) Gish, *The Movies, Mr. Griffith, and Me*, p. 299.

44 *On February 21* . . . Accounting report to Thalberg, February 22, 1927. Fragmentary copy, Photoplay Productions Collection.

not in good . . . Walker, *Garbo*, p. 69.

A five-year . . . Ibid.

Greta Garbo will play . . . Unsourced clipping, Garbo microfilm files, FCMPS.

I did not say . . . Biery, "The Story of Greta Garbo (Part 3)," p. 144.

I think a lot . . . Louella Parsons column, March 18, 1927.

45 *Garbo said he* . . . Swenson, *Greta Garbo*, p. 147.

She was in love . . . St. Johns, *Love, Laughter, and Tears*, p. 247.

When I was starting . . . Biery, "The Story of Greta Garbo (Part 3)," p. 144.

John Gilbert wasn't . . . Crawford, *A Portrait of Joan*, p. 31.

Tired . . . (caption) Hawkins, "A New Slant on Garbo," p. 112.

46 *She is getting* . . . Calhoun, "They Learned about Women from Her," p. 80.

Gott! She looks . . . Ibid., p. 64. The spelling of Geraldine Dvorak's name has been the subject of speculation for both Garbo and Dracula scholars, since her most famous film role was as one of the vampire's wives in the 1931 *Dracula*. Her name sometimes appeared on studio documents as Jeraldine De Vorak or Jeraldine Dvorak. For the sake of consistency, I use the spelling confirmed by horror film scholar David Skal.

Garbo insisted . . . Bainbridge, *Garbo*, p. 133.

I like her . . . Calhoun, "They Learned about Women from Her," p. 80.

as an intestinal . . . Unsourced clipping, Garbo microfilm files, FCMPS.

An internist consulted . . . Letter, Dr. Leland Paddock of Sequim, Washington, to author, June 1, 2004.

We were on it . . . Ricardo Cortez, interview by Kevin Brownlow, excerpt courtesy of Photoplay Productions.

She might look like . . . Lewis, *The Creative Producer*, p. 93.

a recurring ovarian . . . Swenson, *Greta Garbo*, p. 356.

The heavy-lidded . . . (caption) Calhoun, "They Learned about Women from Her," p. 80.

48 *Mr. Behrman said* . . . "Notes between Mr. Behrman and Mr. Davidson," unpublished transcript.

He was her manager . . . Ibid.

I did not know . . . Letter, Barbara Kent to author, May 14, 2004.

Chapter Five

49 *It stinks* . . . Marion, *Off with Their Heads!*, p. 134.

When Thalberg told me . . . Ibid.

Every day at lunch . . . *Hollywood Citizen News*, September 24, 1930.

She is superbly . . . (caption) Belfrage, "That Languid Lure," p. 44.

50 *I was the one* . . . Higham, *Hollywood Cameramen*, p. 67.

Interviews! How . . . Palmborg, *The Private Life of Greta Garbo*, p. 47.

Oh, please, let's . . . Biery, "The Story of Greta Garbo (Part 3)," p. 144.

She was in the . . . Carr, *Four Fabulous Faces*, p. 150.

Gilbert was feeling . . . Bainbridge, *Garbo*, p. 133.

We are making . . . Fountain, *Dark Star*, p. 126.

51 *In her first* . . . Bainbridge, *Garbo*, p. 135.

Peculiar . . . Conway, *The Films of Greta Garbo*, p. 59.

Love? Of course . . . Biery, "The Story of Greta Garbo (Part 3)," p. 144.

Is it that Americans . . . Calhoun, "They Learned about Women from Her," p. 80.

Chapter Six

53 *I am immortal* . . . Golden, "From Stage to Screen," p. 10.

In the time of . . . Hecht, *A Child of the Century*, p. 498.

54 *You are in love* . . . St. Johns, *Love, Laughter, and Tears*, p. 247.

I do not like . . . Calhoun, "They Learned about Women from Her," p. 80.

I was one in . . . Dietz, *Dancing in the Dark*, p. 153.

[Stiller] was her . . . Smith, "Up Speaks a Gallant Loser," p. 120.

I'm going out . . . Dietz, *Dancing in the Dark*, p. 153.

During the past . . . Fountain, *Dark Star*, p. 143.

She doesn't love . . . Borg, "Garbo's One Great Love," p. 19.

A strange creature . . . "The Divine Woman: Continuity by Dorothy Farnum," *The Divine Woman* file, MGM-USC.

It is no lie . . . Pensel, *Seastrom and Stiller in Hollywood*, p. 40.

Hog woman . . . (caption) "'THE DIVINE WOMAN' Cutting Continuity January 11, 1928," *The Divine Woman* file, MGM-USC.

55 *a softer, more* . . . Swenson, *Greta Garbo*, p. 159.

When the picture . . . Tibbetts, *Introduction to the Photoplay*, p. 123.

56 *For you* . . . "'THE DIVINE WOMAN' Cutting Continuity January 11, 1928." *The Divine Woman* file, MGM-USC.

She and Lars . . . Palmborg, *The Private Life of Greta Garbo*, p. 70.

I will be very . . . Ibid., p. 71.

The world has tossed . . . "'THE DIVINE WOMAN' Cutting Continuity January 11, 1928." *The Divine Woman* file, MGM-USC.

57 *She never once* . . . Billquist, *Garbo*, p. 143.

On the other side . . . Ibid., p. 144.

She thinks above . . . Daum, *Walking with Garbo*, p. 134.

At the preview . . . Pensel, *Seastrom and Stiller in Hollywood*, p. 41.

58 *Given a part* . . . Conway, *The Films of Greta Garbo*, p. 63.

Here is a new . . . Ibid.

Many who admit . . . Ibid.

Chapter Seven

60 *A beautiful woman* . . . Letter, Lorna Moon to Irving Thalberg, November 17, 1927, *The Mysterious Lady* file, MGM-USC.

only a spy-woman . . . Interoffice communication, Lorna Moon to Hunt Stromberg, November 28, 1927, *The Mysterious Lady* file, MGM-USC.

She walks over . . . "War in the Dark, Treatment by Benjamin Christensen, November 30, 1927," *The Mysterious Lady* file, MGM-USC.

61 *terror in all their* . . . Berg, *Goldwyn*, p. 173.

Eet is all . . . Fragmentary clipping, author's collection.

Geraldine had . . . (caption) Palmborg, *The Private Life of Greta Garbo*, p. 63.

62 *I am now* . . . Swenson, *Greta Garbo*, p. 161.

No woman could . . . Ibid., p. 161.

Whether I'm filming . . . Billquist, *Garbo*, p. 149.

63 *WAR IN THE* . . . Daily Production Report, May 8, 1928, *The Mysterious Lady* file, MGM-USC.

Miss Garbo 30 min. . . . Daily Production Report, May 9, 1928, *The Mysterious Lady* file, MGM-USC.

Greta was in . . . Louella O. Parsons, *Los Angeles Examiner*, May 11, 1928.

No! . . . *They posed me* . . . Day, *This Was Hollywood*, p. 97.

Why don't you go . . . Davies, *The Times We Had*, p. 116.

65 *I had a big part in* . . . Zierold, *Garbo*, p. 78.

She concentrated . . . Ibid.

The first reel . . . (caption) *Picture Play* (December 1928). Fragmentary copy, Photoplay Productions Collection.

66 *She was unassuming* . . . Billquist, *Garbo*, p. 146.

Miss Garbo takes . . . Conway, *The Films of Greta Garbo*, p. 68.

This Garbo . . . Ibid.

She is the dream . . . Ibid.

Discovered this . . . (caption) Daily Production Report, June 13, 1928, *The Mysterious Lady* file, MGM-USC.

Chapter Eight

67 *I am not the proud* . . . Arlen, *The Green Hat*, p. 57.

It is sordid . . . "Nina Lewton: Reader's Report, August 6, 1924." Fragmentary copy, Photoplay Productions Collection.

This is a naughty . . . Letter, M. F. Lee to Irving Thalberg, August 14, 1924. Fragmentary copy, Photoplay Productions Collection.

In the greatest . . . (caption) Hall, "Garbo-maniacs," p. 61.

68 *Your generation* . . . Arlen, *The Green Hat*, p. 100.

Agree with Hays . . . Cable, Irving Thalberg to J. Robert Rubin, November 8, 1924. Fragmentary copy, Photoplay Productions Collection.

This looks to me . . . Cable, Irving Thalberg to J. Robert Rubin, December 1, 1924. Fragmentary copy, Photoplay Productions Collection.

This period seemed . . . Acosta, *Here Lies the Heart*, p. 128.

Practically everyone . . . Ibid.

grown up to find . . . Fitzgerald, *This Side of Paradise*, p. 7.

There was a rhythm . . . Arlen, *The Green Hat*, p. 121.

Brilliant men . . . Allen, *Only Yesterday*, p. 84.

America was going . . . Robinson, *Hollywood in the Twenties*, p. 20.

Will you immediately . . . Cable, L. A. Shaw to J. Robert Rubin, December 20, 1927. Fragmentary copy, Photoplay Productions Collection.

Is it possible . . . Letter, Will H. Hays to Irving G. Thalberg, no date. Fragmentary copy, Photoplay Productions Collection.

69 *She wanted people* . . . Arlen, *The Green Hat*, p. 343.

Confident can . . . Cable, M. R. Bennett to Greenwood, signed by Irving Thalberg, June 7, 1928. Fragmentary copy, Photoplay Productions Collection.

I am confident . . . Letter, Irving G. Thalberg to Will H. Hays, June 25, 1928. Fragmentary copy, Photoplay Productions Collection.

We have instructed . . . Letter, J. Robert Rubin to Louis B. Mayer, no date. Fragmentary copy, Photoplay Productions Collection.

70 *a completely different* . . . Crawford, *A Portrait of Joan*, p. 31.

I'd rather you . . . Fountain, *Dark Star*, p. 160.

Miss Garbo 20 min . . . "Daily Production August 15, 1928," *A Woman of Affairs* file, MGM-USC.

She would stay . . . "The Greta Garbo Legend Exposed," p. 10.

Gilbert's a funny . . . (caption) Fountain, *Dark Star*, p. 160.

subtle something . . . (caption) *Variety*, January 23, 1929. Fragmentary clipping, author's collection.

71 *One day* . . . Fairbanks, *The Salad Days*, p. 129.

We lit very much . . . Higham, *Hollywood Cameramen*, p. 67.

INDIVIDUAL SHOT . . . (caption) "'A Woman of Affairs,' Continuity by Bess Meredyth, July 26, 1928," *A Woman of Affairs* file, MGM-USC.

72 *And then I* . . . "Masters of Photography," p. 3.

He directed . . . Swenson, *Greta Garbo*, p. 174.

continually tried to . . . Steichen, *A Life in Photography*, p. 8.

For me . . . Brownlow, *The Parade's Gone By*, p. 169.

She has foreign ideas . . . Palmborg, *The Private Life of Greta Garbo*, p. 62.

It is evident . . . (caption) Walker, *The Shattered Silents*, p. 170.

73 *They feared she* . . . Gutner, *Gowns by Adrian*, p. 74.

A sensational . . . Conway, *The Films of Greta Garbo*, p. 73.

The heroine's . . . Ibid.

Not only is the narrative . . . Fragmentary clipping, author's collection.

Despite the change . . . Thames Television Program, courtesy of Photoplay Productions.

Comments from . . . Ibid.

the finest picture . . . Ibid.

74 *John Gilbert* . . . Conway, *The Films of Greta Garbo*, p. 73.

After Stiller . . . (caption) Billquist, *Garbo*, p. 154.

The movie is . . . (caption) Conway, *The Films of Greta Garbo*, p. 68.

Chapter Nine

77 *Nobody in that* . . . "Mr. Colton of 'Rain.'"

We wish to add . . . Letter, Josephine Lovett to Irving Thalberg, November 10, 1927, *Wild Orchids* file, MGM-USC.

78 *Jack Colton* . . . Marx, *Mayer and Thalberg*, p. 43.

Lilyan wasn't . . . Paris, *Garbo*, p. 251.

When Lilyan had . . . Ibid., p. 255.

She puts in . . . Palmborg, "Greta Garbo Goes Home," p. 21.

Here comes John . . . Billquist, *Garbo*, p. 147.

When we were out . . . Bainbridge, *Garbo*, p. 137.

One evening he . . . Swenson, *Greta Garbo*, p. 56.

The story was a . . . Franklin, "We Laughed and We Cried," p. 181.

79 *I just think how* . . . Billquist, *Garbo*, p. 151.

Never before has . . . Palmborg, "Greta Garbo Goes Home," p. 74.

The moment I . . . Bainbridge, *Garbo*, p. 137.

She was doing . . . Palmborg, "Greta Garbo Goes Home," p. 76.

80 *Your message* . . . Swenson, *Greta Garbo*, p. 177.

Greta turned . . . Broman, *The Divine Garbo*, p. 95.

Slowly she walked . . . Palmborg, *The Private Life of Greta Garbo*, p. 76.

A string trio . . . Daum, *Walking with Garbo*, p. 66.

As I passed . . . Broman, *The Divine Garbo*, p. 95.

After Moje died . . . Bainbridge, *Garbo*, p. 141.

Our relationship . . . Franklin, "We Laughed and We Cried," p. 181.

81 *Sidney Franklin* . . . Nils Asther, interview by Kevin Brownlow, January 12, 1967, excerpt courtesy of Photoplay Productions.

It became so . . . Franklin, "We Laughed and We Cried," p. 181.

It was not . . . Ibid.

There is still time . . . Walker, *Garbo*, p. 89.

She was sort of . . . Haworth, "I Loved Garbo," p. 89.

Garbo was a nice . . . (caption) Nils Asther, interview by Kevin Brownlow, January 12, 1967, excerpt courtesy of Photoplay Productions.

82 *pleasingly imaginative* . . . Conway, *The Films of Greta Garbo*, p. 77.

Garbo threw off . . . Haworth, "I Loved Garbo," p. 89.

You are a very . . . St. Johns, *Love, Laughter, and Tears*, p. 247.

The set was . . . (caption) Palmborg, *The Private Life of Greta Garbo*, p. 76.

Sex is . . . (caption) *Variety*, April 3, 1929. Fragmentary clipping, author's collection.

Chapter Ten

83 *I don't like to* . . . Carr, *Four Fabulous Faces*, p. 156.

On the tray . . . Palmborg, *The Private Life of Greta Garbo*, p. 123.

She was always . . . Ibid., p. 169.

People look at me . . . St. Johns, "Garbo, the Mystery of Hollywood," p. 35.

Run like hell . . . Laing, *Greta Garbo*, p. 186.

Gott! Are you . . . Billquist, *Garbo*, p. 166.

A reporter kept . . . Zierold, *Garbo*, p. 100.

Joan of Arc . . . Hall, "The Hollywood Hermit."

84 *She begged me* . . . Haworth, "I Loved Garbo," p. 90.

pimps, professional . . . St. Johns, *The Honeycomb*, p. 28.

Arden Stuart stood . . . "'The Single Standard,' Complete Magazine Story, Copied 7/25/27," *The Single Standard* file, MGM-USC.

85 *[The modern American* . . . Adams, "Now the Siren Eclipses the Flapper," p. 73.

Miss Garbo has . . . "Greta Garbo Appears Once More."

We open up . . . "'Picking Up the Action from the Return of Packy Cannon,' Dictated by Mr. Stromberg, March 13, 1929," *The Single Standard* file, MGM-USC.

I like it when . . . Daum, *Walking with Garbo*, p. 134.

86 *She was sorry* . . . Palmborg, *The Private Life of Greta Garbo*, p. 161.

He was only . . . Billquist, *Garbo*, p. 167.

He says I must . . . Bainbridge, *Garbo*, p. 169.

Gott, I wonder . . . Ibid., p. 156.

She'd had enough . . . Ibid.

He was playing . . . Fountain, *Dark Star*, p. 169.

87 *I'd thought he* . . . Ibid.

an unkind, empty . . . Olivier, *Confessions of an Actor*, p. 127.

John Gilbert, star . . . "Gilbert to Wed Ina Claire."

She turned white . . . "When Greta Isn't Garbo."

Some of the M-G-M . . . Coffee, *Storyline*, p. 187.

88 *The voice* . . . Fountain, *Dark Star*, p. 170.

[She was saying that . . . Coffee, *Storyline*, p. 187.

Thank you . . . Walker, *Garbo*, p. 92.

89 *How does it* . . . Fountain, *Dark Star*, p. 171.

I had an awful . . . Benchley, "This Is Garbo," p. 14.

I used to stand . . . Broman, *The Divine Garbo*, p. 83.

Stop that! . . . Billquist, *Garbo*, p. 150.

The Stafford-Hanley party . . . "'The Single Standard' Retakes by Hunt Stromberg, 5-17-29," *The Single Standard* file, MGM-USC.

Arden Stuart was . . . (caption) "'The Single Standard,' Complete Magazine Story, Copied 7/25/27," *The Single Standard* file, MGM-USC.

90 *What some girls* . . . "Single Standard," *Variety*, July 31, 1929.

Chapter Eleven

92 *Garbo handed me* . . . Palmborg, *The Private Life of Greta Garbo*, p. 120.

Greta Garbo passes . . . Arnheim, *Film Essays and Criticism*, p. 216.

I never will be . . . Palmborg, *The Private Life of Greta Garbo*, p. 170.

did not know how . . . Ibid., p. 139.

When Garbo wasn't . . . Ibid., p. 161.

I always knew when . . . Ibid., p. 168.

93 *There is no doubt* . . . Ibid., p. 194.

It will be the . . . Ibid., p. 259.

She sat silent . . . Walker, *Garbo*, p. 102.

94 *We knew that she* . . . Palmborg, *The Private Life of Greta Garbo*, p. 154.

She told me . . . Viertel, *The Kindness of Strangers*, p. 142.

She often went . . . Palmborg, *The Private Life of Greta Garbo*, p. 174.

Is this a talking . . . Letter, exhibitor to studio, quoted in Eyman, *The Speed of Sound*, p. 268.

I am not sympathetic . . . Berg, *Goldwyn*, p. 165.

I loathe them . . . Walker, *The Shattered Silents*, p. 132.

95 *It's a gorgeous* . . . Hall, "Garbo Explains Her Next Picture."

She says it portrays . . . Marx, *Mayer and Thalberg*, p. 123.

I remember that she . . . (caption) Palmborg, *The Private Life of Greta Garbo*, p. 173.

96 *He was a fine* . . . Zierold, *Garbo*, p. 78.

97 *Now if they had* . . . Rosenberg, *The Real Tinsel*, p. 185.

Ina wanted so badly . . . Fountain, *Dark Star*, p. 171.

I tried once to . . . Ibid.

I watched Jack . . . Hopper, *From Under My Hat*, p. 163.

What do you mean . . . Hawkins, "A New Slant on Garbo," p. 21.

The great stellar . . . Wagner, *You Must Remember This*, p. 165.

I was flabbergasted . . . Ibid., p. 167.

Can't Mr. Ayres . . . Billquist, *Garbo*, p. 168.

I remember her . . . Wagner, *You Must Remember This*, p. 167.

98 *Some day you will* . . . Palmborg, *The Private Life of Greta Garbo*, p. 156.

Garbo had very little . . . Wagner, *You Must Remember This*, p. 167.

I play the wife . . . Hall, "Garbo Explains Her Next Picture."

There was a mood . . . Wagner, *You Must Remember This*, p. 167.

far more shy . . . Ibid.

She always quits . . . Hawkins, "A New Slant on Garbo," p. 21.

If they want to send . . . Palmborg, *The Private Life of Greta Garbo*, p. 180.

I want to send . . . Jordan, "Photographing Garbo," p. 101.

99 *The day Garbo* . . . Bull, *Faces of Hollywood*, p. 23.

100 *She first appears* . . . Hall, "A Silent Miss Garbo."

one of Miss Garbo's . . . "The Kiss," *Variety*, November 20, 1929. Fragmentary clipping, author's collection.

The last stand . . . Conway, *The Films of Greta Garbo*, p. 85.

If any voice . . . Hall, "Garbo Explains Her Next Picture."

Chapter Twelve

103 *What kind of* . . . Swenson, *Greta Garbo*, p. 206.

Be a bull . . . Allen, *Only Yesterday*, p. 258.

104 *The prosperity* . . . Ibid., p. 150.

If you really . . . Broman, *The Divine Garbo*, p. 181.

She said she had no . . . Hall, "Clever Film Actresses."

They are making . . . Broman, *The Divine Garbo*, p. 181.

She looked like . . . Bainbridge, *Garbo*, p. 170.

That's all over . . . "The Day That Garbo Dreaded."

ANNA CHRISTOPHERSON . . . O'Neill, *Anna Christie*, p. 73.

In choosing . . . Conway, *The Films of Greta Garbo*, p. 89.

105 *You don't suppose* . . . Marion, *Off with Their Heads!*, p. 196.

What do I need . . . "The Day That Garbo Dreaded."

bullish enthusiasm . . . Allen, *Only Yesterday*, p. 245.

106 *His voice is* . . . Fountain, *Dark Star*, p. 178.

Gilbert has not . . . Ibid., p. 180.

Obviously John . . . Walker, *The Shattered Silents*, p. 171.

White-hot love . . . Ibid., p. 172.

Mr. Gilbert repeatedly . . . Fountain, *Dark Star*, p. 180.

Jack was young . . . Hopper, *From Under My Hat*, p. 164.

Studios have found . . . Walker, *The Shattered Silents*, p. 171.

It was not Jack's . . . de Mille, *Hollywood Saga*, p. 288.

Quite obviously . . . Walker, *The Shattered Silents*, p. 172.

I was amazed . . . "The Day That Garbo Dreaded."

I was bothered . . . Bickford, *Bulls, Balls, Bicycles, and Actors*, p. 215.

107 *I'm sorry for* . . . Ibid., p. 216.

He brushed the . . . Beauchamp, *Without Lying Down*, p. 250.

To everybody's . . . Lee, *Marie Dressler*, p. 174.

I have learned . . . Marion, *Off with Their Heads!*, p. 197.

She hated to . . . Brownlow, *The Parade's Gone By*, p. 169.

This is it . . . "The Day That Garbo Dreaded."

We sat in the . . . Ibid.

108 *My God!* . . . "William Daniels, September 11, 1967," Thomas/UCLA.

Does that sound . . . "When Greta Isn't Garbo."

But you should have seen . . . "The Day That Garbo Dreaded."

109 *One of the most* . . . Dressler, *My Own Story*, p. 249.

I have never seen . . . Billquist, *Garbo*, p. 171.

characterization . . . "Daily Production Report, October 19, 1929," *Anna Christie* file, MGM-USC.

No one else . . . Hawkins, "A New Slant on Garbo," p. 19.

Garbo was so . . . Billquist, *Garbo*, p. 171.

It was always . . . Marion, *Off with Their Heads!*, p. 197.

Garbo's present contract . . . Walker, *Garbo*, p. 109.

She has the basis . . . Beauchamp, *Without Lying Down*, p. 250.

I made up my . . . Dressler, *My Own Story*, p. 249.

The gigantic edifice . . . Allen, *Only Yesterday*, p. 271.

110 *It's a good campaign* . . . Day, *This Was Hollywood*, p. 99.

I must sit . . . Bainbridge, *Garbo*, p. 172.

She usually went . . . Palmborg, *The Private Life of Greta Garbo*, p. 173.

Garbo is holding . . . Marion, *Off with Their Heads!*, p. 199.

I went to the opening . . . Lee, *Marie Dressler*, p. 175.

Eugene O'Neill might . . . Hamann, *Greta Garbo in the 30s*, p. 6.

Isn't it terrible . . . Palmborg, *The Private Life of Greta Garbo*, p. 218.

Great artistically . . . "Anna Christie (All Dialog)."

Miss Garbo's voice . . . Hall, "Miss Garbo's First Talker."

Her voice is revealed . . . Walker, *Garbo*, p. 110.

The voice that . . . Conway, *The Films of Greta Garbo*, p. 89.

111 *No pyrotechnical* . . . Marion, *Off with Their Heads!*, p. 204.

'Garbo Talks' . . . "Anna Christie (All Dialog)."

Miss Garbo . . . Day, *This Was Hollywood*, p. 100.

I read last night . . . Bainbridge, *Garbo*, p. 174.

Chapter Thirteen

112 *I would make a* . . . Kakutani, "A Drama Recalls a Playwright."

bewitching, brilliant little . . . Sheldon, *Romance*, p. 44.

He is about twenty-eight . . . Ibid., p. 25.

This has already . . . "Reader's Report, December 13, 1926," *Romance* file, MGM-USC.

She shakes her head . . . "ROMANCE, Adaptation and Continuity by F. Hugh Herbert, March 31, 1928," *Romance* file, MGM-USC.

Love . . . Sheldon, *Romance*, p. 57.

113 *Garbo is keenly* . . . Palmborg, *The Private Life of Greta Garbo*, p. 142.

She never likes to . . . Ibid., p. 203.

Greta Garbo and Fifi D'Orsay." Fragmentary clipping, Garbo microfilm files, FCMPS.

Why don't you write . . . Viertel, *The Kindness of Strangers*, p. 143.

Jacques Feyder will . . . "Foreign Language Films." Feyder directed only one of two projected Garbo films in German. Foreign-language revenues did not justify taking either of them away from English-language films.

Right now . . . Palmborg, *The Private Life of Greta Garbo*, p. 142.

Garbo didn't want to . . . Ibid., p. 248.

After a gay . . . Ibid., p. 239.

114 *Nearly every afternoon* . . . Ibid., p. 226.

If they know . . . St. Johns, "The Heart of Garbo," p. 84.

115 *But you can't* . . . Palmborg, *The Private Life of Greta Garbo*, p. 248.

Neither of us . . . Ibid., p. 250.

You'll have to leave . . . "Greta Garbo's Latest Film."

116 *I took a look* . . . George Hurrell, interview by author, December 1, 1975.

She just sat . . . Kapitanoff, "Sixty-three Years of Shooting the Legends."

She was pensive . . . Stine, *The Hurrell Style*, p. 20.

It may have been . . . Kobal, *People Will Talk*, p. 265.

There's a crazy . . . Pepper, *The Man Who Shot Garbo*, p. 23.

I didn't do too well . . . Kobal, *People Will Talk*, p. 265.

After the picture . . . Palmborg, *The Private Life of Greta Garbo*, p. 253.

Until de night . . . "ROMANCE, Continuity by Bess Meredyth and Edwin Justus Mayer, February 6, 1930," *Romance* file, MGM-USC.

Eddie Woods . . . This is the same Edward Woods who was made to switch parts with James Cagney in William Wellman's *Public Enemy*. Cagney became a star; Woods became a footnote.

117 *The audience cheered* . . . Palmborg, *The Private Life of Greta Garbo*, p. 253.

I was cast . . . Viertel, *The Kindness of Strangers*, p. 151.

Playing Anna . . . Ibid., p. 151.

He says this . . . Billquist, *Garbo*, p. 172.

Greta Garbo's peculiarly . . . Hall, "In Old Manhattan."

When Garbo gargles . . . Fragmentary clipping, Garbo microfilm files, FCMPS.

slow, draggy, and lack[ing] . . . Conway, *The Films of Greta Garbo*, p. 93.

She laughed out . . . (caption) Chester W. Schaeffer, interview by author, October 9, 1971.

118 *Hollywood's favorite* . . . Conway, *The Films of Greta Garbo*, p. 93.

There was suddenly . . . Bach, *Marlene Dietrich*, p. 129.

I hate to admit . . . (caption) Unsourced clipping, author's collection.

Chapter Fourteen

120 *Not long ago* . . . Hall, "Garbo-maniacs," p. 61.

You certainly slammed . . . Ibid., p. 60.

If Greta is cold . . . Ibid.

I have 368 . . . Durgnat, *Garbo*, p. 27.

123 *Garbo is often* . . . "Garbo by Her Cameraman."

Socially, I don't . . . Carr, *Four Fabulous Faces*, p. 121.

In silent pictures . . . Hedda Hopper, unsourced clipping, Garbo microfilm files, FCMPS.

We could never get . . . Brownlow, *The Parade's Gone By*, p. 169.

What is the matter . . . Albert, "Did Garbo and Brown Fight?" p. 130.

124 *Greta gets away* . . . Hall, "Garbo-maniacs," p. 60.

Temperamentally Garbo . . . "Garbo by Her Cameraman."

That's silly . . . Albert, "Did Garbo and Brown Fight?" p. 130.

Excuse me, Miss . . . "No Man Is Safe from Her Witchery."

125 *Well, . . . we'll shoot the scene* . . . Albert, "Did Garbo and Brown Fight?" p. 130.

Photographically she . . . "Garbo by Her Cameraman."

Marlene Dietrich . . . "In Studios and Theatres."

Don't you think . . . Billquist, *Garbo*, p. 177.

banal clap-trap . . . Hamann, *Greta Garbo in the 30s*, p. 9.

126 *There is a definite* . . . Parsons, "Famous Actress Wins Acclaim at Chinese Opening."

symbol of glamour . . . Bach, *Marlene Dietrich*, p. 129.

I didn't have sufficient . . . Higham, *Hollywood Cameramen*, p. 67.

I didn't create . . . Ibid., p. 70.

If they had only . . . Boland, "Garbo Likeness Deplored."

She is a rather gaunt . . . (caption) Hamann, *Greta Garbo in the 30s*, p. 11.

128 *Why has she been* . . . Walker, *Dietrich*, p. 40.

Who is Marlene . . . Ibid., p. 92.

I would not direct . . . Hamann, *Greta Garbo in the 30s*, p. 9.

The afternoon . . . Pepper, *The Man Who Shot Garbo*, p. 21.

Well, . . . because she's used . . . Jordan, "Photographing Garbo," p. 100.

mediocre and tiresome . . . "Greta Garbo Back at the Capitol."

chief failing . . . Hall, "A Conception of 'Sapho.'"

Handicapped by . . . Conway, *The Films of Greta Garbo*, p. 97.

The theater yesterday . . . Hamann, *Greta Garbo in the 30s*, p. 9.

Why do people . . . Walker, *Dietrich*, p. 101.

Chapter Fifteen

129 *In many ways* . . . Walker, *Garbo*, p. 110.

As figures at . . . Silverman, "U. S. Film Field for 1930."

Why should some . . . Wilkerson, "Tradeviews."

With crime practically . . . Letter, Jason Joy to Joseph I. Breen, December 15, 1931, *Possessed* file, in the Production Code Administration papers, MPAA Collection, Margaret Herrick Library, Fairbanks Center for Motion Picture Study (hereinafter PCA).

Female picturegoers . . . Aaronson, "B. O. Explodes Idea That Women Dislike War and Crook Pictures."

130 *The smug and contented* . . . Morris, "Sinful Girls Lead in 1931."

Women love dirt . . . "Dirt Craze Due to Women," p. 24.

It has been said . . . Laing, *Greta Garbo*, p. 187.

The rumors of her . . . Grant, "Does Garbo Tank She Go Home Now?"

Greta Garbo broke . . . "Miss Garbo's Plans."

They do say . . . Laing, *Greta Garbo*, p. 187.

131 *Look at that* . . . Lee Garmes, interview by author, October 10, 1971.

How much of . . . Kobal, *Dietrich*, p. 76.

Marlene Dietrich has . . . Ibid., p. 49.

Her hasty rise . . . Dickens, *The Films of Marlene Dietrich*, p. 99.

intimate story of . . . "Synopsis by Ross Wills, April 10, 1925," *Susan Lenox* file, MGM-USC.

Who is Susan Lenox . . . Marx, *Mayer and Thalberg*, p. 87.

132 *Jack would put* . . . Fountain, *Dark Star*, p. 172.

No, you've missed . . . Thomas, *Thalberg*, p. 184.

There's a pint of . . . "Susan Lenox by Wells Root, May 25, 1931," *Susan Lenox* file, MGM-USC.

A star is . . . Samuels, *The King*, p. 159.

The big thrill . . . Hamann, *Greta Garbo in the 30s*, p. 9.

134 *Our aim* . . . "Greta Garbo's New Film."

Some persons have . . . "Jean Hersholt and the Screen."

Plenty of turmoil . . . "Garbo's Six Walkouts One Lenox Headache."

I am not going . . . Acosta, *Here Lies the Heart*, p. 217.

Well, you have managed . . . "From Mr. Bern, June 22, 1931," *Susan Lenox* file, M-G-M story files, FCMPS.

Rodney's change . . . "Retakes by George Kelly, August 8, 1931," *Susan Lenox* file, MGM-USC.

She never marries . . . "Synopsis by Ross Wills, April 10, 1925," *Susan Lenox* file, MGM-USC.

135 *My present prison* . . . Acosta, *Here Lies the Heart*, p. 224.

Absolutely no one . . . Ibid.

136 *Look, Rodney* . . . "Suggested New Ending by L. Coffee, August 8, 1931," *Susan Lenox* file, MGM-USC.

I've changed, too . . . "Retakes by Leon Gordon, August 24, 1931," *Susan Lenox* file, MGM-USC.

Garbo and Gable . . . Unsourced clipping, author's collection.

It is rather . . . Hall, "Miss Garbo's Fine Work."

The film is good . . . Durgnat, *Garbo*, p. 131.

Chapter Sixteen

139 *Now I am* . . . (caption) Hopper, *From Under My Hat*, p. 174.

In my opinion . . . (caption) "What the Audience Thinks," p. 6.

140 *Innocent bystanders* . . . Acosta, *Here Lies the Heart*, p. 229.

Recent associations are . . . Swenson, *Greta Garbo*, p. 259.

one of the most contemptible . . . *The American Film Institute Catalog, 1931–1940*, p. 1340.

If you had been born . . . Billquist, *Garbo*, p. 100.

Miss Garbo has shown . . . "Research in Hollywood."

A half life-size . . . Howe, *Mata Hari*, p. 87.

141 *There is no glitter* . . . "Mata Hari—Changes by Richard L. Sharpe," *Mata Hari* file, MGM-USC.

142 *The evening I met* . . . Acosta, *Here Lies the Heart*, p. 231.

took eight Guadalajaran . . . Hopper, *The Whole Truth and Nothing But*, p. 115.

They said 'We have . . . Pratt, "Interview with Ramon Novarro."

I used to read these . . . Ibid.

Each one was marked . . . "Mata Hari in a Film."

I hope the world . . . Wheelright, Ralph, "When Nordic Met Latin," p. 101.

143 *The ermine* . . . (caption) Parsons, "Sirenic Garbo Sways Public as Mata Hari."

144 *I felt very strange* . . . Wheelright, Ralph, "When Nordic Met Latin," p. 101.

As we posed . . . Ibid., p. 103.

145 *Her emotional intensity* . . . Ibid.

Garbo always wanted . . . Zierold, *Garbo*, p. 90.

She and I staged . . . Pratt, "Interview with Ramon Novarro."

Miss Garbo's understanding . . . Fragmentary clipping from *Mata Hari* reissue press kit, author's collection.

I wanted to illuminate . . . Higham, *Hollywood Cameramen*, p. 57.

146 *The scene played* . . . The scene was cut from the camera negative in 1939 to comply with Production Code requirements for a reissue. Even so, Novarro told a 1960s interviewer: "I am remembered as much for that scene as I am for the chariot race in *Ben-Hur*." (Soares, *Beyond Paradise*, p. 171.)

We have a scene . . . Zierold, *Garbo*, p. 77.

She wore that . . . Wheelright, "When Nordic Met Latin," p. 103.

I wondered how . . . Ibid., p. 89.

148 *Up to this time* . . . "Conference Notes, December 4, 1931," *Mata Hari* file, MGM-USC.

she dances rather . . . Hamann, *Greta Garbo in the 30s*, p. 9.

Chapter Seventeen

150 *I didn't know* . . . Hall, "The Perils of Marlene."

Where did you learn . . . "Alias Marlene Dietrich."

Okay . . . Higham, *Marlene*, p. 114.

The swift-moving . . . "Producer Discusses Pictures."

151 *aquatic Grand Hotel* . . . *The American Film Institute Catalog, 1931–1940*, p. 2257.

There is a new . . . Hamann, *Greta Garbo in the 30s*, p. 19.

An immense amount . . . Marx, *A Gaudy Spree*, p. 56.

made love to his light . . . (caption) Hedda Hopper, unsourced clipping, Garbo microfilm files, FCMPS.

152 *I don't want to do* . . . Thomas, *Joan Crawford*, p. 73.

Yes, but why must . . . Considine, *Bette and Joan*, p. 34.

I took this up . . . Walker, *Garbo*, p. 124.

Thalberg was influenced . . . Marx, *A Gaudy Spree*, p. 56.

154 *Turning on the light* . . . Baum, *Grand Hotel*, p. 116.

Nobody has loved . . . "'Hotel' (Translation of 'Menschen im Hotel') by William A. Drake, December 4, 1930," *Grand Hotel* file, MGM-USC.

The thing that is so . . . "Grand Hotel, Story Cutting Conference, December 9, 1931," *Grand Hotel* file, MGM-USC.

155 *You have two pages* . . . "Grand Hotel, Cutting Conference, Saturday December 26, 1931," *Grand Hotel* file, MGM-USC.

His sunny . . . Marx, *Mayer and Thalberg*, p. 188.

The sound mixers . . . Chester W. Schaeffer, interview by author, October 9, 1971.

I know what . . . Fountain, *Dark Star*, p. 184.

That should take . . . Ibid., p. 186.

Thalberg decided . . . Marx, *Mayer and Thalberg*, p. 188.

She is a fine . . . (caption) Billquist, *Garbo*, p. 184.

156 *I shot my mouth* . . . Parish, *The Best of MGM*, p. 86.

Greta Garbo was . . . Crawford, *A Portrait of Joan*, p. 92.

Greta did agree to . . . Santon, "*Grand Hotel* Revisited with Director Edmund Goulding," p. 101.

Her habit of punctuation . . . Considine, *Bette and Joan*, p. 34.

Here was a Joan . . . Thomas, *Joan Crawford*, p. 75.

How do they light . . . Platt, *Great Stars of Hollywood's Golden Age*, p. 166.

157 *walking personality* . . . *Grand Hotel* press book, copy in author's collection.

I didn't know you . . . Kobler, *Damned in Paradise*, p. 261.

My wife and I . . . Fowler, *Good Night, Sweet Prince*, p. 340.

This is a great . . . Kobler, *Damned in Paradise*, p. 261.

One evening . . . Thomas, *Joan Crawford*, p. 75.

I'm sorry, but . . . Billquist, *Garbo*, p. 184.

You are the most . . . Fowler, *Good Night, Sweet Prince*, p. 340.

I was touched . . . Kobler, *Damned in Paradise*, p. 261.

Rafaela was an . . . (caption) Santon, "*Grand Hotel* Revisited with Director Edmund Goulding," p. 104.

159 *If he wants to see* . . . Hopper, *The Whole Truth and Nothing But*, p. 122.

Do you know him . . . Kotsilibas-Davis, *The Barrymores*, p. 119.

I wasn't there . . . Hedda Hopper, unsourced clipping, Garbo microfilm files, FCMPS.

Not because . . . Acosta, *Here Lies the Heart*, p. 234.

There is no reason . . . York, "One More Garbo Fan," p. 95.

There are no good . . . Alpert, *The Barrymores*, p. 291.

She was nice . . . Hedda Hopper, unsourced clipping, Garbo microfilm files, FCMPS.

Now, Miss Garbo . . . *Grand Hotel* press book, copy in author's collection.

One afternoon . . . Daum, *Walking with Garbo*, p. 149.

Not once did I . . . "What the Audience Thinks (2)."

160 *Worshipers of the* . . . Hall, "The Screen," p. 23.

Here Greta Garbo . . . Conway, *The Films of Greta Garbo*, p. 97.

Chapter Eighteen

161 *One sitting at* . . . Hamann, *Greta Garbo in the 30s*, p. 27.

It will be hard . . . Ibid., p. 26.

the finest actress . . . Ibid., p. 21.

I [didn't] feel any . . . Broman, *Conversations with Greta Garbo*, p. 100.

An electrical thrill . . . Ibid., p. 28.

162 *desirous of increasing* . . . Unsourced clipping, Greta Garbo file, Cinema Television Library, University of Southern California (hereinafter USC).

We fail to see . . . Bach, *Marlene Dietrich*, p. 153.

crazy mystic Spaniard . . . Acosta, *Here Lies the Heart*, p. 233.

After trying to . . . Ibid., p. 231.

163 *One must learn* . . . "'Desperate' by Mercedes de Acosta, January 21, 1931," quoted in Swenson, *Greta Garbo*, p. 274.

Do you want to . . . Acosta, *Here Lies the Heart*, p. 233.

I would like to . . . Hall, "The Hollywood Hermit."

164 *Our contract* . . . Walker, *Garbo*, p. 129.

Greta played . . . Acosta, *Here Lies the Heart*, p. 239.

Forward, like some Norse . . . Unsourced clipping, Garbo file, USC.

Von came up . . . Higham, *Hollywood Cameramen*, p. 71.

We worked for a . . . Hedda Hopper, unsourced clipping, Garbo microfilm files, FCMPS.

Garbo and Pirandello . . . Douglas, *See You at the Movies*, p. 88.

166 *Garbo had an extraordinary* . . . Ibid.

Oh, is that the . . . (caption) Jordan, "Photographing Garbo," p. 100.

167 *She is the only person* . . . Vickers, *Loving Garbo*, p. 41.

What difference does it . . . Beaton, *The Wandering Years*, p. 253.

I at last got through . . . Vickers, *Loving Garbo*, p. 41.

I could now drink . . . Beaton, *The Wandering Years*, p. 257.

I had looked forward . . . Curtiss, *Von Stroheim*, p. 284.

Stroheim was very . . . Ibid., p. 287.

I never knew at . . . Payne, *The Great Garbo*, p. 200.

a scene that was . . . Hedda Hopper, unsourced clipping, Garbo microfilm files, FCMPS.

169 *Well, shall we do* . . . Jordan, "Photographing Garbo," p. 100.

I never got to . . . Douglas, *See You at the Movies*, p. 88.

I have never played . . . Billquist, *Garbo*, p. 187.

On the last . . . Hopper, *From Under My Hat*, p. 175.

Garbo's performance . . . Fragmentary clipping, author's collection.

Garbo has never . . . Conway, *The Films of Greta Garbo*, p. 116.

Why speak of . . . Fragmentary clipping, author's collection.

Chapter Nineteen

171 *Miss Garbo has* . . . "Garbo Off for Europe."

At the beginning . . . Beaton, *Cecil Beaton*, p. 238.

I don't hate . . . Ibid., p. 209.

I used to quake . . . Ibid., p. 210.

Those long years . . . Ibid., p. 238.

The preposterous child . . . Viertel, *The Kindness of Strangers*, p. 152.

I had for some . . . Acosta, *Here Lies the Heart*, p. 251.

Bernhardt and Duse . . . (caption) Shawell, "Garbo or Dietrich?" p. 17.

172 *Mercedes de Acosta looked* . . . Riva, *Marlene Dietrich by Her Daughter*, p. 153.

I believed, without . . . Acosta, *Here Lies the Heart*, p. 76.

Be careful . . . Schanke, *That Furious Lesbian*, p. 163.

After thorough . . . Viertel, *The Kindness of Strangers*, p. 152.

It's a waste . . . Ibid., p. 152.

There is nothing . . . Payne, *The Great Garbo*, p. 208.

The love story . . . Viertel, *The Kindness of Strangers*, p. 162.

Here they should build . . . (caption) Riva, *Marlene Dietrich by Her Daughter*, p. 154.

173 *an opportunity to sing* . . . Baxter, *Just Watch!*, p. 67.

When I had finished . . . Beaton, *Cecil Beaton*, p. 209.

Metro was moving . . . Viertel, *The Kindness of Strangers*, p. 152.

Greta came to . . . Acosta, *Here Lies the Heart*, p. 235.

We'll see whether . . . *Motion Picture*, September 1932, quoted in Swenson, *Greta Garbo*, p. 284.

It came at an . . . "Bank Failure Hits Screen Players."

I'm afraid I am . . . Acosta, *Here Lies the Heart*, p. 217.

174 *Somebody joked* . . . Beaton, *Cecil Beaton*, p. 209.

I had to sign . . . Ibid.

That's Ernst . . . Acosta, *Here Lies the Heart*, p. 240.

I did not know . . . Viertel, *The Kindness of Strangers*, p. 169.

dull political content . . . "Reader's Report, July 29, 1932," *Queen Christina* file, MGM-USC.

The love that . . . Ibid.

As things often go . . . Acosta, *Here Lies the Heart*, p. 169.

175 *The Garbo-Mercedes* . . . Vickers, *Loving Garbo*, p. 4.

Auf wiedersehen . . . Swenson, *Greta Garbo*, p. 287.

After she left . . . Acosta, *Here Lies the Heart*, p. 233.

As you know . . . Viertel, *The Kindness of Strangers*, p. 173.

You had a very bad . . . Ibid., p. 175.

jolly blonde . . . Ibid., p. 174.

176 *My suggestions were* . . . Ibid., p. 175.

What I do . . . "Garbo at Home Drops Cloak of Mystery."

Thalberg had one . . . Riva, *Marlene Dietrich by Her Daughter*, p. 154.

177 *My mother told* . . . Ibid.

I was working . . . Fountain, *Dark Star*, p. 226.

he was furious and fired her . . . The Youssoupoffs sued M-G-M and won a large, undisclosed sum. The scene was cut from the negative of the film, which had been released as *Rasputin and the Empress*.

It will be hard to . . . Schanke, *That Furious Lesbian*, p. 114.

Please come . . . Ibid.

I know that I am . . . Swenson, *Greta Garbo*, p. 303.

We had always . . . Viertel, *The Kindness of Strangers*, p. 170.

Always clever . . . "Greta Garbo—Her Life Story."

We plodded . . . Viertel, *The Kindness of Strangers*, p. 178.

178 *Rouben Mamoulian was* . . . Riva, *Marlene Dietrich by Her Daughter*, p. 160.

Finally the studio . . . Ibid., p. 183.

You think nothing . . . "H. M. Harwood, April 27, 1933," *Queen Christina* file, MGM-USC.

The Christina *script* . . . Viertel, *The Kindness of Strangers*, p. 183.

It sounds all . . . "Notes by H. M. Harwood [undated]," *Queen Christina* file, MGM-USC.

Sex was to . . . Ibid.

The most important . . . "Notes by Salka Viertel, April 22, 1933," *Queen Christina* file, MGM-USC.

179 *We used to do* . . . Beaton, *Cecil Beaton*, p. 257.

Anyone who . . . Hodgekins, "Garbo's Gamble," p. 37.

And here's one . . . Ibid.

Garbo didn't like . . . Unsourced clipping, Garbo file, USC.

180 *a slight man* . . . Riva, *Marlene Dietrich by Her Daughter*, p. 159.

Greta and Harry . . . Unsourced clipping, June 9, 1933, Garbo file, USC.

Contrary to all . . . Viertel, *The Kindness of Strangers*, p. 152.

I learned from . . . Ibid., p. 188.

Sam Behrman . . . Ibid., p. 189.

I think that taking . . . Payne, *The Great Garbo*, p. 218.

brilliant, witty . . . Viertel, *The Kindness of Strangers*, p. 189.

I can't work . . . Haining, *The Legend of Garbo*, p. 197.

We photograph . . . (caption) Chapman, "The Only Man Who Knows Garbo," p. 60.

181 *Why don't you ask* . . . Haining, *The Legend of Garbo*, p. 197.

On her way . . . Hare, "Mamoulian Talks about Garbo," p. 30.

I read the manuscript . . . Kobler, *Damned in Paradise*, p. 263.

Barrymore was . . . Rouben Mamoulian, interview by Kevin Brownlow, excerpt courtesy of Photoplay Productions.

added to the terrific . . . Carr, *Four Fabulous Faces*, p. 121.

I raved . . . Viertel, *The Kindness of Strangers*, p. 190.

My performances . . . Olivier, *Laurence Olivier on Acting*, p. 253.

Christina turns to . . . "'Queen Christina,' Harvey Gates, July 29, 1933," *Queen Christina* file, MGM-USC.

Marlene Dietrich floats . . . Sennwald, "Marlene Dietrich in Mamoulian's Jeweled Version of *The Song of Songs*."

an era that has . . . Shawell, "Garbo or Dietrich?" p. 17.

From a critical . . . Carr, *Four Fabulous Faces*, p. 121.

182 *It was a silent* . . . Haining, *The Legend of Garbo*, p. 265.

I made a rather . . . Hare, "Mamoulian Talks about Garbo," p. 30.

I never had anyone . . . Beaton, *Cecil Beaton*, p. 210.

I understand . . . Haining, *The Legend of Garbo*, p. 197.

We assume . . . Letter, James Wingate to Eddie Mannix, August 7, 1933, *Queen Christina* file, PCA.

So let's have . . . Haining, *The Legend of Garbo*, p. 197.

I never rehearsed . . . Beaton, *Cecil Beaton*, p. 210.

Well, Miss Garbo . . . Haining, *The Legend of Garbo*, p. 198.

183 *Mamoulian had already* . . . Behrman, *People in a Diary*, p. 149.

I didn't want to know . . . Beaton, *Cecil Beaton*, p. 210.

wearing loose lounging . . . Maxwell, "The Amazing Story behind Garbo's Choice of Gilbert," p. 32.

I went boldly . . . Olivier, *Confessions of an Actor*, p. 122.

The stage was set . . . Maxwell, "The Amazing Story behind Garbo's Choice of Gilbert," p. 33.

So she simply . . . Fountain, *Dark Star*, p. 234.

I stayed home . . . Ibid., p. 233.

184 *Garbo's face* . . . Maxwell, "The Amazing Story behind Garbo's Choice of Gilbert," p. 33.

Here I am . . . Fountain, *Dark Star*, p. 234.

I looked at the screen . . . Rouben Mamoulian, interview by Kevin Brownlow, excerpt courtesy of Photoplay Productions.

Larry, I want . . . Olivier, *Confessions of an Actor*, p. 123.

Get down here . . . Fountain, *Dark Star*, p. 234.

Why it's . . . Hamann, *Greta Garbo in the 30s*, p. 38.

She was exactly . . . Billquist, *Garbo*, p. 187.

There's never been . . . St. Johns, *Love, Laughter, and Tears*, p. 252.

Garbo had . . . Fountain, *Dark Star*, p. 234.

You know what started . . . Ibid., p. 233.

I asked Gilbert . . . Broman, *Conversations with Greta Garbo*, p. 123.

I have been struggling . . . Ibid., p. 118.

I can't laugh . . . Haining, *The Legend of Garbo*, p. 198.

Col. [Jason] Joy . . . Memo to SRC files from John V. Wilson, August 11, 1933, *Queen Christina* file, PCA.

I have imagined . . . "Mr. S. Behrman, August 22, 1933," *Queen Christina* file, PCA.

That scene I have . . . Chapman, "The Only Man Who Knows Garbo," p. 60.

You know how noisy . . . Ibid., p. 14.

186 *Mr. Gilbert is* . . . Bainbridge, *Garbo*, p. 208.

This has to be . . . Zierold, *Garbo*, p. 112.

It was a graphic . . . Sarris, *Interviews with Film Directors*, p. 292.

You did not have . . . Broman, *Conversations with Greta Garbo*, p. 122.

All the light . . . Higham, *Hollywood Cameramen*, p. 72.

During most of these . . . Walker, *Garbo*, p. 110.

I did learn . . . Broman, *Conversations with Greta Garbo*, p. 123.

As for the bedroom . . . Walker, *Garbo*, p. 110.

187 *We have received* . . . Letter, James Wingate to Eddie Mannix, September 5, 1933, *Queen Christina* file, PCA.

I wish to . . . Acosta, *Here Lies the Heart*, p. 251.

I was nervous . . . Fountain, *Dark Star*, p. 235.

When Jack was feeling . . . Ibid., p. 126.

I was sick over . . . Ibid., p. 239.

Sometimes he'd be awake . . . Ibid., p. 228.

She knew that I . . . Ibid., p. 235.

To illuminate . . . "When Greta Isn't Garbo."

There was no one . . . Fountain, *Dark Star*, p. 126.

The delays . . . Behrman, *People in a Diary*, p. 149.

I had to spend . . . Viertel, *The Kindness of Strangers*, p. 192.

It's been a difficult . . . Broman, *Conversations with Greta Garbo*, p. 119.

Where is Don Antonio . . . "Dialogue Continuity, Harvey H. Gates, July 28, 1933," *Queen Christina* story files, FCMPS.

188 *I had quite an* . . . Sarris, *Interviews with Film Directors*, p. 291.

a rhythmic progression . . . Ibid.

We needed a device . . . Ibid.

People don't really . . . (caption) "Garbo at Home Drops Cloak of Mystery. "

189 *With a tragic* . . . Sarris, *Interviews with Film Directors*, p. 292.

Garbo always stopped . . . Ibid., p. 291.

What do I express . . . Ibid., p. 292.

I feel I've almost . . . Broman, *Conversations with Greta Garbo*, p. 119.

Soon after entering . . . Hall, "Greta Garbo Appears as Queen Christina of Sweden."

There are two . . . Hamann, *Greta Garbo in the 30s*, p. 44.

registers with voluminous . . . Quigley, *Decency in Motion Pictures*, p. 37.

a perverted creature . . . Walsh, *Sin and Censorship*, p. 97.

It is quite apparent . . . Memo, Joseph I. Breen to James Wingate, January 8, 1934, *Queen Christina* file, PCA.

This jury . . . Letter, Secretary of Jury to Eddie Mannix, January 11, 1934, *Queen Christina* file, PCA.

190 *I am so ashamed* . . . Broman, *Conversations with Greta Garbo*, p. 119.

I tried to be . . . Bainbridge, *Garbo*, p. 211.

It is a great . . . "Tradeviews," *The Hollywood Reporter*, February 13, 1934.

There are times . . . Hamann, *Greta Garbo in the 30s*, p. 44.

clammy Queen Christina . . . Conway, *The Films of Greta Garbo*, p. 131.

handsomely . . . Ibid.

She identified . . . "Notes between Mr. Behrman and Mr. Davidson," unpublished transcript.

No one could have . . . Behrman, *People in a Diary*, p. 151.

Thanks to my . . . (caption) Broman, *Conversations with Greta Garbo*, p. 105.

Chapter Twenty

192 *Finally Acosta* . . . Riva, *Marlene Dietrich by Her Daughter*, p. 158.

She drove . . . Swenson, *Greta Garbo*, p. 303.

I have built . . . Riva, *Marlene Dietrich by Her Daughter*, p. 169.

193 *If he comes back* . . . Hamann, *Greta Garbo in the 30s*, p. 39.

The restless look . . . Ibid.

I was feeling . . . Fountain, *Dark Star*, p. 237.

Metro is chastising . . . Ibid., p. 238.

Mr. Gilbert's makeup . . . Hall, "Miss Garbo and Others."

Where are you . . . Zierold, *Garbo*, p. 68.

Word had gotten around . . . Ibid., p. 241.

In his mid-thirties . . . Niven, *Bring On the Empty Horses*, p. 175.

194 *We were talking* . . . Carr, *Four Fabulous Faces*, p. 120.

Salka was AC/DC . . . Paris, *Garbo*, p. 263.

She was no more . . . Ibid., p. 186.

We'll make them . . . Acosta, *Here Lies the Heart*, p. 258.

When I returned . . . Riva, *Marlene Dietrich by Her Daughter*, p. 169.

Greta for three . . . Ibid.

I believed that Greta . . . Acosta, *Here Lies the Heart*, p. 258.

She talked a great . . . Schanke, *That Furious Lesbian*, p. 120.

196 *I have repressed* . . . Viertel, *The Kindness of Strangers*, p. 197.

pretty strong . . . Letter, Joseph I. Breen to Irving G. Thalberg, April 2, 1934, *The Painted Veil* file, PCA.

197 *If the sale of black* . . . Black, *Hollywood Censored*, p. 100.

A vicious and . . . "Cardinal Bans All Pix."

Purify Hollywood . . . Black, *Hollywood Censored*, p. 167.

Hollywood is . . . Schallert, "Film Producers Shaken by Clean-up Campaign," p. 1.

With the new . . . "Hollywood Cleans House." *New York Times*, July 15, 1934, p. X3.

She and Jehanne . . . Acosta, *Here Lies the Heart*, p. 259.

So complete . . . Schanke, *That Furious Lesbian*, p. 120.

198 *Yet curiously* . . . Acosta, *Here Lies the Heart*, p. 259.

a monogram . . . Hamann, *Greta Garbo in the 30s*, p. 49.

199 *Here was an artistic* . . . Wiles, "What It's Like to Work with Garbo," p. 43.

It was thought . . . Ibid.

During these drenching . . . Ibid., p. 80.

She was so completely . . . Bainbridge, *Garbo*, p. 213.

200 *I could only do* . . . Beaton, *Cecil Beaton*, p. 210.

anxious and straightforward . . . Wiles, "What It's Like to Work with Garbo," p. 80.

Rubbish . . . Broman, *Conversations with Greta Garbo*, p. 152.

I am still not . . . Ibid.

201 *I have never met* . . . Wiles, "What It's Like to Work with Garbo," p. 80.

He praised it . . . Acosta, *Here Lies the Heart*, p. 259.

I'm lying on . . . Broman, *Conversations with Greta Garbo*, p. 153.

Garbo's European . . . Bainbridge, *Garbo*, p. 212.

For the life of . . . Hamann, *Greta Garbo in the 30s*, p. 52.

Garbo does not want . . . Acosta, *Here Lies the Heart*, p. 259.

202 *Sternberg has achieved* . . . Dickens, *The Films of Marlene Dietrich*, p. 115.

Under [Sternberg's] tutelage . . . Ibid.

A ponderous . . . Sennwald, "Mr. von Sternberg Presents Miss Dietrich."

an arty disaster . . . West, *Goodness Had Nothing to Do with It*, p. 196.

The star's clothes . . . Churchill, "Out of the Golden West."

No star . . . Hamann, *W. S. Van Dyke in the 30s*, p. 41.

slow, confused . . . *Variety*, November 3, 1934.

heavy treatment . . . *Motion Picture Daily*, November 5, 1934.

The wedding of . . . "Miscellaneous Sections of Dialogue from Rowland Leigh, September 15, 1934," *Painted Veil* story files, MGM-USC.

Hi, honey . . . Cannom, *Van Dyke and the Mythical City, Hollywood*, p. 373.

Garbo and I did . . . Haining, *The Legend of Garbo*, p. 205.

204 *The script says* . . . Daum, *Walking with Garbo*, p. 149.

Again Greta Garbo . . . Conway, *The Films of Greta Garbo*, p. 126.

It is the height . . . Sennwald, "Greta Garbo Makes Her Semi-Annual Screen Appearance."

Chapter Twenty-one

205 *Miss Garbo, the* . . . (caption) Sennwald, "Greta Garbo as the Star of a New Version of *Anna Karenina*."

206 *The trend to* . . . Lewin, "A Guide to the Study of the Screen Version of Tolstoy's *Anna Karenina*," p. 11.

It did not take . . . Viertel, *The Kindness of Strangers*, p. 197.

We undertook the . . . Lewin, "A Guide to the Study of the Screen Version of Tolstoy's *Anna Karenina*," p. 11.

David wanted . . . Viertel, *The Kindness of Strangers*, p. 197.

She was aghast . . . Lewin, "A Guide to the Study of the Screen Version of Tolstoy's *Anna Karenina*," p. 11.

Miss Dane . . . Niven, *Bring On the Empty Horses*, p. 346.

We did not leave . . . Letter, James Wingate to Joseph Breen, October 23, 1934, *Anna Karenina* file, PCA.

207 *With the dice* . . . Sternberg, *Fun in a Chinese Laundry*, p. 266.

Our first blow . . . Lewin, "A Guide to the Study of the Screen Version of Tolstoy's *Anna Karenina*," p. 12.

To eliminate this . . . Rathbone, *In and Out of Character*, p. 138.

To my mind . . . Haver, *David O. Selznick's Hollywood*, p. 163.

We were sorely . . . Lewin, "A Guide to the Study of the Screen Version of Tolstoy's *Anna Karenina*," p. 12.

How are you getting . . . Letter, Hugh Walpole to George Cukor, December 1, 1934, FCMPS.

I have read . . . Letter, Joseph Breen to Louis B. Mayer, December 21, 1934, *Anna Karenina* file, PCA.

couldn't face all . . . Letter, George Cukor to Hugh Walpole, December 25, 1934, FCMPS.

When working with . . . (caption) *M-G-M: When the Lion Roars*, documentary film.

208 *Mercedes d' Acosta* . . . Schanke, *That Furious Lesbian*, p. 120.

Selznick found . . . Viertel, *The Kindness of Strangers*, p. 198.

We have lost . . . Behlmer, *Memo from: David O. Selznick*, p. 110.

209 *Sam Behrman* . . . Viertel, *The Kindness of Strangers*, p. 198.

I became . . . Behrman, *People in a Diary*, p. 151.

I can give you . . . Hamann, *Greta Garbo in the 30s*, p. 55.

They are trying to . . . Ibid.

Walking up and . . . Viertel, *The Kindness of Strangers*, p. 198.

Her relation with . . . "Notes between Mr. Behrman and Mr. Davidson," unpublished transcript.

210 *I really did* . . . Broman, *Conversations with Greta Garbo*, p. 152.

Anna Karenina is. . . Hamann, *Greta Garbo in the 30s*, p. 56.

If you weren't . . . "Adrian Answers Twenty Questions on Garbo."

As we see it . . . Letter, Joseph Breen to Louis B. Mayer, March 5, 1935, *Anna Karenina* file, PCA.

I am distressed . . . Letter, David O. Selznick to Joseph Breen, March 7, 1935, *Anna Karenina* file, PCA.

Lengthen this . . . "Anna Karenina" notes, March 12, 1935, *Anna Karenina* file, MGM-USC.

avoid shooting . . . Letter, Joseph Breen to David O. Selznick, March 12, 1935, *Anna Karenina* file, PCA.

the sin of Anna . . . Joseph Breen, Annual Report, March 15, 1936, PCA.

211 *When I read the script* . . . Beaton, *Cecil Beaton*, p. 289.

Mr. Selznick drove . . . Rathbone, *In and Out of Character*, p. 138.

In Chapter Twelve . . . Haver, *David O. Selznick's Hollywood*, p. 163.

212 *Formerly it disturbed* . . . "Garbo at Close Range."

Do you mean . . . O'Dowd, "Why Garbo Quit Movies," p. 14.

We would bounce . . . Zierold, *Garbo*, p. 90.

I used to go . . . Haining, *The Legend of Garbo*, p. 223.

I have never met . . . Ibid., p. 224.

It may be argued . . . (caption) *"Anna Karenina," Daily Variety*, June 29, 1935.

If her attitude . . . Rathbone, *In and Out of Character*, p. 141.

213 *As an actress* . . . Parish, *The Best of MGM*, p. 8.

I thought she . . . Daum, *Walking with Garbo*, p. 149.

She knew just . . . Bainbridge, *Garbo*, p. 215.

She made tiny . . . Haining, *The Legend of Garbo*, p. 224.

I told her one . . . Zierold, *Garbo*, p. 90.

Imagine a production . . . Daum, *Walking with Garbo*, p. 79.

I did see her . . . "Notes between Mr. Behrman and Mr. Davidson," unpublished transcript.

I don't think she . . . Stull, "Garbo's Cameraman."

Miss Dietrich and I . . . Walker, *Dietrich*, p. 122.

It is not hard . . . Sennwald, "The Paramount Presents Mr. Sternberg's *Devil Is a Woman*."

Not even Garbo . . . Sarris, *The Films of Josef von Sternberg*, p. 42.

214 *Miss Garbo* . . . Rathbone, *In and Out of Character*, p. 138.

Greta Garbo loves . . . *M-G-M: When the Lion Roars*, documentary film.

I managed to . . . Skolsky, *Don't Get Me Wrong—I Love Hollywood*, p. 133.

I drove out . . . Behrman, *People in a Diary*, p. 151.

216 *Nothing mattered* . . . Paris, *Garbo*, p. 319.

Never before or . . . Selznick, *A Private View*, p. 197.

He said he had . . . Behrman, *People in a Diary*, p. 151.

The picture looks . . . Haver, *David O. Selznick's Hollywood*, p. 164.

Greta Garbo, after . . . Conway, *The Films of Greta Garbo*, p. 132.

a dignified and . . . Sennwald, "Greta Garbo as the Star of a New Version of *Anna Karenina*." Less than five months after writing about Garbo's suicide scene, André Sennwald, whose expressive reviews were such an improvement over his predecessor's, turned on the gas in his two-room penthouse apartment and killed himself. He was twenty-eight, had been married less than a year, and was going blind.

This is a weak . . . Conway, *The Films of Greta Garbo*, p. 132.

Garbo asked me to . . . Haver, *David O. Selznick's Hollywood*, p. 167.

Chapter Twenty-two

217 *Greta Garbo is in* . . . Lewis, *The Creative Producer*, p. 65.

When I walked . . . Ibid.

When you return . . . Acosta, *Here Lies the Heart*, p. 262.

As I was considered . . . Viertel, *The Kindness of Strangers*, p. 199.

two thousand . . . Bach, *Marlene Dietrich*, p. 201.

218 *Lubitsch was* . . . Eyman, *Ernst Lubitsch*, p. 197.

I had to go . . . Riva, *Marlene Dietrich by Her Daughter*, p. 316.

I was dancing . . . McKay, "Interview with Elizabeth Allan."

Marlene was unable . . . Higham, *Marlene*, p. 164.

Thalberg was going . . . Lambert, *On Cukor*, p. 108.

I waited almost . . . Letter, Greta Garbo to Salka Viertel, November 22, 1935, courtesy of Photoplay Productions.

219 *his health* . . . Walker, *Garbo*, p. 148.

My mother admitted . . . Riva, *Marlene Dietrich by Her Daughter*, p. 267.

She behaves . . . Marx, *Mayer and Thalberg*, p. 301.

On my first day . . . Acosta, *Here Lies the Heart*, p. 273.

220 *iron out* . . . Beauchamp, *Without Lying Down*, p. 250.

The play presented . . . Lambert, *On Cukor*, p. 108.

Frances and Jimmy . . . Lewis, *The Creative Producer*, p. 65.

Frances was having . . . Ibid., p. 83.

I'm worried . . . Schanke, *That Furious Lesbian*, p. 129.

something like the . . . Swenson, *Greta Garbo*, p. 350.

Please, you will not . . . Proctor, "Scoop! At Last Garbo Really Talks," p. 35.

221 *You have put too* . . . Letter, Joseph Breen to Louis B. Mayer, May 18, 1936, *Camille* file, PCA.

I read it with. . . Lewis, *The Creative Producer*, p. 83.

She was on the . . . Ibid., p. 87.

We have a problem . . . Thomas, *Thalberg*, p. 306.

Instead of the story . . . Lewis, *The Creative Producer*, p. 85.

After I saw how . . . (caption) Watts, *Behind the Screen*, p. 22.

222 *We discussed* . . . Walker, *Garbo*, p. 150.

Went to Mr. Hyman . . . Ibid.

I sensed that she . . . Watts, *Behind the Screen*, p. 22.

Police had . . . Hamann, *Greta Garbo in the 30s*, p. 67.

We can't miss . . . Marion, *Off with Their Heads!*, p. 265.

I was scared . . . Zierold, *Garbo*, p. 90.

Stage 23 . . . "*Camille* Supplement," p. 4.

Miss Akins and . . . Lewis, *The Creative Producer*, p. 86.

She gave no impression . . . Marion, *Off with Their Heads!*, p. 265.

I was one of the . . . Zierold, *Garbo*, p. 96.

Don't drop . . . (caption) Chester W. Schaeffer, interview by author, February 4, 1973.

223 *I wanted to show* . . . Lambert, *On Cukor*, p. 112.

Of course I was . . . Hamann, *Greta Garbo in the 30s*, p. 68.

Is the feet . . . Bainbridge, *Garbo*, p. 220.

Garbo didn't talk . . . Ibid., p. 223.

During the first . . . Hamann, *Greta Garbo in the 30s*, p. 68.

In an apparent . . . Ibid., p. 67.

She said that when . . . McGilligan, *George Cukor*, p. 109.

George, she's awfully . . . Ibid.

She is a fascinating . . . Thomas, *Thalberg*, p. 308.

While I was explaining . . . Viertel, *The Kindness of Strangers*, p. 210.

On the set she . . . Haining, *The Legend of Garbo*, p. 255.

Greta Garbo has been . . . Hamann, *Greta Garbo in the 30s*, p. 69.

She started giving . . . Zierold, *Garbo*, p. 92.

Armand comes in . . . Lambert, *On Cukor*, p. 109.

224 *She did this memorable* . . . Ibid.

I think we have . . . Lewis, *The Creative Producer*, p. 86.

If only they . . . Marx, *Mayer and Thalberg*, p. 247.

So weighty . . . Hamann, *Greta Garbo in the 30s*, p. 70.

I've been put . . . Thomas, *Thalberg*, p. 308.

We were having coffee . . . Viertel, *The Kindness of Strangers*, p. 212.

I went into the anteroom . . . Lewis, *The Creative Producer*, p. 100.

Only a few . . . Viertel, *The Kindness of Strangers*, p. 212.

There was no one . . . Ibid.

I liked him . . . Broman, *Conversations with Greta Garbo*, p. 65.

I felt that there . . . Acosta, *Here Lies the Heart*, p. 278.

My mother had . . . Long, *George Cukor*, p. 9.

Cukor gave me . . . Broman, *Conversations with Greta Garbo*, p. 152.

Garbo wouldn't . . . Bach, *Marlene Dietrich*, p. 214.

225 *Everything in the film* . . . Lewis, *The Creative Producer*, p. 98.

Garbo wore . . . Hamann, *Greta Garbo in the 30s*, p. 70.

He was so fascinated . . . Lewis, *The Creative Producer*, p. 98.

She often did . . . Lambert, *On Cukor*, p. 114.

I was scared . . . (caption) Zierold, *Garbo*, p. 90.

226 *If I hadn't been so* . . . Broman, *Conversations with Greta Garbo*, p. 158.

I walked her . . . Lewis, *The Creative Producer*, p. 107.

It's finished . . . Ibid., p. 86.

He always seemed . . . McGilligan, *George Cukor*, p. 124.

[Cukor] had that taste . . . Ibid., p. 130.

I have never worked . . . Broman, *Conversations with Greta Garbo*, p. 158.

It was a great . . . Acosta, *Here Lies the Heart*, p. 273.

227 *We had to make* . . . Broman, *Conversations with Greta Garbo*, p. 152.

The screen is just . . . Lambert, *On Cukor*, p. 114.

After three times . . . Zierold, *Garbo*, p. 92.

Garbo was so . . . Isherwood, *Diaries*, p. 761.

Salka Viertel said . . . Lewis, *The Creative Producer*, p. 93.

Garbo always went . . . Haining, *The Legend of Garbo*, p. 255.

If you're going . . . Broman, *Conversations with Greta Garbo*, p. 139.

She told me . . . Paris, *Garbo*, p. 334.

Hyman's new . . . Lewis, *The Creative Producer*, p. 109.

229 *I'll have a new* . . . Ibid., p. 110.

Camille never . . . Broman, *Conversations with Greta Garbo*, p. 162.

It's great! . . . Lewis, *The Creative Producer*, p. 110.

I ran into . . . Ibid., p. 107.

When illness . . . Hamann, *Greta Garbo in the 30s*, p. 72.

Perhaps it is . . . Ibid., p. 73.

It's a brief . . . *Variety*, January 27, 1937.

Greta Garbo's performance . . . Nugent, "Camille."

I heard a plaintive . . . Lewis, *The Creative Producer*, p. 86.

I wouldn't have . . . (caption) Long, *George Cukor*, p. 9.

Chapter Twenty-three

232 *Metro makes*. . . Nugent, "The Great Waltz."

The best Garbo . . . Viertel, *The Kindness of Strangers*, p. 214.

I was thinking about . . . Letter, Greta Garbo to Salka Viertel, July 10, 1935, courtesy of Photoplay Productions.

The story deals . . . Letter, Charles R. Metzger to Joseph I. Breen, December 5, 1935, *Conquest* file, PCA.

We are particularly . . . Letter, Joseph I. Breen to Louis B. Mayer, December 10, 1935, *Conquest* file, PCA.

233 *I began to work* . . . Viertel, *The Kindness of Strangers*, p. 206.

I cannot bear . . . Ibid., p. 212.

I wished to convey . . . Behrman, *People in a Diary*, p. 162.

I was fearful . . . Swindell, *Charles Boyer*, p. 97.

It seemed likely . . . Viertel, *The Kindness of Strangers*, p. 206.

Bernie Hyman was . . . Behrman, *People in a Diary*, p. 158.

no heart, was sophisticated . . . Viertel, *The Kindness of Strangers*, p. 213.

234 *I'm afraid this* . . . Broman, *Conversations with Greta Garbo*, p. 157.

the slightest idea . . . Swenson, *Greta Garbo*, p. 365.

Stoki didn't waste . . . Bainbridge, *Garbo*, p. 226.

235 *My latest physician* . . . Broman, *Conversations with Greta Garbo*, p. 157.

Often I wondered . . . Viertel, *The Kindness of Strangers*, p. 215.

Even when Garbo . . . Beaton, *Cecil Beaton*, p. 248.

You know, I don't . . . McGilligan, *George Cukor*, p. 109.

My last hunt . . . Broman, *Conversations with Greta Garbo*, p. 157.

In one scene . . . Zierold, *Garbo*, p. 88.

What dope . . . Hamann, *Greta Garbo in the 30s*, p. 77.

During the whole . . . Viertel, *The Kindness of Strangers*, p. 216.

236 *G. G., what* . . . Zierold, *Garbo*, p. 88.

I give them . . . Brownlow, *The Parade's Gone By*, p. 148.

I am incredibly . . . Broman, *Conversations with Greta Garbo*, p. 157.

She was tremendously . . . Higham, *Marlene*, p. 180.

Lee Garmes had . . . Ibid., p. 179.

The money M-G-M spent . . . (caption) "Greta Garbo in *Conquest*."

237 *Greta Garbo had* . . . Brownlow, *The Parade's Gone By*, p. 148.

heartbreaking . . . Viertel, *The Kindness of Strangers*, p. 213.

You look tired . . . Bainbridge, *Garbo*, p. 184.

She is wearing . . . Bach, *Marlene Dietrich*, p. 201.

If Conquest *cost* . . . Nugent, "*Conquest*, a Napoleonic Romance."

238 Conquest *is of road* . . . "*Conquest*."

Garbo is completely . . . Hamann, *Greta Garbo in the 30s*, p. 87.

Madame Garbo's . . . Conway, *The Films of Greta Garbo*, p. 142.

The costliest picture . . . Hamann, *Greta Garbo in the 30s*, p. 89.

I have been away . . . Broman, *Conversations with Greta Garbo*, p. 164.

Chapter Twenty-four

239 *Garbo was the only* . . . Griffith, *The Movies*, p. 353.

It never pleased . . . Beaton, *Cecil Beaton*, p. 258.

240 *Garbo was* . . . Eyman, *Ernst Lubitsch*, p. 267.

She had a fanatical . . . Brownlow, *The Parade's Gone By*, p. 169.

After Conquest *was* . . . Viertel, *The Kindness of Strangers*, p. 206.

You are incorrigible! . . . Ibid.

Always smiling . . . Ibid.

Over the years . . . Stanley, "How Garbo Laughed."

241 *There is no reason* . . . "Ninotchka (Love Is Not So Simple) by Melchior Lengyel, August 25, 1937," *Ninotchka* file, MGM-USC.

With the influx . . . Behrman, *People in a Diary*, p. 163.

I walked in . . . Schnayerson, *Irwin Shaw*, p. 117.

The greatest contrasts . . . Reinhardt, *The Genius*, p. 303.

No, I am not going . . . Grinstead, "With Garbo at Home," p. 27.

242 *What makes you* . . . Viertel, *The Kindness of Strangers*, p. 218.

Aldous wants it . . . Dardis, *Some Time in the Sun*, p. 192.

It stinks . . . Viertel, *The Kindness of Strangers*, p. 223.

Anita couldn't . . . Carey, *Anita Loos*, p. 192.

Compare Garbo's . . . (caption) Fragmentary clipping, Garbo file, USC.

243 *As soon as I* . . . Viertel, *The Kindness of Strangers*, p. 238.

On a very large . . . Rathbone, *In and Out of Character*, p. 143.

LEON: Am I . . . "Ninotchka by S. N. Behrman, November 15, 1938," *Ninotchka* file, MGM-USC.

244 *This sort of let* . . . "Telephone: Mr. Reinhardt—Mr. Franklin, November 16, 1938," *Ninotchka* file, MGM-USC.

The minute . . . Eyman, *Ernst Lubitsch*, p. 267.

I just want to prove . . . Zolotow, *Billy Wilder in Hollywood*, p. 80.

245 *I don't like to work* . . . Beaton, *Cecil Beaton*, p. 258.

Because she was funny . . . Kanin, *Hollywood*, p. 87.

Garbo arrived . . . Zierold, *Garbo*, p. 98.

In case M-G-M . . . Hamann, *Greta Garbo in the 30s*, p. 92.

Can you laugh? . . . Kanin, *Hollywood*, p. 88.

I feel it is wicked . . . (caption) Paris, *Garbo*, p. 389.

Greta likes the cooking . . . Hamann, *Greta Garbo in the 30s*, p. 92.

246 *The nice thing* . . . Eyman, *Ernst Lubitsch*, p. 267.

We were in Sidney . . . Ibid.

Brackett, Reisch . . . Madsen, *Billy Wilder*, p. 39.

Boys, I've got . . . Sikov, *The Life and Times of Billy Wilder*, p. 135.

Now that is the . . . Madsen, *Billy Wilder*, p. 39.

It was so much . . . Brackett, Interview with Joan and Robert C. Franklin.

He wasn't just . . . Sikov, *The Life and Times of Billy Wilder*, p. 136.

use of the word . . . Letter, Joseph I. Breen to Louis B. Mayer, May 24, 1939, *Ninotchka* file, PCA.

247 *I don't think that* . . . Lubitsch, "Garbo, as Seen by Her Director."

Garbo was uncommunicative . . . Maxwell, *R.S.V.P.*, p. 241.

My studio is . . . Broman, *Conversations with Greta Garbo*, p. 153.

On her first . . . Hamann, *Greta Garbo in the 30s*, p. 92.

There never was . . . Beaton, *Cecil Beaton*, p. 258.

I remember going . . . Sikov, *The Life and Times of Billy Wilder*, p. 137.

248 *Are you ready* . . . Zierold, *Garbo*, p. 65.

Roses I got to . . . Unsourced clipping, Garbo microfilm files, FCMPS.

Lubitsch came to . . . Viertel, *The Kindness of Strangers*, p. 223.

I was frequently . . . Douglas, *See You at the Movies*, p. 89.

The most hilarious . . . "Notes about *Ninotchka*," *Ninotchka* Souvenir Program excerpt, Garbo file, USC.

She didn't show . . . Douglas, *See You at the Movies*, p. 89.

Lubitsch was clever . . . Beaton, *Cecil Beaton*, p. 239.

I remember one morning . . . Ibid.

Never since I had . . . Acosta, *Here Lies the Heart*, p. 259.

Having worked with . . . Lubitsch, "Garbo, as Seen by Her Director."

249 *She was unable* . . . Douglas, *See You at the Movies*, p. 89.

When we finally . . . Lubitsch, "Garbo, as Seen by Her Director."

The girl in the . . . Higham, *Marlene*, 190.

the equal of Destry . . . Ibid.

I knew Marlene . . . Ibid.

250 *I put you on* . . . Bach, *Marlene Dietrich*, p. 246.

Unless the film . . . Hedda Hopper, *Los Angeles Times*, August 25, 1939, fragmentary clipping, Garbo file, USC.

The lady went . . . Swenson, *Greta Garbo*, p. 399.

She was so excited . . . Ibid., p. 395.

The face . . . Zolotow, *Billy Wilder in Hollywood*, p. 84.

251 *Do you like yourself* . . . Lubitsch, "Garbo, as Seen by Her Director."

My film . . . Broman, *Conversations with Greta Garbo*, p. 186.

On the day . . . Viertel, *The Kindness of Strangers*, p. 242.

Stalin won't . . . Nugent, "*Ninotchka*, an Impious Soviet Satire."

Now that she . . . Conway, *The Films of Greta Garbo*, p. 148.

252 *Exhibitors who* . . . "Ninotchka."

protests and forlorn . . . Nugent, "Entirely a Laughing Matter."

Marlene Dietrich returns . . . Bach, *Marlene Dietrich*, p. 254.

Here is a Dietrich . . . Ibid.

a trouper with . . . Ibid.

Surprise picture . . . Fragmentary clipping, Garbo file, USC.

I still don't know . . . Broman, *Conversations with Greta Garbo*, p. 188.

relief from nervous . . . Ibid., p. 174.

Chapter Twenty-five

254 *When are you coming* . . . Viertel, *The Kindness of Strangers*, p. 247.

I was astonished . . . Behrman, *People in a Diary*, p. 153.

I wouldn't have done . . . Eyman, *Ernst Lubitsch*, p. 270.

She made age-old . . . Ibid.

He said he had several . . . Behrman, *People in a Diary*, p. 153.

255 *A pity that we cannot* . . . Reinhardt, *The Genius*, p. 100.

She was the only . . . Paris, *Garbo*, p. 373.

She talked quite freely . . . Beaton, *Cecil Beaton*, p. 239.

Garbo didn't care . . . Eyman, *Ernst Lubitsch*, p. 267.

The locale was . . . Viertel, *The Kindness of Strangers*, p. 247.

I don't know . . . Broman, *Conversations with Greta Garbo*, p. 189.

Greta Garbo had the local . . . "Not Only Alone, but Unique."

256 *Fur will fly* . . . Swenson, *Greta Garbo*, p. 114.

I gave up . . . Viertel, *The Kindness of Strangers*, p. 247.

I was terribly upset . . . Acosta, *Here Lies the Heart*, p. 314.

The studio made . . . Ibid.

The setting of . . . Viertel, *The Kindness of Strangers*, p. 247.

Garbo picked . . . Gilbert, *Opposite Attraction*, p. 242.

257 *bombardment of jealousy* . . . Ibid.

The conferences with . . . Viertel, *The Kindness of Strangers*, p. 248.

At the time when . . . Ibid.

Watching the view . . . "Notes between Mr. Behrman and Mr. Davidson," unpublished transcript.

Sam Behrman and . . . Viertel, *The Kindness of Strangers*, p. 252.

258 *We certainly didn't* . . . McGilligan, *George Cukor*, p. 165.

In those days . . . Reinhardt, *The Genius*, p. 104.

Due to the fact . . . Letter, Joseph I. Breen to Bernard Hyman, June 17, 1941, *Two-Faced Woman* file, PCA.

They wanted to make . . . Hedda Hopper interview, Garbo microfilm files, FCMPS.

The camera crew . . . "How Cukor Directs Garbo," p. 7.

This is a distance . . . "She Works with Garbo," p. 13.

259 *Griselda Vaughn* . . . "The Twins, August 20, 1941," *Two-Faced Woman* file, MGM-USC.

Behrman did most . . . Oppenheimer, *The View from the Sixties*, p. 155.

We had too many . . . McGilligan, *George Cukor*, p. 166.

I've started work . . . Broman, *Conversations with Greta Garbo*, p. 193.

She held . . . Douglas, *See You at the Movies*, p. 89.

Only four times . . . "How Cukor Directs Garbo," p. 8.

I refused many . . . "She Works with Garbo," p. 13.

I had heard . . . Oppenheimer, *The View from the Sixties*, p. 156.

Two days before . . . Eyman, *Five American Cinematographers*, p. 43.

Isn't that beautiful . . . Joseph Ruttenberg Oral History, American Film Institute.

They tried to put . . . Eyman, *Five American Cinematographers*, p. 43.

260 *Go away* . . . Paris, *Garbo*, p. 378.

261 *There are some* . . . "She Works with Garbo," p. 13.

Robert Alton . . . Oppenheimer, *The View from the Sixties*, p. 156.

If I were to write . . . Beaton, *Cecil Beaton*, p. 258.

I must work in . . . Ibid.

She couldn't impose . . . "Notes between Mr. Behrman and Mr. Davidson," unpublished transcript.

They're trying . . . Haining, *The Legend of Garbo*, p. 35.

I'll soon be finished . . . Broman, *Conversations with Greta Garbo*, p. 195.

Even while we were . . . Lambert, *On Cukor*, p. 109.

It was because . . . Hedda Hopper interview, Garbo microfilm files, FCMPS.

I'm sorry that you're . . . Leonard Stanley, interview by author, September 3, 1993.

Garbo was strange . . . Eyman, *Ernst Lubitsch*, p. 267.

described in graphic . . . Frye, "The Garbo Next Door," p. 232.
Someone sold . . . Oppenheimer, *The View from the Sixties*, p. 156.
262 *Two-Faced Woman was* . . . Frye, "The Garbo Next Door," p. 232.
[Garbo] with curls . . . Gilbert, *Opposite Attraction*, p. 243.
I am old! . . . McGilligan, *George Cukor*, p. 167.
I went out . . . "Notes between Mr. Behrman and Mr. Davidson," unpublished transcript.
Lacking is the . . . "Two-Faced Woman," undated clipping, Garbo file, USC.
The parade of . . . "Two-Faced Woman," unsourced clipping, Garbo file, USC.
The other night . . . "Hedda Hopper's Hollywood," January 25, 1942, fragmentary clipping, Garbo file, USC.
I have finished . . . Broman, *Conversations with Greta Garbo*, p. 196.
263 *Go gay with* . . . "The Gay Garbo."
Two-Faced Woman has . . . "Two-Faced Woman on Legion's 'C' List."
The defunct Hapsburg . . . Viertel, *The Kindness of Strangers*, p. 252.
City Welfare Board . . . "Omaha Deletes Part of Garbo's Picture."
a danger to public . . . "Ban Demanded on Two-Faced Woman."
264 *They've dug* . . . Bainbridge, *Garbo*, p. 89.
It protested vehemently . . . Reinhardt, *The Genius*, p. 104.
flush that filth . . . Ibid.
After a lunch . . . Viertel, *The Kindness of Strangers*, p. 253.
I sat in a dubbing . . . Reinhardt, *The Genius*, p. 104.
The Legion of Decency . . . Fragmentary clipping, Garbo file, USC.
Her pictures are so . . . Swenson, *Greta Garbo*, p. 417.
265 *Don't look now* . . . "At the Capitol."
The screen doesn't . . . Conway, *The Films of Greta Garbo*, p. 154.
An absurd . . . Ibid.
Garbo was humiliated . . . Acosta, *Here Lies the Heart*, p. 315.
266 *People often say* . . . Greenberg, *The Celluloid Muse*, p. 66.

Epilogue
268 *As long as I'm* . . . "Hedda Hopper's Hollywood," January 25, 1942, fragmentary clipping, Garbo file, USC.
One day Bernie Hyman . . . Viertel, *The Kindness of Strangers*, p. 268.
eye to eye . . . Ibid., p. 271.
Even that poor little . . . Ibid.
269 *Mayer knew that* . . . Zierold, *Garbo*, p. 95.
270 *She and Garbo* . . . Higham, *Marlene*, p. 180.
A few jobs were . . . Viertel, *The Kindness of Strangers*, p. 272.
Greta is impatient . . . McGilligan, *George Cukor*, p. 109.
I have been considering . . . Broman, *Conversations with Greta Garbo*, p. 197.
Stars look . . . Daum, *Walking with Garbo*, p. 149.
I know she was fully . . . Lewis, *The Creative Producer*, p. 92.
It's so much harder . . . Beaton, *Cecil Beaton*, p. 238.
The minute the camera . . . Swenson, *Greta Garbo*, p. 477.
271 *How strange that I* . . . Beaton, *Cecil Beaton*, p. 210.
I remember the first . . . Ibid.
She couldn't explain . . . Paris, *Garbo*, p. 334.
Garbo has a magic . . . Levy, *George Cukor, Master of Elegance*, p. 96.
If she had . . . Hedda Hopper, unsourced clipping, Garbo microfilm files, FCMPS.

Bibliography

Books

Acosta, Mercedes de. *Here Lies the Heart*. North Stratford, N.H.: Ayer Company Publishers, 2003.

Allen, Frederick Lewis. *Only Yesterday: An Informal History of the Nineteen-Twenties*. New York: Harper & Row, 1964.

Alpert, Hollis. *The Barrymores*. New York: Dial Press, 1964.

American Film Institute Catalog of Motion Pictures Produced in the United States, 1931–1940, The. Berkeley: University of California Press, 1993.

Ankerich, Michael G. *The Sound of Silence*. Jefferson, N.C.: McFarland & Company, Publishers, 1998.

Ardmore, Jane Kesner. *The Self-Enchanted*. New York: McGraw-Hill, 1959.

Arlen, Michael. *The Green Hat: A Romance for a Few People*. New York: George H. Doran Company, 1924.

Arnheim, Rudolph. *Film Essays and Criticism*. Madison: University of Wisconsin Press, 1997.

Bach, Steven. *Marlene Dietrich: Life and Legend*. New York: William Morrow and Company, 1992.

Bainbridge, John. *Garbo*. New York: Holt, Rinehart, and Winston, 1971.

Balász, Bela. *Theory of the Film*. London: Dennis Dobson, 1952.

Baum, Vicki. *Grand Hotel*. London: Geoffrey Bles, 1930.

Baxter, Peter. *Just Watch! Sternberg, Paramount, and America*. London: British Film Institute Publishing, 1993.

Beaton, Cecil. *Cecil Beaton: Memoirs of the 40s*. New York: McGraw-Hill Book Company, 1972.

———. *The Wandering Years. Diaries: 1922–1939*. Boston: Little, Brown and Company, 1961.

Beauchamp, Cari. *Without Lying Down: Frances Marion and the Powerful Women of Early Hollywood*. New York: Scribner, 1997.

Behlmer, Rudy. *Memo from: David O. Selznick*. New York: Avon Books, 1972.

Behrman, S. N. *People in a Diary: A Memoir*. Boston: Little, Brown and Company, 1972.

Berg, Scott. *Goldwyn: A Biography*. New York: Alfred A. Knopf, 1989.

Bickford, Charles. *Bulls, Balls, Bicycles, and Actors*. New York: Paul Eriksson, 1965.

Billquist, Fritiof. *Garbo*. New York: G. P. Putnam's Sons, 1960.

Black, Gregory D. *Hollywood Censored: Morality Codes, Catholics, and the Movies*. Cambridge, Mass.: Cambridge University Press, 1994.

Broman, Sven. *Conversations with Greta Garbo*. New York: Viking Press, 1992.

———. *The Divine Garbo*. New York: Grosset and Dunlap, 1979.

———. *Garbo on Garbo*. London: Bloomsbury, 1992.

Brownlow, Kevin. *Hollywood: The Pioneers*. New York: Alfred A Knopf, 1979.

———. *The Parade's Gone By*. New York: Ballantine Books, 1969.

Bull, Clarence Sinclair, and Raymond Lee. *Faces of Hollywood*. New York: A. S. Barnes and Co., 1968.

Cannom, Robert W. *Van Dyke and the Mythical City, Hollywood*. Culver City, Calif.: Murray and Gee, 1948.

Carey, Gary. *Anita Loos: A Biography*. New York: Alfred A. Knopf, 1988.

Carr, Larry. *Four Fabulous Faces*. New York: Galahad Press, 1970.

Coffee, Lenore. *Storyline: Recollections of a Hollywood Screenwriter*. London: Cassell and Company, 1973.

Considine, Shaun. *Bette and Joan: The Divine Feud*. New York: E. P. Dutton, 1989.

Conway, Michael, Dion McGregor, and Mark Ricci. *The Films of Greta Garbo*. New York: Bonanza Books, 1965.

Crawford, Joan, with Jane Kesner Ardmore. *A Portrait of Joan*. Garden City, N.Y.: Doubleday and Company, 1962.

Crowther, Bosley. *The Lion's Share*. New York: E. P. Dutton and Company, 1957.

Curtiss, Thomas Quinn. *Von Stroheim*. New York: Farrar, Straus, and Giroux, 1971.

Dardis, Tom. *Some Time in the Sun*. New York: Charles Scribner's Sons, 1976.

Daum, Raymond, and Jeffrey Vance. *Walking with Garbo*. New York: HarperCollins, 1991.

Davies, Marion, and Kenneth Marx. *The Times We Had*. New York: Ballantine Books, 1990.

Davis, Ronald L. *The Glamour Factory: Inside Hollywood's Big Studio System*. Dallas: Southern Methodist University Press, 1993.

Day, Beth. *This Was Hollywood*. Garden City, N.Y.: Doubleday and Company, 1960.

de Mille, William C. *Hollywood Saga*. New York: E. P. Dutton and Company, 1939.

Dickens, Homer. *The Films of Marlene Dietrich*. New York: Citadel Press, 1968.

Dietrich, Marlene. *Marlene*. New York: Grove Press, 1987.

Dietz, Howard. *Dancing in the Dark*. New York: Quadrangle/New York Times Book Co., 1974.

Douglas, Melvyn, and Tom Arthur. *See You at the Movies: The Autobiography of Melvyn Douglas*. New York: University Press of America, 1986.

Dressler, Marie. *My Own Story*. Boston: Little, Brown and Company, 1934.

Durgnat, Raymond, and John Kobal. *Greta Garbo*. London: Studio Vista, 1965.

Eyman, Scott. *Ernst Lubitsch: Laughter in Paradise*. New York: Simon and Schuster, 1993.

———. *Five American Cinematographers*. Metuchen, N.J.: Scarecrow Press, 1987.

———. *The Speed of Sound: Hollywood and the Talkie Revolution, 1926–1930*. New York: Simon and Schuster, 1997.

Fairbanks, Douglas, Jr. *The Salad Days*. New York: Doubleday, 1988.

Fitzgerald, F. Scott. *This Side of Paradise*. New York: Charles Scribner's Sons, 1920.

Fountain, Leatrice Gilbert, with John R. Maxim. *Dark Star*. New York: St. Martin's Press, 1985.

Fowler, Gene. *Good Night, Sweet Prince*. New York: Viking Press, 1944.

Gilbert, Julie. *Opposite Attraction*. New York: Pantheon, 1995.

Gish, Lillian, with Ann Pinchot. *The Movies, Mr. Griffith, and Me*. Englewood Cliffs, N.J.: Prentice-Hall, 1969.

Greenberg, Joel, and Charles Higham. *The Celluloid Muse*. New York: Signet Books, 1972.

Griffith, Richard, and Arthur Mayer. *The Movies*. New York: Simon and Schuster, 1957.

Gutner, Howard. *Gowns by Adrian*. New York: Harry N. Abrams, 2001.

Haining, Peter. *The Legend of Garbo*. London: W. H. Allen, 1990.

Hamann, G. D. *Greta Garbo in the 30s*. Los Angeles: Filming Today Press, 2003.

———. *W. S. Van Dyke in the 30s*. Los Angeles: Filming Today Press, 2003.

Haver, Ronald. *David O. Selznick's Hollywood*. New York: Alfred A. Knopf, 1980.

Hecht, Ben. *A Child of the Century*. New York: Donald Fine, 1985.

Higham, Charles. *Hollywood Cameramen*. Bloomington: Indiana University Press, 1970.

———. *Marlene: The Life of Marlene Dietrich*. New York: W. W. Norton, 1977.

Hopper, Hedda. *From Under My Hat*. New York: McFadden-Bartell, 1964.

Hopper, Hedda, and James Brough. *The Whole Truth and Nothing But*. New York: Pyramid Books, 1963.

Howe, Russell Warren. *Mata Hari: The True Story*. New York: Dodd, Mead, 1986.

Isherwood, Christopher. *Diaries, Volume One: 1939–1960*. New York: HarperCollins Publishers, 1997.

Kanin, Garson. *Hollywood*. New York: Viking Press, 1967.

Kennedy, Matthew. *Edmund Goulding's Dark Victory: Hollywood's Genius Bad Boy*. Madison: University of Wisconsin Press, 2004.

Kobal, John. *Dietrich*. New York: E. P. Dutton and Company, 1968.
———. *People Will Talk*. New York: Alfred A. Knopf, 1985.
Kobler, John. *Damned in Paradise: The Life of John Barrymore*. New York: Atheneum, 1977.
Kotsilibas-Davis, James. *The Barrymores: The Royal Family in Hollywood*. New York: Crown Publishers, 1981.
Laing, E. E. *Greta Garbo: The Story of a Specialist*. London: Ebenezer Baylis and Son, 1946.
Lambert, Gavin. *On Cukor*. New York: G. P. Putnam's Sons, 1972.
Lee, Betty. *Marie Dressler: The Unlikeliest Star*. Lexington: University of Kentucky Press, 1997.
Levy, Emanuel. *George Cukor, Master of Elegance*. New York: William Morrow and Company, 1994.
Lewis, David, with James Curtis. *The Creative Producer: A Memoir of the Studio System*. Metuchen, N.J.: Scarecrow Press, 1993.
Long, Robert Emmett. *George Cukor: Interviews*. Jackson: University of Mississippi Press, 2001.
Madsen, Axel. *Billy Wilder*. London: Secker and Warburg, 1968.
Marion, Frances. *Off with Their Heads!*. New York: Macmillan Company, 1972.
Marx, Samuel. *A Gaudy Spree*. New York: Franklin Watts, 1987.
———. *Mayer and Thalberg, the Make-Believe Saints*. New York: Random House, 1975.
Maxwell, Elsa. *R.S.V.P.: Elsa Maxwell's Own Story*. Boston: Little, Brown, and Company, 1964.
McGilligan, Patrick. *George Cukor: A Double Life*. New York: St. Martin's Press, 1991.
Niven, David. *Bring On the Empty Horses*. New York: Dell Publishing Co., 1976.
Noble, Peter. *Hollywood Scapegoat*. London: Fortune Press, 1950.
Olivier, Laurence. *Confessions of an Actor: An Autobiography*. Boston: G. K. Hall & Co., 1983.
———. *Laurence Olivier on Acting*. New York: Simon and Schuster, 1986.
O'Neill, Eugene. *Anna Christie*. New York: Vintage Books, 1972.
Oppenheimer, George. *The View from the Sixties*. New York: David McKay Company, 1966.
Palmborg, Rilla Page. *The Private Life of Greta Garbo*. Garden City, N.Y.: Doubleday, Doran, and Company, 1931.
Paris, Barry. *Garbo: A Biography*. New York: Alfred A. Knopf, 1995.
Parish, James Robert, and Gregory W. Mank. *The Best of MGM: The Golden Years (1928–59)*. Westport, Conn.: Arlington House Publishers, 1981.
Payne, Robert. *The Great Garbo*. New York: Cooper Square Press, 2002.
Pensel, Hans. *Seastrom and Stiller in Hollywood: Two Swedish Directors in Silent American Films, 1923–1930*. New York: Vantage Press, 1969.
Pepper, Terence, and John Kobal. *The Man Who Shot Garbo*. New York: Simon and Schuster, 1989.
Pirandello, Luigi. *As You Desire Me*. Translated by Samuel Putnam. New York: E. P. Dutton & Co., 1931.
Platt, Frank C. *Great Stars of Hollywood's Golden Age*. New York: Signet Books, 1966.
Quigley, Martin. *Decency in Motion Pictures*. New York: Macmillan, 1937.
Rathbone, Basil. *In and Out of Character*. New York: Limelight Editions, 1997.
Reinhardt, Gottfried. *The Genius: A Memoir of Max Reinhardt by His Son*. New York: Alfred A. Knopf, 1979.
Riva, Maria. *Marlene Dietrich by Her Daughter*. New York: Alfred A. Knopf, 1993.
Robinson, David. *Hollywood in the Twenties*. New York: A. S. Barnes & Co., 1968.
Rosenberg, Bernard, and Harry Silverstein. *The Real Tinsel*. New York: Macmillan Company, 1970.
Samuels, Charles. *The King: A Biography of Clark Gable*. New York: Coward-McCann, 1961.
Sarris, Andrew. *The Films of Josef von Sternberg*. Garden City, N.Y.: Doubleday and Company, 1966.

———. *Interviews with Film Directors*. New York: Bobbs-Merrill Co., 1967.
Schanke, Robert A. *That Furious Lesbian*. Carbondale: Southern Illinois University Press, 2003.
Schnayerson, Michael. *Irwin Shaw*. New York: Putnam and Sons, 1989.
Selznick, Irene. *A Private View*. New York: Alfred A. Knopf, 1983.
Sheldon, Edward. *Romance*. New York: Macmillan Company, 1914.
Sikov, Ed. *The Life and Times of Billy Wilder*. New York: Hyperion, 1998.
Skolsky, Sidney. *Don't Get Me Wrong—I Love Hollywood*. New York: G. P. Putnam's Sons, 1975.
Soares, Andre. *Beyond Paradise*. New York: St. Martin's Press, 2002.
St. Johns, Adela Rogers. *The Honeycomb*. Garden City, N.Y.: Doubleday and Company, 1969.
———. *Love, Laughter, and Tears: My Hollywood Story*. Garden City, N.Y.: Doubleday & Company, 1978.
Steichen, Edward. *A Life in Photography*. London: W. H. Allen, 1963.
Sternberg, Josef von. *Fun in a Chinese Laundry*. New York: Collier Books, 1973.
Stine, Whitney. *The Hurrell Style: Photographs by George Hurrell*. New York: John Day, 1976.
Swenson, Karen. *Greta Garbo: A Life Apart*. New York: Lisa Drew/Scribner, 1997.
Swindell, Larry. *Charles Boyer: The Reluctant Lover*. New York: Doubleday and Co., 1983.
Thomas, Bob. *Joan Crawford*. New York: Bantam Books, 1978.
———. *Thalberg: Life and Legend*. Garden City, N.Y.: Doubleday & Company, 1969.
Tibbetts, John C. *Introduction to the Photoplay: 1929, A Contemporary Account of the Transition to Sound in Film*. Shawnee Mission, Kan., 1977.
Tynan, Kenneth. *Curtains!*. London: Longmans, 1961.
Vickers, Hugo. *Loving Garbo: The Story of Greta Garbo, Cecil Beaton, and Mercedes de Acosta*. New York: Random House, 1994.
Vidor, King. *A Tree Is a Tree*. Hollywood: Samuel French, 1989.
Viertel, Salka. *The Kindness of Strangers*. New York: Holt, Rinehart, and Winston, 1969.
Wagner, Walter. *You Must Remember This*. New York: G. P. Putnam's Sons, 1975.
Walker, Alexander. *Dietrich*. New York: Harper & Row Publishers, 1984.
———. *Garbo*. New York: Macmillan Publishing Co., 1980.
———. *The Shattered Silents: How the Talkies Came to Stay*. New York: William Morrow and Company, 1979.
Wallis, Hal, and Charles Higham. *Star Maker*. New York: Berkley Books, 1981.
Walsh, Frank. *Sin and Censorship: The Catholic Church and the Motion Picture Industry*. New Haven: Yale University Press, 1996.
Watts, Stephen. *Behind the Screen: How Films Are Made*. London: Arthur Barker, 1938.
West, Mae. *Goodness Had Nothing to Do with It*. Englewood Cliffs, N.J.: Prentice-Hall, 1959.
Wylie, Philip. *Generation of Vipers*. New York: Pocket Books, 1955.
Zierold, Norman. *Garbo*. New York: Stein and Day, 1969.
Zolotow, Maurice. *Billy Wilder in Hollywood*. New York: G. P. Putnam's Sons, 1977.

Signed Articles
Aaronson, Charles S. "B. O. Explodes Idea That Women Dislike War and Crook Pictures." *Exhibitors Herald-World*, September 6, 1930, p. 24.
Adams, Mildred. "Now the Siren Eclipses the Flapper." *New York Times*, July 28, 1929, pp. 72–73.
Albert, Katherine. "Did Garbo and Brown Fight?" *Photoplay* (March 1931), pp. 33, 130–31.
Auriol, Jean George, "Faire des Films—V—Avec Qui?" *La Revue du Cinéma*, no. 6 (spring 1947).

Belfrage, Cedric. "That Languid Lure." *The Picturegoer* 15, no. 87 (March 1928), pp. 44–45.
Benchley, Nathaniel. "This Is Garbo." *Collier's*, March 1, 1952.
Biery, Ruth. "The Story of Greta Garbo (Part 1)." *Photoplay* 33, no. 6 (April 1928), pp. 30–31, 78, 102.
———. "The Story of Greta Garbo (Part 2)." *Photoplay* 34, no. 1 (May 1928), pp. 36–37, 127–29.
———. "The Story of Greta Garbo (Part 3)." *Photoplay* 35, no. 2 (June 1928), pp. 64–65, 107–8.
Boland, Elena. "Garbo Likeness Deplored." *Los Angeles Times*, November 23, 1930.
Borg, Sven-Hugo. "Garbo's One Great Love." *Screen Play*, October 1933, pp. 18–20, 56–57.
———. "Garbo's Untold Story." *Screen Play*, September 1933, pp. 20–22, 54–55.
Brayton, Potter Burnell. "The Garbo Legend Exposed." *Hollywood* (October 1930), pp. 9–10, 30.
Calhoun, Dorothy. "They Learned about Women from Her." *Motion Picture Classic* (August 1927), pp. 36–37.
Chapman, Jay Brien. "The Only Man Who Knows Garbo." *Screen Book Magazine* (January 1934), pp. 14, 15, 60.
Churchill, Douglas W. "Out of the Golden West." *New York Times*, November 11, 1934, p. X5.
Frye, William. "The Garbo Next Door." *Vanity Fair*, April 2000, pp. 218, 220, 232–36.
Golden, Eve. "From Stage to Screen: The Film Career of Sarah Bernhardt." *Classic Images* 264 (June 1997), pp. 8–11.
Grant, Jack. "Does Garbo Tank She Go Home Now?" *Motion Picture Classic*, June 25, 1931.
Grinstead, Hettie. "With Garbo at Home." *Screenland* (April 1938), pp. 26–28, 80.
Hall, Leonard. "Garbo-maniacs." *Photoplay* 27, no. 2 (January 1930), pp. 60, 106.
———. "The Perils of Marlene." *Photoplay*, May 1931.
Hall, Mordaunt. "Clever Film Actresses." *New York Times*, March 23, 1930, p. X5.
———. "A Conception of 'Sapho.'" *New York Times*, February 9, 1931.
———. "Garbo Explains Her Next Picture." *New York Times*, July 30, 1929.
———. "Greta Garbo Appears as Queen Christina of Sweden." *New York Times*, December 27, 1933, p. 23.
———. "The Hollywood Hermit." *New York Times*, March 24, 1929, p. X1.
———. "Hollywood Surprises New Swedish Actress." *New York Times*, February 28, 1926.
———. "In Old Manhattan." *New York Times*, August 23, 1930, p. 12.
———. "Miss Garbo and Others." *New York Times*, January 7, 1934, p. X5.
———. "Miss Garbo's Fine Work." *New York Times*, October 25, 1931, p. X5.
———. "Miss Garbo's First Talker." *New York Times*, March 15, 1930, p. 25.
———. "The Screen." *New York Times*, April 13, 1932, p. 23.
———. "A Silent Miss Garbo." *New York Times*, November 16, 1929, p. 28.
Hare, William. "Mamoulian Talks about Garbo." *Hollywood Studio Magazine* (October 1977), pp. 29–31.
Hawkins, Paul. "A New Slant on Garbo." *Screenland* (June 1931), pp. 24–25, 112–13.
Haworth, Gurdi. "I Loved Garbo," *New Movie Magazine* (February 1934), pp. 30–31, 86–90.
Hodgekins, Arline. "Garbo's Gamble." *Photoplay*, July 1933, pp. 37, 99.
Hopper, Hedda. "The Garbo I Know." Unsourced clipping on microfilm in Greta Garbo core collection, Margaret Herrick Library, Fairbanks Center for Motion Picture Study, Academy of Motion Picture Arts and Sciences, Beverly Hills (hereinafter FCMPS).
———. "Garbo Romance Meets Approval of Old Friend." *Los Angeles Times*, April 9, 1938, fragmentary clipping, Garbo microfilm files, FCMPS.
Jordan, Allan. "Photographing Garbo." *Movie Mirror* 2, no. 3 (July 1932), pp. 46, 100–101.

Kakutani, Michiko. "A Drama Recalls a Playwright." *New York Times*, November 8, 1981.

Kapitanoff, Nancy. "Sixty-three Years of Shooting the Legends." *Los Angeles Times Calendar*, December 15, 1991.

Kingsley, Grace. "Two Swedish Players Now En Route Here." *Los Angeles Times*, September 1, 1925, p. A10.

Lubitsch, Ernst. "Garbo, as Seen by Her Director." *New York Times*, October 22, 1939, p. 132.

Markham, Doris. "An Idyll or a Tragedy—Which?" *Motion Picture* 32, no. 5 (December 1926), pp. 23, 99, 100.

Maxwell, Virginia. "The Amazing Story behind Garbo's Choice of Gilbert." *Photoplay* (January 1934), pp. 32, 33, 101.

Morris, George. "Opening Night: A Memoir from the Only Warner Who Was There." *Take One* (January 1978), pp. 30–32, 55–56.

Morris, Ruth. "Sinful Girls Lead in 1931." *Variety*, December 29, 1931, p. 37.

Nugent, Frank S. "*Camille.*" *New York Times*, November 5, 1937, p. 19.

———. "*Conquest*, a Napoleonic Romance." *New York Times*, November 5, 1937, p. 19.

———. "Entirely a Laughing Matter." *New York Times*, November 19, 1939.

———. "*The Great Waltz.*" *New York Times*, November 25, 1938, p. 19.

———. "*Ninotchka*, an Impious Soviet Satire." *New York Times*, November 10, 1939.

O'Dowd, Brian. "Why Garbo Quit Movies." *Hollywood Studio Magazine*, November 1987, pp. 14, 15, 32.

Palmborg, Rilla Page. "Greta Garbo Goes Home." *Motion Picture Classic* (February 1929), pp. 21, 74.

———. "The Private Life of Greta Garbo." *Photoplay* (September 1930), pp. 38–40, 90, 92.

———. "The Private Life of Greta Garbo (Part Two)." *Photoplay* (October 1930), pp. 36–39, 142–43.

Parsons, Louella. "Famous Actress Wins Acclaim at Chinese Opening," *Los Angeles Examiner*, November 26, 1930.

———. "Sirenic Garbo Sways Public as Mata Hari." Unsourced clipping, author's collection.

Proctor, Kay. "Scoop! At Last Garbo Really Talks." *Screen Guide* 1, no. 3 (July 1936), pp. 6, 7, 35.

Quigly, Isabel. "Garbo, Garbo, Garbo." *The Spectator*, September 6, 1963, fragmentary clipping, author's collection.

Roberts, W. Adolph. "Confidences Off-Screen." *Motion Picture* 30, no. 4 (November 1925), p. 53.

Santon, Fredrick. "*Grand Hotel* Revisited with Director Edmund Goulding." *Movie Collector's World*, fragmentary copy, author's collection.

Schallert, Edwin. "Film Producers Shaken by Clean-Up Campaign." *Los Angeles Times*, June 10, 1934.

———. "*Flesh and the Devil.*" *Los Angeles Times*, December 26, 1926, p. 5.

Sennwald, André. "Greta Garbo as the Star of a New Version of *Anna Karenina.*" *New York Times*, August 31, 1935, p. 16.

———. "Greta Garbo Makes Her Semi-Annual Screen Appearance." *New York Times*, December 7, 1934, p. 29.

———. "Marlene Dietrich in Mamoulian's Jeweled Version of *The Song of Songs.*" *The New York Times*, July 20, 1933, p. 22.

———. "Mr. von Sternberg Presents Miss Dietrich." *New York Times*, September 15, 1934, p. 20.

———. "The Paramount Presents Mr. Sternberg's *Devil Is a Woman.*" *New York Times*, May 3, 1935, p. 17.

Shawell, Julia. "Garbo or Dietrich?" *Pictorial Review* (July 1933), pp. 16, 17, 65, 66.

Silverman, Sid. "U. S. Film Field for 1930." *Variety*, December 31, 1930, p. 7.

Smith. Agnes. "Up Speaks a Gallant Loser." *Photoplay* (February 1927), pp. 32–33, 120.

St. Johns, Adela Rogers. "Garbo, the Mystery of Hollywood." *Liberty* (July 27, 1929), pp. 35–37, 77–80.

———. "The Heart of Garbo." *New Movie Magazine* (July 1930), pp. 83–84.

Stanley, Fred. "How Garbo Laughed." *New York Times*, January 4, 1948, p. X4.

Stull, William. "Garbo's Cameraman." *Hollywood*, October 1935.

Sundborg, Åke. "That Gustaffson Girl (Part Two)." *Photoplay* (May 1930), pp. 40–43, 156–59.

Ussher, Kathleen. "A Swedish Siren." *Picturegoer* 13, no. 77 (May 1927), pp. 30, 31, 48.

West, Myrtle. "That Stockholm Venus." *Photoplay* (May 1926), p. 36.

Wheelright, Ralph. "When Nordic Met Latin." *Photoplay*, February 1932, pp. 45, 101–3.

Wiles, Otis. "What It's Like to Work with Garbo." *Photoplay*, November 1934, pp. 43, 80.

Wilkerson, W. R. "Tradeviews." *Hollywood Reporter*, March 23, 1931, p. 1.

———. "Tradeviews." *Hollywood Reporter*, February 13, 1934.

York, Cal. "One More Garbo Fan." *Photoplay* 41, no. 3 (June 1932), pp. 67, 95.

Anonymous Articles

"Adrian Answers Twenty Questions on Garbo." Fragmentary clipping, Garbo microfilm files, FCMPS.

"Alias Marlene Dietrich." *New York Times*, April 5, 1932, p. 109.

"Anna Christie (All Dialog)." *Variety*, March 19, 1930.

"At the Capitol." *New York Times*, January 1, 1942, p. 37.

"Ban Demanded on *Two-Faced Woman.*" *Seattle Times*, December 1, 1941.

"Bank Failure Hits Screen Players." *Hollywood Citizen-News*, June 6, 1932.

"*Camille* Supplement." *Picturegoer*, September 4, 1937, pp. 1–15.

"Cardinal Bans All Pix." *Hollywood Reporter*, June 9, 1934, p. 1.

"*Conquest.*" *Variety*, October 23, 1937, p. 3.

"The Day That Garbo Dreaded." *London Sunday Express*, June 5, 1955.

"Dirt Craze Due to Women." *Variety*, June 16, 1931, pp. 1, 24.

"Foreign Language Films." *New York Times*, November 17, 1929, p. X5.

"Garbo at Close Range." *New York Herald Tribune*, June 30, 1935.

"Garbo at Home Drops Cloak of Mystery." Unsourced clipping, Greta Garbo file, Cinema Television Library, University of Southern California (hereinafter USC).

"Garbo by Her Cameraman." *The Film Weekly*, March 21, 1931.

"Garbo Off for Europe." Unsourced clipping, Garbo microfilm files, FCMPS.

"Garbo's Six Walkouts One Lenox Headache." *Variety*, July 7, 1931.

"The Gay Garbo." *Lion's Roar* 1, no. 3, p. 2.

"Gilbert to Wed Ina Claire." *New York Times*, May 9, 1929, p. 24.

"Greta Garbo and Fifi D'Orsay." Fragmentary clipping, Garbo microfilm files, FCMPS.

"Greta Garbo Appears Once More." *New York Times*, August 4, 1929, p X4.

"Greta Garbo Back at the Capitol." *New York Telegram*, February 7, 1931, unsourced clipping, author's collection.

"Greta Garbo—Her Life Story." M-G-M Biography, Garbo microfilm files, FCMPS.

"Greta Garbo in *Conquest.*" *Literary Digest*, November 20, 1937, p. 34.

"The Greta Garbo Legend Exposed," *Hollywood* Magazine (October 1930), pp. 18–19, 54–55.

"Greta Garbo's Latest Film" *New York Times*, May 4, 1930, p. X6.

"Greta Garbo's New Film." *New York Times*, June 28, 1931, p. X4.

"Hollywood Cleans House." *New York Times*, July 15, 1934, p. X3.

"How Cukor Directs Garbo." *Lion's Roar* 1, no. 3, pp. 6–8.

"In Studios and Theatres." *New York Times*, November 9, 1930, p. X5.

"Jean Hersholt and the Screen." *New York Times*, August 30, 1931, p. X3.

"Masters of Photography." Fragmentary clipping, excerpt from Los Angeles County Museum of Art exhibition catalogue. New York: Camera Three Productions, 1989.

"Mata Hari in a Film." *New York Times*, December 20, 1931, p. X5.

"Miss Garbo's Plans." *New York Times*, December 21, 1930, p. 102.

"Mr. Colton of 'Rain.'" *New York Times*, February 7, 1926.

"Mysterious Lady." *Variety*, August 8, 1928, fragmentary clipping, Garbo microfilm files, FCMPS.

"Ninotchka." *Motion Picture Review Digest* 4, no. 48 (November 27, 1939), pp. 22, 23.

"No Man Is Safe from Her Witchery," *London Sunday Express*, July 3, 1955.

"Not Only Alone, but Unique." *New York Times*, November 30, 1941, p. X5.

"Omaha Deletes Part of Garbo's Picture." Unsourced clipping, Garbo file, USC.

"Producer Discusses Pictures." *New York Times*, May 3, 1931, p. X6.

"Research in Hollywood," *New York Times*, January 3, 1932, p. X4.

"She Works with Garbo." *Lion's Roar* 1, no. 3, p. 13.

"*Two-Faced Woman* on Legion's 'C' List." *Motion Picture Daily*, November 24, 1941, p. 2.

"What the Audience Thinks." *Photoplay* 41, no. 4 (March 1932), pp. 6, 10, 112–15.

"What the Audience Thinks (2)." *Photoplay* 41, no. 5 (April 1932), pp. 6, 14, 16, 121.

"When Greta Isn't Garbo." *Silver Screen*, October 1939.

Unpublished Documents

Brackett, Charles. Interview with Joan and Robert C. Franklin. Oral History Collection, Columbia University.

Franklin, Sidney. "We Laughed and We Cried." Excerpt from incomplete copy in Photoplay Productions Collection. Used by permission of the Sidney Franklin estate.

Lewin, William. "A Guide to the Study of the Screen Version of Tolstoy's *Anna Karenina.*" Garbo microfilm files, FCMPS.

"Notes between Mr. Behrman and Mr. Davidson." Unpublished transcript. Courtesy of Photoplay Productions.

Audiotapes

McKay, Rob. "Interview with Elizabeth Allan, June 6, 1987." Unpublished audiotape in the author's collection.

Pratt, George C. "Interview with Ramon Novarro." Rochester, New York, April 17, 1968. Unpublished audiotape in the author's collection.

Documentary Films

M-G-M: When the Lion Roars. Turner Entertainment documentary, 1992.

Index

Note: Page numbers in *italics* refer to illustrations.